The Police
And Criminal Evidence
Act 1984

AUSTRALIA AND NEW ZEALAND
The Law Book Company Ltd.
Sydney : Melbourne : Perth

CANADA AND U.S.A.
The Carswell Company Ltd.
Agincourt, Ontario

INDIA
N.M. Tripathi Private Ltd.
Bombay
and
Eastern Law House Private Ltd.
Calcutta and Delhi
M.P.P. House
Bangalore

ISRAEL
Steimatzky's Agency Ltd.
Jerusalem: Tel Aviv : Haifa

MALAYSIA : SINGAPORE : BRUNEI
Malayan Law Journal (Pte.) Ltd.
Singapore

PAKISTAN
Pakistan Law House
Karachi

The Police
And Criminal Evidence
Act 1984

BY

MICHAEL ZANDER
Professor of Law, London School of Economics

FOREWORD BY

The Right Honourable
LEON BRITTAN, Q.C., M.P.

LONDON
SWEET & MAXWELL
POLICE REVIEW PUBLISHING COMPANY
1985

Published in 1985 by
Sweet & Maxwell Limited of
11 New Fetter Lane, London
Computer typeset in Great Britain
by The Eastern Press Limited of
London and Reading
Printed in Scotland

British Library Cataloguing in Publication Data
Zander, Michael
The Police and Criminal Evidence Act 1984.
1. Great Britain. Police and Criminal Evidence Act 1984
I. Title
344.205'52   KD4834.5/

ISBN 0–421–32690–5

For my father

ACKNOWLEDGMENTS

The author wrote a series of articles on the Police and Criminal Evidence Bill in the *New Law Journal*. Some of that material has been included here with grateful acknowledgment to the Editor and publishers of the journal for permission to do so. The author also gratefully acknowledges permission of the Comptroller of Her Majesty's Stationery Office to publish the text of the Act and of the Home Office to reproduce the Codes of Practice to be issued under the new Act. (The text of the Codes was supplied to me by the Home Office on April 3, 1985, "in the form in which they are to be printed for tabling before Parliament".) Home Office Ministers and officials were unfailingly helpful in answering questions and making material available. Work on the book was greatly aided by their kind assistance.

The author's personal thanks go in particular to the Home Secretary, the Right Hon. Leon Brittan for agreeing to write an introductory foreword to this book.

FOREWORD

The Police and Criminal Evidence Act effects a long overdue reform and modernisation of the law governing the investigation of crime. The Government's aim has throughout been to ensure that the police have the powers they need to bring offenders to justice, but at the same time to balance those powers with new safeguards to ensure that these powers are used properly, and only where and to the extent that they are necessary.

The Act therefore forms a means of securing our general aim to equip the police to work in a way which commands public confidence: confidence that the law will be enforced effectively and confidence that it will be enforced fairly, responsibly and with proper regard to the rights of the individual who may be suspected of crime. It is for this reason that the Act does not deal with police powers alone. It also effects important reforms of the law of criminal evidence and of the police complaints and discipline procedures. And it provides for consultation between the police and the local community about policing matters.

Although, as Professor Zander rightly points out, we have in this legislation departed in various specific respects from the recommendations of the Royal Commission on Criminal Procedure, the Act is firmly based on the Commission's proposals. The underlying concept of the balance to be struck between powers and safeguards is that proposed by the Commission; and the three tests against which its provisions should be judged are those developed by the Commissions. Are they fair? Are they open? Are they workable?

The Act is therefore a wide-ranging measure; and its success will in large part depend on the extent to which its provisions are generally understood by the public and to which its underlying philosophy is reflected in the actions of the individual police officer.

I therefore very much welcome Professor Zander's book as a contribution towards making the legislation more generally accessible and understood. He is not only a distinguished academic lawyer; he has also taken a close interest in the progress of the Act through Parliament over the past two years and has himself made a number of valuable suggestions for its improvement. He is therefore well qualified to provide this guide to its provisions, and I hope that it will promote understanding of matters which are of concern to everyone in a free society.

October 31, 1984

LEON BRITTAN
HOME SECRETARY

PREFACE

The purpose of this book is to provide a commentary on the Police and Criminal Evidence Act 1984 which it is hoped will help police officers and lawyers as well as law students and others interested in understanding the new law. The book attempts to put the new Act into context by considering both the previous law and the recommendations of the Royal Commission on Criminal Procedure which led up to the formulation of legislative proposals. It deals also with the Codes of Practice which are being issued by the Home Secretary under the Act to deal with stop and search, the detention and questioning of suspects, the search of premises and identification.

The book is not intended to be a complete review of everything that might be included if it were primarily an academic text for scholars. It does not for instance purport in every area to give a comprehensive review of the previous law; and it does not deal with *all* the relevant research and sociological data on the operation of police powers (although much important material is included).

I should perhaps acknowledge some considerable involvement in the debate on this issue as it has evolved since the appointment of the Royal Commission. My article in the May, 1977 issue of the *Criminal Law Review* calling for a major inquiry into the criminal process may have contributed to the decision of the Government of Mr. James Callaghan a few weeks later to set up the Royal Commission. I gave somewhat lengthy written evidence to the Commission and was in addition invited by it to conduct a preliminary seminar for its members. After the Commission's Report was published in January, 1981 I wrote extensively about its proposals and later about the two bills both as Legal Correspondent for *The Guardian* and elsewhere. I also spoke about both the Commission's Report and the first and second Bills at many meetings and conferences and lectured on the subject to lawyers, police officers, law students and others. Whilst the Bill was twice going through Parliament I had repeated contact with both Ministers and officials in the course of trying to get amendments adopted, or of seeking clarification on points of doubt or obscurity. I was given full access to the Ministers' Notes on Clauses that were made available to members of both Houses of Parliament during the Committee stage.

I tried to keep up with the outpouring of memoranda issued by bodies such as The Law Society, the National Council for Civil Liberties, the Justices' Clerks' Society and the various representative bodies of the police service. I read all the parliamentary debates in both Houses of Parliament from start to finish (if both Bills are counted there was a grand total of 120 sittings, including 105 in committee) and struggled throughout to follow the bewildering sequence of hundreds of amendments that poured like confetti from the Home Office. (There can rarely have been a piece of legislation that was subject to so many Government amendments). The House of Lords passed no fewer than 363 and, if one includes the amendments made on the first Bill, the complete tally must be close to or even exceed a thousand.

However, to the best of my ability I have tried not to allow my personal views on the legislation to intrude. I have not attempted here to evaluate the policy options open to the government nor to contribute here to the fierce debate that has raged over the pros and cons of the Conservative Government's legislation. To have done so would obviously have added considerably to the length (and cost) of the book. More important, it would probably have been regarded by most lawyers and police officers and others needing to discover what the new law says, as detracting from, rather than adding to, the value of the book.

I take it to be axiomatic that the law on police powers should be as up to date and accessible as possible. Equally it is plainly helpful to have a statement of all or most of the relevant material in one statute and an accompanying booklet of codes of practice rather than having it scattered through a jumble of disconnected statutes, judicial decisions, Judges' Rules and miscellaneous other sources. One of the great advantages of the new era that will start with the implementation of the Act and its codes is that it will settle many of the old arguments by stating clear new rules where previously there was either no rule or only doubt and obscurity. But even at this stage it is already clear that in many areas the Act leaves important questions unanswered and creates a host of new problems that will keep the courts busy for many years. No doubt the draftsman has used the accident that this bill dragged out its course through two parliamentary sessions to refine and further refine the drafting and no doubt the final product was vastly improved as a result. But the ultimate product can hardly be said to be simple. The officer on the beat will not settle down with the Act and rejoice to have his new powers spelled out in such splendid clarity. The Act has 122 sections with some 685 subsections, running in all to 110 or so pages. In addition there are 26 pages of schedules in small print—not to mention the Codes of Practice which contain over 300 paragraphs.

If this book assists in unravelling the complexities of the new law and stating it in a form that can be followed by those that have to understand or apply it, it will have served its purpose. The method used is to accompany the actual text of the Act and of the Codes with an extended commentary complete with full references and a series of Questions and Answers which have no references. The commentary and the Questions and Answers treat the same subject-matter in different ways—one more descriptive and discursive; the other in a simpler more direct way that is intended to assist particularly those who want a short, broad-brush answer to a problem. The other chief differences between the two approaches is that the commentary proceeds chronologically from section to section whilst the Answers to Questions take their text from whatever material is relevant to the point at issue. There is a very full index which attempts, inter alia, to include all terms which are defined anywhere in the Act.

The manuscript was completed on the day of Royal Assent, October 31, 1984 and was finally revised up to April 10, 1985. It had originally been thought that the Act would come into force around Easter 1985 together with the accompanying Codes of Practice. But the date of implementation has had to be set back considerably because of the dislocation to police manpower caused by the miners' strike. The police persuaded the Home Office that they will need many months after the strike has been settled to get to grips with the job of retraining their personnel. The first part of the Act to come into force on January 1, 1985, was the sections requiring forces to set up consultative committees to obtain the community's views on policing. The Police Complaints Authority was set up at the end of April 1985 and other changes to the complaints procedure and discipline regulations also came into force then. But the whole of the rest of the Act and the four Codes of Practice will not come into force until January 1986.

London   MICHAEL ZANDER
April, 1985

THE BACKGROUND

The Police and Criminal Evidence Act was the result of more than 10 years' travail. Official dissatisfaction with the rules of the criminal process goes back in fact even further to the mid 1960s when the Home Office asked the Criminal Law Revision Committee to inquire into the rules of evidence in criminal cases. Their eight year study culminated in 1972 with the publication of the ill-fated and notorious 11th Report of that prestigious Committee. Their report was received with a barrage of criticism most of which was actually directed at one only of the Committee's many recommendations, that the right of silence in the police station should be abolished. This proposal led to such a storm of abuse that the report was effectively still-born. No Government could implement even the uncontroversial recommendations of a report so widely regarded as fatally flawed.

For some years the Home Office shelved the whole topic. But in June 1977, the Labour Government announced that it was setting up a Royal Commission on Criminal Procedure whose terms of reference were to consider the investigation of offences in the light of police powers and duties as well as the rights and duties of suspects. The Commission was asked to examine the issues, "having regard both to the interests of the community in bringing offenders to justice and to the rights and liberties of persons suspected or accused of crime, and taking into account also the need for the efficient and economical use of resources." The Commission was also asked to look into the problem of the responsibility for the prosecution process, but that part of the Commission's report is not dealt with in this book since the topic was not included in the new Act. The Government introduced the Prosecution of Offences Bill in November 1984.

The Royal Commission's remit was to attempt to reach an agreed solution to a series of highly contentious issues. Its members included representatives of many of the interested groups—a judge, two police officers, a Queen's Counsel, a stipendiary magistrate who had formerly been a justices' clerk, a defence lawyer, and several lay magistrates. The lay members included the chairman, Sir Cyril Philips a Professor of History and former Vice-Chancellor of London University. Under his unassuming but effective leadership the Commission achieved the almost impossible task of obtaining unanimity or near unanimity on all the topics in their report. On many issues there were one or two unidentified dissenters. But virtually all the recommendations in the report were endorsed by the overwhelming majority of the 15 members.

The report was well received by the police and tolerably well received by the legal profession. It was condemned as too prosecution minded by the political Left including organisations like the National Council for Civil Liberties and the Legal Action Group, as well as the official Labour Opposition.

The Home Office showed every sign of wanting to legislate to implement the report. It set up internal working parties to consider the proposals and issued a long list of examination type specific questions for comment by interested groups and persons. In November 1982, only 20 or so months after the Royal Commission had reported, the then Home Secretary Mr. William Whitelaw introduced the first version of the Police and Criminal Evidence Bill. Broadly, it was based on the report of the Philips Royal Commission, though in many respects the Government had exercised its political right to discriminate as to what it would and would not accept of the Royal Commission's proposals. To some extent therefore the carefully constructed package of proposals hammered out over three years around the Royal Commission's table became unstitched. The Government had put together its own somewhat different package.

The Bill proved to be highly controversial and during its passage through the House of Commons in the winter of 1982–83 it was subject to fierce criticism. The debate on the right of silence that sunk the 11th Report of the Criminal Law Revision Committee was barely mentioned this time. The Royal Commission, astutely, had decided that the right of silence in the police station should stay—because it was too important to abolish and moreover so few people were actually silent that it would achieve little to abolish it. The furious debate over the Bill was mainly over the great question of whether the police should have the right to ask to see a doctor's files or the priest's notes of what transpired in the confessional or the records of a citizen's advice bureau. The number of times per year that the police would want to exercise such powers must be rather small, but the heat of the debate suggested that the Government were proposing a serious invasion of fundamental principles. Even the bishops got involved. Eventually the Government retreated and, in addition, amended the Bill on many other less highly publicised issues.

The first Bill failed to pass however because the Prime Minister called a General Election in May, 1983 when it was just completing its Report stage in the House of Commons. At that point a very large number of government amendments had been incorporated in the Bill but a large number of other Government amendments which were already tabled were not reached.

The new Home Secretary Mr. Leon Brittan then spent the summer months considering the Bill. In October, 1983 when he unveiled his Bill Mark II it was found to have included not only all the Government amendments that had already been tabled but a considerable number of further amendments which in some respects departed from policies of his predecessor in office. Thereafter the process of argument and debate continued with interest groups such as the National Council for Civil Liberties assisting the Labour Opposition to mount a sustained campaign against the Bill.

The Committee stage in the House of Commons broke the record for the highest number of sittings. But in spite of all the sound and fury in both Houses and in spite of the fact that the Government moved hundreds of amendments to its own Bill, on the whole they were of relatively minor import. The Bill as it finally emerged at the end of October 1984 is very recognisable as the Bill which was first unveiled a year previously in October, 1983.

Views will inevitably remain divided as to the merits or otherwise of the legislation but whatever opinion one happens to hold, there can be no denying that the whole exercise was an example of the democratic system working. The subject was taken off the shelf by the Labour Government when it set up the Royal Commission in 1977. The Commission had its first meeting in early 1978 and three years later after taking mountains of evidence it had produced a report together with a substantial series of research volumes. There was extensive debate about the proposals before the Conservative Government introduced first one and then a second Bill. Both Bills were massively amended by the Government itself. In a few instances the amendments were made because the Government was swept off course by political tides that were too strong to resist. This was true in particular of the changes made to the first Bill in regard to the search for confidential material and the change on the second Bill giving police officers appealing from serious disciplinary proceedings the right to legal representation (on which the Police Federation formed an unholy alliance with the Law Society and the National Council for Civil Liberties!). But the vast majority of the amendments were moved by the Government because Ministers and officials were persuaded that they represented genuine improvements in the proposed legislation. The Home Office (somewhat uncharacteristically) throughout showed itself willing to listen and to respond constructively to suggestions from a wide variety of bodies and individuals. The end result will not satisfy everyone. Even its own authors will not be completely satisfied with their handiwork. But at least no one who takes any interest in these matters can complain that they lacked time or opportunity to participate in this great and continuing debate.

CONTENTS

CODES OF PRACTICE

APPENDIX

TABLE OF CASES

COMMENTARY ON THE ACT

COMMENTARY ON THE ACT

PART I

POWERS TO STOP AND SEARCH

Definition of powers of stop and search: section 1[1]

The Act begins with one of its most controversial issues—that of stop and search.

The Royal Commission identified two main defects in the existing law. First, police powers to stop and search varied from one part of the country to another. In London for instance the police could use the powers under section 66 of the Metropolitan Police Act 1839 to stop and search for stolen goods and similar local powers existed in Birmingham, Manchester, Liverpool and Rochdale,[2] but equivalent powers did not exist in most other parts of the country. Secondly, existing powers were either inadequate or at best uncertain and required clarification or redefinition. There were some 16 statutes that gave the police powers of stop and search but in other situations the police lacked powers they needed. The police said, "they frequently have to lay themselves open to the risk of civil action by stopping and searching in circumstances where they have no power to do so but where equally they will be criticised for failing to act. One example cited is the carrying of offensive weapons by football supporters."[3]

The Commission proposed first that the police should be given a uniform power of stop and search throughout England and Wales and, secondly, that this should replace all existing powers. Its content would cover searches in a public place of anyone reasonably suspected of conveying stolen goods or of being in possession of anything whose possession in a public place is of itself a criminal offence—for example prohibited drugs, firearms or housebreaking implements.[4] The main innovation, the Commission said, would be in relation to offensive weapons though the Prevention of Crimes Act 1953 already gave the police some powers in this regard. That Act makes it an offence to carry offensive weapons in a public place without lawful authority or reasonable excuse but the police power of arrest in this connection arises only if the suspect's name and address cannot be ascertained or to prevent an offence in which an offensive weapon might be used. The proposed new power permitted search simply on the basis that someone is reasonably suspected of being in possession of offensive weapons.

This topic led to the biggest row in the deliberations of the Royal Commission with two members (Mr. Jack Jones, former General Secretary

---

[1] See also text of the Act at p. 160 below.
[2] For a full list see, Royal Commission on Criminal Procedure, *Law and Procedure Volume* (Cmnd. 8092–1 (1981)). (The Royal Commission's Report is referred to throughout in the notes simply as "Report.")
[3] Report, para. 3.15.
[4] Report, para. 3.20.

of the Transport and General Workers Union, and Canon Wilfrid Wood, a black magistrate) dissenting. In fact Mr. Jones and Canon Wood both signed the report but, somewhat unconventionally, Mr. Jones sent a letter to the press just before publication of the report attacking the Commission's proposals especially on this issue and Canon Wood, seemingly a little reluctantly, associated himself with Mr. Jones' critique.

Mr. Jack Jones and Canon Wood were concerned that this created a danger of random and discriminatory searches "which could further worsen the relationship between the police and young people, particularly black youth."[5]

The majority of the Royal Commission thought, however, that safeguards could be introduced to reduce the danger of random and discriminatory searches. They took the view that "if Parliament has made it an offence to be in possession of a particular article in a public place, the police should be able to stop and search persons suspected on reasonable grounds of committing that offence."[6]

The danger that stops and searches under this proposed general power might be virtually random is illustrated by the statistics regarding the use of existing powers of this kind. The Royal Commission's valuable *Law and Procedure Volume*[7] shows the results of stops and searches nationally for drugs under the Misuse of Drugs Act 1971 and in London for stolen goods under the 1839 Act. The figures for drugs indicate that between 1972 and 1978 in England and Wales, apart from the Metropolitan area, the proportion of persons searched who were found to be in illegal possession of drugs fell from 30 per cent. in 1972 to 22 per cent. in 1978. (Curiously, the "hit rate" declined year by year except for 1977 which saw a slight rise before 1978 in which it dropped to its lowest point). The figures for the Metropolitan area showed that in 1977 34 per cent. of stops under the 1971 Act led to arrests and in 1978 the percentage was 39 per cent. But it is not known how many of the arrests were for illegal possession of drugs. In relation to stolen goods, out of 40,477 stops under the 1839 Act in July 1978, 13 per cent. led to arrests and in January 1979 the figure was 12 per cent. out of 35,298 stops. The difference in the percentage indicates that it is twice as likely that the police will successfully detect a person carrying illegal drugs as stolen goods but even in the case of drugs, between seven and eight stops out of 10 prove unsuccessful.

More recent evidence about the success rate in stop and search in London emerged in the study by the Policy Studies Institute (P.S.I.) published in November 1983. This included a study based on interviews with 2,420 Londoners. It showed that only 3 per cent. of those stopped were arrested and charged with an offence, 5 per cent. had an offence reported and in 1 per cent. of cases the person was arrested but not in fact charged.[8]

On the other hand, there is evidence that a high proportion of arrests result from the exercise of stop and search powers. The P.S.I. survey of police officers showed that no less than 23 per cent. of arrests in the previous six weeks had resulted from a stop.[9] Also the *number* of arrests following on from stops is high. In the Metropolitan Police Area for

[5] Report, para. 3.21.
[6] *Ibid.*
[7] Cmnd. 8092–1 (1981), Apps. 2 and 3.
[8] David J. Smith, *Police and People in London: A Survey of Londoners,* (1983) p. 115.
[9] David J. Smith, *A Survey of Londoners,* (1983) p. 115

instance there are an estimated 1½ million stops per year, about 100,000 of which result in offences being discovered.[10] The P.S.I. study suggested that as many as half of all stops were not recorded.[11]

The Government accepted the Royal Commission's recommendation that stop and search powers should extend to offensive weapons. It also accepted that stop and search powers should be uniform throughout the country. But it did not agree with the Commission's recommendation that one single new statutory provision should replace all existing statutory powers of stop and search.

The Act gives the police the power to search "any person or vehicle" and "anything which is in or on a vehicle, for stolen or prohibited articles" and to detain a person or vehicle for the purpose of such a search (s.1(2)). A constable may not, however, search a person or vehicle under section 1 "unless he has reasonable grounds for suspecting that he will find stolen or prohibited articles" (s.1(3)). Any stolen or prohibited article found in the course of such a search may be seized (s.1(6)). The section does not deal with anything else found in the course of such a search.

An article is "prohibited" for the purpose of the statute if it is either an offensive weapon or it is "made or adapted for use" in the course of or in connection with burglary, theft, taking a motor vehicle without authority or obtaining property by deception or is intended by the person having it with him for such use by him or by some other person (s.1(7)). An offensive weapon is defined as meaning "any article made or adapted for use for causing injury to persons or intended by the person having it with him for such use by him or by some other person" (s.1(9)). This definition is taken from the Prevention of Crime Act 1953, s.1. Note, however, that the power to search for offensive weapons as defined, already existed in Scotland under the Criminal Justice (Scotland) Act 1980, s.4.

One fear of those worried by section 1 is that it might lead to arrests for possession of such potential weapons as a pocket comb, a compass from a geometry set, a sharp pencil or other normally innocent articles on the basis that they could be used as weapons. But if the courts pay any attention to the actual wording of the statute this appears to be unlawful unless the attack has already taken place. A pocket comb for instance might be used as a weapon in a mugging but until the attack has occurred it is difficult to see how a police officer could reasonably have any suspicion that it was to be used for this purpose. A constable would therefore not be entitled to search on suspicion that the person stopped was carrying a normally innocent article, unless there was some outward sign that it was about to be used for offensive purposes or had already been so used.

For discussion of three recent cases on the concept of "reasonable grounds" see S.H. Bailey and D.J. Birch, "Recent Developments in the Law of Police Powers."[12] In the recent study by the Policy Studies Institute the researchers concluded that in about one third of cases when stop and search powers were used there had been no cause for suspicion of the individual concerned, other than the fact that he belonged to a

---

[10] *Ibid.* pp. 311, 346.
[11] *Ibid.* p. 114. See to like effect Carole Willis, *The Use, Effectiveness and Impact of Police Stop and Search Powers*, Home Office Research and Planning Unit, Paper 15 (1983), p. 10
[12] [1982] Crim.L.R. 475–476.

particular group or type or that the stop was made in a particular neighbourhood.[13]

The Home Office view of the meaning of the concept of reasonable suspicion is put very plainly in Annex B of the Code of Practice on Stop and Search. (For discussion of the Codes of Practice see p. 93 below.) This states categorically that "Reasonable suspicion, in contrast to mere suspicion, must be founded on fact. There must be some concrete basis for the officer's belief, related to the individual person concerned, which can be considered and evaluated by an objective third person" (p. 303 below).

Mere suspicion, in contrast, was "a hunch or instinct which cannot be explained or justified to an objective observer," (*ibid*). An officer who had such a hunch or instinct might well be justified in keeping the person under observation but additional grounds were needed to bring suspicion up to the level of "reasonable suspicion."

Such additional grounds could not come from the fact that the person concerned was black even if it was the case that blacks committed more of a particular category of offence than others. Nor was the fact that the person was dressed in a particular way or had a certain hairstyle nor that he had previous convictions for possession of an unlawful article.

The Code puts the point even more strongly: "The degree or level of suspicion required to establish the reasonable grounds justifying the exercise of powers of stop and search is no less than the degree or level of suspicion required to effect an arrest" (*ibid*).

The Notes for Guidance accompanying the Code warn officers that it was important "to ensure that the powers are used responsibly and sparingly". Over use of the powers was "as likely to be harmful to police support in the long term as misuse; both can lead to mistrust of the police among sections of the public" (para. 1A, p. 298 below).

Note that the power conferred by section 1 is a power to stop and search—not a power to stop and question. But in *Daniel* v. *Morrison*[14] the Divisional Court held that the power under section 66 of the 1839 Metropolitan Police Act to stop, search and detain anyone suspected of having stolen goods included the power to question him as well, though only briefly. See to same effect *Geen*[15] in relation to stop and search for prohibited drugs under the Misuse of Drugs Act 1971. The Code of Practice states that a person can only be detained against his will if there are grounds for suspicion beforehand. ("There is no power to stop or detain a person against his will in order to find grounds for a search," (para.2.1). Before carrying out a search the officer could question the person and if a satisfactory explanation of anything suspicious emerged, no search should take place. Section 2(1) of the Act makes the same point when it says that a constable need not conduct a search of someone whom he has detained if it appears to him subsequently that no search is required. The police are therefore not legally at fault if they stop, and do not search but the legality of the stop depends on whether there were or were not grounds for reasonable suspicion before the stop was made.

[13] See D. Smith and J. Gray, *Police and People in London: The Police in Action* (1983, Policy Studies Institute), pp. 232–234.
[14] [1980] Crim.L.R. 181.
[15] [1982] Crim.L.R. 604.

The power of stop and search can be exercised "in any place to which at the time . . . the public or any section of the public has access, on payment or otherwise, as of right or by virtue of express or implied permission; or in any other place to which people have ready access . . . but which is not a dwelling" (s.1(1)). This would cover such places as car parks, pub forecourts, the common parts of a block of flats, and gardens that are readily accessible from the street. So the police can stop and search someone who has aroused reasonable suspicion who is lurking in a garden next to the road.

However, the section makes it clear that if a person is in a garden or yard or other land attached to a dwelling-house, the officer cannot search him unless he has reason to believe that he does not live there and that he does not have the express or implied permission of the person who lives there to be on the premises (s.1(4)). Similar provisions apply equally to a search of a vehicle (s.1(5)). In other words, people and their cars are not to be searched on their own private land.

Safeguards regarding stop and search powers: section 2[16]

Section 2 sets out new procedural safeguards relating to stop and search powers, both under the Act and under any other statutory provisions. These new procedural safeguards apply therefore not only to the police exercising their powers under the Act but also to all the various other statutory powers of stop and search and to similar powers enjoyed by other forces such as the British Transport Police and the Port of London Police. They do not apply however to police at airports, ports and similar places ("statutory undertakers") where vehicles come in and out constantly and routine checks are a regular feature of the movements of such vehicles (s.2(2)(*b*) and s.6).

The provisions broadly follow the recommendations of the Royal Commission. The first is that before searching a person or vehicle or detaining a person or vehicle for the purpose of such a search the officer must take reasonable steps to bring to the person's attention his name, the name of the police station to which he is attached, the object of the search and his grounds for making it (s.2(3)). If he is not in uniform he must produce documentary evidence that he is a police officer. (The House of Lords in fact passed an amendment providing that stop and search powers could only be used by officers in uniform. But this was rejected by the Government when the Bill returned to the House of Commons.) The officer must also inform the person being searched that he is entitled to a record of the search—see section 3(7) and (8) below. However, this duty need not be performed if it appears to the officer that it is not practicable to make a record—for instance because of the size of the group involved (s.(4)).

If the search is of unattended vehicles, the officer must leave a notice stating that he has searched the vehicle, giving the name of his police station, stating that an application for compensation for any damage done should be made to that station and that the owner can request a copy of the record of the search (s.2(6)).

The procedural safeguards apply only to searches. They therefore need not be complied with if the stop does not lead to a search. This is based

---

[16] See also text of the Act at p. 162 below.

on the Royal Commission's view that it would not be desirable, practicable or necessary to require the police to record each occasion on which they stop a member of the public, possibly for an informal conversation. "It is a search following upon a stop and based upon reasonable suspicion that is the main intrusion upon the person and it is that and the reason for it which should be recorded."[17]

The time for which someone may be detained is limited to such time as is reasonably necessary to permit the search to be carried out there or nearby (subs. 8).

It is specifically stated (s.2(9)(*a*)) that no power to stop and search short of arrest authorises a police officer to *require* a person to remove any of his clothing in public other than an outer coat, jacket or gloves. Any such search would therefore have to take place at least out of public view. So if there is no suitable place for a strip search to be conducted nearby it cannot be done at all. But the code does state that a person can be asked to take off more than the statutory minimum voluntarily in (Notes for Guidance, 3A, p. 300 below).

Subsection 9 also makes it clear that only a police officer in uniform can lawfully require a person driving a vehicle to stop for the purpose of any exercise of a power of stop and search (s.2(9)(*b*)). The power to require a driver to stop under section 159 of the Road Traffic Act 1972 is not affected by section 1 and stopping a vehicle under that provision therefore still does not require the test of reasonable suspicion to be satisfied.

Subsection (10) extends the power of stop and search to vessels, aircraft and hovercraft.

Duty to make records concerning searches: section 3[18]

The Royal Commission recommended that as a further control against arbitrary and discriminatory searches police officers should be under a duty to make records of what transpires.[19] Also the individual, it thought, should have a right to a copy of such a record. The Government accepted both recommendations. An officer who has searched someone under statutory powers of stop and search (other than a search by a statutory undertaker—for which see s.6 below), must make a written record of the search, unless this is not practicable, for instance because of the numbers involved (s.3(1)). If he is under a duty to make a record but it is not reasonably practicable to make such a record at the time, it must be done "as soon as is reasonably practicable after the completion of the search" (s.3(2)).

The record must include the object of the search, the grounds for making it, the date, and time when, and the place where, it was made, its result, details of any injury or damage to property caused and the identity of the constable (s.3(6)). It should also identify the name of the person searched, if known—but he may not be detained for the purpose of discovering his name (s.3(3)). If no name is known, the officer is supposed at least to record some description of the person (s.3(4)). The record of a search of a vehicle should describe it (subs.(5)).

Anyone who, or whose vehicle has been searched under stop and search powers will be entitled to ask for a copy of the record made (if any has

---

[17] Report, para. 3.26.
[18] See also text of the Act at p. 163 below.
[19] Report, para. 3.26.

been made)—providing he asks for it within 12 months (s.3(7),(8) and (9)).

The Royal Commission recommended that supervising police officers should scrutinise figures of searches and their results. They should watch for signs "that searches are being carried out at random, arbitrarily or in a discriminatory way."[20] Moreover H.M. Inspectors of Constabulary should give attention to this matter on their annual inspection of each force. Not surprisingly, nothing of this appears in the Act. It is obviously more appropriate to deal with such matters by internal police regulation, and training. Numbers of stops and searches must be contained in the chief constable's annual report so as to make the application of the powers subject to scrutiny by the police authority as will be seen in section 5 of the Act.

The Commission also proposed that failure to provide reasons for a search should make the search unlawful which would entitle the person concerned to resist and also to sue for assault. This recommendation however is not reflected in the Act.

Road checks: section 4[21]

The present police power to set up road blocks derives from section 159 of the Road Traffic Act 1972 which requires drivers to stop when required to do so by a constable in uniform. There is no mention in the section as to the purpose for which the power may be used. The police do use it not only to set up road blocks for road traffic or vehicle excise purposes but also where they believe it to be necessary in connection with a serious crime or when they are hunting an escaped prisoner. Section 159 does not give any power to search a vehicle.

Road blocks are inevitably random in their effect and the Royal Commission said that in general such powers should not be used in connection with crime. "Infringement of a person's liberty to go about his business should be allowed only on suspicion of his involvement in an offence."[22]

But an exception should be made, it thought, for special emergencies. An officer of the rank of assistant chief constable or above should have the power to authorise in writing road checks in two kinds of situation. One would be when a person wanted in connection with a grave offence was thought to be in the area. Second was where it was reasonably thought that a grave offence might be committed in a defined area during a specified period. But the power to establish road blocks should not give the police any right to search vehicles. "That would have to be justified in each case by reference to a suspicion on reasonable grounds that there was evidential material in the vehicle."[23]

The Home Office departed from the Royal Commission's approach in two main particulars. First the Act allows authorisation by an officer of the rank of superintendent, or in a case of urgency by an officer of any rank providing it is subsequently reported to a superintendent or above as soon as practicable (s.4(3), (5), (6) and (7)).

---

[20] *Ibid.*
[21] See also text of the Act at p. 164 below.
[22] Report, para. 3.30.
[23] Report, para. 3.32.

Secondly, the Act substitutes the concept of a "serious arrestable offence" for the Royal Commission's concept of a "grave offence." This has relevance at various points in a comparison between the Act and Commission's report. (For discussion see p. 151 below.)

The Act divides road checks under section 159 of the Road Traffic Act into those involving serious arrestable offences for which the special rules of section 4 are applicable and any other checks. The section 4 road check is permitted to see if a vehicle is carrying someone who has committed a serious arrestable offence, or is a witness to such an offence or someone intending to commit such an offence, or an escaped prisoner (s.4(1)). An officer may only authorise a road check under section 4 where it is reasonably suspected that a person reasonably suspected of having committed a serious arrestable offence or who is unlawfully at large is, or is about to be in the locality; or where the search is for someone intending to commit a serious arrestable offence, that he is or is about to be in the locality (s.4(4)(c)(ii)). When the road check is for potential witnesses it is only necessary for the superintendent to have reasonable grounds for believing that the offence is a serious arrestable one. Authorisation can only be given for seven days at a time but this can be renewed in writing from time to time for a further such period (subss.(11)(12)).

Every authorisation of a road check must specify the ground, the period covered, the locality to which it relates and the name of the officer authorising it. It must also mention the serious arrestable offence in question (s.4(10), (13) and (14)). Where a vehicle is stopped the person in charge of it is entitled to a written statement of the reason for the road check if he asks for it within 12 months (s.4(15)). But there is no requirement that he be told of this right. Road checks which are not under section 4 continue to be legitimate under section 159 of the Road Traffic Act 1972 (see *Lodwick* v. *Sanders* [1985] 1 All E.R. 577).

Reports of recorded searches and road checks: section 5[24]

The chief officer's annual report must contain information about the use made by his force of powers of stop and search and of road checks set up for purposes other than those of road traffic and vehicle excise duties. As the Royal Commission said, this would make the exercise of such powers subject to the independent scrutiny of the police authority and of H.M. Inspectors. Information about searches would not give details of individual cases but it would include the total number of searches in each month for stolen articles and offensive weapons and for other prohibited articles and the total numbers arrested in each month in respect of each such category (s.5(2)). The information about road blocks will have to include the reasons for and the result of each road check (s.5(3)).

Special provisions for statutory undertakers: section 6[25]

Constables employed by a railway, canal, dock or harbour undertaking are given a power under the Act to stop, search and detain for the purpose of searching any vehicle before it leaves parts of the undertaker's premises used for the storage and handling of goods. The special feature of the power is that there is no requirement that the constable have any

---

[24] See also text of the Act at p. 165 below.
[25] See also text of the Act at p. 166 below.

reasonable suspicion that the vehicle is carrying stolen or prohibited goods. Also it extends the power beyond public places.

Its object is to make it possible for statutory undertakings to check outgoing loaded lorries on a random or routine basis as a means of reducing the practice of pilfering. The power is not one that would be likely to affect ordinary members of the public. The power is not entirely new. It is based on similar provisions in section 27 of the Aviation Security Act 1982 in regard to airports. Statutory undertakings for the purposes of this section are defined in section 7(3)—see below. The section does not however confer any power to search the person. This therefore would require reasonable suspicion.

Subsection (3) extends the power to the United Kingdom Atomic Energy Authority's constables in relation to property owned or controlled by British Nuclear Fuels Ltd. and subsection (4) extends the application of subsection (3) to Northern Ireland.

Repeals of existing stop and search powers: section 7[26]

Section 7 repeals six statutory provisions giving constables stop and search powers which are now superseded by section 1. The best known is section 66 of the Metropolitan Police Act 1839. The section also repeals stop and search powers under Acts promoted by local authorities. Other stop and search powers in public general Acts are preserved (s.7(2)(*a*)(i)). Stop and search powers conferred on statutory undertakings are preserved and need not any longer be renewed periodically (s.7(2)(*a*)(ii) and (*b*)).

Subsection 7(3) defines "statutory undertakers."

QUESTIONS AND ANSWERS

1. STOP AND SEARCH

1. Who can exercise the new power of stop and search?

Any police officer whether in uniform or not.

2. Where can the power be exercised?

(1) Any place to which the public have access whether for payment or not (street, park or football ground, but not a private club, school or university); and

(2) any other place which is not a dwelling to which people have ready access (*e.g.* a garden next to the street). But a person cannot be searched in a garden or a yard attached to a dwelling unless it appears that he is not the owner and that he does not have the owner's permission to be there.

3. What does the power consist of?

To stop someone and to speak briefly to him before deciding whether or not to search him. If the decision is to search him he can only be searched superficially. He cannot be required to take off any garments

---

[26] See also text of the Act at p. 166 below.

other than his outer coat, his jacket and his gloves. He can be asked to remove his hat or other items of clothing but if he refuses he cannot be compelled to do so. Also if it is thought right to search him more thoroughly this cannot be done under the stop and search power. For that purpose he would have to be arrested and taken to an appropriate place such as the police station.

4. On what grounds can a person be stopped in order to be searched?

Before stopping the person concerned, the police officer must have reasonable grounds for suspecting that he will find either stolen goods or "prohibited articles" on him or his vehicle.

5. What amounts to reasonable grounds to suspect?

The concept of reasonable grounds to suspect is inevitably somewhat imprecise. But it means basically that there must be some grounds for suspecting that particular individual himself. It is not enough to feel that he is one of a group of a particular type who might be prone to commit that sort of offence—skinheads, young blacks, yobbos or any other category. There must be something about that individual which sparks off suspicion. The concept of "reasonable" suspicion means fairly strong suspicion with a concrete basis that could be evaluated by an objective third person.

6. Can reasonable suspicion be based on the knowledge that the person concerned has committed offences before?

The short answer is No. There must be something about his conduct, manner, appearance, way of moving or other surrounding circumstances which suggest that he has done something recently or is about to do something.

7. What are "prohibited articles"?

The Act establishes two categories of prohibited items. One is something made or adapted for use in connection with burglary, theft, taking a motor vehicle without authority or obtaining property by deception. The other is "offensive weapons".

8. What is meant by an offensive weapon?

An offensive weapon is either something made or adapted for use for causing injury (such as a flick-knife, cosh or knuckle-duster) or something which in itself is innocent but which is intended by the person having it to be used by him or others to cause someone injury.

9. What must the officer do before carrying out a search?

It is an absolute rule that before searching anyone the officer must do his best to inform the person concerned by telling him:

(1) his own name and that of his police station;

(2) the object of the proposed search;

(3) the officer's grounds or reasons for wanting to make it;

(4) that the person searched has the right to ask for a copy of the record of the search at the police station within 12 months.

If the officer is in plain clothes he must also first produce evidence that he is in fact a police officer.

10. What happens if the person concerned does not understand English. Is any search therefore unlawful?

No. The duty is not to inform the person but to "take reasonable steps to bring the information to his attention". If everything has been done that could reasonably be done to get him to understand the relevant information, the officer can proceed to carry out a search.

11. What if the officer wants to search a number of persons in a short space of time which would make it difficult to conform to the duty to give each of them the requisite information?

He must nevertheless do his best to inform them of his name and the name of his station, the object of the search and the reason why he wants to make it. But he is not under a duty to mention the person's right to get a record of the search if the circumstances are such as to make it impracticable to make a record.

12. For how long can a person be detained under the stop and search power?

No longer than is reasonably necessary to carry out the search. (The Notes for Guidance in the Code of Practice (3B, p.300) states, that "such searches should normally be capable of completion within a minute or so."

13. When must a record be made of a stop and search?

A record must be made unless it is not practicable to do so, *e.g.* because considerable numbers have been stopped and searched for instance outside a football ground. But the officer is not exonerated from the duty to make a record where he can in practice make a record later, only if he cannot make one at all. If it is not practicable to make the record on the spot but it is feasible to make it later, the duty is to make it "as soon as practicable."

14. Must a record be made if there is no search?

No. The duty to make a record only arises if there is a search.

15. What is the record supposed to include?

The name of the person searched, if known, and, if not, some description of him including details of his race; the object of the search; the grounds for making it; the date and time; the place; whether anything and if so what was found; and the identity of the officer who made the search.

16. Do the powers to stop and search a person apply to stopping and searching a vehicle?

They do apply in much the same way. But there are some differences. One is that a police officer in uniform has the power to stop any vehicle under section 159 of the Road Traffic Act 1972. That Act does not require the police officer to be suspicious of anything in particular. But a stop under the Road Traffic Act does not entitle the officer to search the vehicle. A search under the 1984 Act requires reasonable grounds to suspect that the vehicle is carrying stolen goods or prohibited articles.

Another difference is that the Act makes special provision for the search of an unattended vehicle where reasonable grounds for suspicion exist. In that case the officer must leave a notice in or on the vehicle stating that he has searched it, giving the name of his police station and stating that the owner can get a copy of the record of the search if he applies within 12 months. The record of a search of a vehicle should describe it.

17. Are there any stop and search powers apart from the 1984 Act?

Yes. There are many statutes which give the police stop and search powers, most of which continue to exist. But the 1984 Act has repealed some of these powers such as the power of the Metropolitan Police dating from 1839 to stop and search persons on reasonable suspicion that they are carrying stolen goods.

18. Can a person be stopped and searched by consent?

Yes, and in that case the various safeguards of the new Act do not apply. The difficulty is in knowing whether a stop is by consent. The Code of Practice states that the code provisions do not affect "the routine searching of a person entering sports grounds or other premises with their consent or as a condition of entry" (Notes for Guidance, 4A, p. 300).

2. ROAD CHECKS

19. At present the police have an unlimited right to stop any vehicle under the Road Traffic Act. How is that right affected by the 1984 Act?

The 1984 Act sets up a procedure for establishing a road check when the purpose is to discover whether a vehicle is carrying someone who has committed a serious criminal offence or someone who is a witness to such an offence or someone intending to commit such an offence or an escaped prisoner.

20. What is the new procedure?

The road check must normally be authorised in advance and in writing by an officer of the rank of superintendent or above. The authorisation must specify the period for which it is to operate (up to a maximum of one week at a time) and the locality in which it is to operate. It must also state the name of the officer giving it; the purpose of the road check; and the nature of the offence in question.

In an emergency where no superintendent is available an officer of any rank can authorise a road check but he must then as soon as is practicable notify a superintendent and make a record of the time at which he granted authority for the road block. The superintendent can then authorise the continuation of the check or can order that it be discontinued.

The person in charge of any vehicle that is stopped in the course of such a check has the right to a written statement as to the grounds for the road check providing he applies for it within 12 months.

21. What grounds justify the setting up of a road block?

There are four possible grounds:

(1) That there are reasonable grounds for believing that someone who has committed a "serious arrestable offence" (for discussion see p. 151 below) is or is about to be in the area.

(2) That the police are looking for a witness to a "serious arrestable offence." In this category there is no requirement that they *expect* to find a witness in the area. They can therefore try their luck without any commitment.

(3) That they are looking for a person who intends to commit a "serious arrestable offence" and that there are reasonable grounds for suspecting that the person is or is about to be in the locality.

(4) That there are reasonable grounds to believe that an escaped prisoner is in the area.

PART II

POWERS OF ENTRY, SEARCH AND SEIZURE

The first study to produce empirical data about police use of powers of entry and search was published by the Royal Commission on Criminal Procedure in its *Law and Procedure Volume*.[1] Ten police forces kept figures for a four-week period in September 1979. The study was not statistically random but the figures based on a total of 341 searches are nevertheless of some interest.

The largest group of all the searches (43 per cent.) were after arrest without a warrant. Thirty-five per cent. were based on a magistrate's warrant, and 13 per cent. were made prior to arrest with the consent (explicit or otherwise) of the householder.

Thirty-nine per cent. of the searches uncovered evidence linking the suspect with the offences under investigation at the time of the search. In one in every 10 searches, material evidence implicating the suspect in other offences came to light during the search. In just under 10 per cent. of the searches evidence was found linking other persons with the offence under investigation or some other offence. In all, 43 per cent. of the searches were successful on at least one of these criteria. In a third of the cases where no evidence was found the suspect was nevertheless charged on the basis of other evidence.[2]

The provisions in the Act regarding entry, search and seizure are partly based on the recommendations of the Royal Commission. But in some important respects they differ from what the Commission proposed. This part of the Act proved to be the one which was most buffeted in the Committee stage on the first version of the Bill and it was here that the Government made the most significant changes to its own Bill.

The Royal Commission recommended[3] that existing powers of entry and search under warrant needed to be supplemented. The existing powers were somewhat haphazard and, there were surprising omissions. There was no power for instance to get a search warrant to search the scene of a murder or a kidnap, apart from the power to search premises after an arrest. In the Commission's view a new compulsory power of search for evidence should be available, though it should be a limited power and one subject to stringent safeguards. ("A compulsory power of search for evidence should be available only as a last resort. It should be granted only in exceptional circumstances and in respect only of grave offences."[4])

Under the existing law the police had authority to enter to search premises under different levels of supervision. In most cases the supervis-

[1] Cmnd. 8092–1 (1981).
[2] App. 7, pp. 126–129.
[3] Report, para. 3.42.
[4] *Ibid.*

ing authority was a magistrate but in some circumstances authority for a search could be given by a senior police officer and in others there had to be the permission of a judge. In the view of the Commission in general the appropriate supervision could be provided by the magistracy. But in cases of great urgency in searching for prohibited goods, a police officer not below the rank of superintendent should be able to authorise a search.

When it came to searches for evidence, however, supervision should be by a judge. The procedure should have two stages. The police should first have to apply for a court order similar to a witness summons in a criminal case or an order for discovery in a civil case. Such an order would require the person to whom it was directed to allow the police to look at the items covered by the order. There should be a right of appeal to the court against the order. If the person refused to comply with the order, the police should have the right to get a warrant. They should also have a right to ask for a warrant forthwith "where there is reason to believe that the evidence will disappear, or be disposed of if the person concerned is alerted to the police interest in it."[5]

An order should be made by a judge only if he was satisfied that other methods of investigation had failed, that the nature of the items was specified with some precision, that there were reasonable grounds for thinking that the items would be found at those premises and that the evidence would be of substantial value to identify those responsible for the crime or to determine the particulars of offences.[6]

The Government gave only partial effect to these proposals. It did not accept the Royal Commission's recommendation that a senior officer should in an emergency be permitted to authorise a search for prohibited goods. But on the other hand, the Government did not agree with the Commission that searches for *evidence* should always require the authority of a judge subject to a two stage process of an order and a warrant. A judge's authority would have to be obtained if the evidence was held on a confidential basis but in other circumstances it would be enough to get a magistrate's permission. The Home Office made the point that there were already some 40 statutes which gave magistrates powers to authorise searches of premises, including in some instances searches for evidence.[7]

When the first Bill was published it gave the police the right to seek a search warrant from a justice of the peace to look for evidence of a serious arrestable offence. The only qualification was that the application to the magistrate had to indicate how the evidence in question related to the inquiry.

Where however the evidence was held on a confidential basis the first Bill provided a special procedure by way of application to a circuit judge. This was in two stages. In the first instance, the police would normally have to ask for an order to produce. If this had already proved abortive or if the order was bound to fail the police could ask for a search warrant.

These provisions were subjected to fierce criticism especially by the medical profession, the clergy, lawyers, journalists, Citizens' Advice Bureaux and other advisory agencies. All were concerned that the powers as they stood would have permitted a judge to authorise search of records

---

[5] *Ibid.*
[6] Report, para. 3.43.
[7] The list is set out in the Commission's *Law and Procedure Volume* (Cmnd. 8092–1 (1981), App. 5).

held in confidence. As a result of the pressure placed upon it the Government made a series of concessions the most important of which were:

(1) to provide that the hearing before the judge would have to be *inter partes* (*e.g.* with both sides present) unless the police could satisfy the judge that there was reason to believe that the person holding the material in question was in some way implicated in the crime;

(2) that certain categories of material would be wholly exempt from any police scrutiny—notably the records of doctors, clergymen and advisory agencies; and

(3) that enforcement of a judicial order to produce confidential material which is not exempt would be by proceedings for contempt and not by a search warrant.

The categories of material exempted ("excluded material") were those subject to legal professional privilege, confidential personal records of doctors and caring professions and advisory agencies, and material held in confidence by journalists. Material held in confidence that is not exempt is called "special procedure" material.

Applications to justices of the peace for search warrants: section 8[8]

Section 8 provides for the issue of warrants to enter and search premises for evidence of serious arrestable offences.

The section gives a justice of the peace, on written application from a constable, power to issue a search warrant where he is satisfied that there are reasonable grounds for believing that a serious arrestable offence (as defined in s.116, see p. 236 below) has been committed. He must also be satisfied:

(1) that there is material on the premises likely to be of substantial value to the investigation s.8(1)(*b*);

(2) that it is likely to be "relevant evidence" (*e.g.* admissible in evidence—subss.8(1)(*c*) and 8(4));

(3) that it is not and does not include "excluded material" (see s.11), or "special procedure material" (see s.14); or material subject to legal privilege (s.10); and

(4) that any of the conditions in subsection (3) applies.

The conditions in subsection (3) are basically that it is not practicable to gain entry to the premises in question without a search warrant. Thus examples are where entry has been refused or no one with authority to grant access can be reached or the purpose of the search may be frustrated unless an officer can gain immediate entry.

Subsection (5) makes it clear that the power to issue a search warrant under subsection (1) is in addition to any existing power to issue warrants. Existing provisions for the issue of search warrants (which are listed in Appendix 5 to the Royal Commission's *Law and Procedure* Volume), include powers to search for evidence of various offences such as under the Gaming Act 1968.

---

[8] See also text of the Act at p. 166 below.

Access to excluded and special procedure material: section 9 and Schedule 1[9]

Section 9 deals with the question of police access to material held on a confidential basis. It also applies the new procedures envisaged under the Act to searches for such material under the authority of other legislation.

Subsection (1) states that the police may only seek access to excluded or special procedure material (as defined in ss.11 and 14 respectively) by applying to a circuit judge under Schedule 1 to the Act. Application must also be made to the judge where the material sought is partly excluded or special procedure and partly other material (Schedule 1, para. 2(*a*) (ii) and 3(*a*). The judge may order the material to be produced or, in exceptional circumstances, may issue a search warrant. But the police can only gain access to excluded material if a search warrant could already be obtained under the previous law for such material (*e.g.* stolen medical records for which a search warrant could have been issued under the Theft Act 1981, s.26(1)). For a full list of all police powers to enter and search premises under warrant or other written authority see Royal Commission, *Law and Procedure Volume*, Appendix 5.

Subsection (2) repeals all existing enactments insofar as they empower judges or magistrates to authorise searches for excluded or special procedure material consisting of documents or records. All applications for searches for such material, whether in connection with a serious arrestable offence (defined in s.116) or not, must now therefore be made under subsection (1) and Schedule 1.

Schedule 1 contains the detailed provisions for making of orders by circuit judges.

The judge must be satisfied that one or other of the two sets of access conditions are satisfied. The first set of access conditions set out in paragraph 2 of the Schedule relate only to special procedure material. The conditions include the requirement that there are reasonable grounds for believing that the material is likely to constitute admissible evidence of a serious arrestable offence; that the material is likely to be of substantial value to the investigation; that other methods of getting the material have been tried and failed or have not been tried because it was likely that they would be bound to fail; and that the public interest would be served by an order requiring access to the material. In weighing the public interest the judge is required to balance the benefit to the investigation of gaining access to the material and "the circumstances under which the person in possession of the material holds it" (para. 2(*c*)).

The second set of access conditions (para. 3) applies to both excluded and special procedure material. The effect of this paragraph in Schedule 1 and section 9 is that a judge can order the production of the material if a warrant could previously have been issued to search for it and the issue of such a warrant would have been appropriate. The material need not relate to a serious arrestable offence.

Paragraph 4 states that an order made by the judge is an order to produce the material to the police or to give the police access to it within seven days or such other time as it specifies.

Paragraph 5 parallels provisions in section 19(4) regarding access to information in a computer and paragraph 6 applies provisions of sections

[9] See also text of the Act at p. 167 and Sched. 1 at p. 239 below.

21 and 22 regarding access and copying and retention of articles seized to items seized under Schedule 1.

Paragraph 7 provides that an application for such an order must be made *inter partes*. This represented a major concession by the Government. When the first Bill was published it provided for such applications to be made *ex parte* (*e.g.* with only the police represented)—as recommended by the Royal Commission.

Paragraphs 8 to 10 deal with the service of notice of the application on the person concerned. Paragraph 11 provides that a person served with such a notice must not "conceal, destroy, alter or dispose of the material," save with the leave of a judge or the written consent of a police officer until the application is either dismissed or abandoned or the order under paragraph 4 is complied with

Paragraph 12 provides for the issue of a search warrant by the judge instead of an order to produce under paragraph 4. An application for a warrant would be made *ex parte* by virtue of section 15(3) of the Act.

Before issuing a search warrant the judge must be satisfied first that one or other of the two sets of access conditions is satisfied and further that any of the conditions in paragraph 14 (see below) are fulfilled. He may also issue a warrant if an order for production has been disobeyed, but only if the order related to material for which a warrant could have been issued under the previous law.

If an order for the production of special procedure material issued under the first set of access conditions is disobeyed no search warrant can be issued. Such an order can only be enforced by proceedings for contempt (paras. 12(*b*) and 15). This again was an important concession by the Government which originally proposed that disobedience of any order for production by the circuit judge should be followed by an application for a search warrant.

The conditions set out in paragraph 14 are:

(1) that it is not practicable to communicate with anyone able to authorise entry to the premises or to give access to the material in question; or

(2) that it is excluded material subject to a restriction or obligation of secrecy under any enactment as mentioned in section 11(2)(*b*) and that the material is likely to be disclosed in breach of such restriction if a warrant is not issued; or

(3) that service of a notice of an application for an order of production might seriously prejudice the investigation.

Meaning of "items subject to legal privilege": section 10[10]

Material covered by legal professional privilege can neither be searched for nor seized by the police. In the first Bill as first published legal privilege was confined to communications between a professional legal adviser and his client made in connection with the giving of legal advice to the client. This was then extended by amendment in Committee to include also communications between a professional legal adviser and his client or between such an adviser or his client and any other person made in connection with or in contemplation of legal proceedings and for the purpose of such proceedings.

Subsequently by further amendment the Government changed the

[10] See also text of the Act at p. 167 below.

definition again. The final version which was adopted in the second Bill and which became law in section 10 described the categories covered as (a) communications in connection with the giving of legal advice between the professional legal adviser and his client "or any person representing his client"; and (b) communications in connection with or in contemplation of legal proceedings and for the purposes of such proceedings made between the professional legal adviser and his client or any person representing his client or between such a legal adviser or his client or any such representative and any other person.

Documents or other articles mentioned or enclosed with such communications are also covered by legal privilege if the communication is in connection either with the giving of legal advice or in connection with or contemplation of legal proceedings and for the purpose of such proceedings and if they are in the possession of someone entitled to possession of them. But documents or articles held with the intention of furthering a criminal purpose are stated not to be items subject to legal privilege.

Meaning of "excluded material": section 11[11]

Section 11 defines "excluded material." Anything which is in this category is totally exempt from any order or warrant under Schedule 1 unless the police could already get a search warrant to look for it, *e.g.* because it is a stolen or forged article for which a search warrant could be obtained under section 26(1) of the Theft Act 1968.

Subsection (1) provides that "excluded material" consists of three categories of material held on a confidential basis: (a) personal records (defined in s.12); (b) samples of human tissue or tissue fluid taken for the purpose of diagnosis or medical treatment and which are held in confidence; and (c) journalistic material (defined in s.13) consisting of documents or records if held in confidence (defined in subs. (3)).

Subsections (2) and (3) define what is meant by the concept of "held in confidence" for excluded material other than journalistic material and for journalistic material respectively.

Excluded material other than journalistic material is held in confidence if it is held subject to an express or implied undertaking to hold it in confidence or it is held subject to a restriction on disclosure or obligation of secrecy contained in any statute. Journalistic material is held in confidence if held subject to such an undertaking, restriction or obligation and it has been continuously so held, whether by one or more than one person, since it was first acquired or created for the purposes of journalism. This last requirement does not apply to other categories of excluded material, apparently because of a sense that they are intrinsically more sensitive.

Meaning of "personal records": section 12[12]

"Personal records" for this purpose are defined to mean documents and other records concerning an individual (whether living or dead) who can be identified from them which relate: (a) to his physical or mental health; or (b) to spiritual counselling or assistance given or to be given to him; or (c) to counselling or assistance given or to be given to him for the purposes

---

[11] See also text of the Act at p. 168 below.
[12] See also text of the Act at p. 168 below.

of his personal welfare and involving counselling given or to be given to him by any voluntary organisation or by any individual who by reason of his office or occupation has responsibility for his personal welfare or by reason of a court order has responsibility for his supervision.

The exemption of personal records as defined from any search by the police is absolute. This was in response to the fierce campaign waged in particular by the British Medical Association, the bishops and Citizens' Advice Bureaux. The definition is obviously very wide. It would cover not simply the records of probation officers, social workers and advisory agencies but school and university personal files and records. It does not however cover "things" such as the bullet taken from a wound, or bloodstained clothing. The contents of a stomach pumped out by the doctors would probably be exempt as human tissue or tissue fluids. So too would be any form of medical record. But the records of accountants or other professional advisers would presumably not qualify—save in so far as they gained exemption through legal privilege. An accountant would probably not be an individual who through his office or occupation had responsibility for the client's "personal welfare" within the meaning of the phrase, though there is no definition of this phrase in the Act. The section is plainly intended to cover the caring professions and their voluntary counterparts.

Meaning of "journalistic material": section 13[13]

Mr. William Whitelaw on the first Bill was persuaded to grant a major exemption from police searches also to the journalists' lobby. Subsequently some journalists and newspaper editors expressed disquiet about the desirability of this special status but Mr. Leon Brittan decided not to respond to their fears. He maintained the concession agreed by his predecessor. As has been seen, excluded material is defined (in s.11(1)(c)) to include journalistic material which consists of documents or other records, held in confidence. Journalistic material is only deemed to be held in confidence in this context if it is both held subject to an undertaking, restriction or obligation to hold it in confidence and if it has been continuously held by one or more persons subject to such an undertaking, restriction or obligation since it was first acquired or created for the purposes of journalism (s.11(2) and (3)).

Journalistic material is defined as material "acquired or created for the purposes of journalism" (s.13(1)). Journalism is not defined but it includes any form of publication. It is not confined to publication for reward nor to full-time or even professional journalists. Material is only journalistic material however if it is in the possession of someone who either acquired or created it for the purposes of journalism (s.13(2)). This would protect material passed by a journalist to his superiors or to the organisation for which he worked. But it would not cover material that was held by someone not involved in journalism. The Act states that a person who receives unsolicited material from someone who intends that he should use it for the purposes of journalism is taken to have acquired it for that purpose (s.13(3)). Journalistic material that does not qualify as "excluded material" could still be "special procedure material."

[13] See also text of the Act at p. 168 below.

Meaning of "special procedure material": section 14[14]

Section 14 defines "special procedure material" for the purposes of section 9 of the Act. In essence it comprises (a) material held on a confidential basis which does not qualify as personal records (as defined in s.12), and (b) journalistic material (as defined in s.13) not held in confidence.

Subsection (2) states that material is special procedure material if (not being excluded material or subject to legal privilege) it is held subject to an express or implied undertaking of confidentiality or a statutory restriction on disclosure or obligation of secrecy (for instance under the Official Secrets Act) by someone who acquired it or created it in the course of a trade, business, profession or other occupation or for the purpose of any office whether paid or unpaid. This would include, say, company accounts or stock records held on behalf of a client by a bank, solicitor or accountant.

Subsection (3) provides that material acquired by employees from their employer or by a company from an associated company is only special procedure material if it was such material immediately before it was acquired. This means that company records cannot be special procedure material simply by virtue of an instruction by an employer to an employee that they should be held in confidence. The special procedure is intended primarily for material held in confidence by a third party. But if it is special procedure material it remains special procedure material even though it may be passed by an employer to an employee—say in an accountants' firm or a bank.

Subsections (4) and (5) make similar provision for special procedure material created by an employee in the course of employment or by a company on behalf of an associated company.

Safeguards for obtaining search warrants: sections 15 and 16[15]

The Royal Commission recommended that new safeguards should be laid down to apply to the issue of all search warrants[16] and these proposals have been incorporated in section 15.

An application for a search warrant must state the grounds for making the application, the statutory authority covering the claim, and in as much detail as possible, the object of the warrant and the premises concerned. The application, which is made *ex parte* (*e.g.* without the person affected being present), must be supported by an information in writing (s.15(3)). The constable must answer on oath any questions put by the justice of the peace (s.15(4)). Each warrant will authorise entry on only one occasion (s.15(5)). If nothing is found, the police therefore cannot return to have another attempt, unless they can get a second warrant. The warrant must specify the name of the person applying for it; the date of issue; the statutory power under which it is issued; the premises to be searched; and, so far as possible, the articles or persons sought and when the search is to take place (s.15(6)).

---

[14] See also text of the Act at p. 169 below.
[15] See also text of the Act at pp. 169–170 below.
[16] Report, paras. 3.46, 3.47.

Two copies must be made—one for the occupier of the premises to keep (see s.16(5)) and one to be retained by the police. The original goes back to the issuing court (see s.16(10)).

Execution of warrants: section 16 and the Code for the searching of premises and the seizure of property[17]

Section 16 contains provisions to ensure that warrants are executed in a proper and reasonable manner. The provisions are supplemented by the code for the searching of premises promulgated under the authority of section 66. The section applies to all warrants executed by the police. In so far as other statutes lay down different conditions they are repealed (s.15(1)).

Subsection (1) provides that any constable may execute any warrant. This overrides provisions in a number of statutes which specify that only the constable named in the warrant may execute it. Subsection (2) states that a warrant may authorise persons to accompany the officer executing it, such as a witness.

The section provides that entry and search under a warrant must be within one month from the date of its issue (subs. (3)). It must be at a "reasonable hour" unless "it appears to the constable executing it that the purpose of a search may be frustrated on an entry at a reasonable hour" (subs. (4)). The test is subjective—qualified only by the condition that his belief must be honest. Where the occupier of the premises is present, the constable must produce a copy of the warrant and must give a copy to him (subs. (5)). If he is not present, a copy must be left there (subs. (7)). An officer executing a warrant must identify himself and if he is not in uniform he must produce documentary evidence that he is a constable even without being asked (subs. 5). If the occupier is not there but someone else is who appears to be in charge, the police should treat him as the occupier for the purposes of this section (subs. (6)).

A search under a warrant "may only be a search to the extent required for the purpose for which the warrant was issued" (subs. (8)). In other words if the search is for large items it would not be legitimate to tear up the floor boards whereas if it were for prohibited drugs such a search might be lawful. This is an important provision.

Subsection (9) requires the police to endorse a warrant stating whether the articles or persons sought were found and whether any other articles were seized. This will enable the courts to monitor the success or otherwise of search warrants since they will receive the original.

Under subsection (10) the police are subject to a duty to return an executed warrant or one which has expired to the court which issued it. This will give the courts the basic information as regards the operation of the power by the police.

Warrants must then be retained by the courts for 12 months. The occupier has the right to inspect the endorsed warrant at any time within the 12 months.

Code on search and seizure

Further requirements concerning the execution of search warrants are laid down in the new Code of Practice for the searching of premises and

[17] See also text of the Act at p. 170 and the Code at p. 292.

the seizure of property (see p. 292 below. For consideration of the status of the Codes see p. 94 below).

Inspector's authority

The code requires first that police officers check their information carefully before applying for a search warrant and that, save in an emergency, no such request should be made without the authority at least of an inspector or, in the case of a production order under Schedule 1, a superintendent (paras. 2.1–2.4). If there is reason to believe that a search "might have a significantly adverse effect on relations between the police and the community" the local police community liaison officer should be consulted save in urgent cases (para. 2.5).

Owner's consent

Where it is proposed to search with the consent of the owner or occupier of the premises in question (there being no search warrant or arrest) the police will normally be required to get such consent in writing (paras. 4.1 and 4.3). Before getting written consent the police officer will have to explain the purpose of the proposed search and inform the person concerned that he is not obliged to consent and that anything seized may be produced in evidence. If the person is not suspected of an offence, the officer should say so (para. 4.2). The Notes for Guidance accompanying this rule state, "In the case of a lodging house or similar accommodation a search should not be made on the basis solely of the landlord's consent unless the tenant is unavailable and the matter is urgent" (para. 4A).

Minimum force

Where premises are entered by force, no more than the minimum degree of force should be used. Searches must be conducted "with consideration for the property and privacy of the occupier searched and with no more disturbance than necessary" (para. 5.9). If the occupier wishes to have a friend to witness the search he should be allowed to do so unless the officer in charge reasonably believes that this would seriously hinder the investigation (para. 5.10).

Special procedure material

A search under warrant for "special procedure" material (*e.g.* one for confidential material authorised by a circuit judge after an application under Schedule 1 to the Act), must be under the authority of an inspector or above who must be there at the time. The officer would be responsible to ensure "that the search is conducted with discretion and in such a manner as to cause the least possible disruption to any business or other activities carried on in the premises" (para. 5.12).

The officer should ask the person in charge of the premises to produce the special procedure material in question. He may also ask to see any index to files and may inspect any files which according to the index appear to contain any of the material sought. But a more extensive search of the premises can only be made if it appears that the index is inaccurate or incomplete, or if "for any other reason the officer in charge has reasonable grounds to believe that such a search is necessary in order to find the material sought" (para. 5.13).

Record

Full records must be made of the details of the search and of what is taken. If a search is under warrant it must be returned to the court that issued it, endorsed to show whether any of the articles specified in the warrant were found, whether any other articles were seized, the date, duration and time of execution and the names of the officers who executed it (para. 7.2).

Entry for purpose of arrest etc.: section 17[18]

Section 17 makes comprehensive provision for the circumstances in which the police may enter premises in order to effect an arrest. It does not however affect statutory provisions giving the police the power to enter premises without a warrant other than to make an arrest (*e.g.* under the Gaming Act 1968, s.43(2) or the Misuse of Drugs Act 1971, s.23(1), which are set out in Tables 5.2 and 6 in Apps. 5 and 6 of the *Law and Procedure Volume* of the Royal Commission's Report).

Subsection (1) gives the police the power to enter and to search for any of the following purposes:

(a)(i) To execute a warrant of arrest arising out of criminal proceedings. This follows the existing common law.

(ii) To execute a warrant committing a fine defaulter to prison when magistrates have issued a warrant under section 76 of the Magistrates' Court Act 1980. This removes the doubt as to whether an entry was lawful to execute a warrant of commitment for failure to pay a fine or maintenance order.

(b) To arrest a person for an arrestable offence. The category of arrestable offence (defined in s.24(1) and (2) see p. 175 below) is slightly wider than under the previous law.

(c) To arrest for some offences under the Public Order Act 1936 or the Criminal Law Act 1977. These powers follow the provisions of section 26(2) (which with Sched. 2 *inter alia* preserves an unqualified power of arrest without warrant of anyone reasonably suspected of being in the act of committing an offence under ss.1, 4 or 5 of the Public Order Act), and section 11 of the Criminal Law Act 1977. The Criminal Law Act powers (which relate to the offences of entering or remaining on property) can only be exercised by a constable in uniform (subs. 3).

(d) To recapture someone unlawfully at large whom he is pursuing. This reproduces the common law power. But the power only exists in hot pursuit. Otherwise, unless the occupier consents or (b) above applies, the police would have to get a warrant of arrest.

(e) To save life or limb or prevent serious damage to property. This restates the common law.

Subsection (2) states that, save when the entry is under (e) above, a constable can only exercise these powers if he has reasonable grounds for believing that the person sought is on those premises. In the case of a block of flats the power to enter and search only applies to the actual flat in which he is suspected to be, and any common parts. There would be no power without a warrant to search all the flats or a number of them.

[18] See also text of the Act at p. 171 below.

Subsection (4) states that the search must be consistent with the purpose of the entry to make an arrest. A general search of the premises would therefore be unlawful.

The only common law power of entry without a warrant that remains now is that to deal with or to prevent a breach of the peace. All the rest are abolished (subss. (5) and (6)).

Entry and search after arrest: section 18[19]

Until recently it had been assumed that the police had power to search the home of an arrested person at least for evidence connected with the crime for which he was arrested, see especially dicta in *Jeffrey* v. *Black*.[20] But in *McLorie* v. *Oxford*,[21] the Divisional Court (Donaldson L.J. and Webster J.) held, somewhat surprisingly, that the police had no right to enter the premises of a person arrested for attempted murder to search for the motorcar which it was alleged had been the weapon used. (The decision was especially striking since the accused had actually been arrested on those same premises, but the police had taken him away and then later wanted to come back to pursue their inquiries.)

The 1929 Royal Commission on the police said the police commonly searched the home of an arrested person and that the position should be regularised by law. The Philips Royal Commission took the same view— subject to the proviso that a search of the arrested person's premises (or vehicle) should only be permitted where there were reasonable grounds for suspicion that relevant evidence might be found there. Search of any other premises should require a warrant. Also, in order to reduce the risk of "fishing expeditions" the decision to search and the reasons should be recorded prior to the search.[22]

This broadly is the scheme adopted in the Act. The police are given power to enter and search "any premises occupied or controlled by a person who is under arrest for an arrestable offence, if he has reasonable grounds for suspecting that there is on the premises evidence other than items subject to legal privilege, that relates (a) to that offence; or (b) to some other arrestable offence which is connected with or similar to that offence" (subs. (1)). This reverses the decision in *McLorie* v. *Oxford*.

If the police suspect that evidence of other unconnected offences may be found on the premises, their only recourse is to get a search warrant or to get the householder's consent to a search. This would apply equally if the arrest was not for an arrestable offence—as defined in section 24.

A search of a person's home after an arrest normally requires the written authority of an inspector or above (subs. (4)). Subsection (5) makes an exception to the requirement when the arrested person is taken straight to his home rather than to the police station (see s.30), in which case there might not be any way of getting prior written authority. If this is not obtained in advance, a report must be made after the event to an officer of that rank (subs. (6)). In either case the inspector must make a written record of the grounds for the search and the nature of the evidence sought (subss. (7)–(8)). Again, a search must not go beyond what is

[19] See also text of the Act at p. 172 below.
[20] [1978] 1 Q.B. 490.
[21] [1982] Q.B. 1290.
[22] Report, para. 3.12.

reasonably required to discover the evidence in question. No general search is permitted (subs. (3)).

Seizure of articles: section 19[23]

One of the most troublesome problems regarding police powers is the extent of the power to seize articles found in the course of a search. Prior to the new Act, at common law, where the search was under warrant the police could seize anything they found which was or which they reasonably believed to be covered by the warrant.[24] If the search was not under warrant the common law had developed to the point of permitting seizure of evidence where: (i) it implicated the owner or occupier of the premises searched in the offence for which the search was conducted[25]; (ii) it implicated the owner or occupier in some other offence[26]; (iii) it implicated third persons in the same offence for which the search was conducted[27]; or (iv) it was taken from someone innocent of involvement in the crime where his refusal to hand it over was wholly unreasonable.[28]

The Royal Commission said that "it defies common sense to expect the police not to seize items incidentally found during the course of a search."[29] At the same time "the risk that premises may be ransacked as soon as a warrant is granted for any offence must be minimised."[30] The present law was "uncertain and of little help in this respect."[31]

The Commission said it wished to avoid legitimising general searches. So the police should only be permitted to seize items found incidentally if they were evidence of a grave offence and then only if the search was carried out lawfully—in accordance with the terms of the warrant and in a manner appropriate to the items being searched for. Items seized otherwise could not be used in evidence.

The Act however defines the power of seizure very much more broadly. It provides that where a constable is searching premises under statutory powers or by consent he may seize anything on the premises (other than something exempted from seizure), if he reasonably believes that it is evidence in relation to an offence which he is investigating *or any other offence* or that it has been obtained in consequence of the commission of an offence, and that it is necessary to seize it in order to prevent its concealment, loss damage, alteration or destruction (subss. (2)–(3)). Items exempted from seizure are those reasonably believed to be subject to legal professional privilege (subs. (6)).

When seizable material is stored in a computer the police officer may require it to be produced in a form in which it is visible and legible (subs.(4)).

The section differs from the recommendation of the Royal Commission in not being limited to grave offences. Indeed it is not even limited to serious arrestable offences.

[23] See also text of the Act at p. 172 below.
[24] *Chic Fashions (West Wales) Ltd.* v. *Jones* [1968] 2 Q.B. 299.
[25] *Ghani* v. *Jones* [1969] 3 All E.R. 1700; *Garfunkel* v. *Metropolitan Police Commissioner* [1972] Crim.L.R. 44; *Frank Truman Export Ltd.* v. *Metropolitan Police Commissioner* [1977] Q.B. 952.
[26] *Ibid.*
[27] *Ghani* v. *Jones* [1969] 3 All E.R. 1700.
[28] *Ibid.*
[29] Report, para. 3.48.
[30] *Ibid.*
[31] *Ibid.*

As will be seen below, the Act also does not give effect to the Royal Commission's view that evidence seized in the course of an unlawfully conducted search should be inadmissible. On the other hand the section goes beyond what the Commission recommended in permitting seizure only if the evidence would otherwise be concealed, lost or destroyed— though this is not likely to prove much of a safeguard since presumably the police would almost always be able to claim that this condition was fulfilled. Note however, that this condition does not apply if the item to be seized is the very one for which the search was authorised. Sections 8(2), 18(2) and Schedule 1, para. 13 give the police an unqualified right to seize anything for which a search was authorised. The condition in section 19 as to what can be seized only applies to *other* items found in the course of the search.

The section extends the common law by permitting seizure of evidence implicating anyone in *any* crime. The pretence in recent cases that the law of seizure provides protection against general searches[32] has been abandoned. Instead the protection against general searches is in future to be found in the provisions on how a search may be conducted—and especially the requirement that searches must be carried out in a manner consistent with the items being looked for (s.16(8)).

Extension of powers of seizure to computerised information: section 20[33]

Section 20 simply extends the powers of seizure available in any act (including any passed after the 1984 Act), to enable the police to require that information contained in a computer be produced in a form in which it can be taken away and in which it is visible and legible. The police in other words can legitimately object if they are simply handed a floppy disc.

Seized articles: access and copying: section 21[34]

Section 21 makes provision for access to property held by the police. There were no previous statutory rules on the subject. The provisions of section 21 apply not only to property seized under section 19 but also to that seized under all other provisions in the Act or any other Act.

Subsection (1) states that a person who can show that he was the occupier of premises from which items have been seized by the police or that he had custody and control immediately before the seizure may request that he be given a record of what was taken and such a request shall be complied with. The record must be supplied within a reasonable time (subs.(2)).

Subject to subsection (8), if requested to do so the investigating officer shall grant that person or someone acting on his behalf, access to such items under the supervision of a police officer (subs.(3)). Similarly and again subject to subsection (8), the investigating officer should either allow that person or someone acting on his behalf access under supervision for the purpose of photographing or copying the items or should have the items photographed or copied for him (subs.(4)).

---

[32] See for instance *Chic Fashions (West Wales) Ltd.* v. *Jones* [1968] 2 Q.B. 299, 301; *Ghani* v. *Jones* [1969] 3 All E.R. 1700, 1703.
[33] See also text of the Act at p. 173 below.
[34] See also text of the Act at p. 173 below.

Photographs or copies made under subsection (4) should then be supplied to the person who made the request within a reasonable time (subss.(6) and (7)). The caveat in subsection (8) is that there is no duty to grant access to the material or to allow its copying where the officer in charge of the investigation has reasonable grounds for believing that to do so would prejudice the investigation of that offence or of other offences or any criminal proceedings.

Retention of seized articles: section 22[35]

At common law the police may retain items seized for such time as is reasonable in all the circumstances. The Act provides the same power with somewhat more detail.

Subject to subsection (4), anything which has been seized by a police officer may be retained so long as is necessary in all the circumstances. In particular anything seized for the purposes of a criminal investigation may be held by the police for use as evidence at the trial or for forensic examination or for investigation in connection with any offence (subs.(2)(*a*)). It may also be retained in order to establish its true owner where there are reasonable grounds for believing that it has been obtained as the result of the commission of a criminal offence (subs.(2)(*b*)).

If the police seize something on the ground that it may be used to cause physical injury or damage to property or to interfere with evidence to assist an escape, it can be kept by the police once the person from whom it was taken has been released from custody (subs.(3)).

No article may be retained by the police if a photograph or a copy would suffice for their purposes (subs.(4)). Subsection (5) saves the provisions of section 1 of the Police (Property) Act 1897. If someone from whom the police have seized something thinks that it has been retained too long he may make an application to the courts under the 1897 Act.

QUESTIONS AND ANSWERS

ENTRY AND SEARCH OF PREMISES, SEIZURE OF PROPERTY

1. In what circumstances can police enter upon premises without a search warrant?

Normally a search warrant is needed for the police to get into private premises. But there are some exceptions, viz:

(1) Where the occupier consents to entry. This justification of entry is in fact a very common one—but the reality of the consent must sometimes be a matter of some doubt. The Code of Practice on the searching of premises and the seizure of property lays down new rules in regard to the obtaining of consent which are directed to this precise point.

The Code states that consent must be in writing and the occupier must be told that he is not obliged to consent and that anything seized may be used in evidence. If the person in question is not himself suspected of any complicity in the alleged crime he must be told so.

---

[35] See also text of the Act at p. 174 below.

(2) To prevent or to stop a breach of the peace which is imminent or taking place, or to save life or limb or to prevent serious damage to property.

(3) To effect an arrest of someone for whom a warrant of arrest has been issued. The police do not need a separate search warrant.

(4) To arrest someone for an arrestable offence.

(5) Where the police enter to search premises of someone who has been arrested for an arrestable offence where they have reasonable grounds for believing that they will find evidence of that offence or of some similar or connected offence.

(6) To search the premises in which an arrested person was immediately before his arrest, for evidence relating to that offence but only if the officer has reasonable grounds for believing that such evidence is there.

(7) To recapture an escaped prisoner.

2. In what circumstances can an officer get a search warrant?

There are a variety of statutes, including the Police and Criminal Evidence Act, which allow an application to be made to the justices for a search warrant. A magistrate can under the Act grant a search warrant if he is satisfied that there are reasonable grounds to believe that:

(1) a "serious arrestable offence" (p. 236) has been committed;

(2) what is sought is likely to be relevant admissible evidence; and

(3) any one of the following conditions applies:

    (i) that there is no practicable way of contacting someone able to grant entry or to grant access to the evidence; or

    (ii) that entry will only be granted if a warrant is produced; or

    (iii) that the purpose of the search may be frustrated or seriously prejudiced if the officers arrive and are then unable to get in immediately—the occupiers would be alerted and could take steps to make the evidence unavailable.

But there are two exceptional categories where no search warrant can be obtained:

1. Items subject to legal privilege or

2. Material given total immunity under the 1984 Act—"excluded material"

There is also a category created by the 1984 Act where the material is not immune but where because of its sensitivity a special procedure is required to get a search warrant—*"special procedure material."* (As will be seen below, to complicate matters, in some rare circumstances "excluded material" does not qualify for full immunity but does have the status of "special procedure material." (see p. 34 below).

3. What is meant by legal privilege?

Legal privilege covers:

(1) Communications between a professional legal adviser and his client (or anyone representing the client) in connection with the giving of legal advice. This need not be in connection with any pending legal proceedings.

(2) Communications between the lawyer and his client (or anyone representing the client) or between the lawyer or the client or the representative and any one else in connection with actual or pending legal proceedings.

When legal proceedings are in contemplation or are actually in being, the privilege is therefore broader since it then includes communications to third parties. So documents sent to an accountant, a handwriting expert or even just to a witness would be covered by the privilege if the communication was made "in connection with or in contemplation of legal proceedings and for the purposes of such proceedings."

(3) Anything enclosed with communications under (1) above for the purposes of getting advice or with communications under (2) above in connection with actual or pending legal proceedings is also privileged if it is in the hands of someone entitled to possession.

4. Whose privilege is it?

The privilege is that of the client not the lawyer. This means that if the material is not privileged it cannot become privileged by the simple expedient of being sent to the lawyer. On the other hand, the client can release the privilege even if the lawyer does not agree.

5. Does the privilege apply if the lawyer himself is implicated in the crime?

No. The law does not prevent the police from getting a search warrant to seek evidence of a conspiracy between lawyer and client. The 1984 Act states that "items held with the intention of furthering a criminal purpose are not items subject to legal privilege." Nor would there be any privilege if the client had a criminal purpose in seeking advice unbeknown to the solicitor.

6. What is included in the category of "excluded material"?

There are three types of "excluded material":
(1) personal records;
(2) journalistic material;
(3) human tissues or tissue fluid taken for the purpose of diagnosis or medical treatment.

7. What do they cover?

(1) *"Personal records"*: are those acquired in the course of a trade, business or profession and held in confidence. They are documents or records that make it possible to identify individuals and which relate to their physical or mental health (*e.g.* medical or psychiatric records); or spiritual counselling or help (*e.g.* the files of priests or clergymen); or counselling or help given for the purposes of the individual's personal welfare by any voluntary agency or by an individual who has responsibility for the person's personal welfare (such as a university or school careers adviser, social worker, or volunteer advisory agency such as a Citizens' Advice Bureau).

(2) *"Journalistic material"* covers anything which comes into existence or is acquired for the purposes of journalism providing it is in the hands of a person who either acquired or created it for that purpose. This would cover for instance the contents of the journalist's notebook, or documents sent to a journalist with a view to their being considered for publication. Once it passes out of the possession of someone who acquired it or created it for the purposes of journalism it ceases to be "excluded material" though, as will be seen, it can still be "special procedure material."

There is no need for the journalism to be of any very exalted kind to attract the total immunity. The Act does not define what is meant by journalism but it covers any form of the activity however humble, paid or unpaid.

(3) *"Human tissue or tissue fluid"* are not further defined and seem to be reasonably unproblematic.

8. What is meant by the fact that items subject to legal privilege, personal records and journalistic material have special immunity?

The immunity means that the police cannot ask a court for permission to search for such material, let alone seize it. If, on the other hand, such material happens to come into the possession of the prosecution, it may be admissible in evidence.

9. In what circumstances must a search warrant be sought from a judge rather than from a magistrate?

The 1984 Act establishes two basic types of "special procedure material" access to which can only be sought from a judge. If and insofar as the previous law already permitted the police to get a search warrant for anything that is now defined as "excluded material," it becomes "special procedure material" and application for access must be made to a circuit judge. In other words the term "excluded material" covers two different categories of material. One is material covered by any of the definitions of excluded material for which the police could search prior to 1984. The new Act does not give such material immunity but it does require the special procedure of an application to the judge. However, anything covered by the definition of excluded material for which the police had no legal right to seek access prior to the Act now gains complete immunity. Secondly, the Act requires an application to a circuit judge for material held on a confidential basis, for instance by a bank. It is special procedure material if it is held in confidence by someone who acquired or created it in the course of a trade, business, profession or other occupation or for the purpose of any paid or unpaid office.

10. What form does the application to the judge take?

An application to the judge is made under Schedule I of the Act. It must normally be in the presence of the person against whom the order is sought who must be given advance notice of the hearing. But this does not apply where advance notice of the application might "seriously prejudice the investigation." Another exception to the principle is where it proves impossible to find anyone able to grant access to the premises or to the material sought.

The normal application under Schedule I is for an order requiring the person concerned within seven days to produce the material in question to the police so that they can take it away or to give them access to it. It is not an application for a search warrant.

But a search warrant can be obtained in two situations. One is where the material could have been the subject of a search warrant before the 1984 Act and an order to give the police access to the material has been disobeyed. The other is where the application by the police was for a search warrant in the first place because advance notice of the hearing would have seriously prejudiced the investigation. This would be the case where the police were able to satisfy the judge that there was good reason to suspect that the person who had the material was himself implicated in the crime.

When the material could have been the subject of a search warrant under the previous law the judge must grant the application for an "order to produce" providing he is satisfied that the issue of the warrant under the old law would have been appropriate. It does not appear what tests the judges should apply to determine this question.

But such cases will be very rare since there were hardly any statutes that authorised search warrants for what is now termed "excluded material." If the police want access to "excluded material" it will almost always come under the new rules which require the judge to be satisfied that there are reasonable grounds for believing that:

(1) a serious arrestable offence (see p. 236) has been committed;

(2) material of the kind sought is on the premises;

(3) it would be likely to be of substantial value to the investigation of the offence in question and would be likely to be relevant admissible evidence;

(4) other means of getting the material have failed or were not tried because it seemed they were bound to fail;

(5) it is in the public interest that the material should be produced having regard both to its value to the investigation and to the circumstances in which it is held.

If a person fails to comply with an order to produce the material or to make it available to the police, the sanction is for the police to return to the judge to ask him to punish the person concerned for contempt. As has been seen, they can only get a search warrant as a remedy for disobedience in the rare case where such a warrant could have been sought before the 1984 Act.

11. What happens if the police want material from premises some of which requires a warrant from the magistrates and some of which requires an order or a warrant from a judge?

The application must be made to the judge who will then deal with it as a whole.

12. Have the rules in regard to search warrants changed?

The 1984 Act establishes a uniform procedure for applying for and executing a search warrant under any past or future act.

(1) This requires a written application stating the grounds on which it is made; the Act under which the warrant would issue; details of the premises in question; and identification "so far as is practicable" of the articles or persons sought.

(2) The application is heard "ex parte," *e.g.* with only the police present.

(3) Answers to questions put by the justice of the peace must be given on oath.

(4) The warrant can only be used once. If the police wish to return to the premises they must get another warrant, unless the occupier is prepared to give consent.

(5) There must be two copies of the warrant—one for the person whose premises are to be searched.

(6) The warrant must be executed within a month. If it is not, and the police wish to try again, another warrant must be obtained.

(7) Entry and search under a warrant should be at a reasonable hour unless it appears to the constable executing it that the purpose of a search may be frustrated on an entry at a reasonable hour. (This seems to leave sufficient scope for the dawn raid in cases where it is thought to be necessary. It is left to the judgment of the officer concerned. Providing he reaches his decision honestly it could not be unlawful even if it was unreasonable.)

The Code of Practice on the searching of premises and the seizure of property lays down further rules in regard to the obtaining of a search warrant.

The Code requires an officer, before applying for a search warrant, to check his information carefully. No such application should be made (save in an emergency) without the approval of an inspector or above. If there is any risk of the search having adverse effects on community relations, contact should be made, if there is time, with the police community liaison officer.

13. What rules govern the process of getting into the premises to be searched?

The rules derive partly from the Act and partly from the Code of Practice for the searching of premises and the seizure of property.

The 1984 Act states that if the person whose premises are to be searched under warrant is there, the officer must identify himself. If he is not in uniform he must produce documentary evidence that he is a police officer. He must produce the search warrant and give the occupier a copy. If the person named is not there but someone else who appears to be in charge is present, then he should be told instead. If there is no one there at all the search may be carried out, but a copy of the warrant must be left in a prominent place on the premises.

14. Once in the premises, what can the police search for?

If the search is under warrant, they must stick to the terms of the warrant and search only for what it authorises. This means that the manner of the search must be determined by what is being sought. A search for large items will obviously be restricted in a way that a search for something very small is not.

If the entry is without a warrant (see pp. 30–31 above for a list of the situations in which that is possible), the search will normally be for a person and must be limited to what is reasonable in such a search. Where the search is of the premises after an arrest, as has been seen, it can only be for evidence of the offence or a similar or connected offence.

The Code of Practice for searches states that a search may not continue after the police have found what they came to find.

15. How should a search be made?

The Code states "Searches must be conducted with due consideration for the property and privacy of the occupier of the premises searched and with no more disturbance than is necessary. Reasonable force may only be used where this is necessary" (para. 5.9). If the occupier wishes to have a friend with him to witness the search this should be allowed unless the officer in charge has reasonable grounds for believing that this would seriously hinder the search. But a search need not be delayed for the purpose.

At the end of the search the premises should be left secure.

Where the search is under Schedule I for special procedure material the police are required to exercise particular circumspection—see Code, pp. 294–5 below.

16. What can be seized during a search?

The police can seize anything they come across in the course of a lawful search which is covered by any warrant or which they have reasonable grounds for believing is either evidence of any offence or has been obtained in consequence of the commission of an offence (such as the proceeds of a robbery). The only exception is anything covered by legal professional privilege—which is immune from seizure.

17. What access must be given to the person from whom the material has been seized?

The person from whom the material has been taken should, if he asks for it, be given a record of what has been seized within a reasonable time. If he requests access to the material or permission to copy or photograph it, this should be allowed (or he should be given police-made copies or photographs) unless the officer in charge of the case reasonably considers that it would prejudice the investigation of any offence or any criminal proceedings.

18. How long can material seized in a search be held?

Items may be held by the police as long as is necessary—for instance for forensic examination or for use as evidence at a trial or for return to the true owner.

19. Must the police make any reports or returns about the success or otherwise of a search of premises?

The Act requires that where a search is conducted under a warrant the officer to whom it was issued must endorse on it a statement as to whether it was executed within the one month time limit and, if so, whether the articles sought or any other articles were found. The warrant must then be returned to the court which issued it.

PART III

ARREST

The Royal Commission, dealing with arrest, said "there is a lack of clarity and an uneasy and confused mixture of common law and statutory powers of arrest, the latter having grown piecemeal and without any consistent rationale."[1] The Commission said it had two main objectives in its proposals: "to restrict the circumstances in which the police can exercise the power to deprive a person of his liberty to those in which it is genuinely necessary . . . and to simplify, clarify and rationalise the existing statutory powers of arrest."[2]

The figures produced to the Commission showed that in 1978, 76 per cent. of those proceeded against for indictable offences were arrested and the remainder were summonsed. Of those arrested, 86 per cent. were bailed from the police station. Of those dealt with for non-indictable offences (excluding motoring offences), 45 per cent. had been arrested. Of these, 88 per cent. were bailed from the police station. The total number arrested in 1979 was no less than 1.4 million. Somewhere between 10 and 20 per cent. of those were released without any charges being preferred against them.[3]

The national figures, however, concealed considerable differences of approach in different police forces. In Cambridgeshire, Cleveland and the Metropolitan District for instance, only 1 per cent. of adults accused of indictable offences were brought to court by way of summons, compared with over 40 per cent. in such places as Thames Valley, West Yorkshire, Wiltshire and North Wales.[4]

The Commission recommended that there should be a statutory definition of the criteria justifying an arrest ("the necessity principle"[5]). It proposed that the definition of arrestable offences should be expanded, in particular to include all offences carrying any sentence of imprisonment.[6] It also recommended that there be a new power given to the police where an officer sees someone committing a non-arrestable offence and he does not know that person's name and address. He should be able to arrest and detain him whilst he discovers his identity.[7] The Commission also favoured a new power to detain temporarily anyone found at the scene of a grave incident such as a murder so as to prevent possible suspects or witnesses from leaving. The power would allow persons to be held while

[1] Report, para. 3.68.
[2] Report, para. 3.75.
[3] Report, para. 3.71.
[4] Report, para. 3.72.
[5] Report, para. 3.76.
[6] Report, para. 3.83.
[7] Report, para. 3.86.

names and addresses were obtained, a suspect was identified or the matter was otherwise resolved.[8]

The Government did not, however, accept all the Royal Commission's recommendations. In particular, the Government thought the definition of arrestable offences proposed by the Royal Commission was too wide but that the definition of the power to arrest for non-arrestable offences was too narrow.

Arrest without warrant for arrestable and other offences: section 24[9]

Section 24 starts by providing that the power of arrest for arrestable offences applies (a) to offences for which the penalty is fixed by law (*e.g.* murder and treason); (b) to offences carrying a penalty of five or more years of imprisonment; and (c) to offences in subsection (2).

The result is to extend the concept of arrestable offences to two categories not previously covered. One is common law offences carrying five or more years imprisonment. These were not covered by the definition of arrestable offences in the Criminal Law Act 1967, s.2(1), because that section stated that the penalty had to arise under an enactment.

Some common law offences in question are quite serious. They include kidnapping, attempting to pervert the course of justice, conspiring to defraud and false imprisonment. There was no power of arrest in relation to these offences. The Act makes them arrestable. Subsection (2) makes into arrestable offences various statutory offences which were not previously "arrestable" (though some did already carry powers of arrest). They include some offences under the Official Secrets Acts, offences of indecent assault on a woman under section 14 of the Sexual Offences Act 1956 and taking a motor vehicle without authority and going equipped for stealing. The former was already deemed to be an arrestable offence by section 12(3) of the Theft Act 1968 and the latter also carried a power of arrest. Now it becomes a full arrestable offence carrying the other investigative powers available for arrestable and serious arrestable offences (see below).

The power of summary arrest for arrestable offences includes also conspiracy to commit, attempting to commit or inciting, aiding, abetting or procuring any such offence (subs.(3)). Section 24(4)–(7) goes on to reproduce section 2(2)–(5) of the Criminal Law Act 1967, on the circumstances in which arrest without a warrant may be effected on reasonable suspicion that an arrestable offence has been committed, is being committed or is about to be committed.

General arrest conditions: section 25[10]

Section 25 is one of the most important provisions in the Act since it gives the police a new general power of arrest for any offence whatever far beyond what the Royal Commission recommended. Not that such offences become arrestable. The Act at various points gives the police special powers that relate to arrestable offences, or serious arrestable offences. The only offences which are arrestable offences are those defined

---

[8] *Ibid.*
[9] See also text of the Act at p. 175 below.
[10] See also text of the Act at p. 176 below.

in section 24. For offences in that category the power of arrest is unqualified.

All other offences are now to carry a limited power of arrest if a constable has reasonable grounds for suspecting that any offence has been committed or attempted or is being committed or attempted and it appears to him that service of a summons is impracticable or inappropriate because "any of the general arrest conditions is satisfied."

The thinking behind the section is that the police should be able to make an arrest for an offence normally not arrestable where it is likely to prove difficult to serve a summons or where it is necessary to prevent or stop a particular social evil.

The first general arrest condition is that the officer does not know and cannot readily ascertain the name and address of the suspect or he reasonably believes that the name and address he has been given are false, or he doubts whether the suspect has given a satisfactory address for service of a summons—either because he has given no address at all or because it is doubtful whether he will be there long enough to accept service and there is no one else who can do so (subs.(3)(*a*)(*b*)(*c*)). This is obviously much wider than the power proposed by the Royal Commission which was confined to cases where the officer actually saw the offence being committed.

The second condition (in subs.(3)(*d*)) is that there are reasonable grounds for believing that the arrest is necessary to prevent the suspect causing: (i) physical harm to himself or to someone else; (ii) loss of or damage to property; (iii) an unlawful obstruction of the highway (this replaces s.137(2) of the Highways Act 1980); or (iv) an offence against public decency in circumstances "where members of the public going about their normal business cannot readily avoid the person to be arrested" (subs. 5). (This last category is seemingly intended to deal for instance with the case of a "flasher.") It is also permissible to arrest someone to protect a child "or other vulnerable person from the person to be arrested" (subs. (3)(*e*)). This broad power was not recommended by the Royal Commission at all.

The Bill did originally include a power for an officer to detain anyone while he verified the name and address given to him, exercisable if it appeared that verification could be carried out quickly. This in essence is the power given to the police in Scotland by section 2(2) of the Criminal Justice (Scotland) Act 1980. However, the power was deleted by the Government on the Report stage in the House of Commons. No such power exists therefore. Another change made in the course of the Bill's passage was the elimination of the definition of "physical harm" as including serious disease.

Repeal of statutory powers of arrest without warrant: section 26[11]

The section provides for the repeal of virtually all statutory powers of arrest without a warrant. With the enactment of the general power of arrest in section 25 these are no longer needed. Statutory powers of arrest are listed in Appendix 9 to the *Law and Procedure Volume* accompanying the Royal Commission's Report (Table 9.3 in the Appendix lists 23 statutes which give the police powers of arrest if name and address cannot be ascertained). The repeal does not affect powers of arrest at common

---

[11] See also text of the Act at p. 176 below.

law to prevent or deal with a breach of the peace nor those dependent on a warrant or order of a court nor those available to persons other than constables (*e.g.* to game keepers under section 2 of the Poaching Act 1828).

Arrest without warrant for fingerprinting: section 27[12]

It will be seen below (p. 79) that section 61(6) of the Act gives the police power to take a persons's fingerprints without his consent if he has been convicted of an offence for which convictions are recorded in national police records (known as "a recordable offence"). As a consequence, the Part of the Act dealing with arrest grants a power for the police to arrest such a person without warrant. However, the power to make an arrest only arises if the person concerned has failed to comply with a request to attend within seven days at a police station to have the fingerprints taken. Such a request can only be made within one month of the conviction and only if the person concerned was not at the time in police detention for that offence. It also grants the Home Secretary power to make regulations by statutory instrument specifying the offences constituting recordable offences, and making provision for such offences to be recorded in national police records (subss. (4)–(5)).

Information to be given on arrest: section 28[13]

The Royal Commission recommended[14] that the common law rule requiring an arrested person to be told that he is under arrest and the grounds of his arrest should be put into statutory form. This section implements this proposal and adds for good measure that when the arrest is by a police officer (but not otherwise) the requirement to inform the suspect that he is under arrest and the grounds applies regardless of whether the fact of the arrest or the ground for it is obvious. It does not apply however, if he escapes before the information can be communicated to him (subs.(5))! Subsection (3) makes the lawfulness of the arrest dependent on the arrested person having been informed at the time of arrest, or as soon as practicable thereafter, of the fact of and the grounds of arrest.

Voluntary attendance at police station: section 29[15]

The police frequently find it convenient to blur the line between freedom and arrest. The newspaper phrase "a man is helping the police with their inquiries" has become a polite euphemism to describe this shadowy area. But in law the position is not in doubt. A person is either under arrest or he is not. If he is not technically under arrest, he is free to go.

The Royal Commission recommended that this be made clear in the statute[16] and section 29 represents a partial attempt by the Home Office to spell out the details. It specifies first that where a person attends voluntarily at a police station or anywhere else "for the purpose of assisting with an investigation," "he shall be entitled to leave at will unless

---

[12] See also text of the Act at p. 177 below.
[13] See also text of the Act at p. 177 below.
[14] Report, para. 3.87.
[15] See also text of the Act at p. 177 below.
[16] Report, para. 3.97.

he is placed under arrest" and "he shall be informed at once that he is under arrest if a decision is taken by a constable to prevent him from leaving at will."

The object of this clause no doubt is to ensure that the suspect should always know that if he has not been told that he is under arrest he is free to go. But in practice, the suspect will often wrongly assume that he is under arrest and will therefore fail to take advantage of his right to leave. By the time he is told that he is under arrest, it will of course be too late. He will then be unable to depart.

The only way to avoid this dilemma would be to give a suspect who is asked whether he would mind coming down to the police station to answer a few questions a warning that this does not mean that he is under arrest and that he is free to come or not to come as he pleases. This would logically complement the later warning that the suspect need not say anything if he does not want to do so.

The Royal Commission's Report did not discuss this issue and made no recommendation that such a warning should be given and there is nothing about it in the Act. The undoubted value of section 29 is therefore somewhat qualified by the fact that the information about his status will usually be communicated to the suspect only at the moment of being cautioned or arrested.

The point was in fact considered expressly in the House of Lords. Lord Hutchinson moved an amendment which would have had the effect of requiring that a person on arrival voluntarily at the police station be informed both orally and in writing that he was free to leave at any time, that he was under no obligation to answer questions, that he was entitled to have someone told that he was at the police station and to consult a solicitor privately.

Lord Denning said that he supported the amendment. If an interview was wholly voluntary, he said, it should be conducted at the person's home. "But to say to him, 'Are you willing to come along to the police station?' or 'Will you come along to the police station?' is half way to making an arrest. When he has got to the police station, the ordinary person can half feel he is under arrest, even though the police are said to be making inquiries. Then is the time to make clear to him that he is there voluntarily and that he can leave at that moment if he likes. This virtually means in many cases that he is under suspicion. In those circumstances he ought to be told, 'Well you can have a solicitor, if you like; you need not say anything' and so forth. In other words, give him all the protection which should surround a man who is under suspicion, because that is why he is there. A clause like that . . . will ensure the protection of the individual."[17]

In reply the Home Office Minister, Lord Elton, said that Lord Hutchinson's amendment would impose "an enormous administrative burden on the police."[18] "A great many people attend police stations voluntarily for all sorts of reasons. They include, for example, victims of burglary, attending to identify property and victims of assault attending to identify a suspect or to provide a statement . . . If these amendments are accepted, the first thing that must happen would be that a policeman would inform them orally and in writing that they were entitled to leave at will unless

[17] House of Lords, *Hansard*, July 5, 1984, col. 502.
[18] *Ibid.*

placed under arrest. Is that the way to treat a shaken victim or a hesitating and irresolute witness? Such people need encouragement to come to the police, and particularly in the case of victims of rape and sexual assault. . . Similarly, the large volume of paper that would be produced by the voluntary attendance forms would be entirely disproportionate to any good it would achieve."[19]

Lord Elton thought that the problem was met adequately by the requirement that a person be cautioned as soon as there were any grounds to believe that he had committed an offence. At that point he must be told of his right to silence, his right to have someone informed of his whereabouts, and his right to legal advice. He went on to assert that "the person must also be told . . . that he is free to leave the police station if he wishes . . . The right to leave is a most fundamental right."[20] But this only arises after the detainee has been cautioned (Code, para. 11.2). If he is cautioned away from the police station and is not then under arrest the same paragraph of the Code requires that he be told so. This would then presumably inform him that he is not under any compulsion to come with the police officer.

Arrest elsewhere than at police station: section 30[21]

The Royal Commission recommended that persons who have been arrested should normally be taken straight to a police station so that their detention could become subject to the general supervisory measures which the Commission proposed for detained persons.[22] Both the Act and the Code contain various rights for suspects and duties for the police which start to operate from the time of arrival at a police station. It is therefore important that these controls and safeguards take effect from the earliest practicable time. In particular, the time-limit clock only starts to run on arrival at the police station. (There is in any event some value in discouraging the police from "taking the scenic route to the police station" as a way of providing additional time and opportunity for questioning away from the scrutiny of station colleagues.)

The Act implements the Royal Commission's proposal by stating that where a person is arrested away from a police station he shall be taken to a police station "as soon as practicable" (subs. (1)). However, the effect of this provision is somewhat weakened by subsection (9) which allows the police to delay taking him to a police station if the presence of that person elsewhere is necessary to carry out investigations of an offence.

If there is such delay the reasons for it must be recorded on first arrival at the police station (subs. (10)).

The section does not however affect the special powers of the police in relation to immigration and terrorism cases nor the right of the police under the Criminal Justice Act 1972, s.34 to take a drunk to a detoxification centre (subss. (11) and (12)). Normally, according to section 30(1) a person who has been arrested must be taken to a "designated police station" (defined in s.35). But he may be taken to a non-designated station if any of three alternative conditions is satisfied. The first is where the officer is working in the area of a non-designated police station—unless it

---

[19] *Ibid.* col. 503
[20] *Ibid.*
[21] See also text of the Act at p. 178 below.
[22] Report, para. 3.102.

appears that the suspect will have to be held for longer than six hours (subss.(3) and (4)(*a*). This would presumably be relatively common. The second is where the person was arrested by a police officer acting on his own, no other officer is available to help him and it appears to the arresting officer that he will not be able to take him to a designated station without the detained person injuring someone (himself, the officer or another person). The third situation in which he may be taken to a non-designated station is where the officer has taken the person into custody from someone other than a police officer (*e.g.* after a citizen's arrest), and again there is no other officer to help him and taking him to a designated station creates a risk of the suspect causing someone injury.

If the officer is satisfied before the arrested person has reached a police station that there are no grounds for keeping him under arrest, he must release him (subs. (6)). He need not take him to the police station in order to book him before allowing him to go. Obviously this creates the possibility of attempts to corrupt the officer as a way of securing immediate release. The Police Federation spokesman in the House of Commons took this sufficiently seriously to argue strenuously during the Committee stage that there ought to be a duty for the arresting officer always to take the suspect to the station. But the Government rejected this view, preferring to trust officers and to give the citizen the advantage of immediate release if preliminary inquiries show that no arrest is necessary.[23] The safeguard, for what it is worth, is that, where someone is released in this way a record of the fact must be made (subs. (7)). Obviously, if a bribe has been taken; it is hardly likely that a record would be made!

Arrest for further offence: section 31[24]

Section 31 addresses the situation of someone at a police station in connection with several offences, and provides that he must be told afresh if there are grounds to arrest him for any second or later offence. Each time that he is notionally arrested again he must be so informed.

However the time limits on detention in the police station under the Act are not affected. Regardless of how many offences are being investigated whilst he is in custody the police have the same amount of time before they have to bring him before a magistrate under section 43. Unless he is released on bail, the time limits are measured as from his first arrest (s. 41(2) and (3)).

Search upon arrest: section 32[25]

Section 32 deals with search after an arrest somewhere other than at a police station and gives the police a power to search that is somewhat broader than that previously enjoyed at common law. The common law allowed the police to search an arrested person for a weapon or for evidence material to the offence for which he was arrested.[26] The Royal

---

[23] See House of Commons, *Hansard,* Standing Committee E, February 2, 1984, cols. 912–928.
[24] See also text of the Act at p. 179 below.
[25] See also text of the Act at p. 179 below.
[26] *Dillon* v. *O'Brien and David* (1887) 16 Cox C.C. 245.

Commission said it had not received any proposals for alteration of these rules and it recommended that they be confirmed in statute.[27]

Subsection (1) allows the police to search someone arrested where there are grounds for believing that he may present a danger to himself or others. The right to search for a weapon is unqualified.

Subsection (2) permits a search of the arrested person for anything that might be used to effect an escape or which might be evidence relating to any offence. In addition, subsection (2) gives the police the power to enter and search the premises in which he was when arrested, or immediately before he was arrested, for evidence relating to the offence for which he was arrested. But the power of search under subsection (2) only exists if there are reasonable grounds for believing that the search might prove productive of something for which a search is permitted (subss. (5) and (6)). Random or automatic searching is therefore not lawful—as was already determined by the courts.[28] Also, a person searched in public cannot be required to take off anything other than his coat, jacket or gloves (subs. (4)).

Where the person is arrested in a block of flats or other premises consisting of two or more separate dwellings, only the premises in which he was when arrested or immediately beforehand and any common parts shared with other occupiers may be searched (subs. (7)).

It will be noticed that the power under this section to search the premises where an arrest takes place is narrower than that under section 18 to enter and search premises of an arrested person. Under section 18 the police may come in and look for evidence relating to the offence for which he was arrested or "to some other offence which is connected with or similar to that offence." Under this section they may look only for evidence relating to the actual offence for which the arrest was made. On the other hand, under this section they can search the arrested person himself for evidence of *any* offence which enlarges the common law power and goes beyond what the Royal Commission recommended.

Execution of warrant not in possession of constable: section 33[29]

The common law was that the constable had to have the warrant with him when he came to execute it. This rule was changed for warrants of arrest by the Magistrates' Courts Act 1980, s.125(3). Section 33 extends the same rule to the various kinds of warrants referred to in the section.

QUESTIONS AND ANSWERS

ARREST

1. What is the difference between "helping the police with their inquiries" and being under arrest?

Being under arrest means being subject to restraint as to one's movements. One is either under arrest or one is not; there is no half-way stage.

---

[27] Report, para. 115.
[28] See *Lindley* v. *Rutter* [1981] Q.B. 128 and *Brazil* v. *Chief Constable of Surrey* [1983] 3 All E.R. 537.
[29] See also text of the Act at p. 180 below.

A person who is "helping the police with their inquiries" is therefore free to go if he pleases.

2. Are the police obliged to inform someone being questioned that he is not under arrest?

In general the answer is No. When the police ask someone to come down to the police station to answer a few questions, they are not obliged to caution him that he is under no compulsion to do so. Nor are they obliged to advise him on arrival at the police station of his rights including his right to legal advice, the right to have someone informed of where he is and the right to leave. If he happens to know of these rights he is free to exercise them.

The first point at which the police must inform him of these rights is when he is cautioned, whether or not in the police station. They must also tell him at the moment when he is under arrest, but by then it is obviously too late for him to leave.

3. What procedures follow when someone is arrested?

The only strict rule on arrest is that the person concerned must as soon as practicable be told that he is under arrest and why he has been arrested—the Act says even if it is obvious. In principle he should then be taken to a police station as soon as possible, though an exception is allowed where his presence is needed elsewhere in the interests of the investigation

4. To what police station should someone who is arrested be taken?

If it is clear that the suspect will have to be detained for longer than several hours, he should be taken to one of the police stations in the area named by the chief constable as "designated stations" for the receipt of persons in custody. If the police station to which he is taken is not a designated one the suspect cannot be held there for longer than six hours. At that point he must be transferred to a designated police station.

5. On what grounds can someone be arrested?

There are two main categories of situations where someone can be arrested. One is broadly the same as under the previous law—on reasonable suspicion of having committed, being about to commit or committing an arrestable offence. The second is where the officer believes that an arrest is necessary for a non-arrestable offence because of the particular circumstances of the case. One ground is that the culprit refuses to supply his name and address or gives a Mickey Mouse name and address. But the broader ground is that the arrest is thought to be necessary to prevent the person concerned from causing physical injury to himself or others; or suffering physical injury; or causing loss of or damage to property; or committing an offence against public decency; or causing an unlawful obstruction of the highway. There also remains the common law power to arrest someone for a breach of the peace.

If someone has been arrested for one offence and it seems to an officer that, if released, he would be liable to be arrested for other offences he should be arrested for those other offences.

6. Can a person who has been arrested be searched and if so, for what reason?

A person who has been arrested can be searched if there are reasonable grounds to think,

(1) that he may present a danger to himself or others; or

(2) that he might have on him evidence of a crime or something which he could use to escape.

The police may enter and search any premises in which he was when arrested or immediately before he was arrested but only to look for evidence of that offence.

The Code states that on arrival at a police station the custody officer (see below) is under a duty to itemise what property he has (unless he is to be held only very briefly) and to that end he may search him for that purpose if it is necessary. Searches may not however take place on a routine basis, without regard to the circumstances.

See further p. 66 and see also pp. 80–81 below on intimate searches and the taking of body samples.

PART IV

DETENTION

The section on detention runs to no less than 19 sections. It establishes a new framework for the regime of detention and, in particular, in relation to time limits, supervision by a custody officer and record keeping.

Lengthy detention in a police station is relatively rare. The Royal Commission said that about three-quarters of suspects were dealt with within six hours and about 95 per cent. within 24 hours. A survey done for the Commission by the Metropolitan Police for three months in 1979 showed that only 0.4 per cent. of 48,343 persons had been held for over 72 hours before being charged or released without charges.[1]

Limitations on police detention: section 34[2]

Section 34 provides in essence that detention in a police station must be in conformity with the provisions of the Act.

Subsection (2) states that the custody officer (see s.36 below) must order the release of anyone whose continued detention by the police cannot be justified under the Act. Subsection (5) requires that release in such a case be unconditional unless further investigation in the matter is needed or future proceedings may be taken against the detained person, in either of which cases the release may be subject to bail.

"Police detention" is defined in section 118(2).

Designated police stations: section 35[3]

Until a late stage the Bill drew no distinction between busy police stations with large numbers of officers available and small rural stations with slight manpower resources. When the Bill was before the House of Lords however the Government introduced amendments to take account of these differences in terms of the functions and duties of the custody officer.

The scheme devised by the Government was to make the full range of custody officer duties and functions available from "designated police stations," whilst other stations would be restricted as to the the time for which they could hold suspects. As has already been seen, section 30 provides that a person may not be held in a non-designated police station for longer than six hours. The distinction between designated and non-designated police stations is spelled out in sections 35 and 36.

The chief officer in each area must designate which "are to be the

---

[1] Report, para. 3.96.
[2] See also text of the Act at p. 180 below.
[3] See also text of the Act at p. 181 below.

stations in that area to be used for the purpose of detaining arrested persons" (s.35(1)). Enough must be designated to meet the needs of the area (subs. (2)). Each designated police station must have one or more custody officers appointed (s.36(1)).

Custody officers at police stations: section 36[4]

Section 36 provides for there to be a custody officer at every designated police station. This follows the recommendation to this effect by the Royal Commission.[5] At other police stations there must simply be someone able to take on the job if the need arises. The appointment of the custody officer must either be by the chief constable himself or by someone acting under delegated powers from the chief constable (s.36(2)). Anyone appointed to be a custody officer must be at least of the rank of sergeant (s.36(3)) but the value of this is somewhat diminished by the terms of the following subsection which allows an officer who is not a sergeant to perform the functions of a custody officer at a designated station "if a custody officer is not readily available to perform them" (subs. (4)).

Section 36(5) makes it plain that at designated police stations the investigative and custodial functions should be basically distinct. Subject to the provisions of section 39 (2) (p. 185 below), "none of the functions of a custody officer . . . shall be performed by an officer who at the time when the functions fall to be performed is involved in the investigation of an offence for which that person is in police detention at that time." But the prohibition on the custody officer undertaking investigative functions is not total. So the custody officer can do anything authorised by the Act or the codes—such as searching a suspect or his clothing. He can undertake duties in connection with the identification of the suspect or his clothing. He can undertake duties in connection with the identification of the suspect such as taking fingerprints and he can do anything required by section 8 of the Road Traffic Act (driving with excess alcohol) such as administering a breath test (subs.(6)).

What if the suspect is taken to a non-designated police station? In that case s.36(7)(*a*) states that the functions which would be those of the custody officer in a designated police station must be carried out by someone not involved in the investigation, "if such officer is readily available." This clearly leaves scope for the police to plead that no such officer was readily available. In that case the functions may be carried out by the officer who took the person concerned to the station "or any other officer" (s.36(7)(*b*)). When this occurs such an "acting custody officer" must as soon as practicable notify an officer of the rank of inspector or above at a designated police station that this is the case (subss. (9) and (10)). There is no requirement that the notification has to be in writing and normally it will be by telephone or radio. The fact that the notification must be as soon as practicable shows that it is intended to operate before any action is taken, so that the inspector at the larger station can consider whether to have the suspect brought there instead.

Subsection (6) provides that a person arrested on suspicion of driving with excess alcohol under section 7(5) of the Road Traffic Act 1972 is

---

[4] See also text of the Act at p. 181 below.
[5] Report, para. 3.112.

arrested for an offence for the purposes of subsection (1). This settles the doubt about the matter raised by *R.* v. *Mackenzie*.[6]

Duties of custody officer before charge: section 37[7]

The purpose of section 37 is to ensure that a person brought to the police station is charged if there is enough evidence to charge him but that if there is not sufficient evidence he should be released unless the custody officer has reasonable grounds for believing that his detention is needed to preserve or obtain evidence of the offence for which he was arrested.

Subsection (1) states that where someone is arrested without a warrant or on a warrant not endorsed for bail, or returns to a police station to answer to bail, the custody officer at any police station to which he is taken must first consider whether there is sufficient evidence to justify a charge for the offence for which he was arrested. The test is laid down in paragraph 17.1 of the Code of Practice on the treatment and questioning of suspects issued under section 66 of the Act. Paragraph 17.1 requires that as soon as the officer questioning someone "believes that a prosecution should be brought against him and that there is sufficient evidence for it to succeed" he should without delay bring him for charging to the custody officer.

The duty laid on the custody officer by subsection (1) to consider whether there is enough evidence to justify a charge must be carried out as soon as practicable after the suspect's arrival at the police station or, where he was arrested at the police station, after the arrest (subs. (10)).

Under subsection (2) of section 37, if the custody officer determines that he does not have enough evidence to charge the person detained, he must be released on bail or unconditionally, unless he "has reasonable grounds for believing that his detention without being charged is necessary to secure or preserve evidence relating to an offence for which he is under arrest or to obtain such evidence by questioning him." If so, further detention may be authorised (subs. (3)). In other words, detention is permitted primarily for the purpose of questioning. However, as Mr. Douglas Hurd, the Home Office Minister, emphasised in the House of Commons, the phrase is that "This detention was necessary—not desirable, convenient or a good idea but necessary.[8]

Detention for questioning was not always permitted. The common law on this point has moved considerably in the past few years. But there is no doubt that in recent years the courts have countenanced detention for questioning. The latest and most authoritative pronouncement to this effect was the decision of the House of Lords in *Mohammed-Holgate* v. *Duke*.[9] But see also *Shaaban Bin Hussein* v. *Chong Fook Kam*[10] and *R.* v. *Houghton*.[11]

Subsection (4) requires that as soon as practicable, the custody officer make a written record of the grounds of detention and under subsection (5) this should normally be done in the presence of the suspect who must be told the grounds by the custody officer. This would not be required

[6] [1971] 1 All E.R. 729.
[7] See also text of the Act at p. 182 below.
[8] House of Commons, *Hansard*. Standing Committee E, February 16, 1984, col. 1229.
[9] [1984] Q.B. 209.
[10] [1969] 3 All E.R. 1626, 1630.
[11] (1979) 68 Cr.App.R. 197, 205.

however if he is not in a fit state to be told (subs. (6)). Under paragraph 1.7 of the Code of Practice the explanation must then be given as soon as practicable.

If there is enough evidence to charge him he must either be charged (in which case the provisions of section 38 apply) or released with or without bail (subss. (7) and (8)). If no decision has been made as to whether he will be prosecuted he should be so informed (subs. (7)). If he is not in a fit state to be charged he may be detained until he is in a fit state (subs. (9)). Such detention cannot however be for more than 24 hours and must cease when he is in a fit state if that is earlier. This follows from the general prohibition on detention for more than 24 hours in section 41 subject to exceptions which do not apply in such a case.

Subsection (11) deals with arrested juveniles (as defined in subs. (12)). It restates provisions in section (5) and section 29(4) of the Children and Young Persons Act 1969 which are not yet in force. Subsection (11) will only be brought into force if and when these provisions of the 1969 Act are made law. Subsections (12) to (14) put upon the custody officer a duty, so far as practicable, to identify the person responsible for the welfare of an arrested juvenile and, after identifying him, to give that person the same information as under subs. (11) has to be given to the juvenile himself regarding whether a prosecution is to be laid and for what offence. But the duty only arises if and when those provisions of the 1969 Act come into force, which does not at present seem likely.

Subsection (11) defines "arrested juvenile" and "endorsed for bail."

Duties of custody officer after charge: section 38[12]

Section 38 establishes the principles on which the custody officer must decide whether to keep someone in custody after he has been charged. Under the previous law this was dealt with solely by section 43 of the Magistrates' Courts Act 1980.

Subsection (1) sets out the detention conditions after charge. Where someone who has been arrested without warrant or under a warrant not endorsed for bail is charged, the custody officer must release him with or without bail unless any of four detention conditions apply:

(1) If it appears that he has not provided a satisfactory address for service of a summons.

(2) If detention is necessary for his own or other people's protection or to prevent loss of or damage to property (e.g. through committing further offences against persons or property or intimidating witnesses).

(3) If there are reasonable grounds for believing that the suspect would fail to appear in court or not answer to bail or would interfere with the course of justice.

(4) If the suspect is a juvenile (defined in s.37(12)) he can also be detained in his own interests. This preserves the effect of section 29(1)(i) of the Children and Young Persons Act 1969. (Under that Act, if a juvenile is charged with an offence he may be kept in custody pending his production in court if it would be in his own interest.) He must be transferred to the custody of the local authority unless the custody officer

---

[12] See also text of the Act at p. 184 below.

certifies that it is impracticable to do so. A typical example might be that of a youngster picked up for an offence after he has run away from home. He cannot be sent home on overnight bail and would very likely be held in custody "in his own interests". Subsections (3), (4) and (5) require that a written record be made of the grounds of detention in the presence of the suspect who must be told the grounds—unless he is not in a fit state.

Subsections (6) and (7) restate the substance of section 29(3) of the Children and Young Persons Act and thereby maintain the presumption against the detention of juveniles in police custody after charge.

Responsibilities in relation to detained persons: section 39[13]

Section 39 concerns the responsibility of the custody officer for the proper treatment of detained persons as recommended by the Royal Commission.[14] Subsection (1) requires the custody officer to ensure that anyone detained at his police station is treated in accordance with the requirements of the Act and of any Codes of Practice made under it. It states that the duties of the custody officer include responsibility also for seeing that everything required to be recorded in the custody record is in fact recorded.

If the custody officer transfers custody of the suspect to the investigating officer, his duties in this regard are taken over by the person who has custody of the suspect (subs. (2)). When he returns the suspect to the custody officer's custody the officer is supposed to report "as to the manner in which this section and the codes of practice have been complied with" (subs. (3)). If an arrested juvenile is handed over to the local authority under section 38(7) the custody officer's responsibility ceases (subs. (4)). The local authority however has a duty to provide with "such advice and assistance as may be appropriate" (subs. (5)).

The Royal Commission recommended[15] that even where the investigating officer outranks the custody officer it should be the latter not the former who has the decisive responsibility. Subsection (6) gives effect to this view, by requiring that if there is any conflict between the two the custody officer must refer the issue at once to a superintendent or more senior officer in charge of the police station. This makes it clear that the custody officer is directly responsible to the divisional or sub-divisional commander.

Reviews of police detention: section 40[16]

The Royal Commission recommended[17] that the need for detention should be reviewed periodically—on arrival at the police station, after six hours and then after 24 hours. The section adopts this approach but makes the requirement somewhat more onerous by specifying that it must be carried out within the first six hours and then at not more than nine hour intervals. Where the person concerned has already been charged the review would be by the custody officer, if not, it would be by an officer not involved in the investigation of the rank of inspector or above. The person performing the

---

[13] See also text of the Act at p. 185 below.
[14] Report, para. 3.112.
[15] *Ibid.*
[16] See also text of the Act at p. 186 below.
[17] Report, para. 3.105.

function would be known as the review officer. His review would be separate from and in addition to the first assessment by the custody officer on the suspect's arrival at the police station under section 37(2) and (3). These reviews must take place even though continued detention under section 42 has been authorised or a warrant of further detention under section 43 has been issued. The purpose of the reviews is to ensure that the detainee is being properly treated and that he is released as soon as possible. The review can be over the telephone if that is the only practicable way of conducting it (Notes for Guidance, 16B). Any conflict between the review officer and a more senior officer involved in the case must be referred at once by the review officer to a superintendent or above (subs. (11)).

A review may be postponed if, having regard to the circumstances, "it is not practicable" to have it at the specified time, or the suspect is actually being questioned at the time and the review officer is satisfied that interruption would prejudice the investigation or if no review officer is readily available (subs. (4)). It must however be conducted as soon as practicable. When the delay is because the suspect is being questioned the review would take place normally in the next break in questioning. The grounds of any delay must be recorded in the custody record. Moreover, when there has been delay the next review must take place within the time limit as measured from the time when the prior review should have taken place not when it did in fact take place. Otherwise the suspect would be penalised by the fact of the delay (subs. (6)).

The grounds for keeping the suspect in detention must be given to the detainee in his presence if practicable. If not the information must be given as soon as practicable and in any case before he is first questioned (Code of Practice, para. 3.1). The grounds must be recorded in the custody record. But before authorising continued detention the review officer must give the suspect (unless he is asleep at the time) or any solicitor representing him who is available at the time, the opportunity of making representations (subs. (12)). But the review officer can refuse to hear oral representations by the suspect himself "if he considers that he is unfit to make such representations by reason of his condition or behaviour" (subs. (14)). In that case he cannot however refuse to hear representations from a solicitor. In the custody officer's discretion, "other persons having an interest in the person's welfare" may also be allowed to make representations on his behalf (Code of Practice, para. 16.1).

Time limits on detention without charge: section 41[18]

Under the previous law the time limit on police detention depended on whether the offence was regarded by the police as "serious." Section 43 of the Magistrates' Court Act 1980 required that where the offence was not serious and the suspect could not be brought before a magistrates' court within 24 hours he had to be released on bail. But where the offence was serious (and there was no definition in the Act) he simply had to be brought before a court "as soon as practicable" (s.43(4)).

The police tended to interpret the phrase "as soon as practicable" to mean "as soon as we have decided whether to charge him," rather than "as soon as a court can be found that is sitting." The result was that some suspects were held for long periods without charges. The only safeguard against this was the rare intervention of an application for habeas corpus

---

[18] See also text of the Act at p. 187 below.

which usually had the effect of forcing the police either to charge or release the suspect.[19]

The Royal Commission took the view that this problem required drastic change and recommended that a proper system of time limits be imposed. The police, they recommended,[20] should not be permitted to hold a suspect without charges for more than 24 hours unless they had sought and obtained permission from a magistrates' court at a full hearing held in private at which the suspect would be entitled to be both present and legally represented. Moreover there should be no power to hold anyone for more than 24 hours unless he was suspected of having committed a grave offence.

Under the Royal Commission's proposed scheme the magistrates' court would have been able to authorise further detention for periods of not more than 24 hours at a time—with no overall limit. After 48 hours however there would have been a right of appeal to a judge.

When the first Bill was first published it showed that the Government had made certain important modifications in the Royal Commission's proposed scheme.

Its basic provision was that holding a suspect without charges for more than 24 hours would require a magistrate's permission. In the first instance an application would be made *ex parte* to a single magistrate. The hearing could be in the magistrate's own home. The suspect would only have had the right to appear before the magistrates after 48 hours. On the other hand, the magistrates could not authorise more than a total of 96 hours detention without charges. The provisions for holding a suspect beyond 24 hours only applied to serious arrestable offences.

These provisions were criticised from different vantage points. Some argued that it was wrong to delay the suspect's right to a full hearing to review further detention as long as 48 hours. Others contended that the application after 24 hours to a single magistrate possibly in his home and without requiring him to be attended by his clerk would tempt the police to shop around for a compliant magistrate. Also it was undesirable to have matters of such moment determined by a magistrate at his home.

The Government eventually decided to amend the scheme by abolishing the *ex parte* application to the magistrates and by advancing the time of the full hearing before the magistrates' court from the 48 hour point to the 36 hour stage. It resisted the argument that it should be brought forward even further to the 24 hour point mainly on the ground of the burden this would throw on all concerned. The number of persons held for more than 24 hours was some 22,000 compared with only a few hundred held for over 36 hours.[21] For the first 24 hours therefore authority for detention would be for the review officer. At the end of 24 hours it would have to be authorised by an officer of the rank of superintendent or above and from 36 hours onwards it could only be authorised by a magistrates' court after a full hearing at which the suspect could be present and legally represented. This scheme is that adopted in the Act.

[19] See generally C. Munro, "Detention after arrest" [1981] Crim.L.R. 802, and D. Wolchover, "The Police Bill and the scope of existing powers of detention for questioning" (1983) 80 L.S.Gaz. 2978. The most important recent cases are: *Houghton and Franciosy* (1978) 68 Cr.App.R. 197; *Hudson* (1981) 72 Cr.App.R. 163; *Re Sherman and Apps* (1981) 72 Cr.App.R. 266 and *Nycander, The Times,* September 9, 1982.
[20] Report, para. 3.106.
[21] House of Commons, *Hansard,* Standing Committee E, February 16, 1984, col. 1218.

Subsection (1) of section 41 provides that, subject to later provisions of the section and to sections 42 and 43, a person may not be detained without charge in police custody for more than 24 hours. This is the basic rule. Unless his further detention is authorised, he must be released with or without bail and cannot be re-arrested for the same offence unless new evidence comes to light (subss. (7) and (9)).

Subsection (2) defines the time from which the period of detention is to be calculated (the "relevant time"). The normal case in paragraph (d) is where the arrest takes place locally for an offence committed in the same area. In such a case time starts to run from the moment that the arrested person first arrives at the first police station after his arrest.

Where the person is arrested outside England and Wales, the time starts to run from the moment that he arrives at the first police station to which he is taken in the area in which the offence for which he was arrested is being investigated, or 24 hours after his arrival in England and Wales, whichever is the earlier. If therefore he has not arrived at his destination within 24 hours of entering England and Wales, time starts to run at that point. (s.41(2)(b)).

If at any stage of being in police detention the detainee is taken to a hospital for medical treatment, time involved in travel there or back or at the hospital counts if he is actually being questioned about any offence but not otherwise (subs. (6)). The Code of Practice (para. 15.2) states that a person in police detention in hospital "may not be questioned without the agreement of a responsible doctor."

In the case of somebody already under arrest who is then arrested for further offences under section 31, time runs from the first offence for which he was brought into custody (subs. (4)). Otherwise time could be extended by the simple expedient of adding more and more arrests. For someone who comes to the police station voluntarily, time starts to run from the moment of his arrest (subs. 2(c)).

But what if the arrested person is actually wanted by police in some other area? According to paragraph (a) of subsection (2), if the arrested person is arrested in one police area in England and Wales but is wanted in another, time starts to run when he comes into the custody of the second police force or 24 hours, whichever is the earlier.

This is stated to be on the assumption that the force which have first arrested him make no inquiries into the alleged offence. If they in fact do start to question him about the offence for which they arrested him, then time starts to run under paragraph (c) from the time that he first comes to a police station in the first area (subs. (3)(c)).

The Code of Practice states however that if a person has been arrested by one police force on behalf of another and lawful detention under section 37 has not yet commenced, he may not be questioned whilst in transit except to clarify a voluntary statement (para. 15.1).

If the suspect is wanted for questioning both where he is and in another area, there would in effect be two relevant times. In relation to the second area the relevant time would be 24 hours after leaving the first area or the moment of arriving at a police station in the second area whichever was the earlier (subs. (5)).

Authorisation of continued detention: section 42[22]

Section 42 permits an officer of the rank of superintendent or above to authorise the detention of a person without charge beyond 24 hours and up to 36 hours if this is necessary for the effective investigation of a serious arrestable offence (defined in s.116).

The preconditions are that the senior officer must be satisfied that the investigation is being conducted diligently and expeditiously and that the detention of the suspect is *necessary* to secure or preserve evidence relating to the offence or to obtain such evidence by questioning him (subs. (1)).

Such an authorisation may not be given more than 24 hours after time has started to run in regard to detention nor before the second review of detention under section 40[23] has taken place (subs. (4)). The purpose of the latter limitation is to ensure that continued detention is not authorised prematurely. If detention is authorised for less than the full 36 hours it may later be extended up to the 36 hours providing the conditions set out in subsection (1) still apply (subs. (2)).

When authorisation for continued detention has been given, the suspect must be told the grounds of the decision and they must be recorded in the custody record (subs. (5)).

The section also requires the police again to give the suspect (or his solicitor or, in the discretion of the custody officer, other persons interested in his welfare) an opportunity to make oral or written representations (subs. (6)). The right of the suspect himself to make oral representations can be withheld if the police officer concerned considers that he is unfit by reason of his condition or behaviour (subs. (8)). If the suspect has not yet exercised his right under sections 56 or 58 (to have someone informed of his whereabouts and to have legal advice), the officer must remind him of those rights and decide whether he should be allowed to exercise them. His decision must be recorded in the custody record, as must the reasons if he is refused permission (subs. (9)).

A person who has not been charged must be released within 36 hours after the detention clock has started to run unless further detention has been authorised by magistrates under section 43 (subs. (10)). If he has been charged, section 46[24] applies (see p. 60 below). A person who has been released may not be re-arrested for the same offence unless new evidence justifying a further arrest has come to light since his release (subs. (11)).

Warrants of further detention: section 43[25]

Section 43 deals with the hearing before a magistrates' court to decide whether the police can hold the suspect for a longer period without any charge after the initial 36 hours. If so, the magistrates grant a warrant of "further detention" (and later perhaps an extension of the warrant—see s.44 below). By contrast, the authority of a superintendent to continue holding a suspect for longer than 24 hours in the police station is called, as has been seen, authorisation of "continued detention."

[22] See also text of the Act at p. 188 below.
[23] p. 186 below.
[24] p. 192 below.
[25] See also text of the Act at p. 190 below.

An application for permission to hold the suspect beyond 36 hours must be made on oath and *inter partes* to a magistrates' court. It must be supported by an information from the police officer a copy of which must have been supplied in advance to the detainee. The court cannot start the hearing unless he has a copy and he is physically present (subs. (2)). If he does not have a lawyer and wishes to have one the hearing has to be adjourned. He can be kept in police custody during such an adjournment (subs. (3)). If satisfied that there are sufficient grounds, the court may issue a warrant of further detention (subs. (1)). The tests for the magistrates are exactly the same as those for the superintendent considering further detention under section 42(1)[26]: that detention is necessary to secure or preserve evidence relating to a serious arrestable offence for which he is under arrest or to obtain such evidence by questioning him and that the investigation is being conducted diligently and expeditiously.

The court would clearly be entitled to take into account the suspect's response to police questioning. If therefore the evidence was that he had refused to answer all or most questions and if the court took the view that the real purpose of prolonging his detention was to break down his silence it would presumably refuse to grant the police application for further time.

The Opposition tried at the Committee stage in the House of Commons to persuade the Government to accept an amendment which would have required the magistrates, when considering an application for a warrant of further detention, to have regard specifically to whether he was answering questions willingly. The Government refused to accept the amendment. But the Home Office Minister, Mr. Douglas Hurd, made it clear that the principle was accepted: "I do not doubt that in practice when interpreting the Bill the court would ask questions and want to hear evidence on how fruitful interviews had been if the application for further detention were based on this ground. That would clearly be an important consideration, and evidence on this subject—because we are talking of an *inter partes* hearing—would be given by the detained person who would be present and would be legally represented."[27]

Mr. Hurd then referred to the fact (already mentioned above) that the phrase in the Act was that detention for questioning must be "*necessary* to secure or preserve evidence relating to an offence . . . or to obtain such evidence by questioning him" (italics supplied) not that such questioning would be, "desirable, convenient or a good idea."[28] He also drew the attention of the Opposition spokesman to the provision in the Bill (now section 43(14)),which laid down what the police officer had to specify in the way of information in support of an application. Subparagraph (*d*) said the police must give, "the reasons for believing the continued detention of that person to be necessary"—"again not convenient, desirable or a good idea but necessary" for the purposes of such further inquiries. A court he said would need to be satisfied on those points.[29]

An application for a warrant of further detention may be made at any time before the detention clock has run for 36 hours, or if it is not practicable for a court to sit when the 36 hours expires but it will sit

---

[26] p. 56 above, p. 188 below.
[27] House of Commons, *Hansard,* Standing Committee E, February 16, 1984, cols. 1228–1229.
[28] *Ibid.* col. 1229.
[29] *Ibid.*

within 6 hours of that time, up to six hours after the expiry of the 36 hours (subs. (5)). In other words, the police can exceed the 36 hour limit by up to six hours where the 36 hour limit would expire, say, at 8 a.m. Otherwise the application might have to be made in the middle of the previous afternoon. But if the court thinks that the application should reasonably have been made within the 36 hour period, they *must* dismiss the application and as a result the suspect would have to be released (subs. (7)). If the suspect is held in police custody beyond the 36 hour point that fact and the reason must be recorded in the custody record (subs. (6)).

The new requirement of such a hearing will plainly require the courts to sit at unsocial hours and the Home Office Minister Mr. Douglas Hurd assured the House of Commons that after consulting the Magistrates' Association and the Justices' Clerks Society he was "glad to be able to tell the Committee that magistrates will be willing to sit outside normal court hours, within reason, on any day of the week to hear applications for [such] warrants."[30] However the Notes for Guidance in the Code states that applications for a warrant of further detention (or its extension) should be made between 10 a.m. and 9 p.m. and if possible during court hours (para. 16A, p. 277 below).

Under subsection (8), if the court is not satisfied that the further detention of the suspect is justified, it must either dismiss the application and thereby require the release of the suspect or, if time permits, adjourn the hearing until some later stage in the 36 hour period. (Obviously the latter would only be possible if the application has been made well prior to the expiry of the 36 hour period.)

The warrant of further detention must state the time at which it is issued and shall authorise the further detention of the suspect for whatever period the magistrates think—up to a maximum of 36 hours (subss. (10), (11) and (12)).

The court can take into account the fact that the police intend to move the suspect to a different police area (subs. (13)).

An information for the purpose of this section must be on oath in writing and must state the nature of the offence, the general nature of the evidence on which he was arrested, what inquiries have already and are still to be made, and the reasons why further detention is necessary for the purpose of such further inquiries (subs. (14)).

When an application is refused, the suspect must then immediately be either charged or released, on bail or unconditionally, unless subsection (16) applies (subs. (15)).

Subsection (16) permits the police to continue to hold the suspect for the full initial 36 hour period notwithstanding that permission to hold him longer than 36 hours from the relevant time has not been granted by the magistrates. This would obviously only apply where application had been made to the magistrate well before the expiry of the 36 hours and where a superintendent had authorised continued detention from the 24 hour to the 36 hour point. The right to hold him for the whole of the 36 hour period is so that the police are not penalised for making an early application. The court is asked whether he can be held beyond 36 hours from the relevant time. A refusal does not mean that detention up to 36 hours is improper.

[30] *Ibid.* col. 1235.

But the right to continue to hold the suspect is of course subject to the overriding principles stated in section 34(2) that the suspect must always be released if there do not appear to be any sufficient grounds to hold him any longer and in section 40 that the need for further detention must be reviewed periodically.

Where an application has been refused, the police cannot make a further application unless further evidence has come to light (subs. (17)).

If a warrant of further detention is issued, the person concerned must be released on or before its expiry unless he has previously been charged (in which case ss.38, 40 and 46 apply) or an extension has been obtained. Someone who has been released on the expiry of a warrant of further detention cannot be re-arrested unless new evidence has come to light (subs. (19) paralleling s.41(9)).

Extension of warrants of further detention: section 44[31]

The police can apply to the magistrates for one or more further extensions of the time period up to the limit of 96 hours. The length of any such extension is in the discretion of the magistrates, save that no single extension can be for more than 36 hours. Such an application must again be made at an *inter partes* hearing and the suspect is entitled to be legally represented. There must again be an information under oath. Subsections (2)(3) and (14) of section 43 apply to such a hearing. If the application is refused the suspect must be either charged or released (subs. (7)), save that he can be held for the full period allowed by the previous application to the court (subs. (8)).

Detention before charge supplementary: section 45[32]

This section makes it clear that a magistrates' court for the purposes of this Part of the Act means a court sitting with two or more justices in private.

It also states that references to periods of time or times of day shall be treated as approximate only. Police officers will therefore not have to worry if they slightly exceed any specified time limit. It will be for the courts to determine what degree of slippage will be regarded as venial. The Home Office Minister assured the House of Commons that there was no suggestion that this would be abused: "The Hon. Lady . . . will accept that in some matters that we have discussed where time limits are contained in the Bill, it is difficult to operate by a stopwatch. It should not be a matter of seconds or minutes either way. There will be circumstances when it would not be entirely reasonable to expect absolute and complete exactitude. That is why the word "approximate" is in the clause. I do not believe that a court will give much leeway because of that word. . . . We do not intend that the word should be used to undermine the important safeguards in the Bill. Equally, I hope that she will accept that some policing matters cannot be conducted with an exact regard for seconds or a few minutes."[33]

[31] See also text of the Act at p. 191 below.
[32] See also text of the Act at p. 192 below.
[33] House of Commons, *Hansard,* Standing Committee E, February 21, 1984, col. 1260–1261.

Detention after charge: section 46[34]

This section clarifies the law as to when a person must be brought before a court after he has been charged. Broadly it provides that he must be brought before a court within 36 hours.

The basic provision is subsection (2) which states that he must be brought before a court "as soon as is practicable" but this hallowed phrase is amplified by the additional provision "and in any event not later than the first sitting after he is charged with the offence."

If there is no sitting arranged for the day when he is charged or the next day the custody officer must inform the clerk to the justices so that a special sitting can be arranged (subs. (3)).

If the suspect is to appear at a court in a different part of the country, he must be taken there as soon as is practicable and must similarly be brought before a court there as soon as is practicable—and in any event not later than the first sitting in that area after his arrival (subs. (4)). Subsection (5) requires the police to inform the justices' clerk if there is no sitting scheduled for that day or the next day.

When the clerk to the justices has received information under subsection (3) or (5), he is under a duty to arrange a special sitting of the court for the day after the charge (or in the case of the person brought from a different part of the country, the day after his arrival in the area where he is to come before the court). Sundays, Good Friday and Christmas Day can be ignored in this context (subss. (7) and (8)). A person in hospital need not be brought to court if he is not well enough (subs. (9)).

Bail after arrest: section 47[35]

Release on bail under this Part of the Act is stated to be under the ordinary provisions of the Bail Act 1976 (subs. 1). A person released on bail subject to a duty to attend at a police station can only be re-arrested without a warrant if new evidence justifying a further arrest comes to light after his release (subs. (2)). Where someone has been granted bail subject to a condition of attending at a police station the custody officer has the power to cancel this by notice in writing (subs. (4)). Conversely, when he attends there he can be detained without charge but only if the custody officer at the police station has reasonable grounds for believing that his detention is necessary to secure or preserve evidence to the offence, or to obtain such evidence by questioning him (subs. (5)). Where this does occur any time that he has already spent in custody prior to getting bail has to be taken into account when calculating time limits for lawful detention (subs. (6)). He is then to be treated for the purposes of Part IV of the Act in the same way as someone arrested for the first time (subs. (7)).

Subsection (8)(*a*) substitutes a new section for section 43 of the Magistrates' Courts Act 1980. Subsections (1), (4) and most of (3) of the 1980 Act are superseded by the provisions of the Police and Criminal Evidence Act.

Subsection (8)(*b*) slightly amends the procedure where someone is arrested on a warrant of commitment for fine default under section 117(2)(*b*) of the 1980 Act. Instead of his having to be taken to a police

---

[34] See also text of the Act at p. 192 below.
[35] See also text of the Act at p. 193 below.

station to have his recognisance taken, it can be taken on the spot and he can then be released on bail. The purpose is to save the journey to the police station where this is unnecessary.

Remands to police custody: section 48[36]

Under section 128(7) of the Magistrates' Courts Act 1980, the magistrates have power to remand a person who has been charged with offences to police custody for up to three days. Normally this is for the purpose of allowing questioning about other offences. The section provides that in relation to such detention the "necessity principle" applies and when there is no longer any need to detain the suspect to question him about other offences he must be brought back to the magistrates' court. Whilst detained, the custody officer is responsible for him and the ordinary rules about regular review by the custody officer apply.

Police detention to count towards custodial sentence: section 49[37]

Section 49 amends section 67 of the Criminal Justice Act 1967 so as to provide that any period spent in police detention (defined in s.118) or under the terrorism legislation shall count towards any subsequent custodial penalty.

Records of detention: section 50[38]

The section requires each police force to keep records of the numbers of cases where persons are detained for longer than 24 hours and then released without charges, the numbers of applications for warrants of further detention, and the results of such applications and the periods of further detention authorised by the courts and the periods actually spent in custody in such cases. The record must also show whether persons detained under such warrants were eventually released without charges. Every annual report of a chief constable and of the Metropolitan Police Commissioner must likewise include such information. The Royal Commission did not include a recommendation to this effect but it parallels other requirements regarding records.

Savings: section 51[39]

Section 51 makes an exception from the provisions of Part IV of the Act for immigration officers in relation to controls of entry, police officers in relation to arrest and detention under the Prevention of Terrorism (Temporary Provisions) Act 1984 or police officers detaining military deserters, absentees or persons under escort.

Paragraph (*d*) of the section also preserves the right of persons detained by the police to apply for a writ of habeas corpus or any other prerogative remedy.

Children: section 52[40]

Section 52 makes it clear that the detention of children under 10 arrested without a warrant for offences other than homicide is not affected

---

[36] See also text of the Act at p. 194 below.
[37] See also text of the Act at p. 195 below.
[38] See also text of the Act at p. 195 below.
[39] See also text of the Act at p. 195 below.
[40] See also text of the Act at p. 196 below.

by the Act but continues to be dealt with as before by section 28(4) and (5) of the Children and Young Persons Act 1969 which provides for detention, where it is considered to be necessary, in a community home or other place of safety.

QUESTIONS AND ANSWERS
DETENTION

1. Who is responsible for the well-being of persons in custody?

The custody officer is required to ensure that persons in custody are treated in accordance with the Act and the Codes of Practice. Custody officers of the rank of sergeant or above must be appointed for all designated police stations. But an officer of any rank can perform the functions of the custody officer if none is readily available. At non-designated police stations the role of custody officer should be played if possible by someone other than the investigation officer, but this is not a requirement.

2. What happens if the custody officer and the investigating officer disagree as to how the suspect should be treated?

The custody officer is supposed to be separate from the investigating officer. It is the custody officer who is basically in charge. If the investigating officer is senior in rank and there is some disagreement between them as to the handling of the detainee, the custody officer is required to refer the matter at once to an officer of the rank of superintendent or above responsible for that police station. (The same applies to review officers, see below.)

3. What are the custody officer's duties before charge?

He must oversee all aspects of the detainee's treatment. He must ensure that the custody record form is properly maintained with all details of what transpires during the period of the suspect's detention. It is the custody officer's duty, *inter alia*, to decide initially whether the detention of the suspect is warranted.

4. On what grounds can someone be detained without charges?

There is only one ground of police detention prior to a charge—namely, that the custody officer reasonably thinks that such detention is "necessary to secure or preserve evidence relating to an offence for which he is under arrest or to obtain such evidence by questioning him" (s.37(2)).

When the suspect first arrives at the police station, it is the custody officer's duty to decide whether there is sufficient evidence to justify charging him. If there is enough evidence he must be charged. If not, the question arises as to whether he should be detained. The question of the suspect's detention must then be kept under periodic review.

5. How often must there be reviews of the need for further detention?

The need for further detention has to be reviewed periodically after the initial consideration of the question by the custody officer. In the case of someone who has not been charged the review should be by a "review officer"of at least the rank of inspector who has not been directly involved in the investigation. The first review is supposed to be not more than six hours after the initial authorisation of detention by the custody officer. Thereafter the review should be at nine hour intervals.

Before deciding whether to authorise continued detention the review officer must give the person concerned or any solicitor representing him who is available at that time the chance to make representations either orally or in writing.

6. What happens if the time limits cannot be adhered to because the suspect is asleep or ill, is being questioned or for some other reason?

The Act allows for the review to be postponed "if . . . it is not practicable to carry out the review at that time" (s.40(4)(*a*)).

7. How long can a suspect be held in the police station without charges?

The basic rule is that if the police wish to hold the suspect for more than 24 hours such extended detention must be authorised by a superintendent or above after inviting representations from the suspect or his solicitor. If the police wish to hold the suspect beyond the 36 hour point approval must be obtained from a magistrate's court. The magistrates cannot authorise detention for longer than a total of 96 hours. There are therefore successive stages.

(1) Initial review of detention by the custody officer as soon as possible after arrival at the police station.

(2) Review of the rightness of further detention after the first six hours by an inspector (the review officer) and then at nine hour intervals.

(3) Review of the rightness of further detention after 24 hours by a superintendent—approval can be given for further detention up to the 36 hour point.

(4) Review of the rightness of further detention after 36 hours by a magistrates' court—the court is permitted to authorise detention for a maximum of 36 hours at one hearing. There must therefore be at least two hearings if the suspect is to be held for the full 96 hours.

8. Must these time limits be strictly adhered to?

The answer is both yes and no. There is a provision in the Act that "Any reference . . . to a period of time or a time of day is to be treated as approximate only" (s.45(2)). This reflects the view that officers are not expected to walk around with stop watches. Also, the actual rules in the Act and Codes make some allowance for the variety of problems that may come up. Thus, as has been seen, the review within the police station may be postponed if it is not practicable to conduct it at the right time. Though when this happens the next review is to be held at the time it should have been held if the first review had been at the correct time.

The hearing in the magistrate's court can be at any stage up to the 36 hour point. But the Act goes further and gives another six hours leeway, thus making a total of 42 hours. So if the 36 hour period would expire say at 6 a.m., the police have a further six hours and can lawfully bring the suspect to the court during the ordinary morning hearing. But if the court takes the view that the application for approval of further detention could and should have been brought within the 36 hour period it must dismiss the application.

Although there is therefore some flexibility in the time limits they are certainly not to be treated lightly.

9. From when is time counted?

In the ordinary case time starts to run from the moment that the suspect arrives at the first police station to which he is taken. But there are some special cases where the rules are different.

If he is arrested in one police force area but is wanted elsewhere, time starts to run from the time that he arrives at the first police station to which he is taken in the area where he is wanted for questioning—or 24 hours, whichever is the shorter. This is on the assumption however that he is not questioned in the area where he was arrested nor on the way to the second area. If he is in fact questioned time starts to run from that time.

If he is wanted in two areas, time starts to run in the second area 24 hours after leaving the first area or the moment when he reaches any police station in the second area—whichever is the earlier.

If he is arrested outside England and Wales, the detention clock starts from the time that he comes to a police station in the area where the case against him is being investigated, or 24 hours whichever is the shorter.

If at any stage he is taken to hospital whilst in police detention, time during which he is actually being questioned, whether en route or at the hospital counts but the rest of the time involved does not count.

10. What sort of hearing is there before the magistrates?

The application must be heard by a magistrates' court with at least two magistrates and a court clerk sitting in private. The hearing cannot start unless the suspect is present and unless he has received a copy of the police application for the warrant of further detention. The suspect is entitled to be legally represented and if he has no lawyer and wishes to have one, the case must be adjourned while a lawyer is found. The costs of such representation are to be borne by the legal aid fund. There will be no means-test and no contribution from the suspect.

The police will make their application and the suspect or his lawyer, or both, will reply. The onus or burden of proof will be on the prosecution to show why his further detention is necessary.

11. On what grounds can the magistrates grant a warrant of further detention?

The grounds on which further detention can be approved by the court are the same as those already applied by the superintendent at the 24 hour point—(1) whether detention is necessary "to secure or preserve evidence relating to an offence for which he is under arrest or to obtain such evidence by questioning him"; (2) that the offence is indeed a serious arrestable one; and (3) that the investigation is being conducted diligently and expeditiously.

12. If the suspect has not been answering police questions can the court grant a warrant for further detention in the hope that that will enable the police to break him down by further questioning?

The answer to this question may in the end require a decision by the courts. But it would seem that the better view is that if that were indeed the reason for granting a warrant of further detention it would be unlawful. If the police have failed to get the suspect to co-operate with them after 36 hours their only hope of changing his attitude would be through conduct that would run the risk of being oppressive.

The justification for the 96 hour period of detention given time and time again by Home Office Ministers was that it would be necessary in a few very complex and important cases. There was never any suggestion that it was needed in order to "crack" the hard cases. On the contrary, this was repeatedly denied.

13. On what grounds can the suspect be held after he has been charged?

Once a person has been charged, the grounds for further detention change. In principle at that point he should not be questioned further—though the Code does now allow slightly more scope for questioning after charge than the old Judges' Rules (see Code, para. 17.5, p. 278 below).

The sole permitted grounds for detention after charge (under s.38(1)) are:

(1) that his name or address have not been satisfactorily established;

(2) that the custody officer has reasonable grounds for believing that detention is necessary—

"for his own protection"; or

"to prevent him from causing physical injury to any other person"; or

"from causing loss of or damage to property"; or

"that he will fail to appear in court to answer to bail"; or

"that his detention is necessary to prevent him from interfering with the administration of justice or with the investigation of offences or a particular offence."

If he is an arrested juvenile there is an additional ground—
"that he ought to be detained in his own interests".

14. How long can the suspect who has been charged be held in custody without being brought before a court?

The old law was that he had to be brought before a court "as soon as practicable." This formula is also that adopted in the 1984 Act (s.46(2)). But it is strengthened by further provisions in the same section. These state that if there is no sitting of a local magistrates' court on the day on which he is charged or the next day (not counting Sundays, Christmas Day or Good Friday), the custody officer must inform the clerk to the justices that there is a person in custody for whom a special hearing will have to be held.

The Act then lays upon the clerk to the justices the duty of arranging a hearing not later than the day after he has been charged (or in the case of someone brought from another police district the day after he arrives in the area).

PART V

QUESTIONING AND TREATMENT OF PERSONS BY POLICE

Abolition of certain powers of constables to search persons: section 53[1]

Section 53 abolishes all common law and statutory powers to search persons at a police station including intimate searches. The only exception is the power under the Prevention of Terrorism (Temporary Provisions) Act 1984, Sched. 3, para. 6(2).

The existing powers to carry out such searches are replaced by sections 54 and 55 of the new Act.

Searches of detained persons: section 54[2]

Prior to the Act there was no statutory basis for searching someone who had been arrested. The common law recognised the right of the police to do what was necessary to prevent the arrested person escaping, injuring himself or others or destroying evidence and the Royal Commission recommended[3] that the power should be put onto a proper statutory basis and that it should include the power of making a full inventory. On the other hand, it said the process could be "humiliating and disturbing" and it should not be done routinely, and save in exceptional circumstances a suspect should not be deprived of his watch.[4]

The section requires the custody officer to take charge of this process. He must make or cause to be made a record of all the suspect's property unless the suspect is to be detained for only a short period and is not to be put in a cell in which case in the officer's discretion it would be enough to make an abbreviated list—listing a handbag, for instance, without itemising the contents separately. (Notes for Guidance, para. 4A, p. 266 below.) The duty to itemize the suspect's property applies when someone is brought to the police station under arrest or after being committed to police custody by order or sentence of a court or when someone is arrested after coming voluntarily to the station. In the case of an arrested person the record becomes part of their custody record. However he may be searched only if the custody officer considers it necessary in order to make a complete list of all his property and only to the extent that the custody officer considers it necessary for that purpose (subs. (6)). This is therefore a broader power than under the previous law since it places the

---

[1] See also text of the Act at p. 196 below.
[2] See also text of the Act at p. 196 below.
[3] Report, para. 3.116.
[4] Report, para. 3.117.

power to search on the need to make an inventory of the detainee's effects. Also it only requires the custody officer's honest belief that a search is necessary for it to be lawful.

A search must be carried out by a constable and only by one who is the same sex as the person being searched (subss. (8) and (9)).

The Code of Practice for detention, treatment and questioning provides that a search involving the removal of more than outer clothing is only allowed "if this is thought by the custody officer to be necessary to remove an article which the detained person would not be allowed to keep." A record must be made of the reasons for any strip search and its result (Annex A, p. 278, below, paras. 5 and 8).

The custody officer may in his discretion retain anything which the arrested person has, except for things subject to legal professional privilege and clothes and personal effects, which are dealt with in subsection (4).

According to subsection (4), the custody officer may only retain clothes and personal effects if the custody officer believes that they might be used by the arrested person to cause physical injury to himself or anyone else, to damage property, to interfere with evidence or to assist him to escape. He may also retain such items if he has reasonable grounds for believing that they may be evidence relating to an offence. Note the difference between the two halves of this provision. The seizure of items that might be used to do harm does not have to be based on reasonable grounds, on the ground that police officers cannot be expected to anticipate what exactly the suspect might do. Seizure of evidence does, however, need to be on reasonable grounds. There is no mention in either the Act or the Code of the Royal Commission's recommendation that a suspect should always be allowed to keep his watch.

Where property is seized, the person from whom it is taken must (under subs. (5)) be told the reason (unless he is or is likely to become violent or is incapable of understanding what is said to him). Section 22(2)(*a*) provides for the retention by the police of items seized.

Intimate searches: section 55 and Code of Questioning, Annex A[5]

The subject of intimate searches of body orifices is dealt with separately in section 55. The Royal Commission recommended[6] that if the search was of intimate parts of the body it should be carried out only by a doctor and only where the offence in question was a grave one. It should require the authorisation of a sub-divisional commander.

The Government did not agree with the Commission's safeguards. When the first Bill was published an intimate search would have required the approval only of a superintendent. Such authorisation could be given if the offence in question was a serious arrestable one and there were reasonable grounds for believing that such a search would produce relevant evidence or that such a search was necessary to establish that the detainee had nothing that could be used to injure himself or others. The second Bill at first qualified this by limiting the ground for an intimate search to a search for something that could be used as a weapon or to injure oneself or others. Searches for evidence (of drugs offences for instance) were not permitted. The decision was largely based on the view

---

[5] See text of the Act at p. 197 and of Code, p. 276 below.
[6] Report, para. 3.118.

of the doctors who, according to the Home Office Minister, Lord Elton, said that they would not be willing to conduct searches without consent to obtain evidence of crime but would do so to protect life.[7] Needless to say the police regarded this alteration as thoroughly unhelpful. Also they criticised the logic of denying the police the right to conduct intimate searches for evidence but retaining the power for Customs and Excise officers at airports and ports. The Home Office Minister Mr. Douglas Hurd conceded that the powers available to the Customs and Excise under the Customs and Excise Management Act 1979, s. 164 were "valuable" and should be retained. For reasons that he did not explain, that, however, was a different issue.[8]

But during the summer recess between the Report stage and the Third Reading in the House of Lords the Government changed its mind again on this controversial issue. It introduced an amendment to the Bill designed after all to permit an intimate search for drugs. But the rules for searches for weapons and searches for drugs are different in certain important respects.

All intimate searches are subject to the following rules: (1) the search must be authorised by an officer of the rank of superintendent or above on the basis of reasonable belief that the arrested person in police detention has concealed on him anything which could be used to cause physical injury to himself or to others and that he might so use it (subs. (1)). (2) Authorisation may be oral or written, but if oral it must be confirmed in writing (subs. (3)). (3) Authorisation may not be given unless there are reasonable grounds for believing that the item in question cannot be found without such a search. If therefore it could be expected to pass through the natural bodily functions and there is time to wait for this to happen, this should be preferred.

The rules diverge however in regard to who may carry out such a search. Searches for weapons can in the last analysis be carried out by police officers. The Home Office Minister Mr. Douglas Hurd said on this issue that all were agreed that if possible intimate searches should be carried out by a doctor both because it was safer and because "it provides a degree of human dignity and reassurance." But it might be that no doctor could be found who could carry out the search within[9] a reasonable time or the doctor might not be willing to carry out such a search. Swift action might be necessary. The British Medical Association he said accepted that in exceptional circumstances there might be a need for an intimate search to be carried out without the person's consent to remove an object which was of immediate danger to the life of the suspect and those in his proximity. Guidance would be made available to doctors by the B.M.A. to that effect. But there was no way of guaranteeing that the particular doctor approached would agree to carry out such a search without the consent of the suspect. It was therefore necessary to have the reserve power that permitted such a search to be conducted by a police officer.[10]

Such a search must be made by a "suitably qualified person" unless an officer of at least the rank of superintendent considers that this is not

[7] House of Lords, *Hansard*, July 19, 1984, col. 710.
[8] House of Commons, *Hansard*, Standing Committee E, February 23, 1984, col. 3059.
[9] *Ibid.*, col. 3039.
[10] *Ibid.*, col. 3040.

practicable" (subs. (5)). The use of the word practicable in this context is not entirely clear. Presumably it is intended to cover the situation where a doctor is asked but refuses to carry out the search without the consent of the suspect. But does it also cover the rather different case where no effort is made to contact a doctor because the police believe there is none likely to be available at that hour of the day or night, or because the police know that any doctor asked would be likely to refuse? A "suitably qualified person" is either a doctor or a registered nurse (subs. (17)). There is no stated requirement on the police to make any attempt to get such a person to carry out the search, nor even to ask the suspect whether he wishes the search to be carried out by a qualified person, though this duty was in an earlier version of the Code.

Where such a search is not carried out by a doctor or nurse it must be carried out by a police officer of the same sex as the suspect and the Code of Questioning, (Annex A, para. 6, p. 279 below) states that when the intimate parts of the body are searched or clothing is removed no one of the opposite sex who is not a doctor may be present. The custody record must show as soon as practicable which parts of the body were searched and why (subss. (10) and (11)). The Code (Annex A, paras. 7 and 8) requires that the record must also show who carried out the search, who was present, the reason for the search and the result.

If the search is for drugs it can only be carried out by a doctor or registered nurse and it cannot be carried out in a police station (subss. (4) and (9)). Intimate searches for drugs are limited to those for hard drugs defined as Class A drugs in Schedule 2 to the Misuse of Drugs Act 1971. (There are over 80 drugs listed in the Schedule. They do not include cannabis.) But the superintendent who authorises the intimate search must reasonably believe not only that the suspect has such drugs concealed in a body orifice but that he was in possession of them at the time of his arrest with intent either to supply or export them (subss. (1)(b)(ii) and (17)). Someone suspected merely of being a user could therefore not be subjected to an intimate search.

Anything found in the course of an intimate search may be seized by the police if it could be used to cause physical injury, or damage to property, interfere with evidence or to assist an escape or if there are reasonable grounds for thinking that it could be evidence relating to an offence (subs. (12)). The power of seizure is therefore broader (in covering evidence) than the power of intimate search.

The chief constable's annual report must include information about the total number of intimate searches, the number carried out by doctors or nurses, the number carried out by someone else in the presence of such a person, and the result of the searches (subss. (14), (15) and (16)).

The right to have someone informed when arrested: section 56 and Code of Questioning para. 5 and Annex B[11]

Section 56 replaces section 62 of the Criminal Law Act 1967. The Royal Commission recommended[12] that this right be retained but that the details be spelled out even more fully than now. This recommendation is reflected in the Act and the Code of Questioning.

---

[11] See also text of the Act at p. 199 and Code at p. 279 below.
[12] Report, para. 4.80.

Section 56 states that when a suspect is under arrest in a police station he is entitled, if he so requests, to have "one friend or relative or other person who is known to him or who is likely to take an interest in his welfare," to be told as soon as practicable that he is under arrest and his whereabouts (subs. (1)). If such a person cannot be contacted the Code says that two alternatives may be nominated. If they too cannot be contacted the custody officer has a discretion to allow further alternates until the information has been conveyed (para. 5.1). If the suspect knows no one to contact, the custody officer should consider contacting any local agency that might be able to help him (Notes of Guidance, 5C). Delay is only permissible in the case of serious arrestable offences[13] and only if authorised by an officer of the rank at least of superintendent (subs. (2)). There is no requirement however that the superintendent be independent of the investigation. An attempt to persuade the Government to accept this requirement failed.[14] Equally it is not required that the serious arrestable offence necessarily be the one for which the suspect was arrested.[15] Under the Code of Questioning (paras. 3.1–2) this right is one of which the suspect must be told both orally and in writing "when a person is brought to a police station under arrest or arrested at the police station having attended there voluntarily". A person who is still voluntarily at the police station is not covered by this requirement since he is deemed to be free to go if he pleases. But there is no doubt that he has a right to have someone informed of his whereabouts and this right is not subject to the provisions for delay. The gounds for delaying are that there are reasonable grounds for believing that telling the named person of the arrest will lead to interference with or harm to evidence or witnesses or the alerting of others involved in such an offence; or the recovery of any property (subs. (5) and Code, Annex B, p. 279 below). If delay is authorised, the suspect must be told of the fact and of the reasons for it and the reasons must be noted on his custody sheet (subs. (6)). When the grounds for delay cease to apply the suspect must be permitted to exercise his right to have someone informed of his whereabouts (subs. (9)). If the suspect is moved from one police station to another, the right to have someone informed of his whereabouts arises again (subs. (8)).

Where an inquiry as to the whereabouts of a detained person is made by his friends or relatives, or a person with an interest in his welfare, they should be told where he is unless the exceptions permitting delay in Annex B apply or unless the suspect himself does not consent to this (Code, para. 5.5). Action taken under this paragraph must be recorded on the custody record. No one may be prevented from notifying the outside world of the fact of his arrest under section 56 for more than 36 hours (subs. (3)), from "the relevant time" as defined in section 41. The time limit is new and it applies even to terrorism cases. However, in regard to terrorism cases there are additional grounds on which delay of exercise of the right up to a total of 48 hours can be approved as recommended by Lord Jellicoe's report:[16] namely where notifying someone would be likely to lead to interference with the gathering of information about acts of

---

[13] See s.116, pp. 151, 236 below.
[14] House of Commons, *Hansard,* Standing Committee E, February 23, 1984, col. 1385.
[15] *Ibid.* col. 1387.
[16] *Review of the Operation of the Prevention of Terrorism (Temporary Provisions) Act,* Cmnd. 8803 (1983), para. 112.

terrorism or make it more difficult to prevent an act of terrorism or to secure the arrest, prosecution or conviction of anyone in connection with terrorism charges (subs. (11)).

Unless the reasons for delay in Annex B apply, the Code states that the detainee may "also speak on the telephone to one person" (para. 5.7). Whether the call is at public expense is in the discretion of the custody officer. Any officer may listen to what is being said, unless the call is to a solicitor, and "may terminate the call if it is being abused" (para. 5.8). The detainee must be given writing materials on request. Unless Annex B applies, any letter or other message must be sent (at his expense) as soon as practicable but all such communications (other than letters to solicitors), can be read (para. 5.6).

The detainee should be cautioned that what he says in any letter, call or message (other than in communication to his solicitor) may be given in evidence (para. 5.8).

Special (and somewhat muddling) rules apply to foreigners and Commonwealth citizens. Under the Code of Questioning (para. 7.1), they may communicate "at any time" with their embassy, consulate or High Commission. In fact where a foreigner from a country with which a Consular Convention is in force[17] is detained (unless he is seeking political asylum), his consulate must be informed as soon as practicable (para. 7.3). In the case of any other foreign national he must be told of his right to communicate with his consul without delay or that the police will inform the consulate of his arrest (para. 7.4). Curiously in regard to Commonwealth citizens the right is only to be told after 24 hours (para. 7.2).

Consular officials are stated to be free to visit one of their nationals "to talk to him and if required to arrange for legal advice" (para. 7.5). Such visits "shall take place out of the hearing of a police officer" (*ibid.*).

The rights of Commonwealth citizens and foreign nationals to inform someone of their whereabouts after arrest cannot be interfered with even when it is a case covered by Annex B (Code, Notes for Guidance, 7A p. 269 below).

Additional rights of children and young persons: section 57[18]

The section replaces section 34(2) of the Children and Young Persons Act 1933 which provides that where a child or young person has been arrested, reasonable steps must be taken to inform his parent or guardian. The Royal Commission recommended[19] that this provision should be reaffirmed and section 57 gives effect to the recommendation. It also goes a little further by obliging the police to inform the supervisor of any juvenile subject to a supervision order or for those in care of the local authority or a voluntary organisation it should be informed. If none of these persons is available the social services of the local authority or another responsible adult should be informed (Code of Questioning, paras. 1.5 and 3.6). If the parents or guardian are suspected of involvement in the offence the Code says it may be desirable for the adult to be some other person (Notes for Guidance, 13A, p. 275 below).

According to the Code of Questioning arrangements should normally be made for the person notified to see the child or young person before

---

[17] A list of such countries appears at App. 31 to the Home Office Consolidated Circular to the Police Crimes and kindred Matters.
[18] See also text of the Act at p. 200 below.
[19] Report, para. 4.80.

he is interviewed and such a person "must not be interviewed or asked to sign a statement in the absence of the appropriate adult unless Annex C applies" (para. 13.1.). The exception is where an officer at least of the rank of superintendent reasonably believes that the delay in contacting such a person "will involve an immediate risk of harm to persons or serious loss of or serious damage to property." (Annex C, p. 280 below).

Access to legal advice: sections 58 and 59; Code of Questioning, paragraph 6[20]

The previous law regarding access to legal advice for suspects in the police station was to be found in the Preamble to the Judges' Rules and in the dicta of judges in a number of, mainly recent, cases.[21] It was generally agreed that few suspects asked to see a solicitor and that, of those who did, the majority were refused such access.[22]

The Royal Commission[23] thought that a suspect should be informed that generally he had a right to see a solicitor privately. The right to see a solicitor should be withheld only in exceptional circumstances which it listed and which should be confined, it thought, to grave offences.[24] Refusal of access to a solicitor it said[25] should require the authority of a sub-divisional commander and the grounds should be specified on the custody sheet. If for any reason a suspect could not be brought before a magistrate within 24 hours, he should be seen by a solicitor whose duty it would be to ensure that he was being properly cared for.[26]

The Act and the Code of Questioning broadly adopt the approach proposed by the Royal Commission. A person held in custody is said to be "entitled, if he so requests, to consult a solicitor privately at any time" (subs. (1)).

The Code (paras. 3.1–2) provides that the right to have legal advice is one of the rights of which the detained person must be informed orally and in writing when the suspect first comes to the police station under arrest or is arrested there after coming to the station voluntarily or in any case before being questioned about any alleged offence. Under an earlier draft of the Code, if he waived the right to have legal advice he had to sign to that effect on the custody record form and if he refused to sign he was deemed to want legal advice. But under the final version he should be asked to state on the custody record that he does or does not want legal advice at that stage (para. 3.4).

The consultation can be either in person, on the telephone, or in writing (Code, para. 6.1). Requests to see a solicitor must be recorded on the custody sheet (subs. (2)). (This requirement does not apply however if the request is made "at a time while he is at court after being charged with an offence" (subs. (3)). The Government's reasoning was that he would then be in the custody of the court rather than of the police.) Normally the request must be allowed as soon as practicable (subs. (4))

---

[20] See also text of the Act at pp. 201–2 and of Code, pp. 267–69 below.
[21] See especially *Allen* [1977] Crim.L.R. 163; *Lemsatef* [1977] 2 All E.R. 835; *Elliott* [1977] Crim.L.R. 552; *Reid* [1982] Crim.L.R. 515.
[22] See, for instance, M. Zander, "Access to a Solicitor in the Police Station" [1972] Crim.L.R. 342; J. Baldwin and M. McConville, "Police Interrogation and the Right to See a Solicitor" [1979] Crim.L.R. 145; P. Softley, "An Observation Study in Four Police Stations" *Royal Commission on Criminal Procedure*, Research Study 4 (1981), p. 68.
[23] Report, para. 4.87.
[24] Report, para. 4.91.
[25] *Ibid.*
[26] Report, para. 3.107.

and in any event it must be allowed within 36 hours (subs. (5)) or in terrorism cases, 48 hours from the time of arrest, not the time of arrival at the police station (subs. (13)(*a*)).

Delay in compliance with a request for a solicitor is only permitted exceptionally where detention is for a serious arrestable offence[27] and where it is authorised by an officer of the rank at least of superintendent. The possible grounds for such delay include all those proposed by the Royal Commission: where there are reasonable grounds for believing that it will lead to interference with or harm to evidence or witnesses; or the alerting of other suspects; or that it will hinder the recovery of the proceeds of the crime (subs. (8)). The gloss put on these words by the Home Office Minister Mr. Douglas Hurd was that, "The only reason under the Bill for delaying access to a legal adviser relates to the risk that he would either intentionally or inadvertently convey information to confederates still at large that would undercut an investigation in progress. What a suspect's legal adviser says to him can never be a ground for delaying a consultation between them, nor can anxiety about what the legal adviser might say to the suspect. Delay can be authorised only on the basis of what the legal adviser may do once the consultation has been completed."[28] The Code specifically states that access to a solicitor may not be delayed or denied on the ground that he may advise the person not to answer questions, nor on the ground that someone else instructed the solicitor to attend—provided that the detained person then wishes to see the solicitor (Annex B, para. 2, p. 279 below).

Strenuous efforts were made in the House of Lords to persuade the Government to narrow the power to delay access to a lawyer in serious arrestable cases. The Law Society was, with much difficulty, persuaded to agree to support an amendment that would have allowed a superintendent to serve a notice on the solicitor requiring that he refrain from doing any specified act for 36 hours so as to reduce the risk that he would, consciously or unconsciously, alert the suspect's associates. Such a notice would plainly invade the normal solicitor-client relationship but the Law Society were eventually convinced that this was the lesser of two evils. However, the Government were not impressed and the amendment moved by Lord Hutchison was defeated by 53 to 45. (See House of Lords, *Hansard*, October 18, 1984, cols.1153–1177.)

But in addition to the power of the police to delay access to a solicitor in cases involving serious arrestable offences there is also a right to start questioning suspects in other cases where a solicitor has not yet arrived if the situation is an emergency or the solicitor is likely not to arrive for a considerable period. This power is defined in the Code (para. 6.3, p. 268 below). There are three situations mentioned which are exceptions to the general rule that a person who asked for legal advice may not be interviewed or continue to be interviewed until he has received it. One is where Annex B applies (*e.g.* the cases mentioned above affecting only serious arrestable offences). The second is where an officer of the rank of superintendent or above has reasonable grounds to believe that delay will involve "an immediate risk of harm to persons or serious loss of or damage to property, or that awaiting the arrival of a solicitor would cause

---

[27] See s.116, pp. 151, 236 below.
[28] House of Commons, *Hansard*, Standing Committee E, February 2, 1984, col. 1417.

unreasonable delay to the processes of investigation" In such cases questioning could commence even though the suspect has exercised his legal right to ask for a solicitor and even though the police are not entitled to postpone calling him. In considering whether this exception applies the police should bear in mind the time the solicitor is likely to take in coming to the station, the time for which detention is permitted, the time of day, whether a rest period is imminent and the requirements of other investigation in progress. (Code, Notes for Guidance, 6A, p. 268 below). The third exception is where the suspect has given his agreement in writing or on tape that the interview may commence at once. Obviously there is a danger in the last case that improper pressure may be brought to bear to help persuade the suspect to agree to sign away his right to wait for the solicitor to arrive.

The Royal Commission did not recommend that the police be required to inform the suspect that a solicitor had come to the police station, in order to advise him on the instructions of someone else. There is nothing about this in the Act nor in the Code of Questioning. Note however, on this question the Court of Appeal's decision in *R.* v. *Sally Jones*[29] that a solicitor is properly retained when asked to go to the police station by a relative or friend and that the police should have told her that he was there to see her even though she had not asked for a solicitor.

If delay is authorised, the detained person must be told the reason for it and the reason must be recorded in the custody record (subs. (9)). There can be no more delay once the reason for authorising delay no longer applies (subs. (11)).

The Code provides that if the suspect wishes to consult a solicitor and does not know of one, he shall be informed of the availability of a Duty Solicitor if there is a scheme and shall be provided with the list of solicitors available (para. 6.1). This was a major advance achieved by the Government in collaboration with the Law Society. The Government announced that it had allocated six million pounds annually for this work. Moreover, it amended the Police and Criminal Evidence Act by adding in section 59 a provision linking duty solicitor schemes in magistrates' courts under the Legal Aid Act 1982 with 24 hour schemes in police stations. The effect of this is to make it possible to *require* solicitors taking part in court schemes also to take part in schemes in police stations.[30] Regulations are to be made to this end under section 1(6) of the Legal Aid Act 1982. Mr. Douglas Hurd told the House of Commons Committee[31] that *free* advice and assistance would be provided in police stations under the Green Form Scheme. There will be no means test to ascertain whether a suspect is eligible and all suspects who want to use the facility will be able to do so free of charge including those who wish to instruct their own normal solicitor instead of the Duty Solicitor. The ordinary limit of work that can be done without prior approval of the legal aid authorities would be raised to £75. The difficulty that arises because the green form does not become effective until it has been signed by the client will be overcome by modifying the normal rules so that a solicitor will be able to claim his proper travel costs to the police station before the form has been signed.

---

[29] [1984] Crim.L.R. 357. The word 'then' in Annex B, para. 2, p. 279 below suggests the same.
[30] House of Commons, *Hansard*, Standing Committee E, February 28, 1984, col. 1434.
[31] *Ibid.*

These special arrangements will be available not only to those who have been arrested. The Government eventually accepted the Law Society's contention that they should extend also to those who come voluntarily to a police station (See House of Lords, *Hansard*, October 18, 1984, col. 1178 and s. 59(*aa*)(i)).

The Government also agreed that the special arrangements would extend to legal representation at the magistrates' hearing of applications for warrants of further detention. Such representation will be through assistance by way of representation with the usual means test and advance approval by the legal aid authorities waived. They will be entitled to free representation. Mr. Hurd said that he hoped that in the light of these announcements it would be accepted by the Committee "that there is no doubt about our concern to make the right of access to legal advice effective."[32]

Visits by solicitors may be within the sight but must be out of the hearing of a police officer. However, in terrorism cases an officer of the rank of Commander or Assistant Chief Constable can order that the interview be in the sight and hearing of an inspector in uniform if he reasonably believes that any of the consequences mentioned in subsection (8) above would otherwise be likely to ensue (subs. (14) to (17)).

Where a solicitor is being called, the police must wait for his arrival before interviewing the suspect unless either the suspect has agreed in writing or on tape to be interviewed without waiting or an officer of the rank of superintendent or above has reasonable grounds to believe that delay involves an immediate risk of harm to persons or serious loss or damage to property or that it will cause unreasonable delay to the processes of investigation having regard to the time limits for detention (Code of Questioning, para. 6.3). This could prove to be a major qualification to the new provisions for better access to solicitors though once the danger is averted a solicitor is supposed to be called (Code, para. 6.4). The officer should try to get an estimate from the solicitor of how long he will take to get there and relate this to the time limits for detention, the time of day, whether a required break in questioning is due and the requirements of other investigations in progress (Notes for Guidance, para. 6A, p. 268 below). The solicitor should be told how long the police are prepared to wait so that he can consider arranging for someone else to give advice (*ibid*).

The Code (para. 6.5) specifies that a person who is permitted to consult a solicitor may have his solicitor present while he is being interviewed and a solicitor may only be required to leave the interview if an police officer of the rank of superintendent or above considers that by his misconduct he has prevented the proper putting of questions to his client. This would seem to give the police only the narrowest of grounds for refusing a suspect permission to have his solicitor present during questioning. Moreover, the Code (Notes for Guidance, 6C, p. 269 below) says that a solicitor is not guilty of misconduct if he seeks to challenge what seems to him to be an improper question to the client or the way in which it is put and he should not be asked to leave unless his interference "clearly goes beyond this".

Following the recommendations of the report of Lord Jellicoe[33] legal advice is now for the first time available also to persons detained in connection with terrorism offences—subject to the same additional pro-

---

[32] *Ibid.* cols. 1434–1435.
[33] *Op. cit.* (n. 16, p. 70 above) paras. 108–110.

visions already mentioned as apply under section 56 (subs. (12)) and Code of Questioning, (Annex B, p. 279 below). The right applies after 48 hours and the Code provides that anyone detained for 48 hours must be reminded of their right and asked whether he wishes to exercise it (*ibid.*, para. 7).

The provisions regarding access to legal advice apply also to someone who comes voluntarily to the police station and is then cautioned (subs. (*a*)(i); Code of Questioning, para. 3.9).

The Code specifies that access to a solicitor means someone who is qualified to practise. But the Act makes it clear that solicitors' clerks can in principle appear for their firms (subs. (*a*)(ii)) and if the solicitor wishes to send a clerk or legal executive, then the police should admit him unless an officer of the rank of inspector or above considers that such a visit will hinder the investigation of crime and directs otherwise (Code of Questioning, para. 6). A clerk can be excluded if he "acts improperly or has done so in the past", (Notes for Guidance, para. 6D). The solicitor who sent him must then be informed at once to enable him to send someone else (*ibid.*, para. 6.10).

Tape recording of interviews: section 60[34]

Section 60 places upon the Home Secretary a duty to issue a code of practice for the tape-recording of police interviews with suspects and to make a statutory instrument requiring such interviews to be tape-recorded. This provision was not in the first Bill. It was introduced by the new Home Secretary Mr. Leon Brittan as earnest of his and the Government's intentions regarding tape-recording.

The statutory instrument will have to be laid before parliament, subject to annulment by resolution in either House. It will be possible to implement the scheme in some areas and not in others (s.121(3)).

Those who believe that tape-recording is an important new development in providing controls and safeguards for both prosecution and defence must welcome this commitment by the Home Office to proceed when the forthcoming experiments are completed.

The Government had already announced that field trials would take place over some two years in six different areas.[35] The experiments started in January 1984 but the Home Secretary stated on the Second Reading of the second Bill that the Government would not necessarily wait for the full two years before taking the next step.[36]

The cynics may object that, if the experiments disclose unexpected difficulties about tape-recording, ways will no doubt be found to avoid complying with the duty to proceed. But a commitment is better than no commitment.

Moreover, the Home Office have produced a booklet of procedural guidance which sketches the way in which the experiment is intended to work and no doubt in which the actual scheme when it is introduced is likely to function.

The Royal Commission on Criminal Procedure recommended[37] that tape-recording be confined at least initially to the final stage of questioning—the formal taking of the statement. The Government to its credit has determined to go much further by requiring the experiment to

---

[34] See also text of the Act at p. 203 below.
[35] House of Commons, *Hansard*, November 15, 1982, cols. 16–17.
[36] House of Commons, *Hansard*, November 7, 1982, col. 32.
[37] Report, para. 4.27.

include tape-recording of the whole interview in the police station. The Royal Commission thought this would be too costly but the Government believes that it has solved the problem of cost by procedures designed to reduce to a minimum the need for transcription of the tapes.

In brief, under the present rules the officer in the case gives as his evidence in chief the substance of the relevant parts of the interview supplemented by the formal identification of the tape-recording. The defence is given prior access to the tape so that both they and the prosecution have the opportunity to come to a measure of agreement on the substance of the interview. It is hoped that transcripts will be required very rarely. The success of the experiment may turn on whether this proves correct.

The experiment covers all offences triable only on indictment, all offences triable either way and some summary offences, viz. indecent exposure, interference with vehicles under the Criminal Attempts Act 1981, s.9; being found on enclosed premises; offences against the Restriction of Offensive Weapons Acts 1959 and 1961; offences against unlawful immigration; and criminal damage where the amount is under £200.

An officer not connected with the inquiry, of the rank of inspector, is however able to authorise the interviewing officer not to tape the interview where it is "not reasonably practicable" owing to mechanical failure, or the non-availability of suitable facilities or where he believes that tape-recording of the interview of a juvenile, mentally handicapped person or other person "at risk" would not be in the interests of the suspect "because *e.g.* it might frighten him."[38]

Taping is supposed to begin as soon as, or as soon as possible after, the person has become a suspect.[39]

Double-deck machines with two tapes are being used. The apparatus is only able to record. Playing back and copying is done on separate machines. One channel is used for recording; the other has a time coding device to reduce the risk of tampering. Tapes are used on one side only to avoid any confusion in turning them over.

One of the two tapes is sealed immediately after the interview and is then subject to the rules laid down for the police to handle exhibits. The seal can only be broken on the authority of a court. The other tape is the working copy from which further copies can be made.

The suspect must be told that the interview is to be recorded. The officer gives his name, rank and that of any other officer present, and the date and time of the interview. He should then caution the suspect that he need not say anything. If the suspect objects, the officer should point out that a tape-recording is likely to be a more accurate record of the interview and that he will keep a note of it in any event.

If the suspect maintains his objection, the officer should state that he is turning it off with his reasons and should then turn it off.[40] But the draft code provides, somewhat obscurely, that if the officer thinks it legitimate nevertheless to continue to tape the interview he may do so "bearing in mind that a decision to continue interviewing in such circumstances may

---

[38] The Tape-recording of Police Interviews with Suspects: Procedural Guidance, Home Office (1983), para. 3.3.
[39] *Ibid.* para. 3.4.
[40] *Ibid.* para. 4.7.

be the subject of comment in court."[41] What appears to be contemplated here is taping without the knowledge of the suspect.

The tapes are to be taken out of their seal in the presence of the suspect. If there are breaks for refreshment, etc., this should be stated on the tape. If the break is substantial the suspect must be cautioned again.[42]

Officers are advised to consider taking a note as well, since transcriptions will generally not be made.[43]

When the interview is complete, the officer should sign an exhibit label for the tape and should ask the suspect to do so as well. The suspect should be handed a notice which explains the use to be made of the tape and the arrangements for access to it.

After the interview is complete the officer should make a note of its salient features in his notebook and prepare a statement of evidence. If in doubt about what was said he will be able to check his recollection by listening to the tape.[44]

When the case goes to the prosecutor the tape goes with the papers. The interviewing officer indicates to the prosecutor whether the tape contains significant matter to help the prosecutor to decide whether to listen to the whole or to parts of it.[45]

Defence solicitors (including their unadmitted employees) and unrepresented defendants will have access to the tape as of right—though the right must be exercised reasonably and at reasonable times.[46] The Law Society has approved a statement that whether the defence solicitor should listen to the tape is a matter for him, depending on his instructions and his view of the case.[47] It will not necessarily be required of him.

The defence must be shown a copy of the police officer's statement of evidence. Prosecution authorities should routinely serve the defence with copies of the officer's statement of evidence so as to enable them to decide whether to listen to the tape.[48] The defence solicitor will be invited to listen to the tape at the police station, but if this is not practicable he should be sent a copy.[49]

The police should consider whether to advise an unrepresented suspect to get legal representation. If he continues to be unrepresented he should be allowed unhindered access to the tape—either at the police station or at home or, if he is in custody, in the cells.

Where the police believe that the material on the tape is "sensitive and should not be disclosed to the defence" those tapes should be treated as "unused material" in accordance with the Guidelines on the Disclosure of Information to the Defence issued by the Attorney General in December 1981.[50]

Transcripts should only be made where absolutely necessary and then only of those parts that are necessary. This should normally be done only if there is a dispute as to what transpired during the interview.

[41] *Ibid.*
[42] *Ibid.* para. 4.13.
[43] *Ibid.* para. 4.14.
[44] *Ibid.* para. 5.2.
[45] *Ibid.* para. 6.3.
[46] *Ibid.* paras. 7.11 and 7.3.
[47] *Ibid.* para. 7.2.
[48] *Ibid.* para. 7.4.
[49] *Ibid.* para. 7.6.
[50] [1981] New L.J. 1305.

In order to avoid the danger of one party ordering a transcript and then having the cost disallowed on taxation, arrangements have been made for prior consent to be obtained. The prosecution and non-legally aided defendants should apply in writing to the judge in relation to cases to be heard on indictment or to the justices' clerk for indictable cases to be heard summarily. Legally aided defendants should apply to the Legal Aid Committee.[51]

The guide says that it should only be necessary to play a tape in court to resolve doubts in the absence of a transcript or to clear up a dispute about the accuracy of a transcript.[52]

The early indications from various sources were that the experiment was proving to be a considerable success and that the police in particular were delighted with the results (see Interim Report, Home Office Research Studies No. 82, 1984).

Fingerprinting: section 61 and Identification Code, paragraph 3[53]

The previous law on fingerprinting in section 49 of the Magistrates' Courts Act 1980, provided that fingerprints could be taken compulsorily only on the order of a magistrates' court, if the person was 14 years old and if proceedings against him had already begun. The Royal Commission recommended[54] that the minimum age should be reduced to ten years and that it should be possible to take fingerprints, where it was necessary for purposes of the investigation, before proceedings were started. It also proposed[55] that supervision or control should be transferred from the magistrates to the police on the ground that in an operational matter of this nature the magistrates could not in practice exercise any real supervision. Section 61 gives effect to those proposals.

It states that, except as provided, no one's fingerprints may be taken without consent, as defined in section 65. Under section 65, consent of a person over 17 must be his own and in the case of someone under 14 the consent must be that of a parent or guardian. For someone between 14 and 17 consent must be his own *and* that of his parent or guardian.

Consent in a police station must be given in writing (s.61(2); Code, para. 3.1). This therefore does not affect the practice of fingerprinting the victims of burglaries in their homes in order to distinguish their prints from any others found there. However, fingerprints may be taken without consent if an officer at least of the rank of superintendent authorises it, and he has reasonable grounds for suspecting the involvement of the person in a criminal offence and that his fingerprints "will tend to confirm or disprove his involvement" (subss. (3)(*a*) and (4)). The compulsory taking of fingerprints for investigative purposes therefore requires the authority of a superintendent.

But fingerprints can also be taken compulsorily without such authority if the person affected is in police detention and he has been charged with or convicted of an offence recordable in national police records (a "recordable offence"), or he has been told that he will be reported for such an offence. Reporting takes place either to consider the issue of a summons or where the institution of proceedings requires the consent of the Attorney General or the Director of Public Prosecutions (subss. (3)(*b*) and (6)).

---

[51] *Op cit.* para. 8.4.
[52] *Ibid.* para. 9.2.
[53] See also text of the Act at p. 203 and the Code at p. 286 below.
[54] Report, paras. 3.128–3.132.   [55] Report, para. 3.131.

National police records of convictions are kept by the National Identification Bureau at New Scotland Yard (N.I.B.). Only serious offences are recorded by N.I.B.—broadly those punishable by imprisonment. N.I.B. records consist of convictions and the national fingerprint collection.

Under section 27(3)[56], as has been seen, police officers are given a power of arrest for the purpose of taking fingerprints for recordable offences and that section requires the Home Secretary to incorporate the list of recordable offences in a statutory instrument.

Where a person's fingerprints are taken without his consent, he must be told the reason beforehand and this must be recorded. If he is detained at a police station at the time, the reason must be put into the custody record (subss. (7) and (8)).

Subsection (9) preserves the power of compulsory fingerprinting contained in immigration and terrorism legislation.

Intimate samples: section 62 and Identification Code, paragraph 5[57]

The Act distinguishes between two kinds of body samples. One are "intimate samples" which (save for urine and saliva) may be taken only with written consent in advance and only by a doctor or dentist. The other category is "non-intimate samples" which may exceptionally be taken without consent and by a police officer. Intimate samples are dealt with in section 62; non-intimate samples in section 63. The definition of both kinds of body samples is to be found in section 65.

Intimate samples (dental impressions, blood, semen, or other tissue fluid, urine, saliva, pubic hair or a swab taken from a person's body orifice), may only be taken if an officer of the rank of superintendent or above gives permission *and* written consent is given by the suspect (and in the case of a juvenile his parent or guardian). The superintendent can only give authority if the offence in question is a serious arrestable one[58] and he has reasonable grounds for believing that the sample will tend to confirm or disprove his involvement in the offence (subs. (2)). The police officer's authorisation if given orally in advance must be confirmed in writing as soon as practicable (subs. (3)).

When consent is being invited any officer must tell the suspect that the authorisation has been given and the grounds for it. He must also state the nature of the offence in which it is suspected that he is involved. There is no requirement to warn the suspect that he need not give his consent, nor that it cannot be taken without his consent. A record must be made as soon as possible of the authorisation, the grounds and the fact of consent. If the sample is taken at a police station, this must be put into the custody record (subss. (7) and (8)). Save in the case of urine or saliva only a doctor may take an intimate sample (subs. (9)).

A late amendment introduced by the Government provided that where the detainee's consent is refused without good cause, in any proceedings against that person the court may draw such inferences from the refusal as appear proper and the refusal may be treated as corroboration of any evidence against him (subs. (10)). It hardly needs to be emphasised that this somewhat dilutes the value of the requirement of consent. On the

---

[56] p. 41, above.
[57] See also text of the Act at p. 204 and the Code at p. 287 below.
[58] See s.116, pp. 151, 236 below.

other hand) the Government agreed to amend the Code so as to provide
that the suspect would have to be warned about the consequences of
refusal of consent. (See Identification Code, para. 5.2.)

Subsection (11) makes it clear that the taking of samples of blood and
urine in connection with offences of drink and driving under the Road
Traffic Act 1972, ss.5 to 12 are not affected.

Taking non-intimate samples: section 63 and Identification Code, paragraph 5[59]

Section 63 provides that non-intimate samples (meaning a sample other
than an intimate sample or a footprint or similar impression of any part
of a person's body, other than a part of his hand) may be taken
compulsorily in certain circumstances.

Normally written consent is required. But an officer of the rank of
superintendent or above can authorise compulsory taking of non-intimate
samples where the offence in question is a serious arrestable one[60] and
there are reasonable grounds for believing that the sample will tend to
confirm or disprove the suspect's involvement. In such a situation an
officer must inform the suspect that authorisation for taking the sample
compulsorily has been given, and the grounds and the nature of the
offence in which it is suspected that he is involved (subss. (6) and (7)).
The reason for taking the sample without consent must be recorded as
soon as practicable.

Taking of photographs: Identification Code, paragraph 4[61]

There is no judicial decision that determines whether the taking of
photographs of suspects by the police without consent is unlawful. The
Royal Commission recommended[62] that photographing of suspects should
be on the same basis as fingerprinting both in regard to the means for
getting written consent and in regard to the rules regarding authorisation
and safeguards where no written consent was forthcoming.

There is nothing in the Act on the subject. But the Identification Code
provides that, save as stated, no photograph of a suspect may be taken at
a police station without his written consent. If the suspect is under 16 the
consent must be that of his parent or guardian (paras. 1.10 and 4.1).

Photographs may be taken without his consent however if he is arrested
at the same time as other persons (or when it is likely that others will be
arrested) and it is considered necessary to make a photographic record to
establish who was arrested, at what time and what place (para 4.2). Force
may not however be used for this purpose (para. 4.3). A photograph may
also be taken without consent if the suspect has been charged with or
reported for an offence a conviction for which will be recorded in national
records (see p. 79 above). It may also be taken without consent where the
person concerned has been convicted of a recordable offence and either
his photograph is not already on record or it is, but it is not a good
likeness of his current appearance (para. 4.2(iii)). Here too, however,
force may not be used and the grounds for taking the photographs must

[59] See also text of the Act at p. 205 and the Code at p. 287 below.
[60] See s.116, pp. 151, 236 below.
[61] See also the Code at p. 287 below.
[62] Report, para. 3.133.

be recorded and the suspect must be told of his right to witness the destruction of the photographs.

Destruction of fingerprints, samples and photographs: section 64 and Identification Code, paragraphs 3.1, 3.4 and 4.4[63]

The Royal Commission recommended[64] that fingerprints and samples taken must be destroyed if the person concerned is cleared. Section 64 gives effect to this recommendation. It provides that fingerprints and samples, whether taken with consent or under compulsion, must be destroyed as soon as practicable after the suspect has been cleared of the offence. For this purpose he is to be treated as having been cleared if it is decided neither to prosecute nor formally to caution him; or if the offence is indictable and he is not committed for trial; or if he is tried for the offence and is acquitted. If fingerprints are destroyed, any copies that have been made must also be destroyed (subs. (5)). A person who asks to be allowed to be present to witness the destruction has a right to do so (subs. (6)) if he asks within one month of being cleared (para. 3.1). Under the Identification Code (para. 4.4) the same applies to photographs.

Definitions relating to fingerprints and samples: section 65[65]

Section 65 defines "appropriate consent," "fingerprints," "intimate sample," "non-intimate sample" and "the terrorism provisions."

QUESTIONS AND ANSWERS

THE SUSPECT'S RIGHTS IN THE POLICE STATION

1. For how long can the police keep someone incommunicado in the police station?

Where someone is in custody in a police station he has the right "to have one friend or relative or other person who is known to him or who is likely to take an interest in his welfare told, *without delay*—except to the extent that delay is permitted" (s.56(1) italics supplied).

The Code states that if that person cannot be contacted, the suspect may choose up to two alternatives. If they too cannot be contacted the custody officer has discretion to allow further attempts until the information has been conveyed.

The right not to be held incommunicado applies every time one is taken to a new police station.

2. In what circumstances can the police delay the suspect's right to have someone informed as to his whereabouts?

Both the Act and the Code specify the circumstances in which delay is permitted. The Code sets these out in Annex B (p. 279 below). Annex B

---

[63] See also text of the Act at p. 205 and the Code at pp. 286, 287 below.
[64] Report, para. 3.131.
[65] See also text of the Act at p. 206.

is based on the identical provisions in the Act itself. Delay is permissible for a limited period if,
  (1) the suspect is detained in connection with a serious arrestable offence;
  (2) an officer of the rank of superintendent or above reasonably believes that exercise of the right:
    (a) would lead to interference with or harm to witnesses or interference with or physical harm to other persons; or
    (b) would lead to the alerting of others suspected of involvement; or
    (c) would hinder the recovery of the proceeds of the crime.
But if these grounds cease to apply the person must be asked as soon as practicable if he wishes to exercise the right and action must then be taken on any affirmative response. The maximum period of delay is 36 hours.

3. If someone rings the police station asking about the detainee must he be told where he is?

The Code provides that when an inquiry is made as to the whereabouts of a detained person by his friends or relatives, the information "shall be given, if he agrees and if Annex B does not apply." But the Notes for a Guidance (5D, p. 267 below) say that "in some circumstances it may not be appropriate to disclose information of this kind over the telephone." The meaning of this caveat is unclear.

4. Does the right not to be held incommunicado apply also to persons held as suspects under the anti-terrorism legislation?

Under the previous law, suspects held under the Prevention of Terrorism (Temporary Provisions) Act had no right to make contact with the outside world while they were held for anything up to one week. But as a result of Lord Jellicoe's 1983 Report into the working of the Act this was changed by the Police and Criminal Evidence Act. Under the 1984 Act a suspect held under the Prevention of Terrorism Act cannot be denied the right to have someone informed of his arrest for longer than 48 hours. The grounds for delaying the exercise of this right are the same as those set out in Annex B that apply to suspects in serious arrestable offence cases. But there are in addition two further grounds on which a superintendent may authorise delay: if he has reasonable grounds for believing that notification will lead to interference with the gathering of information relating to acts of terrorism or that it will, by alerting any person, make it more difficult to prevent an act of terrorism or to secure the arrest, prosecution or conviction of someone involved in terrorism.

5. Can detained persons demand to have visits or to make phone calls, send letters or cables?

The Code has provisions on all these matters. It states that detained persons may receive visits at the custody officer's discretion and that he should exercise his discretion as to visits "in the light of the availability of sufficient manpower to supervise a visit and any possible hindrance to the investigation (Notes for Guidance, 5B)." The detained person may also speak on the telephone to one person—unless Annex B applies. Whether or not the call is at public expense is at the discretion of the custody officer. A police officer may listen to what is said unless the call is to a solicitor. He may terminate the call if it is being abused. If the person does not speak English, an interpreter may make a call for him. The person should be cautioned that what he says in any letter, call or message may be given in evidence.

A detained person should be supplied on request with writing materials. Any letter or other message should be sent at his expense as soon as practicable unless Annex B applies. All letters except those to solicitors may be read by the police.

The only suspects who have an absolute and unqualified right to make a call and to have visits are those from abroad. The Code says that a foreign national or a citizen of a Commonwealth country "may communicate at any time with his High Commissioner, Embassy or Consulate" (para. 7.1). In regard to visits, the Code states that "consular officers may visit one of their nationals who is in police detention to talk to him and, if required, to arrange for legal advice." Such visits should take place out of hearing of a police officer (para. 7.5).

The Notes for Guidance (7A) state that these rules regarding foreign and Commonwealth detainees cannot be suspended even though Annex B does apply.

6. In what circumstances can a suspect get a lawyer in the police station?

The Royal Commission hoped to see a dramatic improvement in the suspect's access to legal advice in the police station. The Government implemented the Commission's recommendations subject to an important reservation.

Under the new Act a person who is not suspected of involvement in a serious arrestable offence has an absolute right to see a lawyer in the police station. But in spite of this right the police are permitted under the Code to start questioning him even though he has asked to see a solicitor if: (1) a superintendent reasonably believes that to delay would involve an immediate risk of harm to persons or serious loss of or damage to property; or (2) a superintendent reasonably believes that to wait for the solicitor to arrive would unreasonably delay the inquiry; or (3) the suspect has agreed in writing or on tape that the interview may be started without waiting for the solicitor.

A person who is suspected of involvement in a serious arrestable offence also has an absolute right to ask for a lawyer. But in such a case the police have the additional right to delay access to legal advice for up to 36 hours in ordinary cases and for up to 48 hours in terrorism cases.

Delay has to be authorised by an officer at least of the rank of superintendent and can be approved only on the same grounds set out in Annex B of the Code as apply to delay in permitting a suspect to tell someone outside the police station of his whereabouts (see p. 82 above).

Once the reason for delaying access to a solicitor ceases to apply the suspect must as soon as practicable be told of the right and asked whether he wishes now to exercise it.

Annex B specifically makes it clear that access to a solicitor cannot be denied or delayed on the ground that the solicitor might advise the suspect to say nothing.

7. How in practice would a suspect go about trying to find the name of a local solicitor?

The Government agreed with the Law Society a new scheme for legal advice, assistance and representation for suspects in police stations. The Act itself gives the Government power to make rules to require solicitors who take part in the criminal legal aid scheme to take their fair share of duty solicitor cases in police stations.

Preparation for this duty solicitor scheme was reasonably well advanced by the time of Royal Assent though it was not then clear as to when it would come into effect.

The Code provides that if he does not know the name of a solicitor to contact the detainee should (1) be told of the availability of the local Duty Solicitor scheme (if any), and (2) be provided with a list of local solicitors who have indicated their willingness to act in such situations.

8. How could suspects in the police station expect to pay for the help of lawyers?

The Government announced during the passage of the Bill that advice and assistance by solicitors in police stations would be exempted from the normal requirement of a means test and a graduated contribution. The service in other words would be free of charge at public expense. The same would be true of the services of solicitors at hearings before magistrates on applications by the police for warrants of further detention.

9. If the detained person wants a lawyer and one has been called, can the police start questioning him before the lawyer arrives?

A person who has asked for legal advice "may not be interviewed or continue to be interviewed until he has received it." But there are three exceptions. The first is where Annex B (see p. 279 below) applies. The second is where an officer of the rank of superintendent or above has reasonable grounds to believe that there is an immediate risk of harm to persons or serious loss of or damage to the property, or that waiting for the arrival of the solicitor would cause unreasonable delay to the investigation. (But when the danger has passed, questioning may not continue until the person has received the legal advice he asked for.) The third is where the detained person has agreed in writing or on tape that the interview can commence without waiting.

10. Can the solicitor remain during the interview with the detained person?

The Code states that unless Annex B applies a person may have his solicitor present while he is interviewed but the solicitor can be asked to withdraw if an officer of the rank of superintendent or above considers that by his misconduct he has prevented the proper putting of questions to his client (Code, paras. 6.6–6.8 and Notes for Guidance, 6E). The officer should consider whether a report to the Law Society is appropriate.

11. If the solicitor sends his clerk or legal executive does he count as a solicitor for these purposes?

The Code states that the word "solicitor" means someone qualified as a solicitor. However clerks or legal executives shall be allowed to perform the same functions "unless an officer of the rank of inspector or above considers that such a visit will hinder the investigation of crime and directs otherwise" (Code, para. 6.9 and Notes for Guidance, 6D).

12. What is the position if a solicitor sent by a friend or relative arrives at the police station but the suspect has not asked for a solicitor?

Neither the Act nor the Codes deal explicitly with the point. But a recent decision of the Court of Appeal held that a solicitor sent to the police station by a friend of the suspect, who had not asked for one, was nevertheless validly instructed. The court held that the police ought to have told her that the solicitor was physically there to see her. (*R.* v. *Sally Jones* [1984] Crim.L.R. 357.)

13. At what point must the person in the police station be told of his rights?

The answer depends on whether he is there voluntarily or under arrest. If he is not under arrest he must be told of his rights only when he is cautioned. If he is under arrest he must be told of his rights when he comes to the police station or, if he comes voluntarily but is then arrested, at that time. (It is the custody officer's duty to consider whether he ought to be detained as soon as practicable after he arrives at the police station, or, if he has been arrested at the station, as soon as practicable after his arrest.)

14. Of what rights must he be informed?

He must be told:
(1) the grounds of his detention;
(2) of the right to have someone informed of his detention;
(3) of the right to consult a copy of the Codes;
(4) of the right to legal advice.

He must be told of these rights orally and must also be given a notice setting them out together with a statement that he is entitled to ask for a copy of the custody record form providing he does so within 12 months.

A person who is at the police station voluntarily and who has been cautioned must be told of the same rights but he must also be told that he has a right to leave if he wishes.

15. To what extent do the rules make special provision for the needs of the young, those with mental handicaps, the deaf, those who cannot speak English, etc.?

There are special rules in the Codes for each of these groups.

(1) *The young.* The Code provides that when a child or young person has been arrested his parent or guardian must be informed. If he is in care, the local authority or the voluntary organisation he is with should be told. Failing the parent or guardian the information should be communicated to a representative of the social services department of the local authority or to another responsible adult who is not a police officer. If the juvenile is subject to a supervision order, the supervisor should, if possible, be informed.

The custody officer should as soon as possible inform the adult who is called of the grounds of detention and his whereabouts and should ask the adult to come to the police station. The information about the suspect's right to legal advice and to consult the Codes must be given to the juvenile in the adult's presence, or if not must be given to him when he arrives at the police station.

The Code (para. 13.1) states categorically "A juvenile whether suspected of crime or not . . . must not be interviewed or asked to provide or sign a written statement in the absence of the "appropriate adult" unless Annex C (p. 280 below) applies." Annex C sets out the circumstances in which a juvenile may be interviewed even though the adult is not there—"If, and only if, an officer of the rank of superintendent or above considers that delay will involve an immediate risk of harm to persons or serious loss of or serious damage to property." Questioning in those circumstances "may not continue once sufficient information to avert the immediate risk has been obtained" (Annex C, para. 2).

If the adult thinks that the juvenile needs legal advice the police are required to treat this as a request for a lawyer by the juvenile himself.

Juveniles may not be interviewed at school unless this is unavoidable in which case the head teacher or his nominee should agree and be present. Where the parents or guardians of a person at risk are themselves suspected of involvement in the offence concerned or are the victims of it, the Notes for Guidance (13B) state it may be desirable for the "appropriate adult" to be someone else. Police are warned that juveniles (like the mentally handicapped and the mentally ill) are "particularly prone in certain circumstances to provide information which is unreliable, misleading or self-incriminating" and that it is important to obtain corroboration of any facts admitted whenever possible. A juvenile should not be arrested at school unless this is unavoidable in which case the head teacher or his nominee should be informed (para. 13.3).

A juvenile should not be placed in police cells unless no other secure accommodation is available or the custody officer considers that it is not practicable to supervise him if he is not in a cell. He may not however be placed in a cell with an adult.

(2) *The mentally ill and the mentally handicapped.* The rules in the Code for the mentally ill and the mentally handicapped are similar to those for juveniles. An appropriate adult must be notified that such a

person is in the police station. The "appropriate adult" in this case would be a relative or guardian responsible for his care, failing whom someone experienced in dealing with such people not employed by the police, failing whom some other responsible adult not employed by the police.

Just as in the case of the juvenile, the custody officer must call the appropriate adult to the police station and must give the same information. The prohibition on interviewing a mentally disordered person on his own are likewise the same as for juveniles—subject to the same exceptions in Annex C. The whole list of special provisions affecting the treatment of the mentally ill and mentally handicapped is to be found in Annex E, p. 281 below.

(3) *The deaf.* The Code (para. 14.4) states that if a person is deaf or there is doubt about his hearing ability he must not be interviewed in the absence of an interpreter unless he agrees in writing or Annex C (see above) applies. The interviewing officer shall ensure that the interpreter makes a note of the interview at the time for use in the event of his being called to give evidence. The suspect should be given an opportunity to read and sign it as correct or to indicate any respects in which he considers it to be inaccurate. Such an interpreter is provided free of charge at public expense.

(4) *Those who cannot speak or understand English.* The Code (para. 14) states that if someone has difficulty in understanding English and either the police officer does not speak the person's own language or he wishes to have an interpreter to be present, "he must not be interviewed in the absence of an adult capable of acting as interpreter." The only exception is again where Annex C (above) applies.

The interviewing officer must ensure that the interpreter makes a note at the time of the interview in the language of the person being interviewed and that he certifies its accuracy. The suspect should be given a chance to read it and to sign it as accurate or to indicate the respects in which he considers it to be inaccurate.

If the suspect makes a statement in a language other than English the interpreter should take down the statement in the language in which it is made; the person making the statement should be invited to sign the statement; and an official English translation should be made in due course.

Interpreters must be provided at public expense and all reasonable efforts must be made to make this clear to the detainee (para. 14.6).

If a person is charged, arrangements have to be made as soon as practicable to have the interpreter explain the offence and any other information given by the custody officer.

(5) *The blind.* The Code states that if a person is blind or visually handicapped the custody officer should ensure that someone appropriate is called to the police station to help him in checking any documentation and to sign any document on his behalf (para. 3.7).

16. Does the suspect have to answer questions put to him by the police?

A police officer has the right to ask any questions and the Code states that citizens have a civic duty to "help police officers to prevent crime and discover offenders." But the citizen has no legal duty to answer; a person detained in the police station, like everyone else in the community, has an absolute "right of silence." The purpose of the caution is precisely to remind him of this right. (In fact the Notes for Guidance (10D) state that if the person cautioned does not understand its significance the officer should explain that it is given because of the general principle of English law that a person need not answer any questions or provide any information which might tend to incriminate him.) The caution must be administered by the police officer at such time as he has grounds to suspect that a person has committed an offence and in any event when arresting him. The phrase "grounds to suspect that a person has committed an offence" is deliberately a weaker test than the former test of "reasonable grounds for belief." He must always be cautioned before any questions or further questions are put to him for the purpose of getting evidence from him. The caution was redrafted in the fourth draft of the Code to read: "You do not have to say anything unless you wish to do so but what you say may be given in evidence." But minor verbal deviations from this formula do not matter and if the person does not understand what the caution means the officer should explain it in his own words.

If the case later comes to court, the rules prohibit both the judge and the prosecution from commenting critically on the defendant's failure to say anything to the police. In particular, the judge is not permitted to suggest to the jury that silence is in any way evidence of guilt. Judges vary somewhat in the way in which they interpret this rule. But the rule itself is firmly established. (The only exceptions the courts have allowed are where the parties are said to be in a state of parity in terms of the power relationship between them. In one case a tenant's silence in the face of an accusation by his landlady that he killed her daughter was held by the court to be admissible evidence of guilt (*Parkes* v. *The Queen* (1976)). In another case an accused's silence in the face of police questioning was held to be some evidence of guilt because he had been accompanied by his solicitor (*R.* v. *Chandler* (1976)).)

On the other hand, although the prosecution are not allowed to suggest that the accused's silence was suspicious, they can inform the jury that the accused was silent. Nothing can prevent the jury from drawing adverse inferences from the fact of silence if they choose to do so. Also, the police need not give the person the false impression that non-cooperation will have no effect on his immediate treatment *e.g.* in terms of being kept in custody.

THE EXERCISE OF POLICE POWERS IN THE POLICE STATION

17. What rules restrict the police in questioning the suspect?

There are rules in the Code about interviews with a suspect;

(1) In any 24 hour period a continuous period of eight hours must be allowed for rest, free from questioning, or travel. If possible, this period should be at night.

(2) Breaks should be made at recognised meal times. In addition there should be short breaks for light refreshment at intervals of approximately two hours. But breaks can be delayed in the interviewing officer's discretion if there are reasonable grounds for believing that the break would involve a risk of harm to persons, or serious loss of or damage to property; or would unnecessarily delay the person's release from custody; or would otherwise prejudice the investigation. Two light and one main meal should be provided in any 24 hour period.

(3) Persons being questioned should not be required to stand whilst being questioned.

(4) If it is necessary to take a person's clothing for investigatory or health and hygiene reasons, adequate replacement clothing must be provided. A person may not be interviewed unless adequate clothing has been offered to him.

(5) No officer should try to obtain answers to questions or to elicit a statement "by the use of oppression."

(6) An officer should not indicate, save in answer to a direct question, what action will be taken by the police if the detainee answers questions, makes a statement or refuses to do so. If the person directly asks the officer such a question, "then the officer may inform the person what action he proposes to take in that event provided that that action is itself proper and warranted." It would therefore now appear to be proper for instance for the officer to say to the suspect "If you make a statement I will let you go home, or let you off the more serious charges or not pursue charges against your wife etc." (This represents a major shift in the rules—see further pp. 110–114 below).

18. In what circumstances can the police fingerprint the detainee?

In general the taking of fingerprints before someone has been convicted requires his consent. But they may be taken without consent even before a charge if an officer of the rank of superintendent or above authorises them to be taken. He can do so only if he has reasonable grounds for suspecting the person's involvement in a criminal offence and for believing that his fingerprints will tend to confirm or disprove his involvement. Fingerprints may be taken from anyone over the age of 10.

The person from whom the fingerprints are taken must be told the reason and that they will be destroyed if he is not charged or he is charged and acquitted. If he wishes, he may be present at the time to witness their destruction.

19. Can a suspect in the police station be photographed?

Normally a person who has been arrested but not convicted must give his consent to be photographed. Moreover the consent is required by the Code to be written.

But a photograph can be taken without the person's consent if he is arrested at the same time as other persons and a photograph is necessary to establish who was arrested, at what time or at what place. Force may not be used however in the taking of a photograph.

All copies and negatives of the photograph must be destroyed if he is not charged in the event or if he is tried but acquitted. Again he must be given the chance of witnessing their destruction if he wishes.

20. In what circumstances can the suspect's personal clothes and effects be taken from him?

A detained person may retain clothing and personal effects at his own risk unless the custody officer considers that he may use them to cause harm to himself or others, or interfere with evidence, or damage property or effect an escape or they are needed as evidence. In that event the custody officer can withhold such articles as he considers necessary. He must tell the person why.

The power of the police to search the suspect, including the right to conduct an intimate search, have been considered already (see pp. 44–45, 66–69).

21. In what circumstances can a search take place of body orifices?

A search of body orifices (an "intimate search") may only take place where an officer of the rank of superintendent or above has reasonable grounds for believing that the arrested person has concealed on him something which could be used to cause physical injury to himself or others and that it cannot be found without an intimate search. With one exception it cannot be a search for evidence of crime. The exception is where a superintendent reasonably believes that the suspect has on him hard drugs (Class A drugs) which he intended to supply to others or to export. The search should in principle be carried out by a doctor or nurse but in an urgent case, if a superintendent thinks it is not practicable, it can be done by a police officer providing he is of the same sex as the person being searched and provided that no officer of the opposit sex is present. But this is not so with searches for drugs. They can only be carried out by a doctor or nurse and cannot be done in a police station. Anything found in the course of an intimate search can be used in evidence.

22. Can a doctor or nurse be compelled to carry out a search of body orifices where the suspect refuses to consent?

The answer is No. It is for them to decide each for him or herself whether or not to conduct an intimate search in such circumstances. However, doctors who decline to carry out searches for drugs would have the support of the British Medical Association which wrote to members of the House of Lords stating that they did not approve of "doctors searching around inside people for evidence." In practice, most of such searches will presumably be carried out by police surgeons.

23. Can samples of body fluids be taken from a suspect?

The 1984 Act distinguishes between "intimate" and "non-intimate" samples. "Intimate samples are blood, semen, urine, saliva, pubic hair or a swab taken from a body orifice." Save for samples of urine or saliva, an intimate sample may only be taken by a doctor and in *all* cases the suspect must give written consent. A superintendent or above must authorise the taking of an intimate sample and can do so only if he reasonably believes that it will tend to confirm or disprove his involvement in a serious arrestable offence.

Non-intimate samples mean samples of hair, other than pubic hair, a sample taken from or under a nail, a footprint or a swab from a part other than a body orifice. Such a sample may be taken without consent from the suspect if a superintendent or above reasonably considers that the sample will tend to confirm or disprove the suspect's involvement in a serious arrestable offence. Otherwise the taking of such a sample requires the suspect's written consent.

PART VI

THE CODES OF PRACTICE

Codes of Practice: sections 66–67 and the Codes[1]

The Royal Commission on Criminal Procedure said that all aspects of the treatment of suspects in custody should be statutory. This would involve the use of primary legislation on some matters. But the rules to regulate the facilities to be provided for, and the treatment to be accorded to suspects and the rules to govern the conduct and recording of interviews should, it thought, be contained in subordinate legislation. "This should be made by the Home Secretary with consultation as appropriate, and subject to the approval of Parliament by affirmative resolution."[2]

The actual method adopted in the Act is, however, somewhat different.

The Act requires the Secretary of State, subject to Parliament's approval, to issue Codes of Practice in relation to: (i) search of the person and of vehicles without an arrest, (ii) the detention, treatment, questioning and identification of persons; and (iii) searches of premises and seizure of property found in searches of persons or premises (s.66(1)). As has been seen above, there is an equivalent duty in respect of the tape recording of interviews with suspects (s. 60).

The Home Secretary, having prepared and published drafts of any Codes of Practice, must consider any representations made on them. He must lay a draft of the Code before both Houses of Parliament. After he has done this—and no time limit is specified—he "may bring the code into operation by order made by statutory instrument" (s.67(4)). Such an order must be approved by a resolution of each House of Parliament (subs. (5)). The same procedure must be followed for any subsequent revision of the whole or any part of the Codes (subs. (7)).

This procedure therefore contemplates two separate stages. The first is publishing of draft Codes. This in fact proved to be a very lengthy process of "open government." The Codes went through successive drafts as a result of comments from a wide range of individuals and organisations. By the time that Parliament would consider them in spring 1985 they had already been extensively amended and re-amended. The pre-parliamentary stage of publishing drafts therefore proved very important in practice.

The second stage is laying them before Parliament and the order bringing them into force. The Home Office made it clear that there would be a debate on the Codes on the floor of the House and that the statutory

---

[1] See also text of the Act at pp. 206, 207 and the Codes at pp. 259–306 below.
[2] Report, para. 4.116.

instrument bringing them into effect would be introduced at a later stage. M.P.s would not be able to move amendments to the draft codes although they would be able to comment on them. However it was made clear that the Home Office would not redraft the codes in the light of further points made during the Parliamentary debates.

The reason given by the Home Office for not following the Royal Commission's recommendation that the Codes be in the form of a statutory instrument, was that it proved an unworkable proposal in the light of the need to make the Codes self-contained. The object was to produce a custody officer's booklet which would give him a comprehensive guide to the various aspects of his duties. Some of the material in the Code it was thought should come from the statute so as to reduce the need to refer to two documents. It was felt that it would be impossible to have a statutory instrument that repeated parts of the primary legislation in different language.

A second reason for having a code rather than a statutory instrument was that the language of a code could be less formal and that this would be valuable since it must be intelligible to police officers.

Thirdly, the Home Office considered that the underlying objectives for making the Codes statutory instruments could all be fulfilled by the procedure adopted in the Act. There could be a parliamentary debate on the content of the Codes and there would therefore be parliamentary accountability. True there would be no opportunity to move amendments—but this would be the same with any statutory instrument.

Whether the Codes would have a higher status in the eyes of the police if they were statutory instruments is impossible to say. The ordinary police officer is not a close student of the niceties of the parliamentary system and is therefore not likely to be aware of the difference between the procedure for passing a statutory instrument as compared with the bringing into force of the Codes of Practice. It is possible that the words "statutory instrument" have more of the ring of law about them than the words "Code of Practice." But again the difference may not be very major.

The crux of the matter is whether the police treat the rules in the Codes of Practice as rules to which they must adhere. The Judges' Rules were not law and the judges over the years showed themselves somewhat lax in enforcing their provisions. Generally breaches of the Rules were not regarded by the judges as a reason to exclude evidence or on appeal to quash a conviction.

In spite of this the Rules were undoubtedly regarded by the police as something of which they had to take account. They formed part of the material a police officer had to study and indeed master. The informal view of police officers tended to be that the Judges' Rules were a bit of a nuisance—which in itself indicates that they did have some real existence. If they had been treated as irrelevant they would have provoked little or no reaction amongst police officers.

A critical question will be what consequences are likely to flow from a breach of the Codes of Practice. On this, section 67 states that a failure on the part of any person to observe any provision of a Code of Practice shall not of itself render him liable to any criminal or civil proceedings, but in any proceedings the code of practice shall be admissible and shall be taken into account if it is thought to be relevant to any question arising in those proceedings. In other words, the extent to which a breach of the

Codes would result in evidence being excluded would be a matter for the judges but they would be obliged to take it into account. Also s.67(8) states that "a police officer shall be liable to disciplinary proceedings for a failure to comply with any provision of such a code" unless the proceedings are precluded by the "double jeopardy rule" under section 104.[3] This reflects the Royal Commission's view that breaches of the Codes should be dealt with primarily through the police disciplinary system. But it is perhaps stronger than might have been expected. It is certainly not mandatory, requiring that disciplinary proceedings *must* follow from a discovered breach. But it at the least seems to suggest that such proceedings could be regarded as a normal consequence of a breach of the Codes. Lord Elton told the House of Lords on the Third Reading that the difference between the Act and the Codes did not lie in their respective force but rather in the ease with which they could be altered (House of Lords, *Hansard*, October 18, 1984, col.1107).

"Police force" for the purpose of the section is defined as "any body of constables," which includes forces such as the British Transport Police. But the section adopts the Royal Commission's view[4] that the Codes shall apply not only to the police but also so far as possible to anyone else "charged with the duty of investigating offences or charging offenders" (subs. (9)). But rather than being under a duty to comply with the Codes they are instead under a duty only to "have regard" to any relevant provisions of their Codes (subs. (9)).

The Codes

The Royal Commission did not itself draft the Codes of Practice. They were prepared by the Home Office. Four Codes of Practice have been promulgated. One concerns the detention, treatment and questioning of suspects and replaces the Judges' Rules and the Administrative Directions Accompanying the Rules. The second replaces the Rules on identification parades and the use of photographs for identification and the third is an entirely new Code on search and seizure. Drafts of the first two Codes were first published in June, 1982 and in a revised form in November, 1982. A revised version of these two Codes was published in April, 1983 and a further draft together with and the new Code on search and seizure were published in October, 1983. A new revision was published in April, 1984. In July, 1984 the Home Office published the first draft of the Code on stop and search. By the time the Bill received the Royal Assent in October 1984 there had been yet another draft of all the Codes followed by another draft in January 1985 and the final draft laid before Parliament in May 1985.

The April 1984 draft of the Codes introduced a new feature—a differentiation between the contents of the Codes themselves and what are called "Notes for Guidance" which follow each section. These are described as not being provisions of the Code but "guidance to police officers and others about its application and interpretation." By contrast the text of the various Annexes are part of the Codes themselves (Questioning Code, para. 1.3). The purpose of the Annexes (which were

---

[3] p. 139 below.
[4] Report, para. 4.135.

also introduced in the April 1984 redraft), is to collect in one place provisions that recur at various points in the main text and would otherwise need to be repeated several times.

The Notes for Guidance are therefore technically of a lower status in terms of their authority. But they contain much of great importance and it is doubtful whether the distinction between the rules in the Codes and the principles in the Notes for Guidance will remain a clear one. One difference however is that presumably a breach of the Notes for Guidance is not in itself automatically a breach of the police disciplinary code.

The Code states that the document containing the Codes, "must be readily available at all police stations for consultation by police officers, detained persons and members of the public" (para. 1.2). They will be distributed by the Home Office free of charge.

The Code for the detention, treatment and questioning of persons suspected of crime[5] (the Code on Questioning)

The Code starts with the statement that "all persons in custody must be dealt with expeditiously and be released as soon as the need for detention has ceased to apply." Those who are at the police station voluntarily should be treated "with no less consideration" than those in custody (Notes for Guidance, para. 1A, p. 263 below).

The custody record: paragraph 2[6]

The Code requires the custody officer to maintain a custody record for every arrested person for the details of all the relevant events of the detention. There will be a uniform custody record form for the whole country. The items that must be stated in the custody record include: the grounds of detention (para. 3.10); the suspect's signature acknowledging receipt of a notice of his rights, or the custody officer's note that he refused to sign (para. 3.2); any waiver by the suspect of his right to have legal advice (para. 3.4); the list of the suspect's effects, signed by him as correct or, if he refuses, with a note to that effect (para. 4.4); details of any intimate search, including the reason for it and its result (Annex A); a statement of reasons for withholding articles from the suspect (para. 4.5); requests to inform a relative or friend of the fact of the arrest and any action taken on such a request (para. 5.9); the ground for delaying notification by the suspect of a friend or relative of the fact of detention and his whereabouts (para. 5.9); Annex B, para. 5); the time of any later grant of this right (para. 5.9); details of all visits to detained persons (*ibid.*); action taken on any request for legal advice (para. 6.11); the grounds for delaying access to legal advice (Annex B, para. 5); the grounds for starting to interview a suspect who has been allowed to call a solicitor before the solicitor arrives (para. 6.12); details of any letters sent out by the suspect (para. 5.9); when a foreigner or Commonwealth citizen is told of his right to inform his Embassy or High Commission and details of any call made on his behalf of a person regarding the fact of his detention (para. 7.7); details of the times at which meals are served to the suspect (para. 8.11); the grounds why a child or young person is placed in police cells (para. 8.12); details of any complaint by a suspect regarding

[5] See also the Code at p. 263 below.
[6] See also the Code at p. 264 below.

his treatment (para. 9.7); details of any medical treatment or action taken regarding a condition requiring medical attention (*ibid.* and 9.8), the record should also show what medication he claims he needs which he does not have with him (para. 9.9); the time and place of any caution (para. 10.6); the time at which the suspect is handed over by the custody officer for questioning (para. 12.9); the grounds for delay of a required break in interviews (para. 12.11); action taken to call an interpreter and any waiver of the right not to be interviewed without one (para. 14.9); the grounds for delaying a review of detention (para. 16.3); the details of any such review (para. 16.5); any complaint or request concerning the provisions of the code (para. 12.8); any decision to interview a mentally disordered person or child or young person without waiting for a responsible person who has been asked to come to be with him (Annex C); the time at which the suspect is cautioned on being charged and details of anything he said (para. 17.7–8).

On release a person is entitled to a copy of any part of the custody record that the police are required to maintain (para. 2.4, p. 3) and he must be told in writing of his right to have a copy (para. 3.2). He or his representative should also be allowed to inspect the original (Note for Guidance, para. 2A).

Information to the person in custody

One of the most important provisions in the Code relates to the information that must be given to the suspect. On arrival of the suspect at the police station under arrest or his arrival voluntarily followed by his later arrest and before he is questioned, the custody officer must tell him the ground of his detention and must tell him both orally and in writing of his right to have someone informed about his arrest, to have legal advice, of his rights under paragraph 5 to send other messages to the outside world and to consult the Codes of Practice. The written notice must include the caution (paras. 3.1–3.4).

Paragraph 5 permits the suspect at his own expense to send letters, telephone calls, or telegrams—providing Annex B[7] does not apply. But the police can monitor such communications—other than letters to a solicitor (para. 5.7).

As has been seen, the custody record must show that the suspect has been told about his rights either by his signed acknowledgement or a note that he refused to sign. If he wishes to waive the right to legal advice this too must be signed or failure to sign recorded (para. 3.4).

The police must caution the suspect that anything he says in a letter, phone call or telegram may be used in evidence (para. 5.8).

Conditions of detention: paragraph 8[8]

The Judges' Rules and Administrative Directions made some but only rather general reference to the conditions of detention. The new Code makes many very detailed new rules.

So far as practicable there should be no more than one person per cell (para. 8.1). Cells and bedding should be reasonably clean (paras. 8.2, 8.3). There should be reasonable access to toilet and washing facilities

---

[7] See p. 279 below.
[8] See also the Code at p. 270 below.

(para. 8.4). Replacement clothing should be of reasonable standard and no questioning must take place unless the suspect has been offered clothing (para. 8.5). There should be at least two light and one main meal per 24 hours and any dietary requirements should be met so far as possible (para. 8.6). Brief outdoor exercise should be permitted if possible (para. 8.7).

A child or young person should not be placed in police cells unless there is no other secure accommodation available or the custody officer thinks that it is not practicable to supervise him if he is not put in a cell. Only an inspector or above can authorise such detention (para. 8.8).

No more than reasonable force may be used by a police officer to secure compliance with reasonable instructions, to prevent the suspect's escape or to restrain him from causing injury to persons or damage to property or evidence (para. 8.9).

If any ill-treatment or unlawful force has been used, any officer who has notice of it should draw it to the attention of the custody officer who in turn must inform an officer of at least the rank of inspector not connected with the investigation. If it involves an assault or the use of force he in turn must summon a police surgeon to examine the suspect (para. 9.1). A complaint from the suspect to this effect must similarly be reported to an inspector or above (*ibid.*).

Medical treatment: paragraph 9[9]

The Code requires that appropriate action be taken by the custody officer to deal with any medical condition—whether or not the person in custody asks for it. The police surgeon should be called immediately if the suspect is injured or appears to be suffering from any physical or mental illness or does not show signs of awareness or fails to respond normally to questions (other than though drunkenness alone) (para. 9.2). The section specifically warns that a person who appears to be drunk may in fact be suffering from illness or the effects of drugs or some injury. (Notes for Guidance, para. 9B). The police, the Notes for Guidance say, "should therefore always call the police surgeon when in any doubt and act with all due speed" (*ibid.*).

If the suspect says he needs medication for a serious condition such as heart disease, diabetes or epilepsy the advice of the police surgeon should be obtained (para. 9.6). If the suspect is thought to be a drug addict only a police surgeon can authorise the administration of drugs (para. 9.5).

Cautions: paragraph 10[10]

The provisions regarding cautions are an elaboration of those in the Judges' Rules. The first caution must be administered when the officer "has grounds to suspect" a person of an offence, (para. 10.1) rather than when he has admissible evidence to that effect. The grounds are not even required to be reasonable. The caution should therefore be administered earlier than under the previous rules. He need not be cautioned in fixed penalty cases not unless questions are put to him to obtain evidence that may be given in court. If he is questioned in order to establish his identity or ownership of a vehicle he would therefore not have to be cautioned. If questioning is interrupted the officer must ensure that he knows that he

[9] See also the Code at p. 271 below.
[10] See also the Code at p. 272 below.

is still under caution and if there is any doubt he should be cautioned again in full (para. 10.5). If the person cautioned is not under arrest the officer should tell him that that is the position, that he is free to leave if he pleases and that he may get legal advice if he wishes (para. 10.2). A person who is under arrest should be cautioned: before being asked questions or further questions for the purpose of obtaining evidence for use in court; when being arrested for any further offence; when being charged and when being told about someone else's written statement or answers to questions. (See also p. 89 above.)

Interviews: paragraph 12[11]

In any period of 24 hours the suspect is supposed to be given eight continuous hours of rest, free from questioning, travel or other interruption and, if possible, at night. If he goes to the police station voluntarily, the period is calculated from arrival there and not from arrest.

No one may be questioned if he cannot understand the significance of the questions through the effect of drink or drugs (para. 12.3). The only exception is where an officer of the rank of superintendent or above considers that delay will involve an immediate risk of harm to persons or serious loss or damage to property (Annex C).

Interview rooms are supposed to be adequately heated, lit and ventilated (para. 12.4). The suspect should not be required to stand (para. 12.5). The interviewing officers should identify themselves and their rank. In addition to meal breaks there should also be short breaks for refreshment approximately every two hours unless this would prejudice the investigation (para. 12.7).

Records of interviews: paragraph 11(b) and Annex D[12]

The provisions in the Code regarding the process of keeping proper records of any interview with the suspect are similar to those in the Judges' Rules and the Administrative Directions.

One important addition to the previous rules, however, is the statement that records of interviews should so far as practicable be made contemporaneously, or failing this as soon as possible after the interview (para. 11.3(b)(ii). Basically, the Code requires that there be a full and accurate record of all interviews with all relevant details such as time, place, those present, details of breaks, *etc.* (para. 11.3). As full and accurate a written record of the interview must be made as is practicable (*ibid.*). Another addition is that where a third person is present at an interview he must be given the opportunity to read the written record of the interview and to sign it as correct or to indicate the respects in which he thinks it is inaccurate. If he refuses to do so, this fact should be recorded (para. 12.15).

Traditionally, at the end of the process of relatively informal questioning, police officers prepare, or help the person being interviewed to prepare, a "statement." This is a summary of the salient features of the interview. The Code sets out in Annex D (p. 281 below) the procedure for the taking of such statements but the Notes for Guidance do also say that if the interview has been contemporaneously recorded and the record has been signed by the person interviewed (or the interview has been

---

[11] See also the Code at p. 273 below.
[12] See also the Code at p. 281 below.

tape-recorded), there is normally no need also for a statement under caution. In those circumstances such a statement should only be taken at the request of the person concerned (para. 12B).

If Annex D applies the officer is required to allow the person to write the statement himself. If he wishes the officer to write it for him he must so signify in written form: ("I . . . wish to make a statement. I want someone to write down what I say").

The rules in Annex D state specifically that if a police officer writes the statement, "he must write down the exact words spoken by the person making the statement; he must not edit or paraphrase it" (para. 5). Faithful compliance with this admonition would transform the taking of statements as it has been done in the past.

Police officers are required to bear in mind that the reliability of admissions made by children, young persons or someone suffering from mental illness or mental handicap are particularly open to suggestion. Corroboration of the facts admitted should therefore be obtained wherever possible (Notes for Guidance, para. 13B).

Questioning of mentally ill or mentally handicapped persons, children and young persons: paragraph 13[13]

The provisions in the Code for questioning of persons with the handicap of mental disorder or youth broadly are a much fuller and greatly improved version of the equivalent provisions in the Judges' Rules and Administrative Directions. If "an officer has any suspicion or is told in good faith that a person . . . may be mentally ill or mentally handicapped or mentally incapable of understanding the significance of questions put to him or his replies he must treat him as such a person (para. 1.4). Similarly, in the absence of evidence to the contrary, he must treat someone as a juvenile if he appears to be under 17 (para. 1.5). In such cases an "appropriate adult" must be informed and asked to come to be with the person in question. In the case of someone who is mentally ill or mentally handicapped this means a relative, guardian or other person responsible for his care, failing whom someone experienced in dealing with such cases not employed by the police, failing whom some other responsible adult who is not a police officer (para. 1.5b). In the case of a juvenile it means a parent or guardian or if he is in care, the local authority or a representative of its social services department or another responsible adult who is not a police officer (para. 1.5a). If he is subject to a supervision order, his supervisor should, if possible be told (para. 3.8). A police surgeon is supposed to be called if there is any suspicion that the person in custody is suffering from mental illness (para. 9.2). The police must inform an adult accompanying a person who is mentally ill or mentally handicapped or a child or young person of the suspect's right to legal advice (para. 3.6). All officers are warned to bear in mind that persons suffering from mental illness or mental handicap may be particularly open to suggestion (Notes for Guidance, para. 13B). Because of this, corroboration of anything admitted should always be obtained if possible. If the responsible adult called to assist the mentally disordered or young person thinks that legal advice is desirable, the interview should not start until such advice has been received. Save in an emergency, no interview

---

[13] See also the Code at p. 275 below.

is supposed to take place of a juvenile or a mentally ill or mentally handicapped person (whether suspected of crime or not) without a responsible adult there (para. 13.1). An interview may however take place in the absence of the responsible adult or lawyer if an officer of the rank of superintendent or above reasonably believes that the delay in waiting for such a person will involve an immediate risk of harm to persons or serious loss of or damage to property (Annex C, para. 1). The Notes for Guidance warn that because of the risks of unreliable evidence, interviews should only be conducted without an appropriate adult being present in exceptional cases when there is a strict need to avert an immediate risk of serious harm (para. E2, p. 283 below).

Where a person who is mentally ill or mentally handicapped or a child is interviewed in the absence of a responsible adult because of a risk of harm to persons or serious loss or damage to property the interview may not continue in the absence of an accompanying adult once the risk of such harm has been averted (Annex C, para. 2).

All the provisions relating to the mentally ill and mentally handicapped are conveniently set out in Annex E to the Code on Questioning.[14]

Interpreters: paragraph 14[15]

The Administrative Directions accompanying the Judges' Rules referred to statements made by those who could not speak English being translated by an interpreter. But they did not positively require an interpreter to be called. The new Code remedies this deficiency and states categorically that a person who has difficulty in understanding English shall not, save in urgent cases under Annex C, be interviewed except in the presence of someone who can act as interpreter (para. 14.1).

An interpreter called to assist a deaf person with obtaining of legal advice should not be a police officer. In other situations he can be, if the person being questioned, or the appropriate adult, agrees in writing (para. 14.7).

Interpreters are to be provided at public expense (and all reasonable steps must be made so to inform the person concerned) (para. 14.6).

Questioning of deaf persons: paragraph 14[16]

The Code also provides that where there is a doubt as to a person's hearing, arrangements should be made to have a competent interpreter (para. 3.5). If he wishes, no interview should take place without the interpreter save in urgent cases under Annex C or if he agrees in writing (para. 14.4). If the deaf person is also mentally disordered or a child or young person the interpreter should be someone different from the appropriate adult.

Charging of persons in custody: paragraph 17[17]

As has been seen, the suspect must be charged as soon as there is enough evidence to charge him (s. 37(7)). The procedure is dealt with in paragraph 17 of the Code. He must be brought to the custody officer who is responsible for the charging process. He must be cautioned, given a

[14] p. 280 below.
[15] See also the Code at p. 275 below.
[16] See also the Code at p. 276 below.
[17] See also the Code at p. 277 below.

written statement of the charge, the name of the officer in the case, of the police station and the police reference number. If the person is a juvenile or someone suffering from mental illness or mental handicap the appropriate adult should be present.

Questions about an offence may not normally be put after the suspect has been charged with that offence. But they can be put exceptionally not only (as before) to, "prevent harm or loss to some other person or to the public or for clearing up an ambiguity" but also "where it is in the interests of justice that the person should have put to him and have an opportunity to comment on information concerning the offence which has come to light since he was charged" (para. 17.5). However, before being asked such questions he must be cautioned again. Questions and answers must be recorded contemporaneously in full and the record signed by the person and any third person present. If he refuses, the officer should sign.

If an officer wants to tell a suspect who has been charged about someone else's statement he must simply show him a copy of the statement or of the record of the interview. He "shall say or do nothing to invite any reply or comment save to caution him" (para. 17.4).

Identification procedures: Identification Code (sections 1 and 2; Annexes A,B,C)

The new identification Code replaces the previous instruction to the police (Home Office Circular No. 109/1978 entitled "Identification parades and the use of photographs for identification.") Partly it repeats previous rules, partly it adds to and expands upon them and partly it introduces new procedures. The whole of the new Code appears at pp. 284–291 below.

It requires that where there is disputed identification evidence and the suspect asks for an identification parade one should be held unless it is not practicable because of his singular appearance or otherwise to assemble sufficient people who resemble him (para. 2.3, p. 285 below). The parade should be organised by an officer of the rank of inspector who is not involved in the investigation. If the suspect declines to take part or a parade is not practicable arrangements should be made for the witness to see the suspect in a group. If neither an identity parade nor a group identification is arranged the suspect may be confronted by the witness. Photographs or identikit pictures may not be used if real life identification is possible.

The suspect must be given both an oral explanation and a written notice regarding: the purpose of the parade or group identification; the procedure, any special arrangements made for juveniles, the mentally handicapped; the fact that he does not have to take part in the procedure but that, if he does not, he may be confronted by a witness, and that evidence may be given at his trial of his refusal to take part.

The procedure for identification parades is set out in detail in Annex A, p. 290 below. The two main new features are provision for one way screens to be used and for the actual identification to be by numbers given to each person on the parade. The procedure for confrontation of a witness is dealt with in Annex B, p. 290 below. The procedure for the showing of photographs to a witness is set out in Annex C, p. 291 below. There is also new provision for street identification (para. 2.11). The Code (paras. 2.9 to 2.12) provides that these three Annexes must be complied with.

QUESTIONS AND ANSWERS

CODES OF PRACTICE

1. Must the Codes of Practice be complied with?

The Codes of Practice have replaced the Judges' Rules. They are far more detailed than the Judges' Rules. They cover a far wider area. Whereas the Judges' Rules were promulgated by a committee of judges, the Codes of Practice are put out by the Home Office under authority of the 1984 Act which requires the Home Secretary to issue them and to bring them into force by a statutory instrument approved by affirmative resolution in both Houses of Parliament. Before that occurs they will have been debated in both Houses.

The judges consulted no one before promulgating the Judges' Rules. The Codes of Practice by contrast will have exposed to a long period of public debate. They have been redrafted several times.

Any breach of the Codes amounts to a disciplinary offence. This is indeed specifically stated to be the case in the Act itself. It does not mean of course that every breach will necessarily be penalised as a disciplinary offence. No doubt breaches of the Codes when discovered to have taken place will often be the subject of guidance and warnings rather than full blown disciplinary charges. But if there has been a breach of the Codes the police authorities would be entitled to bring such proceedings.

2. Is a breach of the Codes a criminal offence?

The answer is No.

3. Can a breach of the Codes lead to civil proceedings for damages?

Civil proceedings based solely on a breach of the Codes would not succeed since the Act states that a failure to observe any provision of a Code of Practice "shall not of itself render him liable to any criminal or civil proceedings." But if the breach of the Code is at the same time a breach of the ordinary law, then an action, say, for damages could succeed.

4. What effect therefore would a breach of the rules have on the criminal proceedings against the person himself?

The Act states that "in all criminal and civil proceedings, any [such] code shall be admissible in evidence, and if any provision of such a code appears to the court or tribunal conducting the proceedings to be relevant to any question arising in the proceedings it shall be taken into account in determining that question."

This means that the court may take such account of the breach of the Codes as it thinks right. It might for instance exclude evidence obtained in breach of the Codes.

It was the view of both the Royal Commission and of the Government that enforcement of the Codes should basically be through internal police disciplinary proceedings rather than through the courts. But probably the most important means to secure compliance with the Codes will be the attitude of the police service. The Codes are a detailed and carefully worked out statement of how suspects are to be treated. They are clearly much more helpful than the Judges' Rules in that they are much fuller and deal with so many issues that were not previously regulated. They have been drafted with great care after consultation with all interested groups and interests—including of course the police. It is to be expected that they will be treated seriously by the police service.

PART VII

DOCUMENTARY EVIDENCE IN CRIMINAL PROCEEDINGS

Evidence from documentary records: section 68[1]

Certain trade and business records are admissible in evidence under the Criminal Evidence Act 1965 as an exception to the rule against hearsay. The Act was passed to cancel the effect of the House of Lords decision in *Myers* v. *D.P.P.*[2] which held that manufacturers' records of car numbers in cylinder blocks were hearsay and inadmissible as evidence in a case involving allegations of conspiracy and receiving stolen cars.

For the evidence to be admissible the records have to be compiled from information supplied by a person who has, or may reasonably be expected to have, personal knowledge of the matters dealt with, provided that the person is dead, unfit to testify, cannot be identified or found or cannot reasonably be expected to have any recollection of the information supplied.

The Act is however limited to trade and business records. The purpose of section 68 is to extend its scope to records in the public sector. The section supersedes the 1965 Act. The proposal in this and the next section follows the recommendations of the Criminal Law Revision Committee in its 11th Report on Evidence.[3] The section has to be read in conjunction with Schedule 3. (The text of Schedule 3 was originally in the section itself but was transferred to a schedule by the draftsman in order to reduce the clutter in the main Act.) Part I of Schedule 3 applies to section 68. Part II applies to section 69 and Part III applies to both sections.

Subsection (1) provides that (subject to s. 69) a statement in a document shall be admissible as evidence of any fact in it for which direct oral evidence would be admissible if: (a) the document is or forms part of a record compiled by someone acting under a duty from information supplied by a person (whether acting under a duty or not) who either had or may reasonably be supposed to have had personal knowledge of the matters dealt with, and (b) the person who supplied the information satisfies one or other of the conditions in subsection (2).

Subsection (2) sets out three conditions, one of which has to be fulfilled. The first is that the person is dead, unfit to testify or abroad and it is not practicable to have him testify; or he cannot be expected to recall the matters in question because of the lapse of time and all the circumstances.

---

[1] See also text of the Act at p. 208 below.
[2] [1965] A.C. 1001.
[3] "Evidence (General)," Cmnd. 4991 1972, para. 258.

The second, is that all reasonable steps have been taken to identify the person who supplied the information but without success. The third is that the identity of the person is known but all reasonable steps to find him have proved unsuccessful.

Subsection (3) provides that nothing in section 68 should prejudice admissibility of any evidence that would be admissible apart from this section—such as an exception to the hearsay rule.

Schedule 3 then deals with the detail. Paragraph 1 of the Schedule provides that section 68(1) applies whether the information was supplied directly or indirectly but, if it came through intermediaries, they must themselves have been acting under a duty. Section 68(1) applies also where the supplier of the information is also the person who compiled the document.

The evidence is admissible only with the leave of the court which can give leave only in the interests of justice, after balancing the contents of the document and the danger that the accused will be prejudiced by its admission without being able to cross-examine the person who supplied the information (para. 2).

Paragraph 3 permits evidence to be introduced to test the credibility or weight of the hearsay evidence admitted under section 68. Subparagraph (*a*) permits evidence going to credibility (such as evidence of bias or a previous inconsistent statement or that he had been convicted of an offence) to be admitted. Subparagraph (*b*) states that, with the leave of the court, evidence may be given which could have been given in cross-examination if the witness had appeared. Subparagraph (*c*) allows for the admissibility of evidence tending to show that the absent witness has made a statement at any time which is inconsistent with the information being introduced in evidence.

A statement admissible under section 68 cannot however corroborate evidence given by the supplier of the information. A witness cannot corroborate himself (para. 4).

Paragraph 7 is similar to section 6(3) of the Civil Evidence Act 1968 and supersedes section 1(3) of the Criminal Evidence Act 1965. It provides that in estimating the weight, if any, to be attached to a statement admissible under section 68, regard must be had to all the circumstances including the contemporaneity (or otherwise) and the question whether anyone who was in a position to do so had any incentive to conceal or misrepresent the facts.

Evidence from computer records: section 69[4]

Section 69 provides for the admissibility of computer records subject to certain conditions.

Recent case law had disclosed serious confusion as to whether and when computer records were admissible in evidence.[5] There were certain statutory provisions making computer records admissible,[6] but apart from these, the courts have tended to allow computer generated information and to disallow computer stored information.

---

[4] See also text of the Act at p. 208 below.
[5] See especially *Pettigrew* (1980) 71 Cr.App.R. 39 and J.C. Smith, "The Admissibility of Statements by Computer" [1981] Crim.L.R. 387.
[6] Under the Banking Act 1979, Sched. 6; Army Act 1955, s.198B; Air Force Act 1955, s.198B; Finance Act 1972, s.34; Finance Act 1980, s.16.

The purpose of section 69 and the Schedule are to put the admissibility of computer evidence on a more sure footing. They are based to a large extent on proposals of the Criminal Law Revision Committee in its 11th Report[7] and are broadly similar to section 5 of the Civil Evidence Act 1968.

Subsection (1) provides that statements in documents produced by computers shall not be admissible evidence of any fact contained in them of which direct oral evidence would be admissible unless the conditions in paragraphs (*a*) to (*c*) are satisfied. Paragraph (*a*) states that there should be no reasonable grounds for believing the statement to be inaccurate because of improper use of the computer. Paragraph (*b*) provides that the computer must have been operating properly at all material times, or if not, that any malfunction shall not have affected the accuracy or production of the statement. Paragraph (*c*) provides that any conditions specified in rules of court made under subsection (2) of section 69 shall be satisfied. Subsection (2) simply provides that the procedure and additional requirements for the admission of computer evidence may be governed by rules of court.

The rest of the rules regulating computer evidence are in Part II (paras. 8–12) and Part III (paras. 13–15) of Schedule 3.

Paragraph 8 allows evidence by certificate for the purpose of identifying a document produced by the computer, giving details of how the document was produced and showing that the conditions in section 69(1) have been fulfilled. The certificate may be stated to the best of the knowledge and belief of the person making it.

Paragraph 9 provides that the court may nevertheless require oral evidence to be given of any of the matters mentioned in the certificate. The Criminal Law Revision Committee said that this clause was desirable because there was no equivalent to the provision in the Civil Evidence Act of notice to the other side of the intention to call hearsay evidence which gave the opponent the opportunity to require oral evidence to be given. ("The provision in subsection (5) of the clause seems desirable in the absence of a requirement to give notice and having regard to the higher standard of proof required for a conviction in criminal proceedings."[7]) Presumably the court would act at the request of either prosecution or defence, or of its own motion.

Paragraph 10 makes it an offence knowingly to make a false statement in a certificate under paragraph 8.

Paragraph 11 is similar to paragraph 7 in Part I of the Schedule (and section 6(3) of the Civil Evidence Act 1968). It sets out considerations to be taken into account when estimating the weight to be given to evidence admissible under section 69.

The final paragraphs of Schedule 3 apply to both sections 68 and 69. Paragraph 13 is similar to section 6(1) of the Civil Evidence Act 1968 in providing that a statement in a document which is admissible under sections 68 and 69 can be proved by the production of a document or of an authenticated copy. The next paragraph provides that, when considering whether to admit a statement in evidence under sections 68 and 69, the court can draw any reasonable inferences from the circumstances in which the document came to be made. This is similar to section 6(2) of the Civil Evidence Act 1968 and supersedes the corresponding provision

---

[7] *Op. cit.* (note 3 above), para. 259.

in section 1(2) of the Criminal Evidence Act 1965. Paragraph 15 provides for rules of court to supplement the provisions of sections 68 and 69.

Microfilm copies: section 71[8]

Under the previous law microfilm copies of certain categories of documents were admissible under certain statutory provisions.[9] It seemed unclear whether other microfilm copies were admissible.

Section 71 is intended to put the matter beyond doubt. It provides that the contents of a document may be proved by the production of an enlargement of a microfilm copy of that document or part of it. The copy must be authenticated "in such manner as the court may approve." The microfilm copy is admissible whether or not the original document is still in existence.

Definitions: section 72[10]

Section 72(1) defines "copy," "statement" and "proceedings." The first two have the same meanings as in Part I of the Civil Evidence Act 1968. The expression "proceedings" if not further defined means criminal proceedings.

Subsection (2) saves any power of a court to exclude evidence at its discretion. It is similar to section 18(5)(*a*) of the Civil Evidence Act 1968. It includes exclusion of evidence by preventing questions from being put or by excusing the witness from answering questions already put or by directing the jury to disregard evidence.

[8] See also text of the Act at p. 209 below.
[9] Banking Act 1979, Sched. 6; Finance Act 1972, ss.34 and 39.
[10] See also text of the Act at p. 209 below.

PART VIII

EVIDENCE IN CRIMINAL PROCEEDINGS— GENERAL

Convictions and acquittals: sections 73 to 75[1]

The Criminal Law Revision Committee in its 11th Report recommended that the law on proof of convictions and acquittals in criminal cases should be tidied up, and sections 73–75 broadly follow the recommendations of the Committee.[2]

Section 73 replaces statutory provisions which contain references to court procedures that are outdated.[3] It provides for proof of a conviction or acquittal by a certificate signed by the appropriate officer of the court, together with evidence identifying the person named in the certificate.

There is also a saving for any other authorised manner of providing evidence of a conviction or acquittal—such as by a person present in court, or by means of fingerprints under section 39 of the Criminal Justice Act 1948, or written statements under sections 2 or 9 of the Criminal Justice Act 1967 or an admission under section 10 of the 1967 Act.

Section 74 amends the law on admissibility of convictions as evidence of the commission of an offence. In accordance with *Hollington* v. *Hewthorn*,[4] evidence that a person other than the accused had been convicted of an offence was not admissible for the purpose of proving that that person committed the offence. The rule was abolished for civil proceedings by the Civil Evidence Act 1968, s.11. The difficulties that the rules gave rise to were illustrated recently in *Spinks*.[5] S. had been convicted of acting with intent to impede the arrest of F., having hidden the knife used by F. in a stabbing. S.'s conviction was quashed on appeal because the only evidence at his trial that F. had committed the offence was inadmissible and F.'s conviction for the stabbing was inadmissible because of the rule in *Hollington* v. *Hewthorn*.

The Criminal Law Revision Committee recommended in its 11th Report[6] that the rule in *Hollington* v. *Hewthorn* should be abolished for criminal cases as well. Section 74 follows the C.L.R.C.'s proposals in regard to convictions of persons other than the accused. In regard to the accused himself the section makes no change in the rules regarding the

---

[1] See also text of the Act at pp. 209–210 below.
[2] *Op. cit.* (note 3, p. 105 above) paras. 217–220.
[3] Evidence Act 1851, s.13; Criminal Procedure Act 1865, s.6; and the Prevention of Crimes Act 1971, s.18.
[4] [1943] K.B. 587.
[5] [1982] 1 All E.R. 587.
[6] *Op. cit.* para. 218.

admissibility of his past misconduct. But it does alter the rules regarding his commission of a previous offence by allowing it to be proved by evidence of his conviction.

Subsection (1) states that the conviction of someone other than the accused is admissible as proof that he committed that offence whether or not any other evidence of the fact is given. So if A is charged with handling goods stolen by B, evidence that B was convicted of stealing the goods will be admissible to prove that they were stolen.

Subsection (2) provides that the person convicted shall be taken to have committed that offence unless the contrary is proved.

Subsection (3) deals with the position of the accused. Where evidence is admissible of the fact that he has committed an offence, insofar as that is relevant to a matter in issue other than a tendency to show a disposition to commit the kind of offence with which he is charged, the conviction shall be taken as proof that he committed that offence unless the contrary is proved. The section however specifically preserves the operation of any statute making a conviction or finding of fact conclusive for the purpose of other proceedings. It is also provided that the admissibility of any conviction which would be admissible apart from the clause, is not prejudiced. (For a similar provision in regard to civil cases, see Civil Evidence Act 1968, s. 11(3).)

Section 75 has supplementary provisions making admissible duly certified copies of documents to prove the facts of the offence including the information, complaint, indictment or charge sheet. Without such factual details it may be difficult to determine whether a previous conviction is or is not relevant. Oral evidence is also admissible. Subsection (3) provides that certain enactments under which a conviction leading to probation or discharge is to be disregarded shall not affect the admissibility of the conviction for evidentiary reasons. The enactments in question prevent the conviction from counting as part of the criminal record for the purpose of sentencing.

Confessions: section 76[7]

One of the most controversial sections in the Act is section 76 which makes a major change in the law on confessions. Under the previous law a confession was only admissible if the prosecution could show that it was voluntary, in the sense that it had not been induced, in the classic phrase, "by fear of prejudice or hope of advantage exercised or held out by a person in authority."[8] Also a confession must not have been obtained by oppression.[9]

In the past the courts took this principle very seriously and interpreted it strictly against the police. Even the mildest threat or inducement has been held to make a resulting confession inadmissible. Thus in *Northam*,[10] a person charged with housebreaking was being questioned about his part in other offences. Before confessing he asked whether the other offence might be taken into consideration at his trial rather than being the subject of a separate trial. The Court of Appeal quashed the conviction because of the police officer's acceptance of this suggestion. In *Zaveckas*[11] the

---

[7] See also text of the Act at p. 211 below.
[8] *R. v. Ibrahim* [1914] A.C. 599.
[9] See especially *Prager* [1972] 1 All E.R. 1114; *R. v. Priestly* (1966) 50 Cr.App.R. 183.
[10] (1967) 52 Cr.App.R. 97.
[11] (1969) 53 Cr.App.R. 202.

Court of Appeal quashed a conviction because the trial judge had admitted a confession made after the defendant asked the police officer whether he could have bail if he made a statement.

In its 1972 11th Report the Criminal Law Revision Committee said that two reasons had been given for the rule. One was that a confession not made voluntarily might not be reliable (the "reliability principle"); and secondly, that the police should be discouraged from using improper methods to obtain a confession (the "disciplinary principle"). It thought that historically the reliability principle underlay the law. This was shown by the authorities and also by the fact that if the police discovered something such as a body or a gun as a result of an involuntary confession, the evidence of that fact was admissible.

After reviewing the case law, the Committee said that it was unsatisfactory.[12] It recommended that only threats or inducements likely to produce an unreliable confession or oppression should cause a confession to be inadmissible. It would be for the judge to imagine that he was present at the interrogation and to consider whether at that point the threat or inducement would have been likely to make a confession unreliable.

Since the report of the C.L.R.C. in 1972 the case law on confessions moved somewhat in the direction of the Committee's proposals. In *D.P.P.* v. *Ping Lin*[13] the suspect, a drugs dealer, asked "If I help the police, will you help me?" The officer replied: "I can make no deal with you but if you show the judge that you have helped the police to trace bigger people I am sure he will bear it in mind when he sentences you." The House of Lords said that the prosecution had to show *as a matter of fact* that the threat or promise had not induced the confession. The judge had been entitled to hold the statement admissible.

In the recent case of *Rennie*[14] this ruling was applied to a confession which the police officer actually admitted had been prompted by the suspect's fear that the police would otherwise interview and perhaps arrest other members of his family. The Lord Chief Justice in a reserved judgment said that the speculation of the police officer as to what prompted the confession was irrelevant and inadmissible. But (at p. 388) he went on: "Even if the appellant had decided to admit his guilt because he hoped that if he did so the police would cease their inquiries into the part played by his mother, it does not follow that the confession should have been excluded."

The law did not require, Lord Lane said, that every confession should be excluded simply because it was prompted in part by some hope of advantage. The question was whether on a common sense view the statement had been made voluntarily which in ordinary parlance meant "of one's own free will." This was a question of fact which should be approached by the judge much in the way that a jury would. The confession was held to be admissible.

Plainly the definition of voluntariness in *Rennie* was wholly different from that in cases like *Northam* and *Zaveckas*. Most of the bite in the rule had been removed.

[12] *Op. cit.* paras. 53–69.
[13] [1976] A.C. 574.
[14] [1982] 1 All E.R. 385.

The Royal Commission[15] criticised the voluntariness test as unrealistic. Even a trained psychologist present during questioning, it suggested, could not determine to what extent any particular confession was truly voluntary.[16] In the Commission's view it would be better to abandon the vain attempt to distinguish between voluntary and involuntary confessions and concentrate instead on the behaviour of the police officer. If the suspect was subjected to torture, violence, the threat of violence or inhuman or degrading treatment any subsequent confession should be inadmissible. This would mark society's "abhorrence of such conduct."[17] But any lesser breach of the rules of questioning should merely lead to the judge warning the jury of the danger of relying on the resulting confession if there was no independent evidence.[18]

The Royal Commission's proposal that the voluntariness test be abandoned altogether was rejected by the Government on the ground that it did not provide adequate protection against the danger of an unreliable confession. The Act adopts two tests on admissibility of confessions. The first rejects as inadmissible any confession obtained by oppression of the accused, which as defined "includes torture, inhuman or degrading treatment, and the use or threat of violence" (subss. (2)(*a*) and (8)). The fact that the definition is stated to "include" the listed forms of oppression indicates that the list is not intended to be exhaustive.

The meaning of "inhuman or degrading treatment" will be for the courts to develop. The concept is taken from the words of the European Convention on Human Rights.[19]

The second category of confession evidence that is wholly excluded is where it has been obtained "in consequence of anything said or done which was likely in the circumstances existing at the time, to render unreliable any confession which might be made by the accused in consequence thereof" (subs. (2)(*b*)).

This adopts the approach recommended by the Criminal Law Revision Committee that reliability should be the test. The fact that the section abandons the old approach of cases like *Northam* and *Zaveckas* is explicitly confirmed in the Code of Questioning. This states that no police officer shall seek to obtain answers to questions by the use of oppression or "shall indicate, except in answer to a direct question, what action will be taken on the part of the police if the person being interviewed answers questions, makes a statement or refuses to do either" (para. 9.1). However, if the suspect directly asks the officer "what action will be taken in the event of his answering questions, making a statement or refusing to do either, the officer may inform him what action he proposes to take in that event provided that the action is itself proper and warranted" (*ibid.*).

In other words, indications of threats or promises within the limits of what is lawful and proper will not render a confession inadmissible if they emerge as a result of questions from the suspect. This is a far cry from the traditional common law approach to these matters. But *Ping Lin* and *Rennie* could be said to have paved the way.

[15] Report, para. 4.73.
[16] The Commission based its view largely on the research of Barrie Irving, "Police Interrogation: A Case Study of Current Practice" *Royal Commission Research Study No. 2* (1980).
[17] Report, para. 4.132.
[18] Report, para. 4.133.
[19] Art. 3. The European Court considered the phrase in *Tyrer* v. *U.K.*, 2 E.H.R.R. 1, 9–12; and *Ireland* v. *U.K.* 2 E.H.R.R. 25, 73–85. For the view of a Northern Irish court see *R.* v. *McCormick* [1977] N.I. 105.

It is for the prosecution to prove beyond reasonable doubt that the confession was not obtained in consequence of something likely to make the confession unreliable even though it may be true (subs. (2)). Moreover the court may of its own motion require the prosecution to prove this even if the defence fails to make representations (subs. (3)).

But how should the court approach the task of deciding whether the confession was unreliable? This crucial question was addressed by the Criminal Law Revision Committee which produced the basic formula that has now been adopted. The essential feature of the test it thought "is that it applies not to the confession which the accused in fact made but to any confession which he might have made in consequence of the threat or inducement. On this scheme the judge should imagine that he was present at the interrogation and heard the threat or inducement. In the light of all evidence given he will consider whether, at the point when the threat was uttered or the inducement offered, any confession which the accused might make as a result of it would be likely to be unreliable. If so, the confession would be inadmissible. For example, if the threat was to charge the suspect's wife jointly with him, the judge might think that a confession even of a serious offence would be likely to be unreliable. If there was a promise to release the accused on bail to visit a sick member of his family, the judge might think that this would be unlikely to render a confession of a serious offence unreliable but likely to do so in the case of a minor offence."[20] The mere fact that the police bring improper pressure (not amounting to oppression) to bear on the suspect would therefore not be enough. It must also be improper pressure which would be likely to make the confession unreliable. There must be some likely causal link between the pressure and an unreliabe confession.

The same question was of course debated in Parliament. The Opposition moved an amendment that no-one should be convicted on the basis of a confession obtained as a result of detention in which there had been any breach of Parts IV and V of the Act (dealing with Detention and the Questioning and Treatment of Persons by the Police), or from a juvenile or someone suffering from a mental disorder in response to police questioning without a responsible adult being present unless there was corroboration of the confession. The Government resisted the amendment but the Home Office Minister Mr. Mellor said that in his view "most, if not all the circumstances set out in the amendment render the confession unreliable."[21] However, apart from these two indications the question is not easy to answer. Obviously it will depend on what judges think makes a confession unreliable. The question will slowly be answered through actual decisions.

When the Bill was first published it contained a provision that evidence could be admitted to prove the truth or falsity of the confession if the court thought that such evidence would assist in determining the issue of admissibility. This rejected the view of the majority of the Judicial Committee of the Privy Council in *Wong Kam-Ming* v. *The Queen*[22] in which it was held that on a *voir dire* as to the admissibility of an extra-judicial statement by an accused the prosecution could not cross-examine him as to the truth of the statement. The sole issue on the *voir dire*, the

---

[20] *Op. cit.* (n. 3, p. 109 above). pp. 43–44.
[21] House of Commons, *Hansard,* Standing Committee E, March 8, 1984, col. 1657.
[22] [1979] 1 All E.R. 939.

majority held, was whether the statement had been made voluntarily, and whether it was true was not relevant to that issue. The subsection adopted the minority view expressed by Lord Hailsham which reflects the decision in *Hammond*.[23] However, the Government was persuaded to drop this provision with the result that the majority view in *Wong Kam-Ming* stands after all.

The section goes on to provide that the inadmissibility of a confession shall not affect the admissibility of (a) facts discovered as a result of the confession (such as the gun with fingerprints); or (b) so much of the confession as is necessary to show that the accused speaks, writes or expresses himself in a particular way where this is relevant (subs. (4)).[24]

Subsection (5) provides that evidence that any fact discovered as a result of an inadmissible confession (or part of a confession (subs. (6)(*b*)) was discovered in this way shall be admissible only if evidence of how it was discovered is given by the accused or on his behalf. It cannot be produced by the prosecution.

Confessions by mentally handicapped persons: section 77[24a]

At a very late stage the Government introduced into the Bill this clause to strengthen the protection for defendants who suffer from some form of mental handicap or disability. The section requires a judge in cases brought against persons who are mentally handicapped to warn the jury of the need for special caution before convicting such an accused in reliance on his confession. The judge will have to give this warning where the case against the accused depends wholly or mainly on his confession where he is satisfied that the confession was not made in the presence of an independent person. If the case is a summary one in a magistrates' court, the bench are required to treat it in the same way "as one in which there is a special need for caution before convicting the accused on his confession" (subs.(2)).

A person is mentally handicapped for the purposes of this section if the court is satisfied that he "is in a state of arrested or incomplete development of mind which includes significant impairment of intelligence and social functioning" (subs.(3)).

Exclusion of unfair evidence: section 78[25]

The English tradition in regard to the exclusion of improperly obtained evidence, other than confessions is that it is basically admissible subject to a rarely exercised judicial discretion to exclude it. This approach is in marked contrast to that of the common law in regard to confession evidence where, as has been seen, the judges adopted a much more rigorous rule.

The leading authority was perhaps *Kuruma, Son of Kaniu v. R.*[26] in which, on an appeal from Kenya, the Judicial Committee of the Privy Council held that if evidence was relevant, it mattered not how it was obtained. The accused in that case had been convicted of being in unlawful possession of ammunition discovered during the course of a search by an officer of a lower rank than the rules required for such searches. But the

[23] (1941) 28 Cr.App.R. 84.
[24] As in *R*. v. *Voisin* [1918] 1 K.B. 531.
[24a] See also text of the Act at p. 212 below.
[25] See also text of the Act at p. 212 below.
[26] [1955] A.C. 197.

Board recognised that a judge always had a discretion to exclude evidence in a criminal case if the rules of admissibility would operate unfairly against the accused.

The continuing existence of the discretion to exclude improperly obtained evidence was confirmed by the Divisional Court in *Jeffrey* v. *Black* reported in 1978.[27] The accused was arrested for the suspected theft of a sandwich in a pub. The police then went to his home where they discovered drugs. The court held that this search had been unlawful since it was not for the offence for which he was arrested. But they went on to consider whether the evidence should nevertheless have been admitted. Lord Widgery, the Lord Chief Justice, said: . . . the magistrates sitting in this case, like any other criminal tribunal in England sitting under the English law, have a general discretion to decline to allow any evidence to be called by the prosecution if they think it would be unfair or oppressive to allow that to be done. . . . It is a discretion which every criminal judge has all the time in respect of all the evidence which is tendered by the prosecution.[28] The discretion, he went on, would be rarely used. "But if the case is exceptional, if the case is such that not only have the police officers entered without authority, but they have been guilty of trickery or they have misled someone, or they have been oppressive or they have been unfair, or in other respects they have behaved in a manner which is morally reprehensible, then it is open to the justices to apply their discretion and decline to allow the particular evidence to be let in as part of the trial."[29]

However, in 1979 the House of Lords in *R.* v. *Sang*[30] reduced the scope of the common law discretion to exclude improperly obtained evidence. The only ground for excluding illegally or improperly obtained evidence in the view of the law lords was that where its probative effect was greatly outweighed by its prejudicial effect.

The Royal Commission on Criminal Procedure was invited by witnesses to recommend some form of exclusionary rule of evidence. In the United States illegally obtained evidence is inadmissible and various bodies giving evidence to the Commission argued for the adoption of such a rule. But the Commission was not persuaded. It said that experience in the United States did not suggest that such a rule significantly deterred improper police conduct. It could only affect the small numbers of cases in which the defendant ultimately pleaded not guilty. It operated many months after the event. The proper way to check police misconduct was through actions for damages or disciplinary action by the police themselves.[31] The Commission's views on this issue were however much criticised in some quarters.[32]

Neither Mr. Whitelaw's nor Mr. Brittan's version of the Police and Criminal Evidence Bill initially addressed the problem. But at a very late stage the question suddenly surfaced as one of importance and the

---

[27] [1978] 1 All E.R. 555.
[28] *Ibid.* at p. 559.
[29] *Ibid.*
[30] [1980] A.C. 402.
[31] Report. paras. 4.123–4.128.
[32] See for instance J. Driscoll, "Excluding Illegally Obtained Evidence—Can we learn from the United States," *Legal Action Group Bulletin,* June, 1981, p. 131. See also generally J. D. Heydon, "Illegally Obtained Evidence" [1973] Crim.L.R. 690; A. J. Ashworth, "Excluding Evidence as Protecting Rights" [1977] Crim.L.R. 723. For a comparison with the U.S.A. see P. Hartman, "Admissibility of Evidence Obtained by Illegal Search and Seizure under the U.S. Constitution,"(1965) 28 M.L.R. 298.

Government decided after all to react to the pressure that was developing. The initiative was taken by Lord Scarman who moved an amendment on the Committee stage to give the courts a discretion to exclude evidence that had arguably been unlawfully obtained unless the prosecution could prove beyond reasonable doubt that it had been lawfully obtained or that the illegality was of no material significance or that the overriding interests of justice required that it be allowed in as evidence notwithstanding that it was obtained unlawfully

The amendment was supported by Lord Denning, Lord Edmund-Davies and Lord Fraser. Lord Elwyn Jones said that although he was a signatory to the amendment he was now doubtful whether it was wise. The Lord Chancellor said that he was against the amendment but that there was a case for some form of discretion to be exercised by the judge when to admit the evidence would be unfair to the accused. On that basis Lord Scarman withdrew his amendment.[33]

On the Report stage in the House of Lords, Lord Scarman returned to the point with a similar, though slightly redrafted, amendment. But this time the Lord Chancellor himself proffered his own amendment which would have given the courts a discretion to exclude evidence but only where it was obtained from the accused himself. The court would have a discretion to exclude any evidence obtained from the accused if it appeared to the court, "that, having regard to all circumstances, including the circumstances in which the evidence was obtained, the admission of the evidence would be so prejudicial to the fairness of those proceedings that the court ought not to allow it to be given."

The House of Lords debated Lord Scarman's amendment first and in the event, it was approved by 125 votes to 118 against the advice of the Lord Chancellor. Lord Denning said that he had changed his mind and spoke against the amendment. None of the other law lords participated in the debate. In the light of the result Lord Hailsham's amendment was not debated.[34]

The Government then had to decide whether to accept Lord Scarman's amendment. In the event they concluded that they could not accept it. Mr. Leon Brittan, the Home Secretary, told the House of Commons that the reason was partly that it would lead to the acquittal of guilty persons for reasons that were insufficiently related to the fairness of the case and partly to avoid excessive burdens on the courts of "trials within trials" (House of Commons, *Hansard*, October 29, 1984, cols. 1012–1013). Instead they brought forward a new Government amendment. This was broadly the same as the clause originally introduced by Lord Hailsham with the difference that the evidence covered by the clause was no longer limited to that obtained from the accused himself. In other words, all evidence (other than confession evidence which, as has been seen, has its own separate rules), is subject to a general exclusionary rule under which the court has a discretion to exclude it if its admission would have an unduly adverse effect on the fairness of the proceedings. Also "adverse effect" replaces "prejudicial" in Lord Hailsham's amendment.

It remains to be seen how the judges will use this discretion. It is conceivable that they will interpret the section narrowly and admit evidence obtained by throughly deplorable methods on the pretext that it

---

[33] House of Lords, *Hansard*, July 11, 1984, cols. 931–948.
[34] House of Lords, *Hansard*, July 31, 1984, cols. 635–675.

does not affect the fairness of the *proceedings*. This would emasculate the discretion. The whole thrust of the policy behind the new section is to give courts the power to express their disapproval of objectionable police methods by excluding the fruits of such action. No doubt it would only be used rarely but the discretion is "at large" and should be interpreted in a broad way.

Time for taking accused's evidence: section 79[35]

Under the previous law the accused had to give evidence before hearing the evidence and cross-examination of any witnesses he intended to call.[36] The Criminal Law Revision Committee in its 11th Report recommended[37] that the court should have a discretion—for instance to allow a witness to be called before the accused who is to speak of an event before the matters about which the accused is to give evidence. Section 79 implements this proposal. The accused gives evidence first "unless the court in its discretion otherwise directs."

Competence and compellability of accused's spouse: section 80[38]

Section 80 deals with the rules of the *incompetence* of the accused's spouse to give evidence (of when she cannot give evidence even when willing to do so), and of the spouse's *compellability* (when she can be required to give evidence even though unwilling to do so). The Criminal Law Revision Committee in its 11th Report proposed changes in these rules and section 80 broadly adopts these recommendations.

Under the previous law the accused's spouse was generally not competent for the prosecution[39] (save when the charge was one of personal violence against her) but was always competent as a defence witness for the accused[40] and was competent as a defence witness for the spouse's co-accused but normally only with the spouse's consent.[41]

The C.L.R.C. said that it had no doubt that a wife should always be competent as a witness for the prosecution in all cases. "If she is willing to give evidence, we think that the law would be showing excessive concern for the preservation of marital harmony if it were to say that she must not do so."[42] Subsection (1) adopts this view, subject to an exception in subsection (4) where the spouse is jointly charged with the same offence. But this exception does not apply where he or she is no longer liable to be convicted for that offence by virtue of having pleaded guilty or otherwise.

Previously the spouse was competent but not compellable for the accused. The C.L.R.C. recommended[43] that the spouse should always be compellable as well as competent as a witness for the accused. Subsection

---

[35] See also text of the Act at p. 212 below.
[36] *R.* v. *Morrison* (1911) 6 Cr.App.R. 159; *R.* v. *Smith* (1968) 52 Cr.App.R. 224.
[37] *Op. cit.* note 3, p. 105 above, para. 107.
[38] See also text of the Act at p. 213 below.
[39] There were certain statutory exceptions including the Evidence Act 1898, s.4(1); Sexual Offences Act 1956, s.39; Theft Act 1968, s.30.
[40] By virtue of the Criminal Evidence Act 1898, s.1. See *Cross on Evidence* (5th ed., 1979), p. 179 for discussion of whether an accused's spouse can give evidence for a co-accused without the accused's consent in sexual offence cases.
[41] Also by virtue of the Criminal Evidence Act 1898, s.1.
[42] *Op. cit.* para. 148.
[43] *Ibid.* para. 153.

(2) gives effect to this recommendation save for the same exception in subsection (4) where they are jointly charged.

There were few cases where the spouse was compellable for the prosecution. Until recently it was thought that at common law a spouse was compellable against the marriage partner if the case involved violence against her (or him). But the House of Lords rejected this view in *Hoskyn* v. *Metropolitan Police Commissioner.*[44]

The C.L.R.C. proposed[45] that a wife should be compellable for the prosecution not only where the case involved violence against her but also in cases of violence towards children under the age of sixteen belonging to the same household as the accused. Often in such cases the wife was in fear of her husband but wanted to give evidence against him. To make her compellable as a witness would make her position easier rather than more difficult. The Committee did not however go so far as to recommend compellability where the child was not from the same household.

The Act goes beyond what the C.L.R.C. recommended. Subsection (3) makes the spouse compellable for the prosecution where the case involves violence against him or her or against *anyone* who was under 16 at the time, or where the offence is a sexual one against a person aged under 16. Again the same exception under subsection (4) applies for the case where the spouses are charged jointly.

The C.L.R.C. also dealt with the problem of one spouse as witness for the co-accused of the other spouse.

A spouse was competent for the defence with the consent of the accused spouse but was not generally compellable. In the view of the C.L.R.C.[46] the accused's spouse should be competent but not compellable for the accused's co-accused regardless of the accused's consent. Subsection (1)(*b*) gives effect to this proposal.

It seemed that a divorced wife was not competent to give evidence about something that occurred during the marriage.[47] The C.L.R.C. proposed[48] that, after the marriage had been dissolved, former spouses should be both competent and compellable as if they had never been married. The Act accepts this proposal (subs. (5)). It applies to anything that occurred whilst they were married. Following the views of the C.L.R.C. it does not apply however unless the marriage has been ended by divorce or annulment. Judicial separation is not enough.

The C.L.R.C. proposed[49] that the prohibition in section 1(*b*) of the Criminal Evidence Act 1898 of comment by the prosecution on the failure by the accused's spouse to give evidence should be abolished. But the Government rejected this recommendation (as it rejected the C.L.R.C.'s other recommendations on the right of silence) and section 1(*b*) is expressly confirmed in subsection (8) of section 80.

The final subsection deals with the privilege of a witness not to answer questions about a communication made to the witness by his or her spouse during the marriage and the right to decline to say whether marital intercourse did or did not take place. The Law Reform Committee recommended in its 16th Report that these privileges should be abolished

---

[44] [1979] A.C. 474.
[45] *Op. cit.* para. 150.
[46] *Ibid.* para. 155.
[47] See *Algar* [1954] 1 Q.B. 279; *Lapworth* [1931] 1 K.B. 117.
[48] *Op. cit.* para. 156.
[49] *Ibid.* para. 154.

for civil cases.[50] This was achieved by sections 16(3) and (4) of the Civil Evidence Act 1968 and the C.L.R.C. made the same recommendation in regard to criminal cases.[51] The Act gives effect to the recommendation in subsection (9).

Advance notice of the defence case: section 81[52]

Under the previous law the only requirement that the defendant reveal any part of his case in advance of the trial concerned an alibi defence. The Royal Commission recommended[53] that the defence should be required to give advance notice also of expert evidence so as to reduce the danger of surprise causing adjournments. The Royal Commission said that obvious examples were defences depending on medical evidence or expert forensic evidence which the prosecution needs an opportunity to evaluate or on which it may wish to call its own expert witnesses.[54]

The Act adopts this suggestion by granting powers for Crown Court Rules to be made to require either party to disclose to the other any expert evidence he proposes to adduce in the proceedings and to prohibit a party who fails to comply with such rules to adduce such evidence, save with leave of the court. The Rules may specify the kinds of expert evidence covered.

Exclusion of evidence: section 82[55]

At the end of the interpretation section for Part VIII of the Act is the sentence: "Nothing in this part of this Act shall prejudice any power of a court to exclude evidence (whether by preventing questions from being put or otherwise) at its discretion." The section is somewhat similar to s. 18(5)(*a*) of the Civil Evidence Act 1968. A judge can protect a witness by preventing objectionable questions being put to him. He can also protect him from answering even if the question has in fact been put by indicating that he need not answer. These judicial functions are preserved by subsection (3). The "or otherwise" in subsection (3) also refers to the power of the court to direct a jury to disregard evidence they have heard. The general power of the court to exclude improperly obtained evidence is now of course regulated by the new provisions in section 78.

QUESTIONS AND ANSWERS

CONFESSIONS

1. How does the new Act alter the law regarding the admissibility of confessions?

The previous law excluded confessions that (1) were obtained as a result of oppression; and (2) that could not be shown by the prosecution to have been voluntary.

"Oppression" was defined by the courts to have two aspects. First, that the presence or absence of oppression was a function of both the

---

[50] "Privilege in Civil Proceedings" Cmnd. 3472 (1967).
[51] *Op. cit.* (note 3, p. 105 above) para. 173.
[52] See also text of the Act at p. 213 below.
[53] Report, para. 8.22.
[54] *Ibid.*
[55] See also text of the Act at p. 214 below.

circumstances of the questioning and the characteristics of the defendant. Secondly, that oppressive questioning was questioning which by its nature or duration or other circumstances so affected the accused that his will crumbled.

The 1984 Act retains the rule that confessions which result from oppressive questioning must be excluded. The judge has no discretion. Oppression is defined in the Act as including "torture, inhuman or degrading treatment, and the use or threat of violence (whether or not amounting to torture)."

But the new Act does alter the law as regards the "voluntariness" test. The old test was whether the confession had been obtained from the accused "by fear of prejudice or hope of advantage exercised or held out by a person in authority." The new test is whether the confession was or may have been obtained "in consequence of anything said or done which was likely, in the circumstances existing at the time, to render unreliable any confession which might be made by him in consequence thereof."

Under the old test the judges were supposed to consider primarily whether there had been any threat or promise. Under the new test they will have to consider the likely impact on the mind of the accused of all the circumstances at the time of his confession and evaluate whether they would be likely to have made the confession unreliable. This will probably prove to be an exceedingly difficult matter for the courts and one anticipates a considerable number of cases in the next few years as they struggle to arrive at a sensible elaboration of the new formula.

One thing however is clear. When the case poses this problem the burden of proof is firmly on the prosecution. The statute says in terms that if the question of the admissibility of the confession is raised "the court shall not allow the confession to be given in evidence against him except in so far as the prosecution proves to the court beyond reasonable doubt that the confession (notwithstanding that it may be true) was not obtained as aforesaid" (*e.g.* by oppression or in circumstances likely to make it unreliable). Indeed the Act has an unusual additional provision that even if the defence fail to make representations about the admissibility of the confession the court can require the prosecution to prove that the confession was not obtained in ways that would make it inadmissible.

2. What is the rule about the admissibility of real evidence (fingerprints, bloodstains, stolen goods, etc.) found as a direct result of an inadmissible confession?

The new Act continues the previous law that such real evidence is admissible even though the confession which led to its discovery is inadmissible. But no evidence can be given by the prosecution about the inadmissible confession and how it led to the discovery of the real evidence unless the *defence* state that that was what had happened.

3. In what circumstances will the court exclude evidence (other than confessions) obtained by improper means?

A court has the power in its absolute discretion to exclude any evidence where, having regard to the circumstances (including the way the evidence in question was obtained), it considers that its admission would have an unduly adverse effect on the fairness of the proceedings. So, if the court takes strong exception to the way that the prosecution have obtained any evidence it can rule that the evidence should not be admitted.

THE EVIDENCE OF SPOUSES

1. In what circumstances can a spouse now be compelled to give evidence against her spouse?

Under the previous law, one spouse could not be compelled to give evidence against the other spouse, even in a case where the charge arose from a violent attack by one on the other.

This rule has been changed by the Act which provides that one spouse can be compelled to give evidence against the other spouse where the offence charged involves an assault on, injury or threat of injury to, the first spouse or against a person under sixteen or a sexual offence against a person under 16.

2. When else is a spouse permitted to give evidence against her husband?

Under the old law, subject to a few exceptions, one spouse could not generally testify against the other. The only important exception was where the charge arose out of personal violence by the accused on the other spouse.

The Act changes the rule by making each spouse eligible ("competent") though not required ("compellable") to give evidence against the other.

3. Is one spouse compellable to give evidence for the other?

The old law generally did not treat one spouse as a compellable witness for the other. But this rule has been changed by the Act which makes husband and wife each compellable to give evidence for each other.

4. What happens if one spouse is charged together with the other?

The Act makes this an exception to the new rules. In other words a wife charged jointly with her husband is neither competent nor compellable to give evidence against him unless she is no longer liable to conviction because she pleaded guilty or for any other reason.

5. How are these rules affected by the fact that the spouses are divorced?

The old law took no notice of divorce. A spouse who had been divorced was in exactly the same position in regard to the question of competence and compellability as beforehand.

The Act changes this by providing that once spouses have been divorced they must be treated as if they had never been married. In other words they are free to give evidence even as to what occurred during the marriage—and can be compelled to do so for the prosecution where the case arises out of physical injury by one spouse on the other or on someone under 16.

PART IX

POLICE COMPLAINTS AND DISCIPLINE

The prior system for dealing with complaints against the police had three main elements. A chief officer who received a complaint against a member of his force had to record it and order that it be investigated either by an officer from another force, failing which by a chief superintendent (or in London a chief inspector). In practice, the chief constable's discipline and complaints functions, other than the actual hearing of charges, were delegated to the deputy chief constable.

Unless the chief officer was satisfied from the report that no criminal offence had been committed, he had to send the report to the Director of Public Prosecutions (D.P.P.). The D.P.P. then advised whether the officer should be charged with an offence. The chief officer had to consider in addition whether or not disciplinary charges should be brought. He also had to send the investigating officer's report to the Police Complaints Board together with a memorandum stating whether he intended to institute disciplinary proceedings and, if not, why not. If the chief officer did not bring charges, the Board could recommend and, in the last resort, could direct that he do so. If charges were brought, the Board would decide whether the hearing should be by the chief officer or by a tribunal consisting of the chief officer with two members of the Board.

The system was therefore the same for all cases however trivial. One criticism advanced was that too much time of senior officers was deployed in investigating minor matters that could have been better dealt with less formally. Also cases had to be referred to the D.P.P. even when the chief officer was clear in his own mind as to whether criminal charges should be brought. Another criticism against the system was that there were no real independent checks on the process of investigation. The D.P.P. was an independent check in regard to criminal prosecution and the Board could review decisions on disciplinary charges. But there was no independent review of the way in which the original complaint was investigated.

In October 1982 the Government published a White Paper, "Police Complaints Procedures"[1] in which it set out its proposals for changes to the complaints system. These were reflected in the Police and Criminal Evidence Bill introduced in November 1982. It would have changed the system in three main respects.

First, in regard to serious complaints, an "independent assessor" would have been appointed by the chairman or deputy chairman of the Police Complaints Board to supervise the inquiry made by an officer from another force.

[1] Cmnd. 8681 (1982).

Secondly, it proposed to make changes in regard to very minor complaints by introducing a new system of informal resolution that would not require full investigation of the complaint.

Thirdly, it proposed changes in the rules requiring reference of cases to the D.P.P. which resulted in the Director being inundated with large numbers of relatively minor cases. The Bill proposed to give the chief officer a discretion as to whether to refer a case to the D.P.P. so that he would only have to refer cases whose gravity warranted such a reference.

During the Committee stage of the Bill this last provision was removed, against the wishes of the Government, by an alliance between the Opposition parties and Mr. Eldon Griffiths, Tory backbencher representing the Police Federation.[2] (See further p. 137 below.)

When Mr. Brittan introduced the second Bill in October 1983, he accompanied it with a second White Paper, "Police Complaints and Discipline Procedures."[3] The second Bill adopted the previous changes in regard to the informal resolution of minor complaints. It restored the proposals to give the chief officer a discretion as to whether to refer a case to the D.P.P. But it made major changes in the arrangements for dealing with the most serious complaints—notably by setting up a new Police Complaints Authority to replace the old Police Complaints Board with powers itself to supervise the actual investigation of serious complaints.

Establishment of the Police Complaints Authority: section 83[4]

Section 83 replaces the Police Complaints Board with the new Police Complaints Authority ("the Authority"—not to be confused with the "police authority" or "the authority" or the appropriate authority," see below). The Authority will have two main functions. One is the powers in relation to the consideration of disciplinary charges held by the old Police Complaints Board. In its discipline function its powers are limited to matters concerning officers up to and including the rank of superintendent. Disciplinary matters involving officers above the rank of chief superintendent will continue to be the province of the police authority.

The Authority's second function will be the supervision of investigations relating to the conduct of police officers of whatever rank and over related disciplinary charges.

Schedule 4 of the Act referred to in subsection (2) of section 83 contains detailed provision as to the status, members, staff, proceedings and financial arrangements of the authority. The provisions are virtually identical to those that governed the Police Complaints Board (in the Schedule to the Police Act 1976). Only two matters call for mention here:

Appointment of chairman and members

Whereas the Chairman of the Police Complaints Board was appointed by the Prime Minister, the chairman of the new Authority is appointed by the Queen. On the other hand, whereas members of the Board have all been appointed by the Prime Minister, the members of the Authority (of whom there will not be more than eight) other than the chairman are appointed by the Home Secretary (Sched. 4, para. 1(3)).

[2] See House of Commons, *Hansard*, Standing Committee J, March 10, 1983, col. 1227.
[3] "Police Complaints and Discipline Procedures," Cmnd. 9072 (1983).
[4] See also text of the Act at p. 214 below.

Regional offices

Unlike the Board, the Authority has the right, if it wishes, to set up regional offices in order to improve its capacity to produce a quick response in investigation (Sched. 4, para. 9(1)).

Handling of complaints: Preliminary: section 84[5]

Section 84 sets out the duties of chief officers of police on receiving a complaint against a member of their force. (See also s.86,[6] in relation to complaints against officers above the rank of chief superintendent).

Subsection (1) places a duty on the chief officer when he receives a complaint to take any steps that appear to him to be desirable for obtaining or preserving evidence relating to the offence. The 1983 White Paper[7] said that the first few hours after receipt of a complaint may often be vital, since evidence may have to be obtained which would be unavailable later. "It is essential that the need to refer cases to the Authority should not delay any necessary preliminary investigations."

The duty to take steps to preserve evidence therefore applies regardless of whether the complaint has been sent to the right place.

Under subsection (2) the chief officer must then decide whether he is "the appropriate authority" to deal with the matter. The appropriate authority is defined in subsection (4) as the police authority in relation to senior officers (above the rank of chief superintendent), the chief constable in relation to all other officers and in London the Commissioner of the Metropolitan force in relation to any officer of his force.

If he decides that he is not the appropriate authority, his duty is to send the complaint (or if it was made orally, details of it) to the appropriate authority and to inform the person by whom or on whose behalf the complaint was made that he has done so (subs. (3)). It is therefore his reponsibility to see that a misdirected complaint gets to the right place.

Complaints consist of any complaint made about the conduct of an officer of his force submitted not only by a member of the public but under a new provision, on behalf of a member of the public and with his written consent (subs. (4)). Providing the complainant agrees, the complaint can be made therefore by an M.P., an advisory agency, the Police Complaints Authority or indeed anyone.

The provisions of Part IX of the Act do not apply however to complaints regarding the "direction or control of a police force" by the chief officer or someone on his behalf (subs. (5)). Such complaints will continue to be dealt with through the police authority calling for a report from the chief constable under section 12(2) of the Police Act 1964. Equally Part IX procedures do not apply if the conduct has already been the subject of criminal or disciplinary proceedings (subs. (6)). If the matter has already been investigated there is no point in registering and investigating it as a formal complaint.

Investigation of complaints: standard procedure: section 85[8]

If the chief constable decides that he is the appropriate authority he must record the complaint (subs. (1)). This replaces the duty to record

---

[5] See also text of the Act at p. 215 below.
[6] See p. 216 below.
[7] *Op. cit.* note 3 above, para. 13.
[8] See also text of the Act at p. 215 below.

complaints placed on chief officers of police by section 49(1) of the Police Act 1964.

The chief officer must next determine whether the complaint ought to be investigated formally or whether it is suitable for informal resolution (see below). If he thinks it right to do so he could appoint an officer of his own force of the rank of chief inspector or above to make preliminary inquiries to assist him to make this decision (subss. (2) and (8)). Also the investigating officer should not be of a lower rank than the officer complained of (subs. 8(*b*)).

A complaint is not suitable for informal resolution unless the member of the public consents and the chief officer is satisfied that, even if proved, the conduct would not justify a criminal or disciplinary charge (subs. (10)). Very minor infringements of the police disciplinary code could therefore be dealt with by informal resolution even though technically they might in theory lead to a disciplinary charge.

If, after attempts have been made to settle the matter informally, it appears to the chief officer that the complaint is not after all suitable for informal resolution or that informal resolution of the matter is impossible, he must appoint an officer from his own force or another force to conduct an investigation. If he requests an officer from another force, the request cannot be refused (subss. (5) and (7)). Unless the investigation is supervised by the Authority, the officer who conducts the investigation must report about it to the chief officer (subs. (9)). If the complaint is considered by the chief officer to be suitable for informal resolution he must (under subs. (4)) seek to have it resolved informally and may appoint an officer from his own force for the purpose.

Informal resolution of complaints

There is nothing about the method of informal resolution of complaints in the Act but the 1983 White Paper went into some detail about the new system. No fixed procedures will be imposed on police officers but they are to receive detailed guidance on the procedures to be adopted.

In some cases an explanation or apology to the complainant will suffice; in others the complainant will be told that the officer in question will be talked to; sometimes a meeting may be arranged with a lay person acting either as an independent presence or simply as a friend of the complainant. But the officer complained against would not be compelled to attend such a meeting.

Informal resolution would not be regarded as concluded until the officer, as well as the complainant, has had the chance of commenting orally or in writing on the allegation. But if the process is concluded satisfactorily, the outcome will have to be recorded in a register available for inspection by the police authority and H.M. Inspectorate. The complainant will be entitled to a copy if he asks within three months of it being made.

No entry of any kind will be entered in the personal record of the officer concerned nor will any admission relating to the matter being resolved informally made by the complainant or the accused officer be admissible in any subsequent criminal, civil or disciplinary proceedings (s. 104(3)). The only exception according to the White Paper is where information that comes to light during informal resolution suggests that the matter is actually more serious than had at first appeared. If this happened, the process of informal resolution would cease and the matter would be referred for investigation.[9]

Oversight of the process of informal resolution will fall to police authorities and H.M. Inspectorate of Constabulary. The register recording the outcome of informal resolution will be required to be maintained in sufficient detail to make it possible for them "to form a view of the appropriateness of informal resolution for the complaints in question, and the means by which it was conducted."[10] Each police authority will have the duty to keep itself informed as to how complaints in its area are being dealt with (s.95).

The Police Complaints Authority will have no specific function in regard to informal resolution machinery or procedures. But the White Paper said that it was hoped that the Authority would take account of all aspects of the complaints system in its reports.

Investigation of complaints against senior officers: section 86[11]

Where a complaint is made about an officer above the rank of chief superintendent it must be recorded by the appropriate authority (see section 84) and, subject to subsection (2), investigated by it. Subsection (2) says that it may deal with the complaint according to its discretion if it is satisfied that the conduct complained of would not, even if proved, justify a criminal or disciplinary charge. The effect of this is to give the police authority a right to determine whether it should be handled by the formal or informal machinery. In such cases therefore the complainant does not have the effective veto over a complaint being handled informally that he enjoys under section 85(10)(*a*) in relation to other complaints. It is for the police authority to decide the matter whether or not the complainant agrees. The alleged justification for this difference is not that senior officers should be treated more favourably but rather that the police authority should be expected to act as an effective watchdog.[12]

The actual method for dealing with complaints against senior officers is similar to that for other officers with the substitution of the police authority for the chief officer. Where the complaint is not to be dealt with informally the authority must appoint an officer of the same force or a different force to investigate (subs. (3)). A request for an officer for such an investigation must be complied with (subs. (4)). The officer to conduct such an inquiry must be at least of the same rank as the officer who is the subject of the complaint (subs. (5)). The investigating officer's report must be submitted to the authority which has appointed him save where the investigation is being supervised by the Police Complaints Authority under section 89.

The Home Office Minister told the House of Commons on the consideration of Lord's amendments that the government would introduce a further change by regulations to protect chief constables from over-hasty or possibly politically biassed suspension. Regulations would provide that any decision by a police authority to suspend an officer of the rank of assistant chief constable or above would have to be satisfied by the Police Complaints Authority. Such an event would be very rare but Mr. Giles

[9] *Op. cit.* (note 3 above), para. 33.
[10] *Ibid.* para. 34.
[11] See also text of the Act at p. 216 below.
[12] House of Lords, *Hansard,* July 11, 1984, col. 990.

Shaw said "It is important that the intention to suspend an officer of senior rank should be subject to review by an independent non-partisan organisation. The proposed arrangements are meant solely as a safeguard for senior officers against the remote possibility of an arbitary or unjust exercise of the power of suspension". House of Commons, *Hansard*, October 29, 1984, cols. 1055–1056.

References of complaints to the Authority: section 87[13]

Certain types of complaints *must* be referred by the chief officer to the Police Complaints Authority. They are complaints alleging that death or serious injury has been caused by an officer in his force (subs. (1)(*a*)(i)). "Serious injury" in this context is defined to mean "a fracture, damage to an internal organ, impairment of bodily function, a deep cut or a deep laceration" (subs. (4)).

The 1983 White Paper stated that such cases must be referred to the Authority "irrespective of whether [the chief officer] considers that police action was or could have been responsible."[14]

Regulations are to be made specifying other types of complaints which must also be notified to the Authority (subs. (1)(*a*)(ii)). But (as will be seen below) whereas those alleging death or serious injury will have to be supervised by the Authority those in this additional list will only be supervised by the Authority if it chooses to do so. It will have a discretion. The White Paper stated that this category will consist of complaints "alleging corruption; cases of assault not involving death or serious injury which have nevertheless resulted in actual bodily harm; and other serious cases reflecting adversely on the reputation of the police service."[15] It is not apparent why they are not listed in the Act itself.

In addition, a chief officer will be entitled but not required to notify the Authority about any other complaint (subs. (1)(*b*)). According to the White Paper the chief officer would exercise this discretion in regard to any complaint which he thinks should be brought to the attention of the Authority "whether by reason of the gravity of the allegation or other exceptional circumstances."[16]

Regulations will specify the time limit within which complaints requiring mandatory reference or notification must be referred to the Authority (subs. (3)). The White Paper states that such references and notifications should be effected "as soon as practicable and normally not later than the day after the complaint is recorded."[17]

The Authority will have the power to require the appropriate authority to submit to them for consideration any complaint which it has not referred to them and that authority (defined in s.84) will have to comply with such a request within specified time limits (subs. (2). In this connection it will be important that the Authority, unlike the Ombudsman, will be permitted to receive complaints direct from members of the public, M.P.s, the Home Secretary or any other source. The Authority will also be able to ask the chief officer to provide all such information as is necessary to enable it to determine whether it wishes to supervise the investigation into the matter.[18]

[13] See also text of the Act at p. 216 below.
[14] *Op cit.* (note 3 above), 1983, para. 14.
[15] *Ibid.* para. 15.
[16] *Ibid.* para. 16.
[17] *Ibid.* para. 13.
[18] *Ibid.* para. 17.

Reference of other allegations to the Authority: section 88[19]

Section 88 enables other matters indicating that an officer may have committed a criminal or disciplinary offence not contained in a complaint to be referred to the Authority, for it to decide whether it ought to supervise the investigation. Such a case might arise for instance where a civil action has been brought against the police or because of a newspaper campaign or local or national notoriety. The appropriate authority would have the right to refer such a case to the Authority in its discretion because of its gravity or exceptional circumstances.

Supervision of investigations by the Authority: section 89[20]

Section 89 sets out the powers, duties and procedures of the Police Complaints Authority in the supervision of complaints investigations.

There are two kinds of cases where supervision is mandatory. The first is where there has been a complaint alleging death or serious injury. The second is any other type of complaint specified in regulations made by the Secretary of State (subs (1)). According to section 100(5) such regulations are subject to the affirmative resolution procedure.

The Authority has a discretion as to whether or not to supervise in relation to any other lesser complaint or any matter referred to them under section 88. The test is simply whether they think that such supervision "is desirable in the public interest" (subs. (2)).

The White Paper[21] said that there will be no restriction to criminal cases in the power of discretionary reference or in the Authority's reserve power to call in cases. Also, when exercising its powers of supervision, the Authority will deal with all aspects of the investigation and not only those relating to alleged criminal conduct.

When the Authority have decided whether or not to exercise their discretionary power to supervise an investigation they must inform the appropriate authority accordingly (subs. (3)).

The Authority may require that it should approve the appointment of an investigating officer in a case it is to supervise (subs. (4)). It will therefore have the right to select a particular individual name or to veto a name selected by the chief officer. The Authority may require that no appointment of an officer be made until it approves his name, or if one has already been made, that it be changed (*ibid.*).

Regulations will be made by the Secretary of State regarding the duty of the Authority to consult and obtain the consent of the D.P.P. before imposing requirements in relation to evidential matters (see subs. (5) and the White Paper, para. 26). However, subject to such regulations, the Authority will have the power to impose requirements as to how the investigation should be conducted. The Home Office Minister, Lord Elton told the House of Lords that this could include requirements as to the resources to be deployed on an investigation not simply as to the manner of the inquiry. But the regulations will require that any such requirement involving disposition of resources will be subject to a duty to consult with the chief constable.[22]

[19] See also text of the Act at p. 217 below.
[20] See also text of the Act at p. 217 below.
[21] *Op. cit.* (note 3 p. 123 above), para. 19.
[22] House of Lords, *Hansard*, July 11, 1984, cols. 993–994.

The White Paper gave some further indications regarding the nature of supervision by the Authority. It will be able, after consulting with the chief officer, to require that an investigation team be augmented in respect of manpower, equipment or other resources.[23] It will have the right to give investigating officers "such reasonable directions as it considers necessary for the proper conduct of the investigation" (subject to the consent of the D.P.P. in matters concerning the collection of evidence for possible criminal proceedings).[24] These powers will enable it to require investigating officers "to account for their actions; to explain the strategy and tactics of their investigation; and to justify particular lines and depth of questioning and any apparent delay in the investigation."[25] The degree of supervision in any particular case will depend on the circumstances but it was expected "that consultation and advice, rather than formal directions will be the usual means by which the Authority will proceed."[26] The members of the Authority will be divided into two divisions—one for investigations and one for discipline cases. No one will consider the same case from the point of view of both functions.

If a member of the Authority had been directed to take direct responsibility for the conduct of an investigation he would have regular contact with the officer in charge of the investigation. He could if he wished visit the scene of the incident or inspect material evidence. But it would not be his function to become directly involved in the process of investigation itself. So he would not for example attend interviews conducted by the investigating officer.

Subsection (6) of section 89 requires the investigating officer to submit his report to the Authority in any case in which it has supervised and to send a copy to the chief officer concerned. After considering this report the Authority must send "an appropriate statement" to the "appropriate authority" (subs. (8)). An appropriate statement is defined in subsection (10) as one as to whether the investigation was or was not conducted to the Authority's satisfaction; specifying any way in which it was not so conducted; and dealing with such other matters as the Home Secretary may specify in regulations.

If it is practicable to do so, the Authority when submitting the appropriate statement under subsection (7) must send a copy of it to the officer whose conduct has been investigated (subs. (8)). Similarly, if the investigation related to a complaint it must, if it is practicable, send a copy to the person by or on behalf of whom the complaint was brought (subs. (9)).

Lord Elton explained in the House or Lords what sort of things might make this "not practicable." "Complainants may move away and not be traceable; the investigation may fail to identify a particular officer; indeed investigation might reveal that the person concerned was not a police officer at all."[27] It is also conceivable that it might turn out that the alleged incident never occurred at all.

The Authority can, if it wishes, issue separate statements on the criminal and disciplinary aspects of an investigation (subs. (11)). No disciplinary charges may be brought before the Authority's statement has been

---

[23] *Op. cit.* (note 3, p. 123 above), para. 21.
[24] *Ibid.* para. 22.
[25] *Ibid.*
[26] *Ibid.*
[27] House of Lords, *Hansard,*. July 11, 1984, col. 994.

submitted to the appropriate authority (subs. (12)). Similarly, neither the appropriate authority nor the Director of Public Prosecutions should normally start criminal proceedings before the appropriate statement has been submitted. But if the D.P.P. thought there were exceptional circumstances which made it undesirable to wait, criminal proceedings could be brought before the Authority's statement has been submitted (subss. (13) and (14)).

The Authority's role in regard to the investigation of the complaint would cease with the issue of its "appropriate statement." It would not be involved in any criminal prosecution.

The Authority's statement will be publicly available. Whilst not naming names or providing evidential details it could record such matters as the numbers of witnesses interviewed and statements recorded; the time taken; and the number and rank of officers involved in the investigation.[28]

The role of the D.P.P.

If a police officer investigating a complaint under the supervision of the Authority wishes to consult the D.P.P. he will be entirely free to do so as before—but he must inform the Authority of this intention and of the result of such consultation. Normally the Authority would wish to be involved in such discussions and it would have the right to do so.[29] Where the Authority was intending to give advice short of a formal direction on any matter relating to the collection of evidence for possible criminal proceedings it should first ensure that such advice conformed to the policy of the D.P.P.[30] Where the Authority finds it necessary to give formal directions on such a matter the White Paper said that it will be important to define the relationship between the Authority and the D.P.P. with care. "The need here is to strike a balance between on the one hand the independent position of the D.P.P. and his responsibilities for prosecution policy, and on the other, the new Authority's role as guardian of the public interest in the investigation of a special category of case of concern also to the D.P.P."[31] The Authority will be required by law to consult the D.P.P. before giving directions on evidential questions and his consent will be required before such directions may be made.[32] ever happened that the D.P.P. refused his consent the Authority would be able to make reference to the fact in the statement it issued at the end of the inquiry.

Steps to be taken after investigation of complaint—general section 90[33]

If the report received by the appropriate authority relates to a senior officer (under section 86(6) or 89(6)) it *has* to be sent to the D.P.P. unless the report "satisfies them that no criminal offence has been committed" (subs. (1)).

But if the report does not relates to a senior officer the procedure is different and is set out in section 90. The Bill originally provided that the chief officer should first consider whether the report indicated that the police officer might have committed a criminal offence. If so, he had then

---

[28] *Op. cit.* (note 3, p. 123 above), para. 27.
[29] *Op. cit.* para. 25.
[30] *Ibid.*
[31] *Ibid.* para. 26.
[32] *Ibid.*
[33] See also text of the Act at p. 218 below.

to consider whether the matter was too serious to be dealt with by disciplinary charges. Seriousness was the only test. Only if he decided that it was too serious for disciplinary charges did he have to refer it to the D.P.P. It was hoped that this would relieve the D.P.P.of the immense burden of sifting through vast numbers of trivial matters. But the Police Federation through its representative Mr. Eldon Griffiths M.P. mounted a major attack on this provision and (as has been seen) succeeded in securing a defeat for the Government in the Committee stage in the House of Commons.

Mr. Griffiths said: "I am well aware that the criminal offences that the Government have in mind may be trivial matters such as riding a bicycle without a light. That is a crime. None the less, I believe that it is wrong that a chief officer should have the discretion to prefer a disciplinary charge on a criminal matter rather than take it to the D.P.P.[34] He cited with approval the Federation's statement that it was convinced that "*the only system that is fair to members of the public and the police alike is to continue to have all complaints of a criminal nature dealt with, in the first instance, by the Director of Public Prosecutions. . . . We are not prepared . . . to support a proposition that police officers should be deprived of their constitutional rights as citizens to be tried in open court, according to the rules of evidence and with all the rights of any other person facing a criminal charge . . . when they are accused of breaches of the criminal law.*"[35] Another reason, he said, was that the D.P.P. was consistent in his approach as between one force and another, whereas chief officers varied in their approach.

The Government did not however accept the principle of this defeat. It redrafted the provisions of the Bill so as to distinguish between criminal and disciplinary considerations. Section 90 now establishes a new and different test for a reference to the D.P.P. Instead of having to consider whether a matter is too serious to be dealt with by disciplinary means, chief officers have to consider whether the investigation discloses a criminal offence with which the officer *ought to be charged* (subs. (3)). Only if he decides that no criminal offence should be brought will the chief officer be able to consider the aspects. Otherwise it must be sent to the D.P.P. (subs. (4)).

This is supposed to put police officers in the same position as other citizens. As Lord Elton put it: "If any offence disclosed would in the chief officer's view merit prosecution then he must send it to the D.P.P.; he cannot deal with it by way of discipline."[36]

Lord Elton said that the advantage of this was that it would still relieve the D.P.P. of a mass of cases in respect of which there was no prospect of a prosecution, "while removing from police officers the possibilty of their being dealt with by disciplinary means for matters which should be prosecuted in court."[37]

After the D.P.P. has dealt with the question of criminal charges the chief officer must (subject to section 91(1) below) send the Authority a memorandum stating whether he has preferred disciplinary charges and if not, his reasons for not doing so (subs. (5)).

---

[34] House of Commons, *Hansard,* Standing Committee E, March 20, 1984, col. 1838.
[35] *Ibid.*
[36] House of Lords, *Hansard,* July 11, 1984, col. 997.
[37] *Ibid.*

But if the chief officer has decided that, although a criminal offence does appear to have been committed, it is not one for which charges should be brought, or alternatively that it appears that no criminal offence was committed, he must send the Authority a memorandum to that affect stating whether he has preferred disciplinary charges and if not, his reasons (subss. (6) and (7)). Such a memorandum must give particulars of (i) any disciplinary charges brought or proposed to be brought; (ii) any exceptional circumstances by reason of which section 94 (below) should apply to the hearing; and (iii) the chief officer's opinion of the whole complaint or matter (subs. (8)).

Where the investigation related to conduct which was the subject of a complaint that was not supervised by the Authority, the chief officer must send the Authority a copy of the complaint and of the report of the investigation at the same time as he sends them his memorandum (subs. (9)). Otherwise there would be no way for the Authority to be sure of getting a copy.

If the chief officer states in his memorandum that he has started or intends to start disciplinary proceedings, he is required by subsection (10) actually to carry out this intention. But this is subject to the provisions of section 93(6) below.

Steps to be taken where accused has admitted charges: section 91[38]

The duty to send the Authority a memorandum under section 90 does not arise where disciplinary charges have been started and the accused officer has admitted the charges and has not withdrawn his admission. This is because the powers of the new Authority like those of the previous Board are to direct or to recommend that charges be brought where the chief officer does not propose to do so. It has no power to recommend or to direct that charges should not be brought where the chief officer has decided to bring them.

At the end of the disciplinary proceedings, the chief officer must send the Authority particulars of the charges brought and of any punishment imposed. If the charges related to conduct which had been the subject of a complaint the investigation of which was not supervised by the Authority, he must also send the Authority a copy of the complaint and of the report of the investigation (subss. (2) and (3)). The purpose of this is to enable it to exercise its powers of directing a reference to the D.P.P. under section 92.

Powers of the Authority to direct reference of reports, etc., to D.P.P.: section 92[39]

Where the Authority has received the report of an investigation from a chief constable acting under section 90 or 91 concerning the conduct of an officer of the rank of chief superintendent or below, it must consider whether a criminal offence may have been committed by him (subs. (1)). If it thinks that the officer should have been charged it is their duty to instruct the chief officer to send the D.P.P. a copy of the report (subs. (2)).

They may at the same time direct the chief officer to send the D.P.P. the information contained in the section 90 memorandum. If the investi-

---

[38] See also text of the Act at p. 220 below.
[39] See also text of the Act at p. 220 below.

gation was of a complaint the Authority will tell the chief officer to send the D.P.P. a copy of the complaint (subs. (4)). All directions under this section must be complied with by the chief officer (subs. (5)).

Powers of the Authority as to disciplinary charges: section 93[40]

Section 93 confers on the Authority the same powers to recommend and direct the bringing of disciplinary charges as the Police Complaints Board had under section 3 of the Police Act 1976.

Subsection (1) states that where a memorandum under section 90 indicates that the chief officer does not intend to prefer disciplinary charges, the Authority may recommend that he bring such charges as it specifies.

If after the Authority has made such a recommendation and has consulted the chief officer, he still declines to bring charges, the Authority may direct him to do so (subs. (3)). Where the Authority give the chief officer a direction under section 93 they must give him written reasons (subs. (4)). The chief officer must comply with any such direction (subs. (5)). Disciplinary charges brought either on the chief officer's initiative or following a recommendation or direction by the Authority cannot be withdrawn save with the leave of the Authority (subs. (2)). However, the Authority can give the chief officer leave not to prefer charges which section 90(10) or section 93(3) would otherwise oblige him to bring or not to proceed with charges which section 90(10) or subsections (2) and (5) of section 93 would otherwise require him to continue (subs. (6)).

The Authority may request the chief officer to give them such information as they may reasonably require to enable them to discharge their duties under section 92 and the chief officer must comply with such a request (subss. (7) and (8)).

Disciplinary tribunals: section 94[41]

Section 94 deals with the Police Complaints Authority's power to order that disciplinary charges be heard by a tribunal chaired by a chief officer of police, rather than by a chief officer sitting alone. Otherwise it gives the Authority the powers previously enjoyed by the Police Complaints Board under section 4 of the Police Act 1976.

The section applies to any case where disciplinary charges have been directed by the Authority or where it directs that it should apply because of exceptional circumstances (subss. (1) and (2)).

The tribunal shall consist of a chief officer as chairman with two members of the Complaints Authority who have not previously been concerned with the case. Punishment is to be determined by the chief officer after consulting the other two members. Guilt shall be determined by the tribunal as a whole (subs. (3)(*a*) and (*b*)).

Normally the chief officer would be the officer's own chief. But under the Police (Discipline) Regulations 1977 the accused's chief officer must remit the case to be heard by another chief officer if he has a personal interest in the case or is a material witness, and he may remit it in any other case. Subsection (7) provides that where the chairman is not the chief officer of the force to which the accused officer belongs and that chief officer does not have a personal interest in the case and is not a

[40] See also text of the Act at p. 220 below.
[41] See also text of the Act at p. 221 below.

133

material witness, then it is he, not the chairman who determines the punishment after considering any recommendation from the chairman, and after the chairman has consulted the other members (subs. (8)).

Subsection (4) sets out different rules as to the chairmanship of such a tribunal where the accused officer belongs to the metropolitan force.

By virtue of subsection (6) a tribunal's decision on guilt may be by a majority.

Information as to the manner of dealing with complaints: section 95[42]

Section 95 requires police authorities and H.M. Inspectorate of Constabulary to keep themselves informed about the way in which complaints against police officers are dealt with. The provision is similar to, but not identical with, section 50 of the Police Act 1964. But whereas that spoke of "the manner in which complaints . . . are dealt with by the chief officer of police," section 95 refers more generally to "the working of sections 84 and 93" The section contemplates in particular the arrangements for the handling of minor complaints by informal means.

Constabularies maintained by authorities other than police authorities: section 96[43]

Section 96 is the equivalent of section 7 of the Police Act 1976 under which the Police Complaints Board had power to exercise its functions in relation to constables maintained by bodies other than police authorities. Such arrangements were in force under the 1976 Act in respect of the Ministry of Defence Police, British Transport Police, Port of London Authority Police, Port of Liverpool Police and the U.K. Atomic Energy Authority Police.

Subsection (1) permits the Authority, with the approval of the Home Secretary, to make such arrangements. Subsection (2) permits the Home Secretary, where no such arrangements are in force, to make them by order after consulting with the Authority and with the body maintaining the constabulary in question (subs. (4)). Any such order must be by way of statutory instrument subject to the negative resolution procedure (subs. (5)).

Reports: section 97[44]

Section 97 provides for the Authority to make annual and triennial reports and special reports as requested by the Secretary of State or on its own initiative. The section is similar to section 8 of the Police Act 1976 save that section 97 requires all such reports to be laid before Parliament and published whereas section 8 required this only in regard to the annual reports.

The Authority must respond to requests for reports from the Home Secretary and may for that purpose carry out research (subs. (1)). It can report to the Home Secretary on any matter to which it wishes to draw his attention because of its gravity or other exceptional circumstances.

---

[42] See also text of the Act at p. 222 below.
[43] See also text of the Act at p. 222 below.
[44] See also text of the Act at p. 223 below.

Restriction on disclosure: section 98[45]

Section 98 restricts the unauthorised disclosure of information received by the Authority in the performance of its duties subject to a fine on summary conviction not exceeding level 5 on the scale laid down by the Criminal Justice Act 1972 (at present £2,000).

Regulations: section 99[46]

Section 99 empowers the Secretary of State to make regulations as to the procedures to be followed under Part IX (Complaints and Discipline), and requires him to make regulations in respect of certain other matters. The regulations that he is required to make concern: (a) the supply to a complainant and the officer concerned of a copy of or a record of the complaint; (b) procedures for the informal resolution of complaints; (c) procedures for allowing an officer to comment orally or in writing on a complaint against him which is to be resolved informally; (d) cases where the complaint is withdrawn and any provisions of the Act are not to apply; (e) to enable the Authority to dispense with any requirement of Part IX; (f) procedures for the reference or submission of complaints to the Authority; (g) the supply of information or documents to the Authority; (i) notification by the Authority to the person concerned of any action or decision taken in regard to whether disciplinary charges should be brought or an investigation report should be sent to the D.P.P.

Regulations—supplementary: section 100[47]

Section 100 enables the Secretary of State to make special provision for special cases, *e.g.* special provision to deal with administrative and constitutional arrangements in the Metropolitan Police. Before making such regulations the Home Secretary must provide the Police Advisory Board for England and Wales with a draft and consider any representations made by the Board (subs. (2)).

Discipline regulations: section 101[48]

Section 101 sets out provisions which may or must be included in police discipline regulations made by the Home Secretary. It largely re-enacts section 10 of the Police Act 1964 in regard to the making of regulations dealing with police discipline. The most significant difference is the provision in subsection (1) for regulations to make racially discriminatory behaviour a specific disciplinary offence. It was one of the few occasions on the Bill when the Government was defeated on a vote. Lord Scarman moved the amendment on the Third Reading in the House of Lords (see House of Lords, *Hansard*, October 19, 1984, col. 1219). Speaking to his amendment, Lord Scarman said that it was designed to improve the confidence of the black community. No doubt racially discriminatory conduct was already the disciplinary offence of 'discreditable conduct'. But that was not enough. "We are here at this moment being asked by this amendment . . . to confirm in as emphatic a way as we can to the whole of our society that racially prejudiced police action on the part of a police officer is something that will not be tolerated, is a specific offence,

[45] See also text of the Act at p. 223 below.
[46] See also text of the Act at p. 223 below.
[47] See also text of the Act at p. 224 below.
[48] See also text of the Act at p. 225 below.

and is not merely to be subsumed under some other, larger, vaguer offence" (col. 1226).

For the Government, Lord Elton warned the House that to pass the amendment the House would be saying that coloured people were different from the rest of the community. "They must be inescapably different because conduct towards them and them alone is to be singled out for specific mention in the law. Of uncivil conduct by a white policeman toward a white man in the street one would be saying, 'Oh that is all right. We can deal with that as we always have dealt with it under the code of discipline'; but of uncivil conduct by a white policeman to a black man . . . one would be saying by statute that that is different, and must be punished. How do your Lordships think that will go down with the police? Will that convince them that all men are equal under the law?" (col. 1223).

Lord Scarman said he was "deeply troubled" by Lord Elton's speech. It appeared to be based "on a misunderstanding, if not complete ignorance, about the feeling among the black communities and the West Indian community in particular." It really was absurd he suggested that race relations was a subject that ought not to be touched upon in the Police and Criminal Evidence Bill (col. 1226).

The House of Lords agreed with Lord Scarman and passed his amendment by 71 to 65. Though it was urged to overturn the amendment in the House of Commons by a revolt of some 30 of its own backbenchers led by Mr. Eldon Griffiths, the Government decided to allow the amendment to stand—see for debate House of Commons, *Hansard*, October 28, 1984, cols. 1061–1105.)

Subsection (1) requires that discipline regulations shall provide for the determination of questions whether discipline offences have been committed and for officers found guilty, to be punished by a variety of penalties—dismissal, requirement to resign, reduction in rank, reduction in pay, fine, reprimand or caution. Such regulations will replace the Police (Discipline) Regulations 1977.

Subsection (2) requires that in the case of a county or combined police force (which means all provincial forces in England and Wales) the regulations shall provide for the functions in subsection (1) to be performed in respect of senior officers (chief constables, deputy chief constables and assistant chief constables) by the Police Authority and in respect of all other ranks by the chief constable. But the chief constable's exercise of these duties is subject to the provisions of section 94 (hearing of charges by a disciplinary tribunal on direction of the Police Complaints Authority) and to the following provisions of section 101.

Where the accused's chief officer has an interest in the case or is a material witness, the regulations must provide for his functions to be performed by another chief constable (subs. (3)). The regulations may also allow a chief officer to hand a case to another chief officer "where he considers it appropriate to do so." In such a case however the other chief officer will only deal with guilt. The punishment will still be for the officer's own chief constable though he must consider any recommendations by the chief officer who heard the case.

Subsection (5) is new, allowing the delegation of some disciplinary power from chief constable to deputy chief constable. Subsection (6) states that one function that cannot be delegated however, is that of taking the chair at a disciplinary tribunal under section 94(3). The regulations can provide for the deputy chief constable to remit any matter back to the chief constable—for instance if his powers are found to be inadequate to deal with a case delegated to him (subs. (7)).

Where the deputy chief constable is to act in place of the chief constable the decision as to whether to bring disciplinary proceedings, and of formulating any charges would have to be taken by the assistant chief constable. The White Paper[49] said that the Government regarded it as a principle of great importance "that the person hearing the charge should not previously have been involved in the case."

But the deputy chief constable will not have power to impose the punishment of dismissal, requirement to resign or reduction in rank (s.101(8)(a)). One effect of this limitation of his powers of punishment is that there cannot be legal representation at such hearings—see section 102. There is a right of appeal to the chief constable (subs. (8)(b)), and on such an appeal the chief constable only has the right of punishment available to the deputy chief constable (subs. (8)(c)). Also the White Paper made it clear[50] that the regulations will provide that if an officer wishes to have the matter heard by the chief constable, that wish would always prevail.

Representation at disciplinary proceedings: section 102[51]

The Police Federation, supported by the Law Society and the National Council for Civil Liberties, mounted a formidable campaign to persuade the Government to grant police officers the right to legal representation at disciplinary hearings. Mr. Eldon Griffiths for the Federation succeeded in mobilising sufficient support on the first Bill to have the Governmment defeated on this issue. The Government had stood firm in its view that an officer should only be allowed to be represented by a fellow officer. The amendment forced through against the Government provided that where the case could result in dismissal or demotion or a fine amounting to more than three months pay, the accused officer would have the right to be represented if he wished by a legally qualified person.

When Mr. Leon Brittan re-introduced the Bill in October 1983 this clause had been deleted. But at the Committee stage the Home Secretary brought forward amendments to give police officers accused of the more serious range of offences the right to have legal representation. These provisions were put into the Bill at Report stage in the House of Commons.

Subsection (1) provides that at a discipline hearing the punishments of dismissal, requirement to resign or reduction in rank may not be imposed unless the officer has been given an opportunity to be legally represented. Representation can be by counsel or solicitor (subs. (2)). If he is not represented by a legally qualified person he can only be represented by a serving police officer as has been the position in the past.

Regulations will provide for the giving of notice by the accused officer of whether he wishes to avail himself of the right to have a lawyer. If he fails to give such notice and states that he does not wish to be legally represented he will still be liable to punishment by loss of job or rank

---

[49] *Op. cit.* (note 3, p.123 above), para. 48.
[50] *Ibid.*
[51] See also text of the Act at p. 226 below.

(subss.(4) and (5)). If he has given notice of his intention to be legally represented the case against him can be presented by a lawyer—even if in the event he is not so represented (subs. (6)).

The Police Federation tried hard to persuade the Government that legal representation for police officers should be paid for out of public funds but this campaign was resisted. Police officers will either have to look to their professional organisation to finance representation or will have to pay for it themselves.

Disciplinary appeals: section 103[52]

Section 103 replaces section 37 of and Schedule 5 to the Police Act 1964 (as amended by s.12 of the Police Act 1976) relating to disciplinary appeals to the Secretary of State. But it also takes account of the need for a prior appeal to the chief constable where he has delegated his functions to his deputy (under s.101(5)).

Under the provisions of section 103 an officer who has been dealt with for an offence against discipline may appeal to the Secretary of State against finding and punishment, save where he has a right of appeal to someone else—in which case he can appeal further to the Secretary of State. The Secretary of State may substitute any penalty that could have been given by the person or tribunal below—providing that it is less severe than the punishment appealed against. An appeal can therefore only result in the punishment being upheld or decreased (new s.37(4) of the 1964 Act).

Under the old Schedule 5 to the 1964 Act the Secretary of State was required to appoint a tribunal to advise him on the appeal unless it seemed to him that the case could be determined without this. The policy of successive governments in this regard had been to refer to a tribunal cases which involved all of the following: first, a finding of guilt after a plea of not guilty on a disciplinary offence not involving criminal conduct, where the penalty was dismissal, a requirement to resign or reduction in rank; and secondly where the officer had appealed against finding *and* punishment and had asked for a tribunal. Other cases were referred to a tribunal on an ad hoc basis.

Such a tribunal had to consist of "one or more persons (one at least of whom shall be a person engaged or experienced in police administration)." (*ibid.*). In practice such a tribunal normally sat with a Queen's Counsel as chairman and a member of H.M. Inspectorate of Constabulary as the second member. The officer had the right to appear in person or to be represented by a police officer, or by a barrister or solicitor. The chief officer also had the right to be legally represented.

The tribunal made a report to the Secretary of State with its recommendations. The Secretary of State was not bound to follow the advice of the tribunal; the final decision was a matter for him. But normally he followed their view.

In 1982, of 1,631 discipline charges laid, 1,455 or nearly 90 per cent. were found proved. In 116 cases out of 1,455, the penalty imposed was dismissal (20), requirement to resign (68) or reduction in rank (28). In 70 per cent. of these 116 cases, there was an appeal.

The practice of ordering a tribunal where the officer has been punished by way of dismissal, requirement to resign or reduction in rank is made

---

[52] See also text of the Act at p. 227 below.

a statutory right by section 103, which substitutes new Schedule 5, to Police Act 1964, para. 3(1)(*b*)). Also the requirement for automatic reference to a tribunal will extend not only as before to cases where the appeal is against finding and punishment but also where the appeal is against punishment only. All officers given the most serious disciplinary penalties will therefore have a right to a tribunal hearing at which they can be legally represented.

Another change increases the size of the tribunal to three—the legally qualified chairman; a serving or former member of the Inspectorate or a chief constable; and thirdly, a retired officer from the ranks represented by the Police Federation—unless the accused officer is a superintendent or chief superintendent in which case the third member would be a retired officer of those ranks (new Sched. 5, para. 3(3) and (4)).

In cases where there is no tribunal hearing a further change is that the Home Secretary will give the officer his reasons for his final decision. The requirement of reasons previously only applied where there was a hearing—by virtue of the Tribunals and Inquiries Act 1971. The last Government gave an undertaking that appellants would in future be provided with a statement of the Home Secretary's reasons for his decisions and this commitment is honoured in new Schedule 5 to the 1964 Act, para. 4(1).

Restrictions on subsequent proceedings: section 104[53]

Subsections (1) and (2) re-enact the "double jeopardy" provisions of the Police Act 1976. Subsection (1) provides that where a police officer has been acquitted or convicted of a criminal offence he shall not be liable to be charged with an offence against discipline which is in substance the same (see further below). However an officer who has been convicted can be charged under the discipline code with "criminal conduct" which is itself an offence (subs.(2)).

Subsection (3) restricts the admissibility of statements made during informal procedures to resolve a complaint—in the same way that "without prejudice" negotiations cannot be produced at any subsequent civil trial. The aim is to encourage honest apologies and admissions in the informal procedure. But if formal disciplinary proceedings are taken in the end the accused officer should not be penalised by his previous honesty. This only applies however if the admission related to the matter being resolved in the informal procedure (subs. (4)).

Guidance concerning discipline, complaints etc.: section 105[54]

Section 105 puts onto a statutory basis the issuing of guidance by the Secretary of State to chief officers of police and requires them to have regard to it. It also empowers the Secretary of State to issue guidance to the Police Complaints Authority on the same basis as his guidance to the Police Complaints Board under section 3(8) of the Police Act 1976.

Subsection (1) deals with guidance in connection with discipline and dealing with complaints and other allegations.

According to the Government's White Paper[55] this means more than simply requiring the chief officer to read the terms of the guidance.

[53] See also text of the Act at p. 229 below.
[54] See also text of the Act at p. 230 below.
[55] "Police Complaints and Discipline Procedures," Cmnd. 9072 (1983).

"Those under such an obligation must explicitly take note of its provisions and thus be prepared to justify any departure from them. One result of this change is that it will now be proper to raise at a discipline appeal any failure by a chief officer to follow any provision of the guidance, and it will then be for him to explain such failure."[56] This is reflected in a new provision but the chief significance of the change will lie in the actual substance of the guidance.

The revised guidance will make it clear that hearings must be in accordance with the principles of natural justice, for instance, through the avoidance normally of hearsay evidence and the removal of material which is unduly prejudicial having regard to its evidential value. It will make clear that officers have the right to be informed "at the earliest possible opportunity of allegations against them, and to consult a friend at all stages of the investigation—and that these rights are subject only to the need to avoid prejudicing the investigation itself."[57]

Subsection (4) requires the Complaints Authority to have regard to guidance issued by the Secretary of State in relation to the bringing of disciplinary charges. This provision is the same as section 3(8) of the 1976 Act. The guidance under that Act originally stated that where the D.P.P. had decided that criminal proceedings should not be brought "there should normally be no disciplinary proceedings if the evidence required to substantiate a disciplinary charge is the same as that required to substantiate the criminal charge" (the full text of the original guidance is set out in Appendix B of the Government's 1983 White Paper). However, in *R. v. Police Complaints Board, ex p. Madden and Rhone*[58] it was held that the guidance was not binding and that it was the duty of both chief officers and the Board to examine afresh the case for disciplinary proceedings notwithstanding any decision on the criminal aspects. This view is now reflected in the revised guidance which will be applicable to the new Authority.[59]

Needless to say, guidance may not be issued in relation to an individual case (subs. (2)). The Authority's annual report must contain a statement of any guidance received during the year (subs. (5)).

QUESTIONS AND ANSWERS

COMPLAINTS AGAINST THE POLICE AND DISCIPLINARY MATTERS

1. What is the simplest and shortest way of describing the changes made to the complaints system by the new Act?

The Act aims to achieve some very significant reforms in the system. Instead of every complaint having to be investigated by a senior officer the most minor complaints are to be siphoned off through a form of local informal settlement as recommended by Lord Scarman in his report on the Brixton riots. Also whereas before *all* complaints had to be investigated by superintendents, the Act applies to the rest of the country the

---

[56] *Ibid.* para. 46.
[57] *Ibid.* para. 47.
[58] [1983] 1 W.L.R. 447.
[59] For full text of the revised guidance see App. at p. 301 below.

practice already available to the Metropolitan Force of using chief inspectors as investigators. Thirdly, the number of cases that have to be sent to the DPP is to be drastically reduced by giving powers of decision over the most minor cases to chief officers. Fourthly, a new Police Complaints Authority will replace the old Police Complaints Board. The main difference is that it will have far greater powers and duties of supervision over the handling of investigations into the most serious complaints and allegations against police officers. The Act also gives legal representation to police officers facing the most serious disciplinary charges.

2. What kind of complaints will be subject to informal resolution?

Only complaints where the chief officer is satisfied that, even if proved, the conduct would not justify criminal or disciplinary proceedings. A chief inspector would consider whether the complaint was suitable for informal resolution. The complainant would have a veto over the decision to send the complaint for informal settlement since he has to give his consent.

3. What would be the procedure for informal resolution?

There is nothing about this in the Act. The Government's White Paper ("Police Complaints and Discipline Procedures," 1983, Cmnd. 9072) gave some preliminary thoughts. However detailed guidance is to be issued to all forces by the Home Office.

4. Will the informal settlement of a complaint go onto an officer's record?

No. The White Paper said as to this that "no entry of any kind relating to attempted or successful informal resolution will be made in the personal record of the accused officer" (para. 32).

5. Can admissions made by an officer during informal settlement discussions be used against him in subsequent disciplinary or criminal proceedings?

No. The White Paper said that no reference would be allowed in any subsequent formal proceedings to what any party said or did during the process of informal resolution. "In particular, no statement made by either the complainant or the accused officer will be admissible at criminal or disciplinary proceedings, or in a civil action brought by either party" (para. 32). This statement was implemented by section 104(3) of the Act. The only exception allowed is where the admission relates to something that was not for informal resolution.

6. Can an informal resolution ever be superseded by a formal investigation?

Yes. If during informal resolution it appears that the case is actually too serious for that procedure the informal process would have to be terminated and a formal investigation commenced.

7. What happens if informal settlement does not work?

The White Paper stated that informal resolution would not be regarded as concluded until both the accused officer and the complainant had had an opportunity of commenting on the allegation. The Act states that if it appears that informal resolution is impossible or that it is for any other reason not suitable for that means of resolution, the chief officer must appoint an officer from his force to investigate the complaint formally. The case would then go forward as a normal complaint.

8. Does the new Police Complaints Authority have any role in regard to informal settlement cases?

Not in a formal sense. Supervision and independent scrutiny of the system will fall rather to police authorities and the Inspectorate of Constabulary. But the White Paper said that the Government nevertheless hoped "that a close and fruitful relationship will develop between all the agencies charged with supervising or overseeing the complaints system, including in this the Inspectorate and police authorities as well as the Authority and the D.P.P." (para. 34). The expectation was that "the Authority's unique position in this field will equip it to act as a point of contact between all of these other bodies, and that it will take account of all aspects of the complaints system in its annual and triennial reports" (para. 34).

9. What then will be the remit of the Police Complaints Authority?

It will have three main functions. One will be to supervise the investigation of the most serious complaints. Secondly it will have the power to "call in" any other case where it believes that independent supervision would be appropriate. It will also continue to have the role played by the old Board to consider whether disciplinary proceedings should have been, or should be, instituted.

10. What sorts of cases will come to the Authority?

Some matters *must* be referred to the Authority; some *may* be referred to it; and some can be summoned by the Authority even though they are not referred.

Those that must be referred are:

(1) All complaints alleging that a police officer's conduct resulted in the death of or serious injury to some other person. (Serious injury is defined to mean "a fracture, damage to an internal organ, impairment of bodily function, a deep cut or a deep laceration.")

(2) All complaints of a description specified for this purpose by the Home Secretary in regulations to be made. The White Paper indicated that the kind of cases that would be required to be notified in the regulations would be any complaint alleging corruption, assault resulting in actual bodily harm which is not already covered by the first category and "other serious cases reflecting adversely on the reputation of the police" (para. 15).

The difference between these two categories of case is that the Authority will be required to supervise the investigation of the first, whereas it will decide whether or not it thinks it right to supervise in the second type of case.

(3) The third class of matter that will come to the Authority is the case that is referred to it by the chief officer as a matter of his discretion. This might, for instance, be a matter of local or national notoriety where the chief officer thinks that it would be desirable to report the matter to the Authority. The chief officer has a discretion to refer either complaints or other matters which have not become actual complaints but which should be referred because of their gravity or exceptional circumstances.

In addition to these three categories of case which must or may be referred to the Authority there is also a very important reserve power for the authority to call for any matter that it wishes to consider. It has the power to inform a chief constable that it wants to consider a particular complaint together with the file and the chief officer will be obliged to comply.

11. What are the powers and duties of the Authority?

Apart from those investigations which it *must* supervise, the Authority also has a duty to supervise any complaint or any matter referred to them "if they consider that it is desirable in the public interest." In other words they have a completely unfettered discretion.

The general function of the Authority, the White Paper said, would be "to ensure in the public interest that [investigations] are carried out expeditiously, thoroughly and impartially" (para. 18). It would be given the powers of direction necessary to perform that function. There is little doubt that the Authority will be in a position, if it wishes, materially to influence the actual handling of the case. How it responds to this challenge will depend on both its leadership and its members. (The former Ombudsman, Sir Cecil Clothier, will be the first Chairman of the new Authority which is, at the time of writing, likely to come into being in Spring 1985.)

At the end of any investigation which the Authority has supervised the investigating officer must submit a report on the investigation to the Authority. The Authority must then issue a statement (known rather unhappily as "an appropriate statement") indicating whether the investigation was or was not conducted to its satisfaction and if not, specifying any respect in which it was not.

The other principal function of the Authority is to review the exercise of discretion by chief officers as to whether or not to bring disciplinary charges. The Authority has the power to recommend to the chief officer that disciplinary charges should be brought. If after they have made such a recommendation and have consulted with the chief officer, he is still unwilling to prefer such charges, the Authority can direct him to prefer such charges as they may specify and the chief officer must comply with such a direction.

If the Authority consider that the officer in question ought to have been charged with a criminal offence it is their duty to instruct the chief officer to send the papers to the D.P.P. They do not however have any power to direct the D.P.P. to commence or to recommend the commencement of criminal proceedings. They can only require that the papers be sent to the D.P.P.

12. What then is the role of the D.P.P.?

Under the previous law the D.P.P. had the function of considering all complaints save those where the chief officer was satisfied that no criminal offence had been committed. The Government's aim was to confine the D.P.P.'s function to those more serious cases which merited his attention. The formula changed somewhat as the Bill was amended but the final wording enshrined in the Act requires the chief officer to consider whether the report of the investigating officer discloses a criminal offence with which the officer concerned *ought to be charged.* If it is not such a case it does not have to be sent to the D.P.P; if it is such a case it must be sent to the D.P.P. This will ensure that the D.P.P. gets all cases which raise for consideration the question whether criminal charges should be brought whilst at the same time the number of cases that have to be sifted by the D.P.P. should be considerably reduced.

13. Were there any significant changes in the disciplinary system?

The two most important changes are probably those regarding the composition of disciplinary tribunals and legal representation for police officers. Where the Police Complaints Authority directs that disciplinary proceedings be brought, the case will have to be heard by a tribunal of three rather than simply by the chief officer sitting alone. The other two members would be members of the Authority who have not been concerned with the case previously.

The decision of the tribunal would be by a majority.

Legal representation will be available at disciplinary proceedings whenever police officers face the possibility of loss of job or loss of rank. The Home Office were most reluctant to concede this to the Police Federation but did so eventually at the Report stage in the House of Lords.

PART X

POLICE GENERAL

Arrangements for obtaining the views of the community on policing: section 106[1]

Lord Scarman in his report on the Brixton riots[2] proposed that there should be appropriate procedures to enable the police to consult with members of local communities about the problems of policing. Section 106 gives effect to this recommendation without however, specifying what form the arrangements should take.

In June 1982, the Home Office gave administrative guidance to the police authorities and chief constables (and in the Metropolitan Police District to the police and each borough and district council) regarding the role and nature of local arrangements. The guidelines said the machinery to be set up should produce a two-way information flow, enabling chief constables and police authorities to take local views into account when doing their job. Membership should be flexible and wide ranging whilst not being so large as to be unwieldy. Local councillors and M.P.s should be part of the system and local services such as probation, education and social services, housing and recreation should also be represented. Some members could be nominated by organisations. At the very local level there should be opportunities for consultation at parish council level through regular meetings with beat officers and station officers. Neighbourhood consultation should be based on the local station. At police division level membership of the consultative body should be broadly based. Section 106 is intended to strengthen the guidance by making the arrangements mandatory rather than optional. Subsection (1) requires that arrangements must be made in each police area "for obtaining the views of people in that area about matters concerning the policing of the area and for obtaining their cooperation with the police in preventing crime in the area." There are 43 police force areas for this purpose—the 41 areas served by individual forces set up under the Police Act 1964 plus the City of London and the Metropolitan Police District.

The arrangements are to be made by the police authority in consultation with the chief constable—except in the City of London and the Metropolitan area (subs. (2)). In the Metropolitan Police District, the arrangements are to be made not by the Home Secretary but by the Commissioner of the Metropolitan Police. Separate arrangements must after consultation with the local council be made for each London Borough, District and

---

[1] See also text of the Act at p. 230 below.
[2] Cmnd. 8427 (1981).

any part of a District that is within its territory. (There are 11 districts in the Metropolitan area in the counties of Essex, Hertfordshire and Surrey.) The arrangements for each area can be very different. (subss. (4) to (7)).

During the Committee stage of the first Bill the Government moved an amendment stating that the Home Secretary may issue guidance to the Commissioner of the Metropolitan police regarding the arrangements to be made in the metropolis for consultation with the community and that "the Commissioner shall take account of any such guidance." Mr. White-law told the Committee that the purpose of the clause was to "enable the Home Secretary to establish policies, without involving him in the detailed arrangements in every area."[3]

The guidance, he said, would urge that consultative groups must reflect as wide a range of community interests as was consistent with efficient working arrangements. The police should be members as of right and M.P.s for constituencies in the Metropolitan area should also be members. The guidance would make it clear that "operational policing is on the agenda" for such consultative machinery.[4] Reports that came in from consultative committees could be made available to the House. In addition it would be right to keep the House informed on a regular basis of the operation of arrangements in the Metropolitan police district. This would be in addition to the Commissioner's annual report.[5]   Mr. Whitelaw said he was consulting with a view to bringing forward a further amendment to enable the Home Secretary to require any of the persons or bodies charged with making consultative arrangements to review them and to report to him. This could be used as a reserve power "to be employed only in circumstances where informal advice or encouragement had failed to resolve the problem."[6]

The Home Secretary also made it clear that guidelines to be issued for the rest of the country outside the Metropolitan area would be couched in somewhat less categorical terms than the guidance in the London area where he had constitutional authority. Thus for instance, he would wish M.P.s to be members of local consultative committees outside London but he would not think it right to insist on it.

The Scarman Report recommended consultation in London at Borough level, and the Act adopts this approach. It makes no mention of any need for consultation with the Greater London Council, which does not contribute to the cost of the Metropolitan Force. (Boroughs and districts, by contrast, do contribute to police finances through the Metropolitan Police precept).

Similar arrangements have to be made by the Commissioner for the City of London for that area, after consultation with the Common Council (subs.(8)).

The Act does not specifically say anything to the effect that the police must participate in the arrangements, but this is plainly the intention. In fact it might be said that a chief constable who refused to co-operate with the consultative machinery and who thereby impeded the police authority in carrying out its statutory duty to establish such consultative arrange-ments would be acting against the interests of force efficiency. The duty

[3] *Hansard*, Standing Committee J, March 22, 1983, col. 1344.
[4] *Ibid*. col. 1345.
[5] *Ibid*. col. 1347.
[6] *Ibid*. col. 1348.

to make arrangements includes the duty to review them from time to time (subs. (9)).

Subsection (10) gives the Home Secretary the power, if he has reason to believe that the arrangements in any area are inadequate, to require the police authority or Commissioner responsible for making the arrangements to submit a report to him about the arrangements. Having considered such a report, the Home Secretary could, under subsection (11), require the body or person who supplied the report to review the arrangements and submit a further report. There is, therefore, no actual power to direct the nature of the arrangements that should be set up. But reading between the lines of section 106, it is intended that the Home Secretary should have considerable power to "influence" the authority.

The section complements the existing legislation on the administration of policing, viz. the police authority's duties under section 4 of the Police Act 1964; the duties of the Commissioners under section 1 of the Metropolitan Police Act 1829 and section 14 of the City of London Police Act 1839 respectively.

The draft guidance prepared by the Home Office in anticipation of the passage of the Police and Criminal Evidence Act said that matters which could usefully be taken up in local consultation included: "discussion of the incidence of and police response to both crime generally and specific types of offence" and "the operation of police procedures and policy in relation to law enforcement." But consultative groups could not intervene in the enforcement of the criminal law. The deployment of police officers and the method and timing of police operations were a matter for the police. The timing and detail of discussions about those issues were also within the discretion of the police There were some operational aspects of policing such as criminal investigations and security matters which it would be wrong to make the subject of local consultation. Nor could consultative groups be the forum for the pursuit of individual cases which might be under investigation or sub judice; nor for the discussion of allegations of crime or of complaints against police officers. But within these well established limits, "issues directly or indirectly concerned with the policing of the local community may be considered so that the decisions which are properly for the police can be more closely informed by the discussion of local needs."

On membership, the draft document recommended that groups should reflect as wide a range of community interests as was consistent with reasonably effective working arrangements. In London, members should include M.P.s, members of the Greater London Council, and up to five local council members. But the police, local councillors, M.P.s, GLC councillors and members of statutory agencies should normally be fewer than the number of community representatives. Groups should encourage a regular turnover of members so that they could not be seen to be exclusive. Local umbrella organisations such as councils for voluntary service, community relations councils, trades councils and chambers of commerce might be able to help select suitable representatives or individual members for the consultative groups. Local representatives of services such as probation, education, social services, housing and recreation would also be suitable members.

Police officers performing duties of higher rank: section 107[7]

Many sections in the Act require that an action or decision be made or taken by an officer of a specified rank. Section 107 provides for the situation where an officer of that rank may not be available and permits an officer of a lower rank to be "made up." The section provides that a chief inspector may act as a superintendent if properly authorised to do so by a chief superintendent and that a sergeant may act as an inspector if authorised to do so by a chief superintendent. There is no reference in the Act however for any special procedure to be followed for such "making up," nor for the authorisation to be in writing.

Deputy chief constables: section 108[8]

Section 108 amends the Police Act 1964 and the Police (Scotland) Act 1967 to create a rank instead of the office of deputy chief constable. The 1964 and 1967 Acts provided for an office of deputy chief constable and the holder was normally an assistant chief constable. In 1976 the Joint Working Party on the Rank Structure of the Police recommended that as deputy chief constables had a different role from other assistant chief constables, this should be recognised by the creation of a properly constituted rank. Section 108 carries out this recommendation.

Subsection (1) abolishes the office of deputy chief constable which existed by virtue of section 6(1) of the Police Act 1964 and section 5(1) of the Police (Scotland) Act 1967. Subsection (2) amends section 6 of the Police Act 1964 by providing that in every police force there shall be a person holding the rank of deputy chief constable and that promotion or appointment to the rank shall be on the same basis as to the rank of assistant chief constable under section 6(4) of the 1964 Act. Subsection (4) does the same for Scotland. Subsections (3) and (5) allow a force exceptionally to have two deputy chief constables.

Amendments relating to the Police Federations: section 109[9]

Subsections (*a*) and (*b*) amend section 44(1) of the Police Act 1964 to enable the Police Federations for England and Wales and for Scotland to represent their members at disciplinary hearings and at any appeals.

An accused officer at a disciplinary hearing may conduct his case either in person or by a fellow officer selected by him and known as his "friend." Although the Police Federation was technically barred by section 44 of the Police Act 1964 from representing an officer in its own right, in practice it often acted as the officer's friend. The Edmund-Davies Report on the structure and role of the police staff associations recommended[10] that they should be able to do so in their capacity as officers of the Federations.[11] The amendment gives effect to this recommendation. But if an official acts in this way he must be a serving police officer.

As has been seen, at the Committee stage of the first Bill the Government was defeated over an amendment to give police officers the right to be legally represented at disciplinary hearings.[12] When the new Bill was

---

[7] See also text of the Act at p. 231 below.
[8] See also text of the Act at p. 231 below.
[9] See also text of the Act at p. 233 below.
[10] "Committee of the Inquiry on the Police," Cmnd. 7633 (1979).
[11] *Ibid.* para. 333.
[12] See House of Commons, *Hansard*, Standing Committee J, March 22, 1983, col. 1393.

introduced in October 1983 this amendment had however been taken out. Legal representation is only permitted therefore on appeals from disciplinary proceedings.

Paragraph (*c*) of section 109 amends section 44(3) of the Police Act 1964 which gives the Secretary of State the power to make regulations regarding the constitution and proceedings of the Police Federations. The Edmund-Davies Report[13] recommended that the regulations should be amended to give the Federations greater freedom to manage their affairs and this amendment is intended to achieve that result. It gives the Home Secretary the power to delegate to the Federations the power to make rules governing some aspects of their internal affairs.

The regulations will continue to deal with such matters as the basic elements of the constitution, provisions on membership, the right to hold meetings and conduct Federation business in duty time, the voluntary nature of the subscriptions and restrictions on the use of Federation funds for political purposes. But the details of the constitution and provisions to govern the proceedings of the Federation would be set out in their own rules.

Functions of special constables in Scotland: section 110[14]

Section 110 consists of two and a half lines which repeal section 17(6) of the Police (Scotland) Act 1967 (restriction on functions of special constables).

Regulations for police forces and police cadets—Scotland: section 111[15]

Section 110 provides for powers of delegation in regard to regulations affecting the government and administration of police forces in Scotland.

Metropolitan police officers: section 112[16]

Section 112 confers the powers and privileges of a constable under the local law on an officer of the Metropolitan Police in Scotland or Northern Ireland when assigned to the protection of any person or property there. It fills a gap in the law affecting officers guarding, say, the Royal Family or Ministers who go with them to Scotland or Northern Ireland.

Officers in the Metropolitan Force get their powers under section 19 of the Police Act 1964. Those guarding Royal residences get their powers under section 7 of the Metropolitan Police Act 1839 which enables the Commissioner to administer an oath conferring the powers and privileges of a constable within the Royal Palaces and 10 miles surrounding them. But it was recently realised for the first time that section 7 of the 1839 Act did not extend to other parts of the country. Nor has there been any statutory authority for the carrying out by officers of the Metropolitan force of protection duties for members of the Royal Family or other public figures in Scotland and Northern Ireland.

---

[13] *Op. cit.* paras. 97, 98 and 171.
[14] See also text of the Act at p. 233 below.
[15] See also text of the Act at p. 233 below.
[16] See also text of the Act at p. 233 below.

PART XI

MISCELLANEOUS AND SUPPLEMENTARY

Application of act to armed forces: section 113[1]

Section 113 provides for some parts of the Act to apply to the Armed Forces.

Subsection (1) permits the Secretary of State for Defence to apply any of the provisions of the Act relating to the investigation of offences (subject to any qualifications he may specify) to the investigation of offences under the Army Act 1955, the Air Force Act 1955 and the Naval Discipline Act 1957 and to persons under arrest under any of those Acts.

Subsections (3), (4) and (5) state that the Home Secretary shall issue Codes of Practice for persons other than police officers concerned with investigations in the armed services. These will be suitably adapted versions of the codes applicable to police officers. They will be laid before Parliament, subject to the negative resolution procedure, rather than the affirmative procedure applicable to the codes for the police.

Subsection (12) provides that the Secretary of State may modify the application of Parts VII (Documentary Evidence in Criminal Proceedings) and VIII (Evidence in Criminal Proceedings—General) in regard to court martials or a Standing Civilian Court which tries civilian personnel for offences against military law overseas.

Application of act to Customs and Excise: section 114[2]

Many of the activities of the customs and excise are similar to those of the police. The section is broadly intended to apply the same regime to customs officials as apply under the Act to the police, where and to the extent that this has been decreed by Treasury Order.

However, in one respect Customs and Excise officers will be in a different position from the police. This is in regard to searches for what the Act terms "excluded material" under section 11 and "special procedure material" under section 14 and Schedule 1. Section 114(2) provides that the Treasury may direct that for the purpose of Customs and Excise investigations, material held in commercial confidence which would otherwise fall within the definition of excluded material or special procedure material will not do so. It is felt not appropriate to apply to Customs and Excise officers the Act's regime for exemption and application to a judge for orders to produce confidentially held material. The effect of the exclusion is that Customs and Excise's powers to get search warrants to

---

[1] See also text of the Act at p. 234 below.
[2] See also text of the Act at p. 235 below.

search for evidence will not be affected by section 9 of the Act which provides that existing enactments under which a search warrant may be issued shall be replaced by the procedure set out in Schedule 1.

Expenses: section 115[3]

Section 115 makes financial provision out of central funds for expenditure incurred under the Act. The Explanatory and Financial Memorandum attached to the Bill said that Parts I to VI might increase the workload of police and Customs and Excise officers. The size of the increase was not quantifiable but was unlikely to be large. Some £6 million have been set aside for increases in legal advice by persons in police custody as a result of sections 58 and 59. The resource implications of tape-recording would have to await the field trials.

The total annual cost of the Police Complaints Authority was expected to be around £0.75 million in the early years compared with £0.5 million for the Police Complaints Board. The new rules for referring police discipline appeals to tribunals in section 103 would increase the cost of the appeals system by no more than £0.15 million per year.

Meaning of "serious arrestable offence": section 116[4]

The Royal Commission on Criminal Procedure recommended that the police should have additional powers to deal with what it termed "grave offences." It said that it thought that this category should cover the following broad categories of offences: serious offences against the person or serious sexual offences (murder, manslaughter, causing grievous bodily harm, armed robbery, kidnapping, rape); serious offences of damaging property (arson, causing explosions); serious dishonesty offences (counterfeiting, corruption, and burglary, theft and fraud where major amounts are involved); and a miscellaneous group (the supply, importation or exportation of controlled drugs, perversion of the course of justice and blackmail).[5]

The Government did not, however, accept the recommendation that special powers should be so narrowly confined. Instead it defined a category of "serious arrestable offences."

Various sections in the Act give the police special powers when a "serious arrestable offence" is under consideration. This arises in section 4 (road checks); section 9 (orders and warrants issued by judges under Sched. 1); section 42 (authority to detain without charge for up to 36 hours); sections 43 and 44 (magistrates' warrants of further detention); section 56 (delay in allowing notification of a person's arrest); section 58 (delay in allowing access to legal advice); section 62 (authority to take an intimate sample); and section 63 (authority to take samples without consent).

When the first Bill was published the definition of a "serious arrestable offence" was simply that the person exercising a power under the Act considered the offence to be sufficiently serious to justify his exercising that power. This wholly circular definition was criticised from all sides and the Home Office made several attempts to find a more acceptable definition.

[3] See also text of the Act at p. 235 below.
[4] See also text of the Act at p. 236 below.
[5] Report, para. 3.5.

The definition divides offences into two categories. One is that of offences that are so serious that they would always be serious arrestable offences. These are listed in Schedule 5 and are treason, murder, manslaughter, rape, kidnapping, incest or intercourse with a girl under 13; buggery with a boy under 16 or someone who has not consented; indecent assault which amounts to gross indecency; possession of firearms with intent to injure; carrying firearms with criminal intent; use of firearms or imitation firearms to resist arrest; causing explosions likely to endanger life or property; hostage taking and hijacking. Attempts or conspiracies are treated as if they were completed. Offences under sections 1, 9 or 10 of the Prevention of Terrorism (Temporary Provisions) Act 1984 are also always serious arrestable offences.

The sexual offences in the list were added by the House of Commons on Report stage. Fears have been expressed about the inclusion in the list of offences of indecent assault amounting to acts of gross indecency. The effect, it has been said, could be to give the police the means of harassment of the homosexual community. The offence of committing an act of gross indecency with another man under section 13 of the Sexual Offences Act 1956 is only an arrestable offence if one is over 21 and the other is under 21. But if one is over 21 and the other is under 21, it could be a serious arrestable offence if there is an assault—and the fact of the assault would result from the incapacity of the person under 21 to give valid consent to what takes place.

Any other arrestable offence is serious only if its commission has led or is likely to lead to any of the consequences specified in subsection (6)—namely: (a) serious harm to the security of the State or public order; (b) serious interference with the administration of justice or with the investigation of offences; (c) the death of anyone; (d) serious injury to anyone; (e) substantial financial gain to anyone; and (f) serious financial loss to anyone in the sense that having regard to all the circumstances, it is serious, for the person suffering the loss. The definition of "loss" therefore takes into account the particular circumstances of the person in question. The application of this definition obliges the police officer to consider the matter from the point of view of the person who has suffered the loss—an exercise that is obviously fraught with difficulty. But the test is whether the loss is serious not whether it is felt to be serious by the person concerned. His feeling that the loss is serious is only evidence of whether it is in fact serious. Nevertheless the definition could result in the theft of £20 from an old age pensioner being a serious arrestable offence!

Subsection (8) defines injury in such a way as to make it clear that it includes disease and impairment of a person's mental as well as physical condition. This is very imprecise but it would presumably include at least severe mental distress even though the physical abuse was minor (as in some sexual offences). However, if the judges were to hold that "impairment of a person's mental condition" covered also "upset" it would drive the proverbial coach and four through the definition.

Power of constables to use reasonable force: section 117[6]

Early drafts of the Bill referred in a number of sections to the right of the police to exercise a power with reasonable force. At a certain point

---

[6] See also text of the Act at p. 236 below.

the draftsman must have decided that it would be better to deal with this issue in one brief section which would apply to all such powers. Section 117 permits the use of reasonable force where any provision of the Act confers a power on the police and does not provide that the power may only be used with consent.

The sections of the Act affected are:

powers of search and detention for the purposes of a search (ss.1 and 2)

entry and search of premises to execute a search warrant (s.16)

entry and search premises to make an arrest (s.17)

entry and search of premises following arrest for an arrestable offence (s.18)

seizure of evidence (s.19)

arrest (ss.24, 25, 27, 31)

search of the person on arrest (s.32)

detention of a person at a station (ss.36 and 37)

search of a detained person at a police station (s.54)

intimate searches of detained persons (s.55)

fingerprinting without consent (s.61)

taking a non-intimate sample without consent (s.63)

General interpretation: section 118[7]

Section 118 defines or indicates the source of the definition for the following terms: "arrestable offence"; "designated police station"; "document"; "intimate search"; "item subject to legal privilege"; "premises"; "vessel."

The section also defines the term "police detention" as where a person has been taken to a police station after being arrested and is detained there or is detained elsewhere in the charge of a constable or, where he is arrested at a police station, after going there voluntarily (subs.(2)).

Amendments and repeals: section 119[8]

Section 119 provides for consequential amendments in Schedule 6 and for the repeal of enactments mentioned in Schedule 7.

Extent: section 120[9]

Section 120 details the sections which apply to the different parts of the United Kingdom.

Commencement: section 121[10]

Sections 120, 121 and 122 came into force on Royal Assent. The rest of the Act comes into force when the Secretary of State appoints by statutory instrument and different dates may be appointed for different provisions

---

[7] See also text of the Act at p. 236 below.
[8] See also text of the Act at p. 237 below.
[9] See also text of the Act at p. 237 below.
[10] See also text of the Act at p. 238 below.

and different purposes. It is likely, at the time of writing, that the bulk of the Act will be brought into force on January 1, 1986. The arrangements for tape-recording under section 60 can be brought into force at different dates for different parts of the country (subs. (2)).

Short title: section 122[11]

The short title of the Act is the Police and Criminal Evidence Act 1984.

[11] See also text of the Act at p. 239 below.

POLICE AND CRIMINAL EVIDENCE ACT 1984

POLICE AND CRIMINAL EVIDENCE ACT 1984

CHAPTER 60

PART I

POWERS TO STOP AND SEARCH

PART II

POWERS OF ENTRY, SEARCH AND SEIZURE

Search warrants

Entry and search without search warrant

Seizure

Part II—Supplementary

157

Police and Criminal Evidence Act 1984

General

PART X

POLICE—GENERAL

PART XI

MISCELLANEOUS AND SUPPLEMENTARY

PART I

POWERS TO STOP AND SEARCH

Power of constable to stop and search persons, vehicles etc.

1.—(1) A constable may exercise any power conferred by this section—

    (*a*) in any place to which at the time when he proposes to exercise the power the public or any section of the public has access, on payment or otherwise, as of right or by virtue of express or implied permission; or

(*b*) in any other place to which people have ready access at the time when he proposes to exercise the power but which is not a dwelling.

(2) Subject to subsection (3) to (5) below, a constable—

(*a*) may search—
(i) any person or vehicle;
(ii) anything which is in or on a vehicle,
for stolen or prohibited articles; and

(*b*) may detain a person or vehicle for the purpose of such a search.

(3) This section does not give a constable power to search a person or vehicle or anything in or on a vehicle unless he has reasonable grounds for suspecting that he will find stolen or prohibited articles.

(4) If a person is in a garden or yard occupied with and used for the purposes of a dwelling or on other land so occupied and used, a constable may not search him in the exercise of the power conferred by this section unless the constable has reasonable grounds for believing—

(*a*) that he does not reside in the dwelling; and

(*b*) that he is not in the place in question with the express or implied permission of a person who resides in the dwelling.

(5) If a vehicle is in a garden or yard or other place occupied with and used for the purposes of a dwelling or on other land so occupied and used a constable may not search the vehicle or anything in or on it in the exercise of the power conferred by this section unless he has reasonable grounds for believing—

(*a*) that the person in charge of the vehicle does not reside in the dwelling; and

(*b*) that the vehicle is not in the place in question with the express or implied permission of a person who resides in the dwelling.

(6) If in the course of such a search a constable discovers an article which he has reasonable grounds for suspecting to be a stolen or prohibited article, he may seize it.

(7) An article is prohibited for the purposes of this Part of this Act if it is—

(*a*) an offensive weapon; or

(*b*) an article—
(i) made or adapted for use in the course of or in connection with an offence to which this sub-paragraph applies; or
(ii) intended by the person having it with him for such use by him or by some other person.

(8) The offences to which subsection (7)(*b*)(i) above applies are—

(*a*) burglary;

(*b*) theft;

(*c*) offences under section 12 of the Theft Act 1968 (taking motor vehicle or other conveyance without authority); and

(*d*) offences under section 15 of that Act (obtaining property by deception).

(9) In this Part of this Act—

"offensive weapon" means any article—

(*a*) made or adapted for use for causing injury to persons; or

(*b*) intended by the person having it with him for such use by him or by some other person; and

Provisions relating to search under s.1 and other powers

2.—(1) A constable who detains a person or vehicle in the exercise—

    (*a*) of the power conferred by section 1 above; or

    (*b*) of any other power—

        (i) to search a person without first arresting him; or

        (ii) to search a vehicle without making an arrest,

need not conduct a search if it appears to him subsequently—

        (i) that no search is required; or

        (ii) that a search is impracticable.

(2) If a constable contemplates a search, other than a search of an unattended vehicle, in the exercise—

    (*a*) of the power conferred by section 1 above; or

    (*b*) of any other power, except the power conferred by section 6 below and the power conferred by section 27(2) of the Aviation Security Act 1982—

        (i) to search a person without first arresting him; or

        (ii) to search a vehicle without making an arrest,

it shall be his duty, subject to subsection (4) below, to take reasonable steps before he commences the search to bring to the attention of the appropriate person—

        (i) if the constable is not in uniform, documentary evidence that he is a constable; and

        (ii) whether he is in uniform or not, the matters specified in subsection (3) below,

and the constable shall not commence the search until he has performed that duty.

(3) The matters referred to in subsection (2)(ii) above are—

    (*a*) the constable's name and the name of the police station to which he is attached;

    (*b*) the object of the proposed search;

    (*c*) the constable's grounds for proposing to make it; and

    (*d*) the effect of section 3(7) or (8) below, as may be appropriate.

(4) A constable need not bring the effect of section 3(7) or (8) below to the attention of the appropriate person if it appears to the constable that it will not be practicable to make the record in section 3(1) below.

(5) In this section "the appropriate person" means—

    (*a*) if the constable proposes to search a person, that person; and

    (*b*) if he proposes to search a vehicle, or anything in or on a vehicle, the person in charge of the vehicle.

(6) On completing a search of an unattended vehicle or anything in or on such a vehicle in the exercise of any such power as is mentioned in subsection (2) above a constable shall leave a notice—

    (*a*) stating that he has searched it;

    (*b*) giving the name of the police station to which he is attached;

    (*c*) stating that an application for compensation for any damage caused by the search may be made to that police station; and

    (*d*) stating the effect of section 3(8) below.

(7) The constable shall leave the notice inside the vehicle unless it is not reasonably practicable to do so without damaging the vehicle.

(8) The time for which a person or vehicle may be detained for the purposes of such a search is such time as is reasonably required to permit a search to be carried out either at the place where the person or vehicle was first detained or nearby.

(9) Neither the power conferred by section 1 above nor any other power to detain and search a person without first arresting him or to detain and search a vehicle without making an arrest is to be construed—

(*a*) as authorising a constable to require a person to remove any of his clothing in public other than an outer coat, jacket or gloves; or

(*b*) as authorising a constable not in uniform to stop a vehicle.

(10) This section and section 1 above apply to vessels, aircraft and hovercraft as they apply to vehicles.

Duty to make records concerning searches

3.—(1) Where a constable has carried out a search in the exercise of any such power as is mentioned in section 2(1) above, other than a search—

(*a*) under section 6 below; or

(*b*) under section 27(2) of the Aviation Security Act 1982,

he shall make a record of it in writing unless it is not practicable to do so.

(2) If—

(*a*) a constable is required by subsection (1) above to make a record of a search; but

(*b*) it is not practicable to make the record on the spot,

he shall make it as soon as practicable after the completion of the search.

(3) The record of a search of a person shall include a note of his name, if the constable knows it, but a constable may not detain a person to find out his name.

(4) If a constable does not know the name of a person whom he has searched, the record of the search shall include a note otherwise describing that person.

(5) The record of a search of a vehicle shall include a note describing the vehicle.

(6) The record of a search—

(*a*) shall state—

   (i) the object of the search;

   (ii) the grounds for making it;

   (iii) the date and time when it was made;

   (iv) the place where it was made;

   (v) whether anything, and if so what, was found;

   (vi) whether any, and if so what, injury to a person or damage to property appears to the constable to have resulted from the search; and

(*b*) shall identify the constable making it.

(7) If a constable who conducted a search of a person made a record of it, the person who was searched shall be entitled to a copy of the record if he asks for one before the end of the period specified in subsection (9) below.

(8) If—

(*a*) the owner of a vehicle which has been searched or the person who was in charge of the vehicle at the time when it was searched asks for a copy of the record of the search before the end of the period specified in subsection (9) below; and

(*b*) the constable who conducted the search made a record of it,

the person who made the request shall be entitled to a copy.

(9) The period mentioned in subsections (7) and (8) above is the period of 12 months beginning with the date on which the search was made.

(10) The requirements imposed by this section with regard to records of searches of vehicles shall apply also to records of searches of vessels, aircraft and hovercraft.

Road checks

4.—(1) This section shall have effect in relation to the conduct of road checks by police officers for the purpose of ascertaining whether a vehicle is carrying—

(a) a person who has committed an offence other than a road traffic offence or a vehicles excise offence;

(b) a person who is a witness to such an offence;

(c) a person intending to commit such an offence; or

(d) a person who is unlawfully at large.

(2) For the purposes of this section a road check consists of the exercise in a locality of the power conferred by section 159 of the Road Traffic Act 1972 in such a way as to stop during the period for which its exercise in that way in that locality continues all vehicles or vehicles selected by any criterion.

(3) Subject to subsection (5) below, there may only be such a road check if a police officer of the rank of superintendent or above authorises it in writing.

(4) An officer may only authorise a road check under subsection (3) above—

(a) for the purpose specified in subsection (1)(a) above, if he has reasonable grounds—

    (i) for believing that the offence is a serious arrestable offence; and

    (ii) for suspecting that the person is, or is about to be, in the locality in which vehicles would be stopped if the road check were authorised;

(b) for the purpose specified in subsection (1)(b) above, if he has reasonable grounds for believing that the offence is a serious arrestable offence;

(c) for the purpose specified in subsection (1)(c) above, if he has reasonable grounds—

    (i) for believing that the offence would be a serious arrestable offence; and

    (ii) for suspecting that the person is, or is about to be in the locality in which vehicles would be stopped if the road check were authorised;

(d) for the purpose specified in subsection (1)(d) above, if he has reasonable grounds for suspecting that the person is, or is about to be, in that locality.

(5) An officer below the rank of superintendent may authorise such a road check if it appears to him that it is required as a matter of urgency for one of the purposes specified in subsection (1) above.

(6) If an authorisation is given under subsection (5) above, it shall be the duty of the officer who gives it—

(a) to make a written record of the time at which he gives it; and

(b) to cause an officer of the rank of superintendent or above to be informed that it has been given.

(7) The duties imposed by subsection (6) above shall be performed as soon as it is practicable to do so.

(8) An officer to whom a report is made under subsection (6) above may, in writing, authorise the road check to continue.

(9) If such an officer considers that the road check should not continue, he shall record in writing—

(a) the fact that it took place; and

(b) the purpose for which it took place.

(10) An officer giving an authorisation under this section shall specify the locality in which vehicles are to be stopped.

(11) An officer giving an authorisation under this section, other than an authorisation under subsection (5) above—

    (*a*) shall specify a period, not exceeding seven days, during which the road check may continue; and

    (*b*) may direct that the road check—

        (i) shall be continuous; or

        (ii) shall be conducted at specified times, during that period.

(12) If it appears to an officer of the rank of superintendent or above that a road check ought to continue beyond the period for which it has been authorised he may, from time to time, in writing specify a further period, not exceeding seven days, during which it may continue.

(13) Every written authorisation shall specify—

    (*a*) the name of the officer giving it;

    (*b*) the purpose of the road check; and

    (*c*) the locality in which vehicles are to be stopped.

(14) The duties to specify the purposes of a road check imposed by subsections (9) and (13) above include duties to specify any relevant serious arrestable offence.

(15) Where a vehicle is stopped in a road check, the person in charge of the vehicle at the time when it is stopped shall be entitled to obtain a written statement of the purpose of the road check, if he applies for such a statement not later than the end of the period of twelve months from the day on which the vehicle was stopped.

(16) Nothing in this section affects the exercise by police officers of any power to stop vehicles for purposes other than those specified in subsection (1) above.

Reports of recorded searches and of road checks

5.—(1) Every annual report—

    (*a*) under section 12 of the Police Act 1964; or

    (*b*) made by the Commissioner of Police of the Metropolis,

shall contain information—

        (i) about searches recorded under section 3 above which have been carried out in the area to which the report relates during the period to which it relates; and

        (ii) about road checks authorised in that area during that period under section 4 above.

(2) The information about searches shall not include information about specific searches but shall include—

    (*a*) the total numbers of searches in each month during the period to which the report relates—

        (i) for stolen articles;

        (ii) for offensive weapons; and

        (iii) for other prohibited articles;

    (*b*) the total number of persons arrested in each such month in consequence of searches of each of the descriptions specified in paragraph (*a*)(i) to (iii) above.

(3) The information about road checks shall include information—

    (*a*) about the reason for authorising each road check; and

    (*b*) about the result of each of them.

Statutory undertakers etc.

6.—(1) A constable employed by statutory undertakers may stop, detain and search any vehicle before it leaves a goods area included in the premises of the statutory undertakers.

(2) In this section—

"goods area" means any area used wholly or mainly for the storage or handling of goods.

(3) For the purposes of section 6 of the Public Stores Act 1875, any person appointed under the Special Constables Act 1923 to be a special constable within any premises which are in the possession or under the control of British Nuclear Fuels Limited shall be deemed to be a constable deputed by a public department and any goods and chattels belonging to or in the possession of British Nuclear Fuels Limited shall be deemed to be Her Majesty's Stores.

(4) In the application of subsection (3) above to Northern Ireland, for the reference to the Special Constables Act 1923 there shall be substituted a reference to paragraph 1(2) of Schedule 2 to the Emergency Laws (Miscellaneous Provisions) Act 1947.

Part I—Supplementary

7.—(1) The following enactments shall cease to have effect—
  (a) section 8 of the Vagrancy Act 1824;
  (b) section 66 of the Metropolitan Police Act 1839;
  (c) section 11 of the Canals (Offences) Act 1840;
  (d) section 19 of the Pedlars Act 1871;
  (e) section 33 of the County of Merseyside Act 1980; and
  (f) section 42 of the West Midlands County Council Act 1980.

(2) There shall also cease to have effect—
  (a) so much of any enactment contained in an Act passed before 1974, other than—
    (i) an enactment contained in a public general Act; or
    (ii) an enactment relating to statutory undertakers, as confers power on a constable to search for stolen or unlawfully obtained goods; and
  (b) so much of any enactment relating to statutory undertakers as provides that such a power shall not be exercisable after the end of a specified period.

(3) In this Part of this Act "statutory undertakers" means persons authorised by any enactment to carry on any railway, light railway, road transport, water transport, canal, inland navigation, dock or harbour undertaking.

PART II

POWERS OF ENTRY, SEARCH AND SEIZURE

Search warrants

Power of the justice of peace to authorise entry and search of premises

8.—(1) If on an application made by a constable a justice of the peace is satisfied that there are reasonable grounds for believing—
  (a) that a serious arrestable offence has been committed; and
  (b) that there is material on premises specified in the application which is likely to be of substantial value (whether by itself or

together with other material) to the investigation of the offence; and

(*c*) that the material is likely to be relevant evidence; and

(*d*) that it does not consist of or include items subject to legal privilege, excluded material or special procedure material; and

(*e*) that any of the conditions specified in subsection (3) below applies,

he may issue a warrant authorising a constable to enter and search the premises.

(2) A constable may seize and retain anything for which a search has been authorised under subsection (1) above.

(3) The conditions mentioned in subsection (1)(*e*) above are—

(*a*) that it is not practicable to communicate with any person entitled to grant entry to the premises;

(*b*) that it is practicable to communicate with a person entitled to grant entry to the premises but it is not practicable to communicate with any person entitled to grant access to the evidence;

(*c*) that entry to the premises will not be granted unless a warrant is produced;

(*d*) that the purpose of a search may be frustrated or seriously prejudiced unless a constable arriving at the premises can secure immediate entry to them.

(4) In this Act "relevant evidence", in relation to an offence, means anything that would be admissible in evidence at a trial for the offence.

(5) The power to issue a warrant conferred by this section is in addition to any such power otherwise conferred.

Special provisions as to access

9.—(1) A constable may obtain access to excluded material or special procedure material for the purposes of a criminal investigation by making an application under Schedule 1 below and in accordance with that Schedule.

(2) Any Act (including a local Act) passed before this Act under which a search of premises for the purposes of a criminal investigation could be authorised by the issue of a warrant to a constable shall cease to have effect so far as it relates to the authorisation of searches—

(*a*) for items subject to legal privilege; or

(*b*) for excluded material; or

(*c*) for special procedure material consisting of documents or records other than documents.

Meaning of "items subject to legal privilege"

10.—(1) Subject to subsection (2) below in this Act "items subject to legal privilege" means—

(*a*) communications between a professional legal adviser and his client or any person representing his client made in connection with the giving of legal advice to the client;

(*b*) communications between a professional legal adviser and his client or any person representing his client or between such an adviser or his client or any such representative and any other person made in connection with or in contemplation of legal proceedings and for the purposes of such proceedings; and

(*c*) items enclosed with or referred to in such communications and made—

(i) in connection with the giving of legal advice; or

(ii) in connection with or in contemplation of legal proceedings and for the purposes of such proceedings,
when they are in the possession of a person who is entitled to possession
of them.

(2) Items held with the intention of furthering a criminal purpose are
not items subject to legal privilege.

Meaning of "excluded material"

11.—(1) Subject to the following provisions of this section, in this Act
"excluded material" means—

    (*a*) personal records which a person has acquired or created in the
course of any trade, business, profession or other occupation
or for the purposes of any paid or unpaid office and which he
holds in confidence;

    (*b*) human tissue or tissue fluid which has been taken for the
purposes of diagnosis or medical treatment and which a person
holds in confidence;

    (*c*) journalistic material which a person holds in confidence and
which consists—

        (i) of documents; or

        (ii) of records other than documents.

(2) A person holds material other than journalistic material in confidence for the purposes of this section if he holds it subject—

    (*a*) to an express or implied undertaking to hold it in confidence;
or

    (*b*) to a restriction on disclosure or an obligation of secrecy
contained in any enactment, including an enactment contained
in an Act passed after this Act.

(3) A person holds journalistic material in confidence for the purposes
of this section if—

    (*a*) he holds it subject to such an undertaking, restriction or
obligation; and

    (*b*) it has been continuously held (by one or more persons) subject
to such an undertaking, restriction or obligation since it was
first acquired or created for the purposes of journalism.

Meaning of "personal records"

12. In this Part of this Act "personal records" means documentary and
other records concerning an individual (whether living or dead) who can
be identified from them, and relating—

    (*a*) to his physical or mental health;

    (*b*) to spiritual counselling or assistance given or to be given to
him;

    (*c*) to counselling or assistance given or to be given to him, for the
purposes of his personal welfare, by any voluntary organisation
or by any individual who—

        (i) by reason of his office or occupation has responsibilities
for his personal welfare; or

        (ii) by reason of an order of a court, has responsibilities for
his supervision.

Meaning of "journalistic material"

13.—(1) Subject to subsection (2) below, in this Act "journalistic
material" means material acquired or created for the purposes of
journalism.

(2) Material is only journalistic material for the purposes of this Act if it is in the possession of a person who acquired or created it for the purposes of journalism.

(3) A person who receives material from someone who intends that the recipient shall use it for the purposes of journalism is to be taken to have acquired it for those purposes.

Meaning of "special procedure material"

14.—(1) In this Act "special procedure material" means-
    (*a*) material to which subsection (2) below applies; and
    (*b*) journalistic material, other than excluded material.

(2) Subject to the following provisions of this section, this subsection applies to material, other than items subject to legal privilege and excluded material, in the possession of a person who—
    (*a*) acquired or created it in the course of any trade, business, profession or other occupation or for the purpose of any paid or unpaid office and
    (*b*) holds it subject—
        (i) to an express or implied undertaking to hold it in confidence; or
        (ii) to a restriction or obligation such as is mentioned in section 11(2)(*b*) above.

(3) Where material is acquired—
    (*a*) by an employee from his employer and in the course of his employment; or
    (*b*) by a company from an associated company,
it is only special procedure material if it was special procedure material immediately before the acquisition.

(4) Where material is created by an employee in the course of his employment, it is only special procedure material if it would have been special procedure material had his employer created it.

(5) Where material is created by a company on behalf of an associated company, it is only special procedure material if it would have been special procedure material had the associated company created it.

(6) A company is to be treated as another's associated company for the purposes of this section if it would be so treated under section 302 of the Income and Corporation Taxes Act 1970.

Search warrants—safeguards

15.—(1) This section and section 16 below have effect in relation to the issue to constables under any enactment, including an enactment contained in an Act passed after this Act, of warrants to enter and search premises, and an entry on or search of premises under a warrant is unlawful unless it complies with this section and section 16 below.

(2) Where a constable applies for any such warrant, it shall be his duty—
    (*a*) to state—
        (i) the ground on which he makes the application; and
        (ii) the enactment under which the warrant would be issued;
    (*b*) to specify the premises which it is desired to enter and search; and
    (*c*) to identify, so far as is practicable, the articles or persons to be sought.

(3) An application for such a warrant shall be made ex parte and supported by an information in writing.

(4) The constable shall answer on oath any question that the justice of the peace or judge hearing the application asks him.

(5) A warrant shall authorise an entry on one occasion only.
(6) A warrant—
    (*a*) shall specify—
        (i) the name of the person who applies for it;
        (ii) the date on which it is issued;
        (iii) the enactment under which it is issued; and
        (iv) the premises to be searched; and
    (*b*) shall identify, so far as is practicable, the articles or persons to be sought.
(7) Two copies shall be made of a warrant.
(8) The copies shall be clearly certified as copies.

Execution of warrants

16.—(1) A warrant to enter and search premises may be executed by any constable.
(2) Such a warrant may authorise persons to accompany any constable who is executing it.
(3) Entry and search under a warrant must be within one month from the date of its issue.
(4) Entry and search under a warrant must be at a reasonable hour unless it appears to the constable executing it that the purpose of a search may be frustrated on an entry at a reasonable hour.
(5) Where the occupier of premises which are to be entered and searched is present at the time when a constable seeks to execute a warrant to enter and search them, the constable—
    (*a*) shall identify himself to the occupier and, if not in uniform, shall produce to him documentary evidence that he is a constable;
    (*b*) shall produce the warrant to him; and
    (*c*) shall supply him with a copy of it.
(6) Where—
    (*a*) the occupier of such premises is not present at the time when a constable seeks to execute such a warrant; but
    (*b*) some other person who appears to the constable to be in charge of the premises is present,
subsection (5) above shall have effect as if any reference to the occupier were a reference to that other person.
(7) If there is no person present who appears to the constable to be in charge of the premises, he shall leave a copy of the warrant in a prominent place on the premises.
(8) A search under a warrant may only be a search to the extent required for the purpose for which the warrant was issued.
(9) A constable executing a warrant shall make an endorsement on it stating—
    (*a*) whether the articles or persons sought were found; and
    (*b*) whether any articles were seized, other than articles which were sought.
(10) A warrant which—
    (*a*) has been executed; or
    (*b*) has not been executed within the time authorised for its execution, shall be returned—
        (i) if it was issued by a justice of the peace, to the clerk to the justices for the petty sessions area for which he acts; and
        (ii) if it was issued by a judge, to the appropriate officers of the court from which he issued it.

(11) A warrant which is returned under subsection (10) above shall be retained for 12 months from its return—

    (*a*) by the clerk to the justices, if it was returned under paragraph (i) of that subsection; and

    (*b*) by the appropriate officer, if it was returned under paragraph (ii).

(12) If during the period for which a warrant is to be retained the occupier of the premises to which it relates asks to inspect it, he shall be allowed to do so.

Entry and search without search warrant

Entry for purpose of arrest, etc.

17.—(1) Subject to the following provisions of this section, and without prejudice to any other enactment, a constable may enter and search any premises, for the purpose—

    (*a*) of executing—

        (i) a warrant of arrest issued in connection with or arising out of criminal proceedings; or

        (ii) a warrant of commitment issued under section 76 of the Magistrates' Courts Act 1980;

    (*b*) of arresting a person for an arrestable offence;

    (*c*) of arresting a person for an offence under—

        (i) section 1 (prohibition of uniforms in connection with political objects), 4 (prohibition of offensive weapons at public meetings and processions) or 5 (prohibition of offensive conduct conducive to breaches of the peace) of the Public Order Act 1936;

        (ii) any enactment contained in sections 6 to 8 or 10 of the Criminal Law Act 1977 (offences relating to entering and remaining on property);

    (*d*) of recapturing a person who is unlawfully at large and whom he is pursuing; or

    (*e*) of saving life or limb or preventing serious damage to property.

(2) Except for the purpose specified in paragraph (*e*) of subsection (1) above, the powers of entry and search conferred by this section—

    (*a*) are only exercisable if the constable has reasonable grounds for believing that the person whom he is seeking is on the premises; and

    (*b*) are limited, in relation to premises consisting of two or more separate dwellings, to powers to enter and search—

        (i) any parts of the premises which the occupiers of any dwelling comprised in the premises use in common with the occupiers of any other such dwelling; and

        (ii) any such dwelling in which the constable has reasonable grounds for believing that the person whom he is seeking may be.

(3) The powers of entry and search conferred by this section are only exercisable for the purposes specified in subsection (1)(*c*)(ii) above by a constable in uniform.

(4) The power of search conferred by this section is only a power to search to the extent that is reasonably required for the purpose for which the power of entry is exercised.

(5) Subject to subsection (6) below, all the rules of common law under which a constable has power to enter premises without a warrant are hereby abolished.

(6) Nothing in subsection (5) above affects any power of entry to deal with or prevent a breach of the peace.

Entry and search after arrest

18.—(1) Subject to the following provisions of this section, a constable may enter and search, any premises occupied or controlled by a person who is under arrest for an arrestable offence, if he has reasonable grounds for suspecting that there is on the premises evidence other than items subject to legal privilege, that relates—

    (*a*) to that offence; or

    (*b*) to some other arrestable offence which is connected with or similar to that offence.

(2) A constable may seize and retain anything for which he may search under subsection (1) above.

(3) The power to search conferred by subsection (1) above is only a power to search to the extent that is reasonably required for the purpose of discovering such evidence.

(4) Subject to subsection (5) below, the powers conferred by this section may not be exercised unless an officer of the rank of inspector or above has authorised them in writing.

(5) A constable may conduct a search under subsection (1) above—

    (*a*) before taking the person to a police station; and

    (*b*) without obtaining an authorisation under subsection (4) above,

if the presence of that person at a place other than a police station is necessary for the effective investigation of the offence.

(6) If a constable conducts a search by virtue of subsection (5) above, he shall inform an officer of the rank of inspector or above that he has made the search as soon as practicable after he has made it.

(7) An officer who—

    (*a*) authorises a search; or

    (*b*) is informed of a search under subsection (6) above,

shall make a record in writing—

    (i) of the grounds for the search; and

    (ii) of the nature of the evidence that was sought.

(8) If the person who was in occupation or control of the premises at the time of the search is in police detention at the time the record is to be made, the officer shall make the record as part of his custody record.

Seizure etc.

General power of seizure

19.—(1) The powers conferred by subsections (2), (3), and (4) below are exercisable by a constable who is lawfully on any premises.

(2) The constable may seize anything which is on the premises if he has reasonable grounds for believing—

    (*a*) that it has been obtained in consequence of the commission of an offence; and

    (*b*) that it is necessary to seize it in order to prevent it being concealed, lost, damaged, altered or destroyed.

(3) The constable may seize anything which is on the premises if he has reasonable grounds for believing—

    (*a*) that it is evidence in relation to an offence which he is investigating or any other offence; and

    (*b*) that it is necessary to seize it in order to prevent the evidence being concealed, lost, altered or destroyed.

(4) The constable may require any information which is contained in a computer and is accessible from the premises to be produced in a form in which it can be taken away and in which it is visible and legible if he has reasonable grounds for believing—

(*a*) that—
> (i) it is evidence in relation to an offence which he is investigating or any other offence; or
> (ii) it has been obtained in consequence of the commission of an offence; and

(*b*) that it is necessary to do so in order to prevent it being concealed, lost, tampered with or destroyed.

(5) The powers conferred by this section are in addition to any power otherwise conferred.

(6) No power of seizure conferred on a constable under any enactment (including an enactment contained in an Act passed after this Act) is to be taken to authorise the seizure of an item which the constable exercising the power has reasonable grounds for believing to be subject to legal privilege.

Extension of powers of seizure to computerised information

20.—(1) Every power of seizure which is conferred by an enactment to which this section applies on a constable who has entered premises in the exercise of a power conferred by an enactment shall be construed as including a power to require any information contained in a computer and accessible from the premises to be produced in a form in which it can be taken away and in which it is visible and legible.

(2) This section applies—
> (*a*) to any enactment contained in an Act passed before this Act;
> (*b*) to sections 8 and 18 above;
> (*c*) to paragraph 13 of Schedule 1 to this Act; and
> (*d*) to any enactment contained in an Act passed after this Act.

Access and copying

21.—(1) A constable who seizes anything in the exercise of a power conferred by any enactment, including an enactment contained in an Act passed after this Act, shall, if so requested by a person showing himself—
> (*a*) to be occupier of premises on which it was seized; or
> (*b*) to have had custody or control of it immediately before the seizure,

provide that person with a record of what he seized.

(2) The officer shall provide the record within a reasonable time from the making of the request for it.

(3) Subject to subsection (8) below, if a request for permission to be granted access to anything which—
> (*a*) has been seized by a constable; and
> (*b*) is retained by the police for the purpose of investigating an offence,

is made to the officer in charge of the investigation by a person who had custody or control of the thing immediately before it was so seized or by someone acting on behalf of such a person the officer shall allow the person who made the request access to it under the supervision of a constable.

(4) Subject to subsection (8) below, if a request for a photograph or copy of any such thing is made to the officer in charge of the investigation by a person who had custody or control of the thing immediately before it was so seized, or by someone acting on behalf of such a person, the officer shall—
> (*a*) allow the person who made the request access to it under the supervision of a constable for the purpose of photographing or copying it; or

173

(*b*) photograph or copy it, or cause it to be photographed or copied.

(5) A constable may also photograph or copy, or have photographed or copied, anything which he has power to seize, without a request being made under subsection (4) above.

(6) Where anything is photographed or copied under subsection (4)(*b*) above, the photograph or copy shall be supplied to the person who made the request.

(7) The photograph or copy shall be so supplied within a reasonable time from the making of the request.

(8) There is no duty under this section to grant access to, or to supply a photograph or copy of, anything if the officer in charge of the investigation for the purposes of which it was seized has reasonable grounds for believing that to do so would prejudice—

    (*a*) that investigation;

    (*b*) the investigation of an offence other than the offence for the purposes of investigating which the thing was seized; or

    (*c*) any criminal proceedings which may be brought as a result of—

        (i) the investigation of which he is in charge; or

        (ii) any such investigation as is mentioned in paragraph (*b*) above.

Retention

22.—(1) Subject to subsection (3) below, anything which has been seized by a constable or taken away by a constable following a requirement made by virtue of section 19 or 20 may be retained so long as is necessary in all the circumstances.

(2) Without prejudice to the generality of subsection (1) above—

    (*a*) anything seized for the purposes of a criminal investigation may be retained, except as provided by subsection (4) below,—

        (i) for use as evidence at a trial for an offence; or

        (ii) for forensic examination or for investigation in connection with an offence; and

    (*b*) anything may be retained in order to establish its lawful owner, where there are reasonable grounds for believing that it has been obtained in consequence of the commission of an offence.

(3) Nothing seized on the ground that it may be used—

    (*a*) to cause physical injury to any person;

    (*b*) to damage property;

    (*c*) to interfere with evidence; or

    (*d*) to assist in escape from police detention or lawful custody, may be retained when the person from whom it was seized is no longer in police detention or the custody of a court or is in the custody of a court but has been released on bail.

(4) Nothing may be retained for either of the purposes mentioned in subsection (2)(*a*) above if a photograph or copy would be sufficient for that purpose.

(5) Nothing in this section affects any power of a court to make an order under section 1 of the Police (Property) Act 1897.

Part II—Supplementary

Part II—Interpretation

23. In this Act—

    "premises" includes any place and, in particular, includes—

(*a*) any vehicle, vessel, aircraft or hovercraft;
(*b*) any offshore installation; and
(*c*) any tent or movable structure; and
"offshore installation has the meaning given to it by section 1 of the Mineral Workings (Offshore Installations) Act 1971.

PART III

ARREST

Arrest without warrant for arrestable and other offences

24.—(1) The powers of summary arrest conferred by the following subsections shall apply—
    (*a*) to offences for which the sentence is fixed by law;
    (*b*) to offences for which a person of 21 years of age or over (not previously convicted) may be sentenced to imprisonment for a term of five years (or might be so sentenced but for the restrictions imposed by section 33 of the Magistrates' Courts Act 1980); and
    (*c*) to the offences to which subsection (2) below applies,
and in this Act "arrestable offence" means any such offence.
  (2) The offences to which this subsection applies are—
    (*a*) offences for which a person may be arrested under the customs and excise Acts, as defined in section 1(1) of the Customs and Excise Management Act 1979;
    (*b*) offences under the Official Secrets Act 1911 and 1920 that are not arrestable offences by virtue of the term of imprisonment for which a person may be sentenced in respect of them;
    (*c*) offences under section 14 (indecent assault on a woman), 22 (causing prostitution of women) or 23 (procuration of girl under 21) of the Sexual Offences Act 1956;
    (*d*) offences under section 12(1) (taking motor vehicle or other conveyance without authority etc.) or 25(1) (going equipped for stealing, etc.) of the Theft Act 1968; and
    (*e*) offences under section 1 of the Public Bodies Corrupt Practices Act 1889 (corruption in office) or section 1 of the Prevention of Corruption Act 1906 (corrupt transactions with agents).
  (3) Without prejudice to section 2 of the Criminal Attempts Act 1981, the powers of summary arrest conferred by the following subsections shall also apply to the offences of—
    (*a*) conspiring to commit any of the offences mentioned in subsection (2) above;
    (*b*) attempting to commit any such offence;
    (*c*) inciting, aiding, abetting, counselling or procuring the commission of any such offence,
and such offences are also arrestable offences for the purposes of this Act.
  (4) Any person may arrest without a warrant—
    (*a*) anyone who is in the act of committing an arrestable offence;
    (*b*) anyone whom he has reasonable grounds for suspecting to be committing such an offence.
  (5) Where an arrestable offence has been committed, any person may arrest without a warrant—
    (*a*) anyone who is guilty of the offence;
    (*b*) anyone whom he has reasonable grounds for suspecting to be guilty of it.

(6) Where a constable has reasonable grounds for suspecting that an arrestable offence has been committed, he may arrest without a warrant anyone whom he has reasonable grounds for suspecting to be guilty of the offence.

(7) A constable may arrest without a warrant—

(a) anyone who is about to commit an arrestable offence;

(b) anyone whom he has reasonable grounds for suspecting to be about to commit an arrestable offence.

General arrest conditions

25.—(1) Where a constable has reasonable grounds for suspecting that any offence which is not an arrestable offence has been committed or attempted, or is being committed or attempted, he may arrest the relevant person if it appears to him that service of a summons is impracticable or inappropriate because any of the general arrest conditions is satisfied.

(2) In this section, "the relevant person" means any person whom the constable has reasonable grounds to suspect of having committed or having attempted to commit the offence or of being in the course of committing or attempting to commit it.

(3) The general arrest conditions are—

(a) that the name of the relevant person is unknown to, and cannot be readily ascertained by, the constable;

(b) that the constable has reasonable grounds for doubting whether a name furnished by the relevant person as his name is his real name;

(c) that—

(i) the relevant person has failed to furnish a satisfactory address for service; or

(ii) the constable has reasonable grounds for doubting whether an address furnished by the relevant person is a satisfactory address for service;

(d) that the constable has reasonable grounds for believing that arrest is necessary to prevent the relevant person—

(i) causing physical harm to himself or any other person;

(ii) suffering physical injury;

(iii) causing loss of or damage to property;

(iv) committing an offence against public decency; or

(v) causing an unlawful obstruction of the highway;

(e) that the constable has reasonable grounds for believing that arrest is necessary to protect a child or other vulnerable person from the relevant person.

(4) For the purposes of subsection (3) above an address is a satisfactory address for service if it appears to the constable—

(a) that the relevant person will be at it for a sufficiently long period for it to be possible to serve him with a summons; or

(b) that some other person specified by the relevant person will accept service of a summons for the relevant person at it.

(5) Nothing in subsection (3)(d) above authorises the arrest of a person under sub-paragraph (iv) of that paragraph except where members of the public going about their normal business cannot reasonably be expected to avoid the person to be arrested.

(6) This section shall not prejudice any power of arrest conferred apart from this section.

Repeal of statutory powers of arrest without warrant or order

26.—(1) Subject to subsection (2) below, so much of any Act (including a local Act) passed before this Act as enables a constable—

  (*a*) to arrest a person for an offence without a warrant; or

  (*b*) to arrest a person otherwise than for an offence without a
      warrant or an order of a court,

shall cease to have effect.

  (2) Nothing in subsection (1) above affects the enactments specified in
Schedule 2 to this Act.

Fingerprinting of certain offenders

  27.—(1) If a person—

  (*a*) has been convicted of a recordable offence;

  (*b*) has not at any time been in police detention for the offence;
      and

  (*c*) has not had his fingerprints taken—

      (i) in the course of the investigation of the offence by the
         police; or

      (ii) since the conviction;

any constable may at any time not later than one month after the date of
the conviction require him to attend a police station in order that his
fingerprints may be taken.

  (2) A requirement under subsection (1) above—

  (*a*) shall give the person a period of at least 7 days within which he
      must so attend; and

  (*b*) may direct him to so attend at a specified time of day or
      between specified times of day.

  (3) Any constable may arrest without warrant a person who has failed
to comply with a requrement under subsection (1) above.

  (4) The Secretary of State may by regulations make provision for
recording in national police records convictions for such offences as are
specified in the regulations.

  (5) Regulations under this section shall be made by statutory instrument
and shall be subject to annulment in pursuance of a resolution of either
House of Parliament.

Information to be given on arrest

  28.—(1) Subject to subsection (5) below, when a person is arrested
otherwise than by being informed that he is under arrest, the arrest is not
lawful unless the person arrested is informed that he is under arrest as
soon as is practicable after his arrest.

  (2) Where a person is arrested by a constable subsection (1) above
applies regardless of whether the fact of the arrest is obvious.

  (3) Subject to subsection (5) below, no arrest is lawful unless the person
arrested is informed of the ground for the arrest at the time of, or as soon
as is practicable after, the arrest.

  (4) Where a person is arrested by a constable, subsection (3) above
applies regardless of whether the ground for the arrest is obvious.

  (5) Nothing in this section is to be taken to require a person to be
informed—

  (*a*) that he is under arrest; or

  (*b*) of the ground for the arrest,

if it was not reasonably practicable for him to be so informed by reason
of his having escaped from arrest before the information could be given.

Voluntary attendance at police station etc.

  29. Where for the purpose of assisting with an investigation a person
attends voluntarily at a police station or at any other place where a

constable is present or accompanies a constable to a police station or any such other place without having been arrested—

    (*a*) he shall be entitled to leave at will unless he is placed under arrest;

    (*b*) he shall be informed at once that he is under arrest if a decision is taken by a constable to prevent him from leaving at will.

Arrest elsewhere than at police station

    30.—(1) Subject to the following provisions of this section, where a person

    (*a*) is arrested by a constable for an offence; or

    (*b*) is taken into custody by a constable after being arrested for an offence by a person other than a constable;

at any place other than a police station he shall be taken to a police station by a constable as soon as practicable after the arrest.

    (2) Subject to subsections (3) and (4) below, the police station to which an arrested person is taken under subsection (1) above shall be a designated police station.

    (3) A constable to whom this subsection applies may take an arrested person to any police station unless it appears to the constable that it may be necessary to keep the arrested person in police detention for more than six hours.

    (4) Subsection (3) above applies—

    (*a*) to a constable who is working in a locality covered by a police station which is not a designated police station; and

    (*b*) to a constable belonging to a body of constables maintained by an authority other than a police authority.'

    (5) Any constable may take an arrested person to any police station if—

    (*a*) either of the following conditions is satisfied—

       (i) the constable has arrested him without the assistance of any other constable and no other constable is available to assist him;

       (ii) the constable has taken him into custody from a person other than a constable without the assistance of any other constable and no other constable is available to assist him; and

    (*b*) it appears to the constable that he will be unable to take the arrested person to a designated police station without the arrested person injuring himself, the constable or some other person.

    (6) If the first police station to which an arrested person is taken after his arrest is not a designated police station he shall be taken to a designated police station not more than six hours after his arrival at the first police station unless he is released previously

    (7) A person arrested by a constable at a place other than a police station shall be released if a constable is satisfied, before the person arrested reaches a police station, that there are no grounds for keeping him under arrest.

    (8) A constable who releases a person under subsection (7) above shall record the fact that he has done so.

    (9) The constable shall make the record as soon as is practicable after the release.

    (10) Nothing in subsection (1) above shall prevent a constable delaying taking a person who has been arrested to a police station if the presence of that person elsewhere is necessary in order to carry out such investigations as it is reasonable to carry out immediately.

(11) Where there is delay in taking a person who has been arrested to a police station after his arrest, the reasons for the delay shall recorded when he first arrives at a police station.

(12) Nothing in subsection (1) above shall be taken to affect—

(*a*) paragraphs 16(3) or 18(1) of Schedule 2 to the Immigration Act 1971;

(*b*) section 34(1) of the Criminal Justice Act 1972; or

(*c*) paragraph 5 of Schedule 3 to the Prevention of Terrorism (Temporary Provisions) Act 1984 or any provision contained in an order under section 13 of that Act which authorises the detention of persons on board a ship or aircraft.

(13) Nothing in subsection (9) above shall be taken to affect paragraph 18(3) of Schedule 2 to the Immigration Act 1971.

Arrest for further offence

31. Where—

(*a*) a person—

(i) has been arrested for an offence; and

(ii) is at a police station in consequence of that arrest; and

(*b*) it appears to a constable that, if he were released from that arrest, he would be liable to arrest for some other offence,

he shall be arrested for that other offence.

Search upon arrest

32.—(1) A constable may search an arrested person, in any case where the person to be searched has been arrested at a place other than a police station, if the constable has reasonable grounds for believing that the arrested person may present a danger to himself or others.

(2) Subject to subsections (3) to (5) below, a constable shall also have power in any such case—

(*a*) to search the arrested person for anything—

(i) which he might use to assist him to escape from lawful custody; or

(ii) which might be evidence relating to an offence; and

(*b*) to enter and search any premises in which he was when arrested or immediately before he was arrested for evidence relating to the offence for which he has been arrested.

(3) The power to search conferred by subsection (2) above is only a power to search to the extent that is reasonably required for the purpose of discovering any such thing or any such evidence.

(4) The powers conferred by this section to search a person are not to be construed as authorising a constable to require a person to remove any of his clothing in public other than an outer coat, jacket or gloves.

(5) A constable may not search a person in the exercise of the power conferred by subsection (2)(*a*) above unless he has reasonable grounds for believing that the person to be searched may have concealed on him anything for which a search is permitted under that paragraph.

(6) A constable may not search premises in the exercise of the power conferred by subsection (2)(*b*) above unless he has reasonable grounds for believing that there is evidence for which a search is permitted under that paragraph on the premises.

(7) In so far as the power of search conferred by subsection (2)(*b*) above relates to premises consisting of two or more separate dwellings, it is limited to a power to search—

(*a*) any dwelling in which the arrest took place or in which the person arrested was immediately before his arrest; and

(*b*) any parts of the premises which the occupier of any such dwelling uses in common with the occupiers of any other dwellings comprised in the premises.

(8) A constable searching a person in the exercise of the power conferred by subsection (1) above may seize and retain anything he finds, if he has reasonable grounds for believing that the person searched might use it to cause physical injury to himself or to any other person.

(9) A constable searching a person in the exercise of the power conferred by subsection (2)(*a*) above may seize and retain anything he finds, other than an item subject to legal privilege, if he has reasonable grounds for believing—

(*a*) that he might use it to assist him to escape from lawful custody; or

(*b*) that it is evidence of an offence or has been obtained in consequence of the commission of an offence.

(10) Nothing in this section shall be taken to affect the power conferred by paragraph 6 of Schedule 3 to the Prevention of Terrorism (Temporary Provisions) Act 1984.

Execution of warrant not in possession of constable

33. In section 125 of the Magistrates' Courts Act 1980—

(*a*) in subsection (3), for the words "arrest a person charged with an offence" there shall be substituted the words "which this subsection applies";

(*b*) the following subsection shall be added after that subsection—

"(4) The warrants to which subsection (3) above applies are—

(*a*) a warrant to arrest a person in connection with an offence;

(*b*) without prejudice to paragraph (a) above, a warrant under section 186(3) of the Army Act 1955, section 186(3) of the Air Force Act 1955, section 105(3) of the Naval Discipline Act 1957 or Schedule 5 to the Reserve Forces Act 1980 (desertion etc.);

(*c*) a warrant under—

(i) section 102 or 104 of the General Rate Act 1967 (insufficiency of distress);

(ii) section 18(4) of the Domestic Proceedings and Magistrates' Courts Act 1978 (protection of parties to marriage and children of family); and

(iii) section 55, 76, 93 or 97 above.".

PART IV

DETENTION

Detention—conditions and duration

Limitations on police detention

34.—(1) A person arrested for an offence shall not be kept in police detention except in accordance with the provisions of this Part of this Act.

(2) Subject to subsection (3) below, if at any time a custody officer—

(*a*) becomes aware, in relation to any person in police detention, that the grounds for the detention of that person have ceased to apply; and

(*b*) is not aware of any other grounds on which the continued

detention of that person could be justified under the provisions
of this Part of this Act,
it shall be the duty of the custody officer, subject to subsection (4) below,
to order his immediate release from custody.

(3) No person in police detention shall be released except on the
authority of a custody officer at the police station where his detention was
authorised or, if it was authorised at more than one station, a custody
officer at the station where it was last authorised.

(4) A person who appears to the custody officer to have been unlawfully
at large when he was arrested is not to be released under subsection (2)
above.

(5) A person whose release is ordered under subsection (2) above shall
be released without bail unless it appears to the custody officer—

    (*a*) that there is need for further investigation of any matter in
        connection with which he was detained at any time during the
        period of his detention; or

    (*b*) that proceedings may be taken against him in respect of any
        such matter,

and if it so appears, he shall be released on bail.

(6) For the purposes of this Part of this Act a person arrested under
section 7(5) of the Road Traffic Act 1972 is arrested for an offence.

Designated police stations

35.—(1) The chief officer of police for each police area shall designate
the police stations in his area which, subject to section 30(3) and (4)
above, are to be the stations in that area to be used for the purpose of
detaining arrested persons.

(2) A chief officer's duty under subsection (1) above is to designate
police stations appearing to him to provide enough accommodation for
that purpose.

(3) Without prejudice to section 12 of the Interpretation Act 1978
(continuity of duties) a chief officer—

    (*a*) may designate a station which was not previously designated;
        and

    (*b*) may direct that a designation of a station previously made shall
        cease to operate.

(4) In this Act "designated police station" means a police station for
the time being designated under this section.

Custody officers at police stations

36.—(1) One or more custody officers shall be appointed for each
designated police station.

(2) A custody officer for a designated police station shall be
appointed—

    (*a*) by the chief officer of police for the area in which the designated
        police station is situated; or

    (*b*) by such other police officer as the chief officer of police for
        that area may direct.

(3) No officer may be appointed a custody officer unless he is of at least
the rank of sergeant.

(4) An officer of any rank may perform the functions of a custody
officer at a designated police station if a custody officer is not readily
available to perform them.

(5) Subject to the following provisions of this section and to section
39(2) below, none of the functions of a custody officer in relation to a
person shall be performed by an officer who at the time when the function

falls to be performed is involved in the investigation of an offence for which that person is in police detention at that time.

(6) Nothing in subsection (5) above is to be taken to prevent a custody officer—

> (*a*) performing any function assigned to custody officers—
>> (i) by this Act; or
>> (ii) by a code of practice issued under this Act;
> (*b*) carrying out the duty imposed on custody officers by section 39 below;
> (*c*) doing anything in connection with the identification of a suspect; or
> (*d*) doing anything under section 8 of the Road Traffic Act 1972 1972.

(7) Where an arrested person is taken to a police station which is not a designated police station, the functions in relation to him which at a designated police station would be the functions of a custody officer shall be performed—

> (*a*) by an officer who is not involved in the investigation of an offence for which he is in police detention, if such an officer is readily available; and
> (*b*) if no such officer is readily available, by the officer who took him to the station or any other officer.

(8) References to a custody officer in the following provisions of this Act include references to an officer other than a custody officer who is performing the functions of a custody officer by virtue of subsection (4) or (7) above.

(9) Where by virtue of subsection (7) above an officer of a force maintained by a police authority who took an arrested person to a police station is to perform the functions of a custody officer in relation to him, the officer shall inform an officer who—

> (*a*) is attached to a designated police station; and
> (*b*) is of at least the rank of inspector,

that he is to do so.

(10) The duty imposed by subsection (9) above shall be performed as soon as it is practicable to perform it.

Duties of custody officer before charge

37.—(1) Where

> (*a*) a person is arrested for an offence—
>> (i) without a warrant; or
>> (ii) under a warrant not endorsed for bail, or
> (*b*) a person returns to a police station to answer to bail

the custody officer at each police station where he is detained after his arrest shall determine whether he has before him sufficient evidence to charge that person with the offence for which he was arrested and may detain him at the police station for such period as is necessary to enable him to do so.

(2) If the custody officer determines that he does not have such evidence before him, the person arrested shall be released either on bail or without bail, unless the custody officer has reasonable grounds for believing that his detention without being charged is necessary to secure or preserve evidence relating to an offence for which he is under arrest or to obtain such evidence by questioning him.

(3) If the custody officer has reasonable grounds for so believing, he may authorise the person arrested to be kept in police detention.

(4) Where a custody officer authorises a person who has not been charged to be kept in police detention, he shall, as soon as is practicable, make a written record of the grounds for the detention.

(5) Subject to subsection (6) below, the written record shall be made in the presence of the person arrested who shall at that time be informed by the custody officer of the grounds for his detention.

(6) Subsection (5) above shall not apply where the person arrested is, at the time when the written record is made—

    (*a*) incapable of understanding what is said to him;

    (*b*) violent or likely to become violent; or

    (*c*) in urgent need of medical attention.

(7) Subject to section 41(6) below, if the custody officer determines that he has before him sufficient evidence to charge the person arrested with the offence for which he was arrested, the person arrested—

    (*a*) shall be charged; or

    (*b*) shall be released without charge, either on bail or without bail.

(8) Where—

    (*a*) a person is released under subsection (7)(*b*) above; and

    (*b*) at the time of his release a decision whether he should be prosecuted for the offence for which he was arrested has not been taken,

it shall be the duty of the custody officer so to inform him.

(9) If the person arrested is not in a fit state to be dealt with under subsection (7) above, he may be kept in police detention until he is.

(10) The duty imposed on the custody officer under subsection (1) above shall be carried out by him as soon as practicable after the person arrested arrives at the police station or, in the case of a person arrested at the police station, as soon as practicable after the arrest.

(11) Where—

    (*a*) an arrested juvenile who was arrested without a warrant is not released under subsection (2) above; and

    (*b*) it appears to the custody officer that a decision falls to be taken in pursuance of section 5(2) of the Children and Young Persons Act 1969 whether to lay an information in respect of an offence alleged to have been committed by the arrested juvenile,

it shall be the duty of the custody officer to inform him, and if it is reasonably practicable to do so, his parent or guardian, that such a decision falls to be taken and to specify the offence.

(12) It shall also be the duty of custody officer—

    (*a*) to take such steps as are practicable to ascertain the identity of a person responsible for the welfare of the arrested juvenile; and

    (*b*) if—

        (i) he ascertains the identity of any such person; and

        (ii) it is practicable to give that person the information which subsection (11) above requires the custody officer to give to the arrested juvenile,

to give that person the information as soon as it is practicable to do so.

(13) For the purposes of subsection (12) above the persons who may be responsible for the welfare of an arrested juvenile are—

    (*a*) his parent or guardian; and

    (*b*) any other person who has for the time being assumed responsibility for his welfare.

(14) If it appears to the custody officer that a supervision order, as defined in section 11 of the Children and Young Persons Act 1969, is in force in respect of the arrested juvenile, the custody officer shall also give the information to the person responsible for the arrested juvenile's supervision, as soon as it is practicable to do so.

(15) In this Part of this Act—

"arrested juvenile" means a person arrested with or without a warrant who appears to be under the age of 17 and is not excluded from this Part of this Act by section 52 below;

"endorsed for bail" means endorsed with a direction for bail in accordance with section 117(2) of the Magistrates' Courts Act 1980.

Duties of custody officer after charge

38.—(1) Where a person arrested for an offence otherwise than under a warrant endorsed for bail is charged with an offence, the custody officer shall order his release from police detention, either on bail or without bail, unless—

(a) if the person arrested is not an arrested juvenile—

(i) his name or address cannot be ascertained or the custody officer has reasonable grounds for doubting whether a name or address furnished by him as his name or address is his real name or address;

(ii) the custody officer has reasonable grounds for believing that the detention of the person arrested is necessary for his own protection or to prevent him from causing physical injury to any other person or from causing loss of or damage to property; or

(iii) the custody officer has reasonable grounds for believing that the person arrested will fail to appear in court to answer to bail or that his detention is necessary to prevent him from interfering with the administration of justice or with the investigation of offences or of a particular offence;

(b) if he is an arrested juvenile—

(i) any of the requirements of paragraph (a) above is satisfied; or

(ii) the custody officer has reasonable grounds for believing that he ought to be detained in his own interests.

(2) If the release of a person arrested is not required by subsection (1) above, the custody officer may authorise him to be kept in police detention.

(3) Where a custody officer authorises a person who has been charged to be kept in police detention he shall, as soon as practicable, make a written record of the grounds for the detention.

(4) Subject to subsection (5) below the written record shall be made in the presence of the person charged who shall at that time be informed by the custody officer of the grounds for his detention.

(5) Subsection (4) above shall not apply where the person charged is, at the time when the written record is made—

(a) incapable of understanding what is said to him;

(b) violent or likely to become violent; or

(c) in urgent need of medical attention.

(6) Where a custody officer authorises an arrested juvenile to be kept in police detention under subsection (1) above, the custody officer shall, unless he certifies that it is impracticable to do so, make arrangements for the arrested juvenile to be taken into the care of a local authority and detained by the authority, and it shall be lawful to detain him in pursuance of the arrangements.

(7) A certificate made under subsection (6) above in respect of an arrested juvenile shall be produced to the court before which he is first brought thereafter.

(8) In this Part of this Act "local authority" has the same meaning as in the Children and Young Persons Act 1969.

Responsibilities in relation to persons detained

39.—(1) Subject to subsections (2) and (4) below, it shall be the duty of the custody officer at a police station to ensure—

- (*a*) that all persons in police detention at that station are treated in accordance with this Act and any code of practice issued under it and relating to the treatment of persons in police detention; and
- (*b*) that all matters relating to such persons which are required by this Act or by such codes of practice to be recorded are recorded in the custody records relating to such persons.

(2) If the custody officer, in accordance with any code of practice issued under this Act, transfers or permits the transfer of a person in police detention

- (*a*) to the custody of a police officer investigating an offence for which that person is in police detention;
- (*b*) to the custody of an officer who has charge of that person outside the police station
  - (i) the custody officer shall cease in relation to that person to be subject to the duty imposed on him by subsection (1)(*a*) above; and
  - (ii) it shall be the duty of the officer to whom the transfer is made to ensure that he is treated in accordance with the provisions of this Act and of any such codes of practice as are mentioned in subsection (1) above.

(3) If the person detained is subsequently returned to the custody of the custody officer, it shall be the duty of the officer investigating the offence to report to the custody officer as to the manner in which this section and the codes of practice have been complied with while that person was in his custody.

(4) If an arrested juvenile is transferred to the care of a local authority in pursuance of arrangements made under section 38(7) above, the custody officer shall cease in relation to that person to be subject to the duty imposed on him by subsection (1) above.

(5) It shall be the duty of a local authority to make available to an arrested juvenile who is in the authority's care in pursuance of such arrangements such advice and assistance as may be appropriate in the circumstances.

(6) Where—

- (*a*) an officer of higher rank than the custody officer gives directions relating to a person in police detention; and
- (*b*) the directions are at variance—
  - (i) with any decision made or action taken by the custody officer in the performance of a duty imposed on him under this Part of this Act; or
  - (ii) with any decision or action which would but for the directions have been made or taken by him in the performance of such a duty,

the custody officer shall refer the matter at once to an officer of the rank of superintendent or above who is responsible for the police station for which the custody officer is acting as custody officer.

Review of police detention

40.—(1) Reviews of the detention of each person in police detention in connection with the investigation of an offence shall be carried out periodically in accordance with the following provisions of this section—

    (*a*) in the case of a person who has been arrested and charged, by the custody officer; and

    (*b*) in the case of a person who has been arrested but not charged, by an officer of at least the rank of inspector who has not been directly involved in the investigation.

(2) The officer to whom it falls to carry out a review is referred to in this section as a "review officer".

(3) Subject to subsection (4) below—

    (*a*) the first review shall be not later than six hours after the detention was first authorised;

    (*b*) the second review shall be not later than nine hours after the first;

    (*c*) subsequent reviews shall be at intervals of not more than nine hours.

(4) A review may be postponed—

    (*a*) if, having regard to all the circumstances prevailing at the latest time for it specified in subsection (3) above, it is not practicable to carry out the review at that time;

    (*b*) without prejudice to the generality of paragraph (*a*) above—

        (i) if at that time the person in detention is being questioned by a police officer and the review officer is satisfied that an interruption of the questioning for the purpose of carrying out the review would prejudice the investigation in connection with which he is being questioned; or

        (ii) if at that time no review officer is readily available.

(5) If a review is postponed under subsection (4) above it shall be carried out as soon as practicable after the latest time specified for it in subsection (3) above.

(6) If a review is carried out after postponement under subsection (4) above, the fact that it was so carried out shall not affect any requirement of this section as to the time at which any subsequent review is to be carried out.

(7) The review officer shall record the reasons for any postponement of a review in the custody record.

(8) Subject to subsection (9) below, where the person whose detention is under review has not been charged before the time of the review, section 37(1) to (6) above shall have effect in relation to him, but with the substitution—

    (*a*) of references to the person whose detention is under review for references to the person arrested; and

    (*b*) of references to the review officer for references to the custody officer;

(9) Where a person has been kept in police detention by virtue of section 37(9) above, section 37(1) to (6) shall not have effect in relation to him but it shall be the duty of the review officer to determine whether he is yet in a fit state.

(10) Where the person whose detention is under review has been charged before the time of the review, section 38(1) to (6) above shall have effect in relation to him, but with the substitution of references to the person whose detention is under review for references to the person arrested.

(11) Where—

    (*a*) an officer of higher rank than the custody officer gives direc-
        tions relating to a person in police detention;
    (*b*) the directions are at variance—
        (i) with any decision made or action taken by the review
            officer in the performance of a duty imposed on him
            under this Part of this Act; or
        (ii) with any decision or action which would but for the
            directions have been made or taken by him in the per-
            formance of such a duty,
the review officer shall refer the matter at once to an officer of the rank
of superintendent or above who is responsible for the police station for
which the review officer is acting as review officer in connection with the
detention.

    (12) Before determining whether to authorise a person's continued
detention the review officer shall give—
    (*a*) that person (unless he is asleep); or
    (*b*) any solicitor representing him who is available at the time of
        the review,
an opportunity to make representations to him about the detention.

    (13) Subject to subsection (14) below, the person whose detention is
under review or his solicitor may make representations under subsection
(11) above either orally or in writing.

    (14) The review officer may refuse to hear oral representations from
the person whose detention is under review if he considers that he is unfit
to make such representations by reason of his condition or behaviour.

Limits on period of detention without charge

    41.—(1) Subject to the following provisions of this section and to
sections 42 and 43 below, a person shall not be kept in police detention
for more than 24 hours without being charged.

    (2) The time from which the period of detention of a person is to be
calculated (in this Act referred to as "the relevant time")—
    (*a*) in the case of a person to whom this section applies, shall
        be—
        (i) the time at which that person arrives at the relevant
            police station, or
        (ii) the time 24 hours after the time of that person's arrest,
            whichever is the earlier;
    (*b*) in the case of a person arrested outside England and Wales,
        shall be
        (i) the time at which that person arrives at the first police
            station to which he is taken in the police area in England
            or Wales in which the offence for which he was arrested
            is being investigated; or
        (ii) the time 24 hours after the time of that person's entry
            into England and Wales, whichever is the earlier.
    (*c*) in the case of a person who—
        (i) attends voluntarily at a police station; or
        (ii) accompanies a constable to a police station without having
            been arrested,
         and is arrested at the police station, the time of his arrest;
    (*d*) in any other case, except when subsection (5) below applies,
        shall be the time at which the person arrested arrives at the
        first police station to which he is taken after his arrest.

    (3) Subsection (2)(*a*) above applies to a person if—
    (*a*) his arrest is sought in one police area in England and Wales;
    (*b*) he is arrested in another police area; and

    (c) he is not questioned in the area in which he is arrested in order to obtain evidence in relation to an offence for which he is arrested,

and in sub-paragraph (i) of that paragraph "the relevant police station" means the first police station to which he is taken in the police area in which his arrest was sought.

    (4) Subsection (2) above shall have effect in relation to a person arrested under section 31 above as if every reference in it to his arrest or his being arrested were a reference to his arrest or his being arrested for the offence for which he was originally arrested.

    (5) If—

      (a) a person is in police detention in a police area in England and Wales ("the first area"); and

      (b) his arrest for an offence is sought in some other police area in England and Wales ("the second area"); and

      (c) he is taken to the second area for the purposes of investigating that offence, without being questioned in the first area in order to obtain evidence in relation to it,

the relevant time shall be—

        (i) the time 24 hours after he leaves the place where he is detained in the first area; or

        (ii) the time at which he arrives at the first police station to which he is taken in the second area,

whichever is the earlier.

    (6) When a person who is in police detention is removed to hospital because he is in need of medical treatment, any time during which he is being questioned in hospital or on the way there or back by a police officer for the purpose of obtaining evidence relating to an offence shall be included in any period which falls to be calculated for the purposes of this Part of this Act, but any other time while he is in hospital or on his way there or back shall not be so included.

    (7) Subject to subsection (8) below, a person who at the expiry of 24 hours after the relevant time is in police detention and has not been charged shall be released at that time either on bail or without bail.

    (8) Subsection (7) above does not apply to a person whose detention for more than 24 hours after the relevant time has been authorised or is otherwise permitted in accordance with section 42 or 43 below.

    (9) A person released under subsection (7) above shall not be re-arrested without a warrant for the offence for which he was previously arrested unless new evidence justifying a further arrest has come to light since his release.

Authorisation of continued detention

    42.—(1) Where a police officer of the rank of superintendent or above who is responsible for the police station at which a person is detained has reasonable grounds for believing that—

      (a) the detention of that person without charge is necessary to secure or preserve evidence relating to an offence for which he is under arrest or to obtain such evidence by questioning him;

      (b) an offence for which he is under arrest is a serious arrestable offence; and

      (c) the investigation is being conducted diligently and expeditiously, he may authorise the keeping of that person in police detention for a period expiring at or before 36 hours after the relevant time.

    (2) Where an officer such as is mentioned in subsection (1) above has authorised the keeping of a person in police detention for a period

expiring less than 36 hours after the relevant time, such an officer may authorise the keeping of that person in police detention for a further period expiring not more than 36 hours after that time if the conditions specified in subsection (1) above are still satisfied when he gives the authorisation.

(3) If it is proposed to transfer a person in police detention to another police area, the officer determining whether or not to authorise keeping him in detention under subsection (1) above shall have regard to the distance and the time the journey would take.

(4) No authorisation under subsection (1) above shall be given in respect of any person—

    (*a*) more than 24 hours after the relevant time; or

    (*b*) before the second review of his detention under section 40 above has been carried out.

(5) Where an officer authorises the keeping of a person in police detention under subsection (1) above, it shall be his duty—

    (*a*) to inform that person of the grounds for his continued detention; and

    (*b*) to record the grounds in that person's custody record.

(6) Before determining whether to authorise the keeping of a person in detention under subsection (1) or (2) above, an officer shall give—

    (*a*) that person; or

    (*b*) any solicitor representing him who is available at the time when it falls to the officer to determine whether to give the authorisation,

an opportunity to make representations to him about the detention.

(7) Subject to subsection (8) below, the person in detention or his solicitor may make representations under subsection (6) above either orally or in writing.

(8) The officer to whom it falls to determine whether to give the authorisation may refuse to hear oral representations from the person in detention if he considers that he is unfit to make such representations by reason of his condition or behaviour.

(9) Where—

    (*a*) an officer authorises the keeping of a person in detention under subsection (1) above; and

    (*b*) at the time of the authorisation he has not yet exercised a right conferred on him by section 56 or 58 below,

the officer—

      (i) shall inform him of that right;

     (ii) shall decide whether he should be permitted to exercise it;

    (iii) shall record the decision in his custody record; and

    (iv) if the decision is to refuse to permit the exercise of the right, shall also record the grounds for the decision in that record.

(10) Where an officer has authorised the keeping of a person who has not been charged in detention under subsection (1) or (2) above, he shall be released from detention, either on bail or without bail, not later than 36 hours after the relevant time, unless—

    (*a*) he has been charged with an offence; or

    (*b*) his continued detention is authorised or otherwise permitted in accordance with section 43 below.

(11) A person released under subsection (10) above shall not be re-arrested without a warrant for the offence for which he was previously arrested unless new evidence justifying a further arrest has come to light since his release.

Warrants of further detention

43.—(1) Where, on an application on oath made by a constable and supported by an information, a magistrates' court is satisfied that there are reasonable grounds for believing that the further detention of the person to whom the application relates is justified, it may issue a warrant of further detention authorising the keeping of that person in police detention.

(2) A court may not hear an application for a warrant of further detention unless the person to whom the application relates—

(*a*) has been furnished with a copy of the information; and

(*b*) has been brought before the court for the hearing.

(3) The person to whom the application relates shall be entitled to be legally represented at the hearing and, if he is not so represented, but wishes to be so represented—

(*a*) the court shall adjourn the hearing to enable him to obtain representation; and

(*b*) he may be kept in police detention during the adjournment.

(4) A person's further detention is only justified for the purposes of this section or section 44 below if—

(*a*) his detention without charge is necessary to secure or preserve evidence relating to an offence for which he is under arrest or to obtain such evidence by questioning him;

(*b*) an offence for which he is under arrest is a serious arrestable offence; and

(*c*) the investigation is being conducted diligently and expeditiously.

(5) Subject to subsection (7) below, an application for a warrant of further detention may be made—

(*a*) at any time before the expiry of 36 hours after the relevant time; or

(*b*) in a case where—

(i) it is not practicable for the magistrates' court to which the application will be made to sit at the expiry of 36 hours after the relevant time; but

(ii) the court will sit during the 6 hours following the end of that period,

at any time before the expiry of the said 6 hours.

(6) In a case to which subsection (5)(*b*) above applies—

(*a*) the person to whom the application relates may be kept in police detention until the application is heard; and

(*b*) the custody officer shall make a note in that person's custody record—

(i) of the fact that he was kept in police detention for more than 36 hours after the relevant time; and

(ii) of the reason why he was so kept.

(7) If—

(*a*) an application for a warrant of further detention is made after the expiry of 36 hours after the relevant time; and

(*b*) it appears to the magistrates' court that it would have been reasonable for the police to make it before the expiry of that period,

the court shall dismiss the application.

(8) Where on an application such as is mentioned in subsection (1) above a magistrates' court is not satisfied that there are reasonable grounds for believing that the further detention of the person to whom the application relates is justified, it shall be its duty—

(*a*) to refuse the application; or

(*b*) to adjourn the hearing of it until a time not later than 36 hours after the relevant time.

(9) The person to whom the application relates may be kept in police detention during the adjournment.

(10) A warrant of further detention shall—

(*a*) state the time at which it is issued;

(*b*) authorise the keeping in police detention of the person to whom it relates for the period stated in it.

(11) Subject to subsection (12) below, the period stated in a warrant of further detention shall be such period as the magistrates' court thinks fit, having regard to the evidence before it.

(12) The period shall not be longer than 36 hours.

(13) If it is proposed to transfer a person in police detention to a police area other than that in which he is detained when the application for a warrant of further detention is made, the court hearing the application shall have regard to the distance and the time the journey would take.

(14) Any information submitted in support of an application under this section shall state—

(*a*) the nature of the offence for which the person to whom the application relates has been arrested;

(*b*) the general nature of the evidence on which that person was arrested;

(*c*) what inquiries relating to the offence have been made by the police and what further inquiries are proposed by them;

(*d*) the reasons for believing the continued detention of that person to be necessary for the purposes of such further inquiries.

(15) Where an application under this section is refused the person to whom the application relates shall forthwith be charged or, subject to subsection (16) below, released, either on bail or without bail.

(16) A person need not be released under subsection (15) above—

(*a*) before the expiry of 24 hours after the relevant time; or

(*b*) before the expiry of any longer period for which his continued detention is or has been authorised under section 42 above.

(17) Where an application under this section is refused, no further application shall be made under this section in respect of the person to whom the refusal relates, unless supported by evidence which has come to light since the refusal.

(18) Where a warrant of further detention is issued, the person to whom it relates shall be released from police detention, either on bail or without bail, upon or before the expiry of the warrant unless he is charged.

(19) A person released under subsection (18) above shall not be re-arrested without a warrant for the offence for which he was previously arrested unless new evidence justifying a further arrest has come to light since his release.

Extension of warrants of further detention

44.—(1) On an application on oath made by a constable and supported by an information a magistrates' court may extend a warrant of further detention issued under section 43 above if it is satisfied that there are reasonable grounds for believing that the further detention of the person to whom the application relates is justified.

(2) Subject to subsection (3) below, the period for which a warrant of further detention may be extended shall be such period as the court thinks fit, having regard to the evidence before it.

(3) The period shall not—

(*a*) be longer than 36 hours; or

(b) end later then 96 hours after the relevant time.

(4) Where a warrant of further detention has been extended under subsection (1) above, or further extended under this subsection, for a period ending before 96 hours after the relevant time, on an application such as is mentioned in that subsection a magistrates' court may further extend the warrant if it is satisfied as there mentioned; and subsections (2) and (3) above apply to such further extensions as they apply to extensions under subsection (1) above.

(5) A warrant of further detention shall, if extended or further extended under this section, be endorsed with a note of the period of the extension.

(6) Subsections (2), (3) and (14) of section 43 above shall apply to an application made under this section as they apply to an application made under that section.

(7) Where an application under this section is refused, the person to whom the application relates shall forthwith be charged or, subject to subsection (8) below, released, either on bail or without bail.

(8) A person need not be released under subsection (7) above before the expiry of any period for which a warrant of further detention issued in relation to him has been extended or further extended on an earlier application made under this section.

Detention before charge—supplementary

45.—(1) In sections 43 and 44 of this Act "magistrates' court" means a court consisting of two or more justices of the peace sitting otherwise than in open court.

(2) Any reference in this Part of this Act to a period of time or a time of day is to be treated as approximate only.

Detention—miscellaneous

Detention after charge

46.—(1) Where a person—
    (a) is charged with an offence; and
    (b) after being charged—
        (i) is kept in police detention; or
        (ii) is detained by a local authority in pursuance of arrangements made under section 38(7) above,
he shall be brought before a magistrates' court in accordance with the provisions of this section.

(2) If he is to be brought before a magistrates' court for the petty sessions area in which the police station at which he was charged is situated, he shall be brought before such a court as soon as is practicable and in any event not later than the first sitting after he is charged with the offence.

(3) If no magistrates' court for that area is due to sit either on the day on which he is charged or on the next day, the custody officer for the police station at which he was charged shall inform the clerk to the justices for the area that there is a person in the area to whom subsection (2) above applies.

(4) If the person charged is to be brought before a magistrates' court for a petty sessions area other than that in which the police station at which he was charged is situated, he shall be removed to that area as soon as is practicable and brought before such a court as soon as is practicable after his arrival in the area and in any event not later than the first sitting of a magistrates' court for that area after his arrival in the area.

(5) If no magistrates' court for that area is due to sit either on the day on which he arrives in the area or on the next day—

(*a*) he shall be taken to a police station in the area; and

(*b*) the custody officer at that station shall inform the clerk to the justices for the area that there is a person in the area to whom subsection (4) applies.

(6) Subject to subsection (8) below, where a clerk to the justices for a petty sessions area has been informed—

(*a*) under subsection (3) above that there is a person in the area to whom subsection (2) above applies; or

(*b*) under subsection (5) above that there is a person in the area to whom subsection (4) above applies,

the clerk shall arrange for a magistrates' court to sit not later than the day next following the relevant day.

(7) In this section "the relevant day"—

(*a*) in relation to a person who is to be brought before a magistrates' court for the petty sessions area in which the police station at which he was charged is situated, means the day on which he was charged; and

(*b*) in relation to a person who is to be brought before a magistrates' court for any other petty sessions area, means the day on which he arrives in the area.

(8) Where the day next following the relevant day is Christmas Day, Good Friday or a Sunday, the duty of the clerk under subsection (6) above is a duty to arrange for a magistrates' court to sit not later than the first day after the relevant day which is not one of those days.

(9) Nothing in this section requires a person who is in hospital to be brought before a court if he is not well enough.

Bail after arrest

47.—(1) Subject to subsection (2) below, a release on bail of a person under this Part of this Act shall be a release on bail granted in accordance with the Bail Act 1976.

(2) Nothing in the Bail Act 1976 shall prevent the rearrest without warrant of a person released on bail subject to a duty to attend at a police station if new evidence justifying a further arrest has come to light since his release.

(3) Subject to subsection (4) below, in this Part of this Act references to "bail" are references to bail subject to a duty—

(*a*) to appear before a magistrates' court at such time and such place; or

(*b*) to attend at such police station at such time,

as the custody officer may appoint.

(4) Where a custody officer has granted bail to a person subject to a duty to appear at a police station, the custody officer may give notice in writing to that person that his attendance at the police station is not required.

(5) Where a person arrested for an offence who was released on bail subject to a duty to attend at a police station so attends, he may be detained without charge in connection with that offence only if the custody officer at the police station has reasonable grounds for believing that his detention is necessary—

(*a*) to secure or preserve evidence relating to the offence; or

(*b*) to obtain such evidence by questioning him.

(6) Where a person is detained under subsection (5) above, any time during which he was in police detention prior to being granted bail shall be included as part of any period which falls to be calculated under this Part of this Act.

(7) Where a person who was released on bail subject to a duty to attend at a police station is re-arrested, the provisions of this Part of this Act shall apply to him as they apply to a person arrested for the first time.

(8) In the Magistrates' Courts Act 1980—

(*a*) the following section shall be substituted for section 43—
"Bail on arrest

43.—(1) Where a person has been granted bail under the Police and Criminal Evidence Act 1984 subject to a duty to appear before a magistrates' court, the court before which he is to appear may appoint a later time as the time at which he is to appear and may enlarge the recognizances of any sureties for him at that time.

(2) The recognizance of any surety for any person granted bail subject to a duty to attend at a police station may be enforced as if it were conditioned for his appearance before a magistrates' court for the petty sessions area in which the police station named in the recognizance is situated."; and

(*b*) the following subsection shall be substituted for section 117(3)—
"(3) Where a warrant has been endorsed for bail under subsection (1) above—

(*a*) where the person arrested is to be released on bail on his entering into a recognizance without sureties, it shall not be necessary to take him to a police station, but if he is so taken, he shall be released from custody on his entering into the recognizance; and

(*b*) where he is to be released on his entering into a recognizance with sureties, he shall be taken to a police station on his arrest, and the custody officer there shall (subject to his approving any surety tendered in compliance with the endorsement) release him from custody as directed in the endorsement.

Remands to police custody

48. In section 128 of the Magistrates' Courts Act 1980—

(*a*) in subsection (7) for the words "the custody of a constable" there shall be substituted the words "detention at a police station";

(*b*) after subsection (7) there shall be inserted the following subsection—
"(8) Where a person is committed to detention at a police station under subsection (7) above—

(*a*) he shall not be kept in such detention unless there is a need for him to be so detained for the purposes of inquiries into other offences;

(*b*) if kept in such detention, he shall be brought back before the magistrates' court which committed him as soon as that need ceases;

(*c*) he shall be treated as a person in police detention to whom the duties under section 39 of the Police and Criminal Evidence Act 1984 (responsibilities in relation to persons detained) relate;

(*d*) his detention shall be subject to periodic review at the times set out in section 40 of that Act (review of police detention).".

Police detention to count towards custodial sentence

49.—(1) In subsection (1) of section 67 of the Criminal Justice Act 1967 (computation of custodial sentences) for the words from "period", in the first place where it occurs, to "the offender" there shall be substituted the words "relevant period, but where he".

(2) The following subsection shall be inserted after that subsection—

"(1A) In subsection (1) above "relevant period" means—

(a) any period during which the offender was in police detention in connection with the offence for which the sentence was passed; or

(b) any period during which he was in custody—

(i) by reason only of having been committed to custody by an order of a court made in connection with any proceedings relating to that sentence or the offence for which it was passed or any proceedings from which those proceedings arose; or

(ii) by reason of his having been so committed and having been concurrently detained otherwise than by order of a court.".

(3) The following subsections shall be added after subsection (6) of that section—

"(7) A person is in police detention for the purposes of this section—

(a) at any time when he is in police detention for the purposes of the Police and Criminal Evidence Act 1984; and

(b) at any time when he is detained under section 12 of the Prevention of Terrorism (Temporary Provisions) Act 1984.

(8) No period of police detention shall be taken into account under this section unless it falls after the coming into force of section 49 of the Police and Criminal Evidence Act 1984."

Records of detention

50.—(1) Each police force shall keep written records showing on an annual basis—

(a) the number of persons kept in police detention for more than 24 hours and subsequently released without charge;

(b) the number of applications for warrants of further detention and the results of the applications; and

(c) in relation to each warrant of further detention—

(i) the period of further detention authorised by it;

(ii) the period which the person named in it spent in police detention on its authority; and

(iii) whether he was charged or released without a charge.

(2) Every annual report—

(a) under section 12 of the Police Act 1964; or

(b) made by the Commissioner of Police of the Metropolis,

shall contain information about the matters mentioned in subsection (1) above in respect of the period to which the report relates.

Savings

51. Nothing in this Part of this Act shall affect—

(a) the powers conferred on immigration officers by section 4 of and Schedule 2 to the Immigration Act 1971 (administrative provisions as to control on entry etc.);

195

(b) the powers conferred by or by virtue of section 12 or 13 of the Prevention of Terrorism (Temporary Provisions) Act 1984 (powers of arrest and detention and control of entry and procedure for removal);

(c) any duty of a police officer under—

    (i) section 129, 190 or 202 of the Army Act 1955 (duties of governors of prisons and others to receive prisoners, deserters, absentees and persons under escort);

    (ii) section 129, 190 or 202 of the Air Force Act 1955 (duties of governors of prisons and others to receive prisoners, deserters, absentees and persons under escort); or

    (iii) section 107 of the Naval Discipline Act 1957 (duties of governors of civil prisons etc.); or

    (iv) paragraph 5 of Schedule 5 to the Reserve Forces Act 1980 (duties of governors of civil prisons); or

(d) any right of a person in police detention to apply for a writ of habeas corpus or other prerogative remedy.

Children

52. This Part of this Act does not apply to a child (as for the time being defined for the purposes of the Children and Young Persons Act 1969) who is arrested without a warrant otherwise than for homicide and to whom section 28(4) and (5) of that Act accordingly apply.

PART V

QUESTIONING AND TREATMENT OF PERSONS BY POLICE

Abolition of certain powers of constables to search persons

53.—(1) Subject to subsection (2) below, there shall cease to have effect any Act (including a local Act) passed before this Act in so far as it authorises—

(a) any search by a constable of a person in police detention at a police station; or

(b) an intimate search of a person by a constable,

and any rule of common law which authorises a search such as is mentioned in paragraph (a) or (b) above is abolished.

(2) Nothing in subsection (1) (a) above shall affect paragraph 6(2) of Schedule 3 to the Prevention of Terrorism (Temporary Provisions) Act 1984.

Searches of detained persons

54.—(1) The custody officer at a police station shall ascertain and record or cause to be recorded everything which a person has with him when he is—

(a) brought to the station after being arrested elsewhere or after being committed to custody by an order or sentence of a court; or

(b) arrested at the station after having attended voluntarily there or having accompanied a constable there without having been arrested.

(2) In the case of an arrested person the record shall be made as part of his custody record.

(3) Subject to subsection (4) below, a custody officer may seize and retain any such thing or cause any such thing to be seized and retained.

(4) Clothes and personal effects may only be seized if the custody officer—

    (*a*) believes that the person from whom they are seized may use them—

        (i) to cause physical injury to himself or any other person;

        (ii) to damage property;

        (iii) to interfere with evidence; or

        (iv) to assist him to escape; or

    (*b*) has reasonable grounds for believing that they may be evidence relating to an offence.

(5) Where anything is seized, the person from whom it is seized shall be told the reason for the seizure unless he is—

    (*a*) violent or likely to become violent; or

    (*b*) incapable of understanding what is said to him.

(6) Subject to subsection (7) below, a person may be searched if the custody officer considers it necessary to enable him to carry out his duty under subsection (1) above and to the extent that the custody officer considers necessary for that purpose.

(7) An intimate search may not be conducted under this section.

(8) A search under this section shall be carried out by a constable.

(9) The constable carrying out a search shall be of the same sex as the person searched.

Intimate searches

55.—(1) Subject to the following provisions of this section if an officer of at least the rank of superintendent has reasonable grounds for believing—

    (*a*) that a person who has been arrested and is in police detention may have concealed on him any thing which

        (i) he could use to cause physical injury to himself or others; and

        (ii) he might so use while he is police detention or in the custody of a court; or

    (*b*) that such a person—

        (i) may have a Class A drug concealed on him; and

        (ii) was in possession of it with the appropriate criminal intent before his arrest,

he may authorise such a search* of that person.

(2) An officer may not authorise an intimate search of a person for anything unless he has reasonable grounds for believing that it cannot be found without his being intimately searched.

(3) An officer may give an authorisation under subsection (1) above orally or in writing but, if he gives it orally, he shall confirm it in writing as soon as is practicable.

(4) An intimate search which is only a drug offence search shall be way of examination by a suitably qualified person.

(5) Except as provided by subsection (4) above, an intimate search shall be by way of examination by a suitably qualified person unless an officer of at least the rank of superintendent considers that this is not practicable.

---

* There is plainly a drafting error here. The words "an intimate" should have replaced "such a".

(6) An intimate search which is not carried out as mentioned in subsection (5) above shall be carried out by a constable.

(7) A constable may not carry out an intimate search of a person of the opposite sex.

(8) No intimate search may be carried out except—

    (*a*) at a police station;

    (*b*) at a hospital;

    (*c*) at a registered medical practitioner's surgery; or

    (*d*) at some other place used for medical purposes.

(9) An intimate search which is only a drug offence search may not be carried out at a police station.

(10) If an intimate search of a person is carried out, the custody record relating to him shall state—

    (*a*) which parts of his body were searched; and

    (*b*) why they were searched.

(11) The information required to be recorded by subsection (10) above shall be recorded as soon as practicable after the completion of the search.

(12) The custody officer at a police station may seize and retain anything which is found on an intimate search of a person, or cause any such thing to be seized and retained—

    (*a*) if he believes that the person from whom it is seized may use it—

        (i) to cause physical injury to himself or any other person;

        (ii) to damage property;

        (iii) to interfere with evidence; or

        (iv) to assist him to escape; or

    (*b*) if he has reasonable grounds for believing that it may be evidence relating to an offence.

(13) Where anything is seized under this section, the person from whom it is seized shall be told the reason for the seizure unless he is

    (*a*) violent or likely to become violent; or

    (*b*) incapable of understanding what is said to him.

(14) Every annual report—

    (*a*) under section 12 of the Police Act 1964; or

    (*b*) made by the Commissioner of Police of the Metropolis,

shall contain information about searches under this section which have been carried out in the area to which the report relates during the period to which it relates.

(15) The information about such searches shall include—

    (*a*) the total number of searches;

    (*b*) the number of searches conducted by way of examination by a suitably qualified person;

    (*c*) the number of searches not so conducted but conducted in the presence of such a person; and

    (*d*) the result of the searches carried out.

(16) The information shall also include, as separate items—

    (*a*) the total number of drug offence searches; and

    (*b*) the result of those searches.

(17) In this section—

    "the appropriate criminal intent" means an intent to commit an offence under—

        (*a*) section 5(3) of the Misuse of Drugs Act 1971 (possession of controlled drug with intent to supply to another); or

        (*b*) section 68(2) of the Customs and Excise Management Act 1979 (exportation etc. with intent to evade a prohibition or restriction);

    "Class A drug" has the meaning assigned to it by section 2(1)(*b*) of the Misuse of Drugs Act 1971;

"drug offence search" means an intimate search for a Class A drug
   which an officer has authorised by virtue of subsection (1)(*b*)
   above; and
"suitably qualified person" means—
      (*a*) a registered medical practitioner; or
      (*b*) a registered nurse.

Right to have someone informed when arrested

56.—(1) Where a person has been arrested and is being held in custody
in a police station or other premises, he shall be entitled, if he so requests,
to have one friend or relative or other person who is known to him or
who is likely to take an interest in his welfare told, as soon as is practicable
except to the extent that delay is permitted by this section, that he has
been arrested and is being detained there.

(2) Delay is only permitted—
      (*a*) in the case of a person who is in police detention for a serious
            arrestable offence; and
      (*b*) if an officer of at least the rank of superintendent authorises it.

(3) In any case the person in custody must be permitted to exercise the
right conferred by subsection (1) above within 36 hours from the relevant
time, as defined in section 41(2) above.

(4) An officer may give an authorisation under subsection (2) above
orally or in writing but, if he gives it orally, he shall confirm it in writing
as soon as is practicable.

(5) An officer may only authorise delay where he has reasonable
grounds for believing that telling the named person of the arrest—
      (*a*) will lead to interference with or harm to evidence connected
            with a serious arrestable offence or interference with or physical
            injury to other persons; or
      (*b*) will lead to the alerting of other persons suspected of having
            committed such an offence but not yet arrested for it; or
      (*c*) will hinder the recovery of any property obtained as a result of
            such an offence.

(6) If a delay is authorised—
      (*a*) the detained person shall be told the reason for it; and
      (*b*) the reason shall be noted on his custody record.

(7) The duties imposed by subsection (6) above shall be performed as
soon as is practicable.

(8) The rights conferred by this section on a person detained at a police
station or other premises are exercisable whenever he is transferred from
one place to another, and this section applies to each subsequent occasion
on which they are exercisable as it applies to the first such occasion.

(9) There may be no further delay in permitting the exercise of the
right conferred by subsection (1) above once the reason for authorising
delay ceases to subsist.

(10) In the foregoing provisions of this section references to a person
who has been arrested include references to a person who has been
detained under the terrorism provisions and "arrest" includes detention
under those provisions.

(11) In its application to a person who has been arrested or detained
under the terrorism provisions—
      (*a*) subsection (2)(*a*) above shall have effect as if for the words
            "for a serious arrestable offence" there were substituted the
            words "under the terrorism provisions";
      (*b*) subsection (3) above shall have effect as if for the words from

"within" onwards there were substituted the words "before the end of the period beyond which he may no longer be detained without the authority of the Secretary of State"; and

(c) subsection (5) above shall have effect as if at the end there were added "or

(d) will lead to interference with the gathering of information about the commission, preparation or instigation of acts of terrorism; or

(e) by alerting any person, will make it more difficult—
 (i) to prevent an act of terrorism; or
 (ii) to secure the apprehension, prosecution or conviction of any person in connection with the commission, preparation or instigation of an act of terrorism.".

Additional rights of children and young persons who are arrested

57. The following subsections shall be substituted for section 34(2) of the Children and Young Persons Act 1933—

"(2) Where a child or young person is in police detention, such steps as are practicable shall be taken to ascertain the identity of a person responsible for his welfare.

(3) If it is practicable to ascertain the identity of a person responsible for the welfare of the child or young person, that person shall be informed, unless it is not practicable to do so—

(a) that the child or young person has been arrested;
(b) why he has been arrested; and
(c) where he is being detained.

(4) Where information falls to be given under subsection (3) above, it shall be given as soon as it is practicable to do so.

(5) For the purposes of this section the persons who may be responsible for the welfare of a child or young person are—

(a) his parent or guardian; or
(b) any other person who has for the time being assumed responsibility for his welfare.

(6) If it is practicable to give a person responsible for the welfare of the child or young person the information required by subsection (3) above, that person shall be given it as soon as it is practicable to do so.

(7) If it appears that at the time of his arrest a supervision order, as defined in section 11 of the Children and Young Persons Act 1969, is in force in respect of him, the person responsible for his supervision shall also be informed as described in subsection (3) above as soon as it is reasonably practicable to do so.

(8) The reference to a parent or guardian in subsection (5) above is—

(a) in the case of a child in the care of a local authority, a reference to that authority; and
(b) in the case of a child or young person in the care of a voluntary organisation in which parental rights and duties with respect to him are vested by virtue of a resolution under section 64(1) of the Child Care Act 1980, that organisation.

(9) The rights conferred on a child or young person by subsections (2) to (7) above are in addition to his rights under section 56 of the Police and Criminal Evidence Act 1984.

(10) The reference in subsection (2) above to a child or young person who is in police detention includes a reference to a child or young person who has been detained under the terrorism provisions, and in subsection (7) above "arrest" includes such detention.

(11) In subsection (10) above "the terrorism provisions" has the meaning assigned to it by section 65 of the Police and Criminal Evidence Act 1984.".

Access to legal advice

58.—(1) A person who is in police detention shall be entitled, if he so requests, to consult a solicitor privately at any time.

(2) Subject to subsection (3) below, a request under subsection (1) above and the time at which it was made shall be recorded in the custody record.

(3) Such a request need not be recorded in the custody record of a person who makes it at a time while he is at a court after being charged with an offence.

(4) If a person makes such a request, he must be permitted to consult a solicitor as soon as is practicable except to the extent that delay is permitted by this section.

(5) In any case he must be permitted to consult a solicitor within 36 hours from the relevant time, as defined in section 41(2) above.

(6) Delay in compliance with a request is only permitted—

    (*a*) in the case of a person who is in police detention for a serious arrestable offence; and

    (*b*) if an officer of at least the rank of superintendent authorises it.

(7) An officer may give an authorisation under subsection (6) above orally or in writing but, if he gives it orally, he shall confirm it in writing as soon as is practicable.

(8) An officer may only authorise delay where he has reasonable grounds for believing that the exercise of the right conferred by subsection (1) above at the time when the person in police detention desires to exercise it—

    (*a*) will lead to interference with or harm to evidence connected with a serious arrestable offence or interference with or physical injury to other persons; or

    (*b*) will lead to the alerting of other persons suspected of having committed such an offence but not yet arrested for it; or

    (*c*) will hinder the recovery of any property obtained as a result of such an offence.

(9) If delay is authorised—

    (*a*) the person in police detention shall be told the reason for it; and

    (*b*) the reason shall be noted on his custody record.

(10) The duties imposed by subsection (9) above shall be performed as soon as is practicable.

(11) There may be no further delay in permitting the exercise of the right conferred by subsection (1) above once the reason for authorising delay ceases to subsist.

(12) The reference in subsection (1) above to a person who is in police detention includes a reference to a person who has been detained under the terrorism provisions.

(13) In the application of this section to a person who has been arrested or detained under the terrorism provisions—

    (*a*) subsection (5) above shall have effect as if for the words from "within" onwards there were substituted the words "before the end of the period beyond which he may no longer be detained without the authority of the Secretary of State";

    (*b*) subsection (6)(*a*) above shall have effect as if for the words "for a serious arrestable offence" there were substituted the words "under the terrorism provisions"; and (*c*) subsection (8) above shall have effect as if at the end there were added "or

(*d*) will lead to interference with the gathering of information about the commission, preparation or instigation of acts of terrorism; or

(*e*) by alerting any person, will make it more difficult—
   (i) to prevent an act of terrorism; or
   (ii) to secure the apprehension, prosecution or conviction of any person in connection with the commission, preparation or instigation of an act of terrorism."

(14) If an officer of appropriate rank has reasonable grounds for believing that, unless he gives a direction under subsection (15) below, the exercise by a person arrested or detained under the terrorism provisions of the right conferred by subsection (1) above will have any of the consequences specified in subsection (8) above (as it has effect by virtue of subsection (13) above), he may give a direction under that subsection.

(15) A direction under this subsection is a direction that a person desiring to exercise the right conferred by subsection (1) above may only consult a solicitor in the sight and hearing of a qualified officer of the uniformed branch of the force of which the officer giving the direction is a member.

(16) An officer is qualified for the purpose of subsection (15) above if—

(*a*) he is of at least the rank of inspector; and

(*b*) in the opinion of the officer giving the direction he has no connection with the case.

(17) An officer is of appropriate rank to give a direction under subsection (15) above if he is of at least the rank of Commander or Assistant Chief Constable.

(18) A direction under subsection (15) above shall cease to have effect once the reason for giving it ceases to subsist.

Legal aid for persons in police stations

59. In section 1 of the Legal Aid Act 1982 (duty solicitors)—

(*a*) in subsection (1) the following paragraph shall be inserted after paragraph (*a*)—
"(*aa*) for the making, by such committees, of arrangements whereby advice and assistance under section 1 of the principal Act is provided for persons
   (i) such as an mentioned in section 29 of the Police and Criminal Evidence Act 1984; or
   (ii) arrested and held in custody who—
      (i) exercise the right to consult a solicitor conferred on them by section 58(1) of that Act; or
      (ii) are permitted to consult a representative of a solicitor; and";

(*b*) in paragraph (*b*), after the word "representation" there shall be inserted the words "or advice and assistance";

(*c*) the following subsection shall be inserted after that subsection—
"(1A) A scheme under section 15 of the principal Act which relates to advice and representation at magistrates' courts may provide that arrangements made under it may be so framed as to preclude solicitors from providing such advice and representation if they do not also provide advice and assistance in pursuance of arrangements made by virtue of a scheme under that section which relates to the provision

of advice and assistance for persons such as are mentioned in section 29 of the Police and Criminal Evidence Act 1984 and for persons arrested and held in custody";

and

(*d*) in subsection (5), for the words "such arrangements as are mentioned in subsection (1) above" there shall be substituted the words "arrangements made under subsection (1) above for the provision of advice and representation at the court."

Tape-recording of interviews

60.—(1) It shall be the duty of the Secretary of State—

(*a*) to issue a code of practice in connection with the tape-recording of interviews of persons suspected of the commission of criminal offences which are held by police officers at police stations; and

(*b*) to make an order requiring the tape-recording of interviews of persons suspected of the commission of criminal offences, or of such descriptions of criminal offences as may be specified in the order, which are so held, in accordance with the code as it has effect for the time being.

(2) An order under subsection (1) above shall be made by statutory instrument and shall be subject to annulment in pursuance of a resolution of either House of Parliament.

Fingerprinting

61.—(1) Except as provided by this section no person's fingerprints may be taken without the appropriate consent.

(2) Consent to the taking of a person's fingerprints must be in writing if it is given at a time when he is at a police station.

(3) The fingerprints of a person detained at a police station may be taken without the appropriate consent—

(*a*) if an officer of at least the rank of superintendent authorises them to be taken; or

(*b*) if—

(i) he has been charged with a recordable offence or informed that he will be reported for such an offence; and

(ii) he has not had his fingerprints taken in the course of the investigation of the offence by the police.

(4) An officer may only give an authorisation under subsection (3)(*a*) above if he has reasonable grounds—

(*a*) for suspecting the involvement of the person whose fingerprints are to be taken in a criminal offence; and

(*b*) for believing that his fingerprints will tend to confirm or disprove his involvement.

(5) An officer may give an authorisation under subsection (3)(*a*) above orally or in writing but, if he gives it orally, he shall confirm it in writing as soon as is practicable.

(6) Any person's fingerprints may be taken without the appropriate consent if he has been convicted of a recordable offence.

(7) In a case where by virtue of subsection (3) or (6) above a person's fingerprints are taken without the appropriate consent—

(*a*) he shall be told the reason before his fingerprints are taken; and

(*b*) the reason shall be recorded as soon as is practicable after the fingerprints are taken.

(8) If he is detained at a police station when the fingerprints are taken, the reason for taking them shall be recorded on his custody record.

(9) Nothing in this section—

    (*a*) affects any power conferred by paragraph 18(2) of Schedule 2 to the Immigration Act 1971; or

    (*b*) applies to a person arrested or detained under the terrorism provisions.

Intimate samples

62.—(1) An intimate sample may be taken from a person in police detention only—

    (*a*) if a police officer of at least the rank of superintendent authorises it to be taken; and

    (*b*) if the appropriate consent is given.

(2) An officer may only give an authorisation if he has reasonable grounds—

    (*a*) for suspecting the involvement of the person from whom the sample is to be taken in a serious arrestable offence; and

    (*b*) for believing that the sample will tend to confirm or disprove his involvement.

(3) An officer may give an authorisation under subsection (1) above orally or in writing but, if he gives it orally, he shall confirm it in writing as soon as is practicable.

(4) The appropriate consent must be given in writing.

(5) Where—

    (*a*) an authorisation has been given; and

    (*b*) it is proposed that an intimate sample shall be taken in pursuance of the authorisation,

an officer shall inform the person from whom the sample is to be taken—

    (i) of the giving of the authorisation; and

    (ii) of the grounds for giving it.

(6) The duty imposed by subsection (5)(ii) above includes a duty to state the nature of the offence in which it is suspected that the person from whom the sample is to be taken has been involved.

(7) If an intimate sample is taken from a person—

    (*a*) the authorisation by virtue of which it was taken;

    (*b*) the grounds for giving the authorisation; and

    (*c*) the fact that the appropriate consent was given,

shall be recorded as soon as is practicable after the sample is taken.

(8) If an intimate sample is taken from a person detained at a police station, the matters required to be recorded by subsection (7) above shall be recorded in his custody record.

(9) An intimate sample, other than a sample of urine or saliva, may only be taken from a person by a medical practitioner.

(10) Where the appropriate consent to the taking of an intimate sample from a person was refused without good cause, in any proceedings against that person for an offence—

    (*a*) the court, in determining—

        (i) whether to commit that person for trial; or

        (ii) whether there is a case to answer; and

    (*b*) the court or jury, in determining whether that person is guilty of the offence charged,

may draw such inferences from the refusal as appear proper; and the refusal may, on the basis of such inferences, be treated as, or as capable of amounting to, corroboration of any evidence against the person in relation to which the refusal is material.

(11) Nothing in this section affects sections 5 to 12 of the Road Traffic Act 1972.

Other samples

63.—(1) Except as provided by this section a non-intimate sample may not be taken from a person without the appropriate consent.

(2) Consent to the taking of a non-intimate sample must be given in writing.

(3) A non-intimate sample may be taken from a person without the appropriate consent if—

(*a*) he is in police detention or is being held in custody by the police on the authority of a court; and

(*b*) an officer of at least the rank of superintendent authorises it to be taken without the appropriate consent.

(4) An officer may only give an authorisation under subsection (3) above if he has reasonable grounds—

(*a*) for suspecting the involvement of the person from whom the sample is to be taken in a serious arrestable offence; and

(*b*) for believing that the sample will tend to confirm or disprove his involvement.

(5) An officer may give an authorisation under subsection (3) above orally or in writing but, if he gives it orally, he shall confirm it in writing as soon as is practicable.

(6) Where—

(*a*) an authorisation has been given; and

(*b*) it is proposed that a non-intimate sample shall be taken in pursuance of the authorisation,

an officer shall inform the person from whom the sample is to be taken—

(i) of the giving of the authorisation; and

(ii) of the grounds for giving it.

(7) The duty imposed by subsection (6)(ii) above includes a duty to state the nature of the offence in which it is suspected that the person from whom the sample is to be taken has been involved.

(8) If a non-intimate sample is taken from a person by virtue of subsection (3) above—

(*a*) the authorisation by virtue of which it was taken; and

(*b*) the grounds for giving the authorisation,

shall be recorded as soon as is practicable after the sample is taken.

(9) If a non-intimate sample is taken from a person detained at a police station, the matters required to be recorded by subsection (8) above shall be recorded in his custody record.

Destruction of fingerprints and samples

64.—(1) If—

(*a*) fingerprints or samples are taken from a person in connection with the investigation of an offence; and

(*b*) he is cleared of that offence,

they must be destroyed as soon as is practicable after the conclusion of the proceedings.

(2) If—

(*a*) fingerprints or samples are taken from a person in connection with such an investigation; and

(*b*) it is decided that he shall not be prosecuted for the offence and he has not admitted it and has been dealt with by way of being cautioned by a constable,

they must be destroyed as soon as is practicable after that decision is taken.

(3) If—

(*a*) fingerprints or samples are taken from a person in connection with the investigation of an offence; and

(*b*) that person is not suspected of having committed the offence, they must be destroyed as soon as they have fulfilled the purpose for which they were taken.

(4) Proceedings which are discontinued are to be treated as concluded for the purposes of this section.

(5) If fingerprints are destroyed, any copies of them shall also be destroyed.

(6) A person who asks to be allowed to witness the destruction of his fingerprints or copies of them shall have a right to witness it.

(7) Nothing in this section—

(*a*) affects any power conferred by paragraph 18(2) of Schedule 2 to the Immigration Act 1971; or

(*b*) applies to a person arrested or detained under the terrorism provisions.

Fingerprints and samples—supplementary

65. In this Part of this Act—

"appropriate consent" means—

(*a*) in relation to a person who has attained the age of 17 years, the consent of that person;

(*b*) in relation to a person who has not attained that age but has attained the age of 14 years, the consent of that person and his parent or guardian; and

(*c*) in relation to a person who has not attained the age of 14 years, the consent of his parent or guardian;

"fingerprints" includes palm prints;

"intimate sample" means a sample of blood, semen or any other tissue fluid, urine, saliva or pubic hair, or a swab taken from a person's body orifice

"non-intimate sample" means—

(*a*) a sample of hair other than pubic hair,

(*b*) a sample taken from a nail or from under a nail;

(*c*) a swab taken from any part of a person's body other than a body orifice;

(*d*) a footprint or a similar impression of any part of a person's body other than a part of his hand;

"the terrorism provisions" means—

(*a*) section 12(1) of the Prevention of Terrorism (Temporary Provisions) Act 1984; and

(*b*) any provision conferring a power of arrest or detention and contained in an order under section 13 of that Act; and

"terrorism" has the meaning assigned to it by section 14(1) of that Act.

PART VI

CODES OF PRACTICE—GENERAL

Codes of practice

66. The Secretary of State shall issue codes of practice in connection with—

(*a*) the exercise by police officers of statutory powers—

(i) to search a person without first arresting him; or

(ii) to search a vehicle without making an arrest;
(b) the detention, treatment, questioning and identification of persons by police officers;
(c) searches of premises by police officers; and
(d) the seizure of property found by police officers on persons or premises.

Codes of practice—supplementary

67.—(1) When the Secretary of State proposes to issue a code of practice to which this section applies, he shall prepare and publish a draft of that code, shall consider any representations made to him about the draft and may modify the draft accordingly.

(2) This section applies to a code of practice under Section 60 or 66 above.

(3) The Secretary of State shall lay before both Houses of Parliament a draft of any code of practice prepared by him under this section.

(4) When the Secretary of State has laid the draft of a code before Parliament, he may bring the code into operation by order made by statutory instrument.

(5) No order under subsection (4) above shall have effect until approved by a resolution of each House of Parliament.

(6) An order bringing a code of practice into operation may contain such transitional provisions or savings as appear to the Secretary of State to be necessary or expedient in connection with the code of practice thereby brought into operation.

(7) The Secretary of State may from time to time revise the whole or any part of a code of practice to which this section applies and issue that revised code, and the foregoing provisions of this section shall apply (with appropriate modifications) to such a revised code as they apply to the first issue of a code.

(8) A police officer shall be liable to disciplinary proceedings for a failure to comply with any provision of such a code, unless such proceedings are precluded by section 104 below.

(9) Persons other than police officers who are charged with the duty of investigating offences or charging offenders shall in the discharge of that duty have regard to any relevant provision of such a code.

(10) A failure on the part
(a) of a police officer to comply with any provision of such a code; or
(b) of any person other than a police officer who is charged with the duty of investigating offences or charging offenders to have regard to any relevant provision of such a code in the discharge of that duty.
shall not of itself render him liable to any criminal or civil proceedings.

(11) In all criminal and civil proceedings any such code shall be admissible in evidence, and if any provision of such a code appears to the court or tribunal conducting the proceedings to be relevant to any question arising in the proceedings it shall be taken into account in determining that question.

(12) In this section "criminal proceedings" includes—
(a) proceedings in the United Kingdom or elsewhere before a court-martial constituted under the Army Act 1955, or the Air Force Act 1955 or the Naval Discipline Act 1957 or a disciplinary court constituted under section 50 of the said Act of 1957;
(b) proceedings before the Courts-Martial Appeal Court; and
(c) proceedings before a Standing Civilian Court.

PART VII

DOCUMENTARY EVIDENCE IN CRIMINAL PROCEEDINGS

Evidence from documentary records

68.—(1) Subject to section 69 below, a statement in a document shall be admissible in any proceedings as evidence of any fact stated therein of which direct oral evidence would be admissible if—

(*a*) the document is or forms part of a record compiled by a person acting under a duty from information supplied by a person (whether acting under a duty or not) who had, or may reasonably be supposed to have had, personal knowledge of the matters dealt with in that information; and

(*b*) any condition relating to the person who supplied the information which is specified in subsection (2) below is satisfied.

(2) The conditions mentioned in subsection (1)(*b*) above are—

(*a*) that the person who supplied the information—

(i) is dead or by reason of his bodily or mental condition unfit to attend as a witness;

(ii) is outside the United Kingdom and it is not reasonably practicable to secure his attendance; or

(iii) cannot reasonably be expected (having regard to the time which has elapsed since he supplied or acquired the information and to all the circumstances) to have any recollection of the matters dealt with in that information;

(*b*) that all reasonable steps have been taken to identify the person who supplied the information but that he cannot be identified; and

(*c*) that, the identity of the person who supplied the information being known, all reasonable steps have been taken to find him, but that he cannot be found.

(3) Nothing in this section shall prejudice the admissibility of any evidence that would be admissible apart from this section.

Evidence from computer records

69.—(1) In any proceedings, a statement contained in a document produced by a computer shall not be admissible as evidence of any fact stated therein unless it is shown—

(*a*) that there are no reasonable grounds for believing that the statement is inaccurate because of improper use of the computer;

(*b*) that at all material times the computer was operating properly, or if not, that any respect in which it was not operating properly or was out of operation was not such as to affect the production of the document or the accuracy of its contents; and

(*c*) that any relevant conditions specified in rules of court under subsection (2) below are satisfied.

(2) Provision may be made by rules of court requiring that in any proceedings where it is desired to give a statement in evidence by virtue of this section such information concerning the statement as may be required by the rules shall be provided in such form and at such time as may be so required.

Provisions supplementary to sections 68 and 69

70.—(1) Part I of Schedule 3 to this Act shall have effect for the purpose of supplementing section 68 above.

(2) Part II of that Schedule shall have effect for the purpose of supplementing section 69 above.

(3) Part III of that Schedule shall have effect for the purpose of supplementing both sections.

Microfilm copies

71. In any proceedings the contents of a document may (whether or not the document is still in existence) be proved by the production of an enlargement of a microfilm copy of that document or of the material part of it, authenticated in such manner as the court may approve.

Part VII—supplementary

72.—(1) In this Part of this Act—

"copy" and "statement" have the same meanings as in Part I of the Civil Evidence Act 1968; and

"proceedings" means criminal proceedings, including—

(*a*) proceedings in the United Kingdom or elsewhere before a court martial constituted under the Army Act 1955 or the Air Force Act 1955

(*b*) proceedings in the United Kingdom or elsewhere before the Courts-Martial Appeal Court—

(i) on an appeal from a court-martial so constituted or from a court-martial constituted under the Naval Discipline Act 1957; or

(ii) on a reference under section 34 of the Courts-Martial (Appeals) Act 1968; and

(*c*) proceedings before a Standing Civilian Court.

(2) Nothing in this Part of this Act shall prejudice any power of any court to exclude evidence (whether by preventing questions from being put or otherwise) at its discretion.

PART VIII

EVIDENCE IN CRIMINAL PROCEEDINGS—GENERAL

Convictions and acquittals

Proof of convictions and acquittals

73.—(1) Where in any proceedings the fact that a person has in the United Kingdom been convicted or acquitted of an offence otherwise than by a Service court is admissible in evidence, it may be proved by producing a certificate of conviction or, as the case may be, of acquittal relating to that offence, and proving that the person named in the certificate as having been convicted or acquitted of the offence is the person whose conviction or acquittal of the offence is to be proved.

(2) For the purposes of this section a certificate of conviction or of acquittal—

(*a*) shall, as regards a conviction or acquittal on indictment, consist of a certificate, signed by the clerk of the court where the conviction or acquittal took place, giving the substance and effect (omitting the formal parts) of the indictment and of the conviction or acquittal; and

(*b*) shall, as regards a conviction or acquittal on a summary trial, consist of a copy of the conviction or of the dismissal of the information, signed by the clerk of the court where the conviction or acquittal took place or by the clerk of the court, if any, to which a memorandum of the conviction or acquittal was sent;

and a document purporting to be a duly signed certificate of conviction or acquittal under this section shall be taken to be such a certificate unless the contrary is proved.

(3) References in this section to the clerk of a court include references to his deputy and to any other person having the custody of the court record.

(4) The method of proving a conviction or acquittal authorised by this section shall be in addition to and not to the exclusion of any other authorised manner of proving a conviction or acquittal.

Conviction as evidence of commission of offence

74.—(1) In any proceedings the fact that a person other than the accused has been convicted of an offence by or before any court in the United Kingdom or by a Service court outside the United Kingdom shall be admissible in evidence for the purpose of proving, where to do so is relevant to any issue in those proceedings, that that person committed that offence, whether or not any other evidence of his having committed that offence is given.

(2) In any proceedings in which by virtue of this section a person other than the accused is proved to have been convicted of an offence by or before any court in the United Kingdom or by a Service court outside the United Kingdom, he shall be taken to have committed that offence unless the contrary is proved.

(3) In any proceedings where evidence is admissible of the fact that the accused has committed an offence, in so far as that evidence is relevant to any matter in issue in the proceedings for a reason other than a tendency to show in the accused a disposition to commit the kind of offence with which he is charged, if the accused is proved to have been convicted of the offence—

(*a*) by or before any court in the United Kingdom; or
(*b*) by a Service court outside the United Kingdom,

he shall be taken to have committed that offence unless the contrary is proved.

(4) Nothing in this section shall prejudice—

(*a*) the admissibility in evidence of any conviction which would be admissible apart from this section; or
(*b*) the operation of any enactment whereby a conviction or a finding of fact in any proceedings is for the purposes of any other proceedings made conclusive evidence of any fact.

Provisions supplementary to s.74

75.—(1) Where evidence that a person has been convicted of an offence is admissible by virtue of section 74 above, then without prejudice to the reception of any other admissible evidence for the purpose of identifying the facts on which the conviction was based—

(*a*) the contents of any document which is admissible as evidence of the conviction; and
(*b*) the contents of the information, complaint, indictment or charge-sheet on which the person in question was convicted,

shall be admissible in evidence for that purpose.

(2) Where in any proceedings the contents of any document are admissible in evidence by virtue of subsection (1) above, a copy of that

document, or of the material part of it, purporting to be certified or otherwise authenticated by or on behalf of the court or authority having custody of that document shall be admissible in evidence and shall be taken to be a true copy of that document or part unless the contrary is shown.

(3) Nothing in any of the following—

(a) section 13 of the Powers of Criminal Courts Act 1973 (under which a conviction leading to probation or discharge is to be disregarded except as mentioned in that section);

(b) section 392 of the Criminal Procedure (Scotland) Act 1975 (which makes similar provision in respect of convictions on indictment in Scotland); and

(c) section 8 of the Probation Act (Northern Ireland) 1950 (which corresponds to section 13 of the Powers of Criminal Courts Act 1973) or any legislation which is in force in Northern Ireland for the time being and corresponds to that section,

shall affect the operation of section 74 above; and for the purposes of that section any order made by a court of summary jurisdiction in Scotland under section 182 or section 183 of the said Act of 1975 shall be treated as a conviction.

(4) Nothing in section 74 above shall be construed as rendering admissible in any proceedings evidence of any conviction other than a subsisting one.

Miscellaneous

Confessions

76.—(1) In any proceedings a confession made by an accused person may be given in evidence against him in so far as it is relevant to any matter in issue in the proceedings and is not excluded by the court in pursuance of this section.

(2) If, in any proceedings where the prosecution proposes to give in evidence a confession made by an accused person, it is represented to the court that the confession was or may have been obtained—

(a) by oppression of the person who made it; or

(b) in consequence of anything said or done which was likely, in the circumstances existing at the time, to render unreliable any confession which might be made by him in consequence thereof,

the court shall not allow the confession to be given in evidence against him except in so far as the prosecution proves to the court beyond reasonable doubt that the confession (notwithstanding that it may be true) was not obtained as aforesaid.

(3) In any proceedings where the prosecution proposes to give in evidence a confession made by an accused person, the court may of its own motion require the prosecution, as a condition of allowing it to do so, to prove that the confession was not obtained as mentioned in subsection (2) above.

(4) The fact that a confession is wholly or partly excluded in pursuance of this section shall not affect the admissibility in evidence—

(a) of any facts discovered as a result of the confession; or

(b) where the confession is relevant as showing that the accused speaks, writes or expresses himself in a particular way, of so much of the confession as is necessary to show that he does so.

(5) Evidence that a fact to which this subsection applies was discovered as a result of a statement made by an accused person shall not be admissible unless evidence of how it was discovered is given by him or on his behalf.

(6) Subsection (5) above applies—
    (*a*) to any fact discovered as a result of a confession which is wholly excluded in pursuance of this section; and
    (*b*) to any fact discovered as a result of a confession which is partly so excluded, if that fact is discovered as a result of the excluded part of the confession.

(7) Nothing in Part VII of this Act shall prejudice the admissibility of a confession made by an accused person.

(8) In this section "oppression" includes torture, inhuman or degrading treatment, and the use or threat of violence (whether or not amounting to torture).

Confessions by mentally handicapped persons

77.—(1) Without prejudice to the general duty of the court at a trial on indictment to direct the jury on any matter on which it appears to the court appropriate to do so, where at such a trial—
    (*a*) the case against the accused depends wholly or substantially on a confession by him; and
    (*b*) the court is satisfied—
        (i) that he is mentally handicapped; and
        (ii) that the confession was not made in the presence of an independent person,
the court shall warn the jury that there is special need for caution before convicting the accused in reliance on the confession, and shall explain that the need arises because of the circumstances mentioned in paragraphs (*a*) and (*b*) above, but in doing so shall not be required to use any particular form of words.

(2) In any case where at the summary trial of a person for an offence it appears to the court that a warning under subsection (1) above would be required if the trial were on indictment, the court shall treat the case as one in which there is a special need for caution before convicting the accused on his confession.

(3) In this section—
    "independent person" does not include a police officer or a person employed for, or engaged on police purposes;
    "mentally handicapped", in relation to a person, means that he is in a state of arrested or incomplete development of mind which includes significant impairment of intelligence and social functioning; and
    "police purposes" has the meaning assigned to it by section 64 of the Police Act 1964.

Exclusion of unfair evidence

78.—(1) In any proceedings the court may refuse to allow evidence on which the prosecution proposes to rely to be given if it appears to the court that, having regard to all the circumstances, including the circumstances in which the evidence was obtained, the admission of the evidence would have such an adverse effect on the fairness of the proceedings that the court ought not to admit it.

(2) Nothing in this section shall prejudice any rule of law requiring a court to exclude evidence.

Time for taking accused's evidence

79. If at the trial of any person for an offence—
    (*a*) the defence intends to call two or more witnesses to the facts of the case; and
    (*b*) those witnesses include the accused,

the accused shall be called before the other witness or witnesses unless the court in its discretion otherwise directs.

Competence and compellability of accused's spouse

80.—(1) In any proceedings the wife or husband of the accused shall be competent to give evidence—

(*a*) subject to subsection (4) below, for the prosecution; and

(*b*) on behalf of the accused or any person jointly charged with the accused.

(2) In any proceedings the wife or husband of the accused shall, subject to subsection (4) below, be compellable to give evidence on behalf of the accused.

(3) In any proceedings the wife or husband of the accused shall, subject to subsection (4) below, be compellable to give evidence for the prosecution or on behalf of any person jointly charged with the accused if and only if—

(*a*) the offence charged involves an assault on, or injury or a threat of injury to, the wife or husband of the accused or a person who was at the material time under the age of sixteen; or

(*b*) the offence charged is a sexual offence alleged to have been committed in respect of a person who was at the material time under that age; or

(*c*) the offence charged consists of attempting or conspiring to commit, or of aiding, abetting, counselling, procuring or inciting the commission of, an offence falling within paragraph (*a*) or (*b*) above.

(4) Where a husband and wife are jointly charged with an offence neither spouse shall at the trial be competent or compellable by virtue of subsection (1)(*a*), (2) or (3) above to give evidence in respect of that offence unless that spouse is not, or is no longer, liable to be convicted of that offence at the trial as a result of pleading guilty or for any other reason.

(5) In any proceedings a person who has been but is no longer married to the accused shall be competent and compellable to give evidence as if that person and the accused had never been married.

(6) Where in any proceedings the age of any person at any time is material for the purposes of subsection (3) above, his age at the material time shall for the purposes of that provision be deemed to be or to have been that which appears to the court to be or to have been his age at that time.

(7) In subsection (3)(*b*) above "sexual offence" means an offence under the Sexual Offences Act 1956, the Indecency with Children Act 1960, the Sexual Offences Act 1967, section 54 of the Criminal Law Act 1977 or the Protection of Children Act 1978.

(8) The failure of the wife or husband of the accused to give evidence shall not be made the subject of any comment by the prosecution.

(9) Section 1(*d*) of the Criminal Evidence Act 1898 (communications between husband and wife) and section 43(1) of the Matrimonial Causes Act 1965 (evidence as to marital intercourse) shall cease to have effect.

Advance notice of expert evidence in Crown Court

81.—(1) Crown Court Rules may make provision for—

(*a*) requiring any party to proceedings before the Court to disclose to the other party or parties any expert evidence which he proposes to adduce in the proceedings; and

(*b*) prohibiting a party who fails to comply in respect of any evidence with any requirement imposed by virtue of paragraph (*a*) above from adducing that evidence without the leave of the court.

(2) Crown Court Rules made by virtue of this section may specify the kinds of expert evidence to which they apply and may exempt facts or matters of any description specified in the rules.

Part VIII—Supplementary

Interpretation of Part VIII

82.—(1) In this Part of this Act—

"confession" includes any statement wholly or partly adverse to the person who made it, whether made to a person in authority or not and whether made in words or otherwise;

"court-martial" means a court-martial constituted under the Army Act 1955, the Air Force Act 1955 or the Naval Discipline Act 1957 or a disciplinary court constituted under section 50 of the said Act of 1957;

"proceedings" means criminal proceedings, including—

    (*a*) proceedings in the United Kingdom or elsewhere before a court-martial constituted under the Army Act 1955 or the Air Force Act 1955;

    (*b*) proceedings in the United Kingdom or elsewhere before the Courts-Martial Appeal Court—

        (i) on an appeal from a court-martial so constituted or from a court-martial constituted under the Naval Discipline Act 1957; or

        (ii) on a reference under section 34 of the Courts-Martial (Appeals) Act 1968; and

    (*c*) proceedings before a Standing Civilian Court; and

    "Service court" means a court-martial or a Standing Civilian Court.

(2) In this Part of this Act references to conviction before a Service court are references—

    (*a*) as regards a court-martial constituted under the Army Act 1955 or the Air Force Act 1955, to a finding of guilty which is, or falls to be treated as, a finding of the court duly confirmed;

    (*b*) as regards—

        (i) a court-martial; or

        (ii) a disciplinary court,

    constituted under the Naval Discipline Act 1957, to a finding of guilty which is, or falls to be treated as, the finding of the court;

and "convicted" shall be construed accordingly.

to exclude evidence (whether by preventing questions from being put or otherwise) at its discretion.

PART IX

POLICE COMPLAINTS AND DISCIPLINE

The Police Complaints Authority

Establishment of the Police Complaints Authority

83.—(1) There shall be an authority, to be known as "the Police Complaints Authority" and in this Part of this Act referred to as "the Authority.".

(2) Schedule 4 to this Act shall have effect in relation to the Authority.

(3) The Police Complaints Board is hereby abolished.

Handling of complaints etc.

Preliminary

84.—(1) Where a complaint is submitted to the chief officer of police for a police area, it shall be his duty to take any steps that appear to him to be desirable for the purpose of obtaining or preserving evidence relating to the conduct complained of.

(2) After performing the duties imposed on him by subsection (1) above, the chief officer shall determine whether he is the appropriate authority in relation to the officer against whom the complaint was made.

(3) If he determines that he is not the appropriate authority, it shall be his duty—

    (*a*) to send the complaint or, if it was made orally, particulars of it, to the appropriate authority, and

    (*b*) to give notice that he has done so to the person by or on whose behalf the complaint was made.

(4) In this part of this Act—

"complaint" means any complaint about the conduct of a police officer which is submitted—

    (*a*) by a member of the public; or

    (*b*) on behalf of a member of the public and with his written consent;

"the appropriate authority means—

    (*a*) in relation to an officer of the metropolitan police, the Commissioner of Police of the Metropolis; and

    (*b*) in relation to an officer or any other police force—

        (i) if he is a senior officer, the police authority for the force's area; and

        (ii) if he is not a senior officer, the chief officer of the force;

    "senior officer" means an officer holding a rank above the rank of chief superintendent.

(5) Nothing in this Part of this Act has effect in relation to a complaint in so far as it relates to the direction or control of a police force by the chief officer or the person performing the functions of the chief officer.

(6) If any conduct to which a complaint wholly or partly relates is or has been the subject of criminal or disciplinary proceedings, none of the provisions of this Part of this Act which relate to the recording and investigation of complaints have effect in relation to the complaint in so far as it relates to that conduct.

Investigation of complaints: standard procedure

85.—(1) If a chief officer determines that he is the appropriate authority in relation to an officer, about whose conduct a complaint has been made and who is not a senior officer, he shall record it.

(2) After doing so he shall consider whether the complaint is suitable for informal resolution and may appoint an officer from his force to assist him.

(3) If it appears to the chief officer that the complaint is not suitable for informal resolution, he shall appoint an officer from his force or some other force to investigate it formally.

(4) If it appears to him that it is suitable for informal resolution, he shall seek to resolve it informally and may appoint an officer from his force to do so on his behalf.

(5) If it appears to the chief officer, after attempts have been made to resolve a complaint informally,—

(*a*) that informal resolution of the complaint is impossible; or

(*b*) that the complaint is for any other reason not suitable for informal resolution,

he shall appoint an officer from his force or some other force to investigate it formally.

(6) An officer may not be appointed to investigate a complaint formally if he has previously been appointed to act in relation to it under subsection (4) above.

(7) If a chief officer requests the chief officer of some other force to provide an officer of his force for appointment under subsection (3) or (5) above, that chief officer shall provide an officer to be so appointed.

(8) No officer may be appointed under this section unless he is—

(*a*) of at least the rank of chief inspector; and

(*b*) of at least the rank of the officer against whom the complaint is made.

(9) Unless investigation under this section is supervised by the Authority under section 89 below, the investigating officer shall submit his report on the investigation to the chief officer.

(10) A complaint is not suitable for informal resolution unless—

(*a*) the member of the public concerned gives his consent; and

(*b*) the chief officer is satisfied that the conduct complained of, even if proved, would not justify a criminal or disciplinary charge.

Investigation of complaints against senior officers

86.—(1) Where a complaint about the conduct of a senior officer—

(*a*) is submitted to the appropriate authority; or

(*b*) is sent to the appropriate authority under section 84(3) above,

it shall be the appropriate authority's duty to record it and, subject to subsection (2) below, to investigate it.

(2) The appropriate authority may deal with the complaint according to the appropriate authority's discretion, if satisfied that the conduct complained of, even if proved, would not justify a criminal or disciplinary charge.

(3) In any other case the appropriate authority shall appoint an officer from the appropriate authority's force or from some other force to investigate the complaint.

(4) A chief officer shall provide an officer to be appointed, if a request is made to him for one to be appointed under subsection (3) above.

(5) No officer may be appointed unless he is of at least the rank of the officer against whom the complaint is made.

(6) Unless an investigation under this section is supervised by the Authority under section 89 below, the investigating officer shall submit his report on it to the appropriate authority.

References of complaints to Authority

87.—(1) The appropriate authority—

(*a*) shall refer to the Authority—

(i) any complaint alleging that the conduct complained of resulted in the death of or serious injury to some other person; and

(ii) any complaint of a description specified for the purposes of this section in regulations made by the Secretary of State, and (*b*) may refer to the Authority any complaint which is not required to be referred to them.

(2) The Authority may require the submission to them for consideration of any complaint not referred to them by the appropriate authority, and it shall be the appropriate authority's duty to comply with any such requirement not later than the end of a period specified in regulations made by the Secretary of State.

(3) Where a complaint falls to be referred to the Authority under subsection (1)(*a*) above, it shall be the appropriate authority's duty to refer it to them not later than the end of a period specified in such regulations.

(4) In this Part of this Act "serious injury" means a fracture, damage to an internal organ, impairment of bodily function, a deep cut or a deep laceration.

References of other matters to Authority

88. The appropriate authority may refer to the Authority any matter which—

(*a*) appears to the appropriate authority to indicate that an officer may have committed a criminal offence or an offence against discipline; and

(*b*) is not the subject of a complaint,

if it appears to the appropriate authority that it ought to be referred by reason—

(i) of its gravity; or

(ii) of exceptional circumstances.

Supervision of investigations by Authority

89.—(1) The Authority shall supervise the investigation—

(*a*) of any complaint alleging that the conduct of a police officer resulted in the death or a serious injury to some other person; and

(*b*) of any other description of complaint specified for the purposes of this section in regulations made by the Secretary of State.

(2) The Authority shall supervise the investigation—

(*a*) of any complaint the investigation of which they are not required to supervise under subsection (1) above; and

(*b*) of any matter referred to them under section 88 above,

if they consider that it is desirable in the public interest that they should supervise that investigation.

(3) Where the Authority have made a determination under subsection (2) above, it shall be their duty to notify it to the appropriate authority.

(4) Where an investigation is to be supervised by the Authority they may require—

(*a*) that no appointment shall be made under section 85(3) or 86(3) above unless they have given notice to the appropriate authority that they approve the officer whom that authority propose to appoint; or

(*b*) if such an appointment has already been made and the Authority are not satisfied with the officer appointed, that—

(i) the appropriate authority shall, as soon as is reasonably practicable, select another officer and notify the Authority that they propose to appoint him; and

(ii) the appointment shall not be made unless the Authority give notice to the appropriate authority that they approve that officer.

(5) It shall be the duty of the Secretary of State by regulations to provide that the Authority shall have power, subject to any restrictions or conditions specified in the regulations, to impose requirements as to a particular investigation additional to any requirements imposed by virtue of subsection (4) above and it shall be the duty of a police officer to comply with any requirement imposed on him by virtue of the regulations.

(6) At the end of an investigation which the Authority have supervised, the investigating officer—

(a) shall submit a report on the investigation to the Authority and

(b) shall send a copy to the appropriate authority.

(7) After considering a report submitted to them under subsection (6) above the Authority shall submit an appropriate statement to the appropriate authority.

(8) If it is practicable to do so, the Authority, when submitting the appropriate statement under subsection (7) above, shall send a copy to the officer whose conduct has been investigated.

(9) If—

(a) the investigation related to a complaint; and

(b) it is practicable to do so,

the Authority shall also send a copy of the appropriate statement to the person by or on behalf of whom the complaint was made.

(10) In subsection (7) above "appropriate statement" means a statement—

(a) whether the investigation was or was not conducted to the Authority's satisfaction;

(b) specifying any respect in which it was not so conducted; and

(c) dealing with any such other matters as the Secretary of State may by regulations provide.

(11) The power to issue an appropriate statement includes power to issue separate statements in respect of the disciplinary and criminal aspects of an investigation.

(12) No disciplinary charge shall be brought before the appropriate statement is submitted to the appropriate authority.

(13) Subject to subsection (14) below, neither the appropriate authority nor the Director of Public Prosecutions shall bring criminal proceedings before the appropriate statement is submitted to the appropriate authority.

(14) The restriction imposed by subsection (13) above does not apply if it appears to the Director that there are exceptional circumstances which make it undesirable to wait for the submission of the appropriate statement.

Steps to be taken after investigation—general

90.—(1) It shall be the duty of the appropriate authority, on receiving—

(a) a report concerning the conduct of a senior officer which is submitted to them under section 86(6) above; or

(b) a copy of a report concerning the conduct of a senior officer which is sent to them under section 89(7) above,

to send a copy of the report to the Director of Public Prosecutions unless the report satisfies them that no criminal offence has been committed.

(2) Nothing in the following provisions of this section or in sections 91 to 93 below has effect in relation to senior officers.

(3) On receiving—

(a) a report concerning the conduct of an officer who is not a senior officer which is submitted to him under section 85(9) above; or (*b*) a copy of a report concerning the conduct of such an officer which is sent to him under section 89(7) above—

it shall be the duty of a chief officer of police—

> (i) to determine whether the report indicates that a criminal offence may have been committed by a member of the police force for his area; and
>
> (ii) if he determines that it does, to determine whether the offence indicated is such that the officer ought to be charged with it.

(4) If the chief officer—

(*a*) determines that the report does indicate that a criminal offence may have been committed by a member of the police force for his area; and

(*b*) considers that the offence indicated is such that the officer ought to be charged with it,

he shall send a copy of the report to the Director of Public Prosecutions.

(5) Subject to section 91(1) below, after the Director has dealt with the question of criminal proceedings, the chief officer shall send the Authority a memorandum, signed by him and stating whether he has preferred disciplinary charges in respect of the conduct which was the subject of the investigation and, if not, his reasons for not doing so.

(6) If the chief officer—

(*a*) determines that the report does indicate that a criminal offence may have been committed by a member of the police force for his area; and

(*b*) considers that the offence indicated is not such that the officer ought to be charged with it,

he shall send the Authority a memorandum to that effect, signed by him and stating whether he proposes to prefer disciplinary charges in respect of the conduct which was the subject of the investigation and, if not, his reasons for not proposing to do so.

(7) Subject to section 91(1) below, if the chief officer considers that the report does not indicate that a criminal offence may have been committed by a member of the police force for his area, he shall send the Authority a memorandum to that effect, signed by him and stating whether he has preferred disciplinary charges in respect of the conduct which was the subject of the investigation and, if not, his reasons for not doing so.

(8) A memorandum under this section—

(*a*) shall give particulars—

> (i) of any disciplinary charges which a chief officer has preferred or proposes to prefer in respect of the conduct which was the subject of the investigation; and
>
> (ii) of any exceptional circumstances affecting the case by reason of which he considers that section 94 below should apply to the hearing; and

(*b*) shall state his opinion of the complaint or other matter to which it relates.

(9) Where the investigation—

(*a*) related to conduct which was the subject of a complaint; and

(*b*) was not supervised by the authority,

the chief officer shall send the Authority—

> (i) a copy of the complaint or of the record of the complaint; and
>
> (ii) a copy of the report of the investigation

at the same time as he sends them the memorandum.

(10) Subject to section 93(6) below—

(*a*) if a chief officer's memorandum states that he proposes to

prefer disciplinary charges, it shall be his duty to prefer and proceed with them; and
(b) if such a memorandum states that he has preferred such charges, it shall be his duty to proceed with them.

Steps to be taken where accused has admitted charges

91.—(1) No memorandum need be sent to the Authority under section 90 above if disciplinary charges have been preferred in respect of the conduct which was the subject of the investigation and the accused has admitted the charges and has not withdrawn his admission.

(2) In any such case the chief officer shall send to the Authority, after the conclusion of the disciplinary proceedings (including any appeal to the Secretary of State), particulars of the disciplinary charges preferred and of any punishment imposed.

(3) If—
(a) the charges related to conduct which was the subject of a complaint; and
(b) the investigation of the complaint was not supervised by the Authority,
the chief officer shall also send the Authority—
(i) a copy of the complaint or of the record of the complaint; and
(ii) a copy of the report of the investigation.

Powers of Authority to direct reference of reports etc. to Director of Public Prosecutions

92.—(1) When a chief officer of police has performed all duties imposed on him by section 90 and 91 above in relation to the report of an investigation concerning the conduct of an officer who is not a senior officer, it shall be the duty of the Authority—
(a) to determine whether the report indicates that a criminal offence may have been committed by that officer; and
(b) if so, the offence is such that the officer ought to be charged with it.

(2) If the Authority determine that the officer ought to be charged, it shall be their duty to direct the chief officer to send the Director of Public Prosecutions a copy of the report.

(3) When the Authority give a direction under subsection (2) above, they may also direct the chief officer to send the Director the information contained in the memorandum under section 90 above.

(4) If the investigation was an investigation of a complaint, the Authority shall direct the chief officer to send the Director a copy of the complaint or of the record of the complaint.

(5) It shall be the duty of a chief officer to comply with any direction under this section.

(6) Sections 90 and 91 above shall apply where a copy of a report is sent to the Director under this section as they apply where a copy is sent to him under section 90(4) above.

Powers of Authority as to disciplinary charges

93.—(1) Where a memorandum under section 83 above states that a chief officer of police has not preferred disciplinary charges or does not propose to do so, the Authority may recommend him to prefer such disciplinary charges as they may specify.

(2) Subject to subsection (6) below, a chief officer may not withdraw charges which he has preferred in accordance with a recommendation under subsection (1) above.

(3) If after the Authority have made a recommendation under this section and consulted the chief officer he is still unwilling to prefer such charges as the Authority consider appropriate, they may direct him to prefer such charges as they may specify.

(4) Where the Authority give a chief officer a direction under this section, they shall furnish him with a written statement of their reasons for doing so.

(5) Subject to subsection (6) below, it shall be the duty of a chief officer to prefer and proceed with charges specified in such a direction.

(6) The Authority may give a chief officer leave—

    (*a*) not to prefer charges which section 90(10) above or subsection (5) above would otherwise oblige him to prefer; or

    (*b*) not to proceed with charges with which section 90(10) above or subsection (2) or (5) above would otherwise oblige him to proceed.

(7) The Authority may request a chief officer of police to furnish them with such information as they may reasonably require for the purpose of discharging their functions under this section.

(8) It shall be the duty of a chief officer to comply with any such request.

Disciplinary tribunals

94.—(1) Where a chief officer of police prefers a disciplinary charge in respect of a matter to which a memorandum under section 90 above relates, this section applies—

    (*a*) to the hearing of any charge in pursuance of a direction under section 93 above; and

    (*b*) to the hearing of any other charge to which the Authority direct that it shall apply.

(2) The Authority may direct that this section shall apply to the hearing of a charge if they consider that to be desirable by reason of any exceptional circumstances affecting the case.

(3) Where this section applies to the hearing of a disciplinary charge—

    (*a*) the function of determining whether the accused is guilty of the charge shall be discharged by a tribunal consisting of—

        (i) a chairman who shall, subject to subsection (4) below, be the chief officer of police by whom that function would fall to be discharged apart from this section; and

        (ii) two members of the Authority nominated by the Authority, being members who have not been concerned with the case; and

    (*b*) the function of determining any punishment to be imposed shall, subject to subsection (7) below, be discharged by the chairman after consulting the other members of the tribunal.

(4) Where—

    (*a*) the accused is a member of the metropolitan police force; and

    (*b*) the function of determining whether he is guilty of the charge would, apart from this section, fall to be discharged by a person or persons other than a chief officer of police (whether the Commissioner of Police of the Metropolis or the chief officer of another police force),

the chairman of the tribunal shall be—

        (i) a person nominated by the Commissioner, being either an Assistant Commissioner of Police of the Metropolis or an officer of the metropolitan police force of such rank as may be prescribed by regulations made by the Secretary of State; or

(ii) in default of any such nomination, the Commissioner.

(5) The Secretary of State may by regulations provide for the procedure to be followed by tribunals constituted under this section.

(6) The decision of the tribunal as to whether the accused is guilty of the charge may be a majority decision.

(7) Where—

    (a) the chairman of the tribunal is not the chief officer of police of the police force to which the accused belongs, and

    (b) that chief officer is neither interested in the case otherwise than in his capacity as such nor a material witness,

the function of determining any punishment to be imposed shall be discharged by that chief officer after considering any recommendation as to punishment made by the chairman.

(8) Before making any recommendation the chairman shall consult the other members of the tribunal.

(9) Where—

    (a) this section applies to the hearing of a disciplinary charge; and

    (b) there is another disciplinary charge against the accused which, in the opinion of the chief officer of police of the police force to which he belongs, can conveniently and fairly be determined at the same time,

the chief officer may direct that this section shall apply also to the hearing of the other charge.

Information as to the manner of dealing with complaints

95. Every police authority in carrying out their duty with respect to the maintenance of an adequate and efficient police force, and inspectors of constabulary in carrying out their duties with respect to the efficiency of any police force, shall keep themselves informed as to the working of sections 84 to 93 above in relation to the force.

Constabularies maintained by authorities other than police authorities

96.—(1) An agreement for the establishment in relation to any body of constables maintained by an authority other than a police authority of procedures corresponding to any of those established by or by virtue of this Part of this Act may, with the approval of the Secretary of State, be made between the Authority and the Authority maintaining the body of constables.

(2) Where no such procedures are in force in relation to any body of constables, the Secretary of State may by order establish such procedures.

(3) An agreement under this section may at any time be varied or terminated with the approval of the Secretary of State.

(4) Before making an order under this section the Secretary of State shall consult—

    (a) the Authority; and

    (b) the authority maintaining the body of constables to whom the order would relate.

(5) The power to make orders under this section shall be exercisable by statutory instrument; and any statutory instrument containing such an order shall be subject to annulment in pursuance of a resolution of either House of Parliament.

(6) Nothing in any other enactment shall prevent an authority who maintain a body of constables from carrying into effect procedures established by virtue of this section.

(7) No such procedures shall have effect in relation to anything done by a constable outside England and Wales.

Reports

97.—(1) The Authority shall, at the request of the Secretary of State, report to him on such matters relating generally to their functions as the Secretary of State may specify, and the Authority may for that purpose carry out research into any such matters.

(2) The Authority may make a report to the Secretary of State on any matters coming to their notice under this Part of this Act to which they consider that his attention should be drawn by reason of their gravity or of other exceptional circumstances; and the Authority shall send a copy of any such report to the police authority and to the chief officer of police of any police force which appears to the Authority to be concerned or, if the report concerns any such body of constables as is mentioned in section 96 above, to the authority body maintaining it and the officer having the direction and the control of it.

(3) As soon as practicable after the end of each calendar year the Authority shall make to the Secretary of State a report on the discharge of their functions during that year.

(4) The Authority shall keep under review the working of sections 84 to 92 above and shall make to the Secretary of State a report on it at least once in every three years after the coming into force of this section.

(5) The Secretary of State shall lay before Parliament a copy of every report received by him under this section and shall cause every such report to be published.

(6) The Authority shall send to every police authority—
  (*a*) a copy of every report made by the Authority under subsection (3) above; and
  (*b*) any statistical or other general information which relates to the year dealt with by the report and to the area of that authority and which the Authority consider should be brought to the police authority's attention in connection with their functions under section 95 above.

Restriction on disclosure of information

98.—(1) No information received by the Authority in connection with any of their functions under section 84 to 97 above or regulations made by virtue of section 99 below shall be disclosed by any person who is or has been a member, officer or servant of the Authority except—
  (*a*) to the Secretary of State or to a member, officer or servant of the Authority or, so far as may be necessary for the proper discharge of the functions of the Authority, to other persons;
  (*b*) for the purposes of any criminal, civil or disciplinary proceedings; or
  (*c*) in the form of a summary or other general statement made by the Authority which does not identify the person from whom the information was received or any person to whom it relates.

(2) Any person who discloses information in contravention of this section shall be guilty of an offence and liable on summary conviction to a fine of an amount not exceeding level 5 on the standard scale, as defined in section 75 of the Criminal Justice Act 1982.

Regulations

99.—(1) The Secretary of State may make regulations as to the procedure to be followed under this Part of this Act.

(2) It shall be the duty of the Secretary of State to provide by regulations—

(a) that, subject to such exceptions as may be specified by the regulations, a chief officer of police shall furnish, in accordance with such procedure as may be so specified, a copy of, or of the record of, a complaint against a member of the police force for his area—
  (i) to the person by or on behalf of whom the complaint was made; and
  (ii) to the officer against whom it was made;
(b) procedures for the informal resolution of complaints of such descriptions as may be specified in the regulations, and for giving the person who made the complaint a record of the outcome of any such procedure if he applies for one within such period as the regulations may provide;
(c) procedures for giving a police officer against whom a complaint is made which falls to be resolved informally an opportunity to comment orally or in writing on the complaint;
(d) for cases in which any provision of this Part of this Act is not to apply where a complaint, other than a complaint which falls to be resolved by an informal procedure, is withdrawn or the complainant indicates that he does not wish any further steps to be taken;
(e) for enabling the Authority to dispense with any requirement of this Part of this Act;
(f) procedures for the reference or submission of complaints or other matters to the Authority;
(g) for the time within which the Authority are to give a notification under section 89(3) above;
(h) that the Authority shall be supplied with such information or documents of such description as may be specified in the regulations at such time or in such circumstances as may be so specified;
(j) that any action or decision of the Authority which they take in consequence of their receipt of a memorandum under section 90 above shall be notified if it is an action or decision of a description specified in the regulations, to the person concerned and that, in connection with such a notification, the Authority shall have power to furnish him with any relevant information;
(k) that chief officers of police shall have power to delegate any functions conferred on them by or by virtue of the foregoing provisions of this Part of this Act, other than their functions under section 94(3) above.

Regulations—supplementary

100.—(1) Regulations under this Part of this Act may make different provision for different circumstances and may authorise the Secretary of State to make provision for any purposes specified in the regulations.

(2) Before making regulations under this Part of this Act the Secretary of State shall furnish a draft of the regulations to the Police Advisory Board for England and Wales, and take into consideration any representations made by that Board.

(3) Any power to make regulations under this Part of this Act shall be exercisable by statutory instrument.

(4) Subject to subsection (5) below, regulations under this Part of this Act shall be subject to annulment in pursuance of a resolution of either House of Parliament.

(5) Regulations to which this subsection applies shall not be made unless a draft of them has been approved by resolution of each House of Parliament.

(6) Subsection (5) above applies to regulations made by virtue—

    (*a*) of section 87(1)(*a*)(ii) or 89(1)(*b*) or (6) above;

    (*b*) of section 99(2)(*b*) or (*e*) above.

Amendments of discipline provisions

Discipline regulations

101.—(1) Regulations under section 33(2)(*e*) of the Police Act 1964 (discipline regulations) shall provide—

    (*a*) for the determination of questions whether offences against discipline have been committed;

    (*b*) for racially discriminatory behaviour to be made a specific disciplinary offence; and

    (*c*) for members of police forces who are found to have committed such offences to be punished by way of dismissal, requirement to resign, reduction in rank, reduction in rate of pay, fine, reprimand or caution.

(2) In the case of a police force maintained under section 1 of that Act (county or combined police force) the regulations shall provide for the functions mentioned in subsection (1)(*a*) or (*b*) above to be discharged—

    (*a*) in relation to the chief constable, any deputy chief constable and any assistant chief constable, by the police authority;

    (*b*) in relation to any other member of the police force, by the chief constable,

but subject, in a case within paragraph (*b*) of this subsection, to section 94 above and the following provisions of this section.

(3) The regulations shall provide for the functions mentioned in subsection (1)(*a*) and (*b*) above to be discharged by another chief officer of police if, in a case within subsection (2)(*b*) above, the chief constable—

    (*a*) is interested in the case otherwise than in his capacity as such; or

    (*b*) is a material witness.

(4) Without prejudice to subsection (3) above, the regulations may, as respects any case within subsection (2)(*b*) above, provide—

    (*a*) for enabling a chief constable, where he considers it appropriate to do so, to direct that his function under subsection (1)(*a*) above shall be discharged by another chief officer of police; and

    (*b*) where such a direction is given, for the function mentioned in subsection (1)(*b*) above to be discharged by the chief constable after considering any recommendation as to punishment made by the other chief officer of police.

(5) Subject to subsection (6) below, the regulations may provide for enabling a chief constable to direct that his functions under subsection (1) above may be discharged by a deputy chief constable in any case—

    (*a*) which is within subsection (2)(*b*) above;

    (*b*) in which the decision that a disciplinary charge is to be brought is taken, in accordance with the regulations, by an assistant chief constable; and

    (*c*) in which it appears appropriate to the chief constable so to direct.

(6) In subsection (5) above the reference to functions under subsection (1) above does not include the functions mentioned in section 94(3) above.

(7) If regulations provide by virtue of subsection (5) above that any of the functions of a chief constable may be discharged by a deputy chief constable, they may provide that the deputy chief constable shall have power or shall be under a duty to remit any matter to the chief constable in such circumstances as the regulations may specify.

(8) If regulations provide as mentioned in subsection (5) above, they shall also provide—

> (a) that a deputy chief constable shall have power to punish only by way of reduction in rate of pay, fine, reprimand or caution;
>
> (b) that a police officer dealt with by a deputy chief constable may appeal to the chief constable; and
>
> (c) that on such an appeal the chief constable shall have no power to award a punishment greater than the punishment awarded by the deputy chief constable.

(9) Subsections (2) to (8) above shall apply in the case of the City of London police force as they apply in the case of a police force maintained under section 1 of the Police Act 1964 but with the substitution—

> (a) subject to paragraph (b) below, for references to a deputy chief constable or an assistant chief constable of references to an assistant commissioner of police for the City of London and any officer holding a rank appearing to the Secretary of State to correspond to that of assistant chief constable in a force maintained under that section;
>
> (b) for the reference in subsection (5) to a deputy chief constable of a reference to an officer of the City of London police force holding a rank such as is mentioned in paragraph (a) above but who is not the officer who has taken the decision mentioned in paragraph (b) of that subsection; and
>
> (c) for references to the chief constable of references to the Commissioner of Police for the City of London.

Representation at disciplinary hearings

102.—(1) On the hearing of a disciplinary charge against a police officer of the rank of chief superintendent or below the punishment of dismissal, requirement to resign or reduction in rank may not be awarded unless he has been given an opportunity to elect to be legally represented at the hearing.

(2) Where such an officer so elects, he may be represented at the hearing, at his option, either by counsel or by a solicitor.

(3) Except in a case where such an officer has been given an opportunity to elect to be legally represented and has so elected, he may only be represented at the hearing of a disciplinary charge by another member of a police force.

(4) Regulations under section 33(2)(e) of the Police Act 1964 shall specify—

> (a) a procedure for notifying an officer of the effect of subsections (1) to (3) above;
>
> (b) when he is to be so notified and when he is to give notice whether or not he wishes to be legally represented at the hearing.

(5) If an officer—

> (a) fails without reasonable cause to give notice in accordance with the regulations that he wishes to be legally represented: or
>
> (b) gives notice in accordance with the regulations that he does not wish to be legally represented,

any such punishment as is mentioned in subsection (1) above may be awarded without his being legally represented.

(6) If an officer has given notice in accordance with the regulations that he wishes to be legally represented, the case against him may be presented by counsel or a solicitor whether or not he is actually so represented.

Disciplinary appeals

103.—(1) The following section shall be substituted for section 37 of the Police Act 1964—

"Disciplinary appeals to Secretary of State

37.—(1) A member of a police force who is dealt with for an offence against discipline may appeal to the Secretary of State—

    (*a*) against the decision on the disciplinary charge which was preferred against him;

    (*b*) against any punishment awarded,

except where he has a right of appeal to some other person; and in that case he may appeal to the Secretary of State from any decision of that other person.

(2) On an appeal the Secretary of State may make an order allowing or dismissing the appeal.

(3) Subject to subsection (4) below, in any case where it appears to him that it is appropriate to do so, he may substitute some other punishment.

(4) The Secretary of State may not substitute another punishment unless it appears to him—

    (*a*) that the person or tribunal who heard the disciplinary charge could have awarded it; and

    (*b*) that it is less severe than the punishment awarded by that person or tribunal.

(5) The Secretary of State may direct an appellant to pay the whole or any part of his own costs, but, subject to any such direction, all the costs and expenses of an appeal under this section, including the costs of the parties, shall be defrayed out of the police fund.

(6) Schedule 5 to this Act shall have effect in relation to any appeal under this section.".

(2) The following Schedule shall be substituted for Schedule 5 to that Act—

"SCHEDULE 5   Section 37

DISCIPLINARY APPEALS

Notice of appeal

1. Any appeal under section 37 of this Act (in this Schedule referred to as 'the principal section') shall be instituted by giving a notice of appeal within the time prescribed under this Schedule.

Respondent

2.—(1) On any appeal under the principal section against the decision of a police authority the respondent shall be that authority.

(2) On any other appeal under that section the respondent shall be the chief officer of police of the police force to which the appellant belongs or such other person as the Secretary of State may direct; and the Secretary of State may direct any respondent under this sub-paragraph to act in relation to the appeal in consultation with such other person or persons as the Secretary of State may specify.

227

Inquiries

3.—(1) The Secretary of State may appoint three persons to hold an inquiry into and report to him on any appeal under the principal section other than an appeal from a decision of a police authority and, subject to such paragraph (2) below, shall do so where—

    (*a*) it appears to him that the appeal cannot be properly determined without taking evidence; or

    (*b*) the appellant has been punished by way of dismissal, requirement to resign or reduction in rank and has requested that such persons be appointed.

(2) The Secretary of State need not make an appointment under sub-paragraph (1) above if he is satisfied that there are sufficient grounds for allowing the appeal without an inquiry.

(3) The persons appointed under sub-paragraph (1) above shall be—

    (*a*) a barrister or solicitor, who shall be chairman;

    (*b*) a serving or retired inspector of constabulary or a retired chief officer; and

    (*c*) a retired officer of appropriate rank within the meaning of sub-paragraph (4) below.

(4) A retired officer of appropriate rank means—

    (*a*) where the appellant was, immediately before the disciplinary proceedings, of the rank of chief superintendent or superintendent, a retired police officer who at the time of his retirement was of either of those ranks; and

    (*b*) in any other case, a retired police officer who at the time of his retirement was of the rank of chief inspector or below.

(5) The Secretary of State may appoint one or more persons to hold an inquiry into and report to him on an appeal under the principal section from a decision of a police authority.

(6) The Secretary of State may require persons appointed under this paragraph to deal in their report with any particular matter specified by him.

(7) Subsections (2) and (3) of section 250 of the Local Government Act 1972 shall apply to any inquiry under this paragraph as they apply to an inquiry under that section.

(8) The Secretary of State may require persons appointed under this paragraph to hold a hearing.

(9) Persons so appointed shall hold a hearing in any case where they are not required to do so under sub-paragraph (8) above, unless it appears to them that it is unnecessary to do so.

(10) A decision whether to hold a hearing shall not be taken under sub-paragraph (9) above unless both the appellant and the respondent have been afforded an opportunity to make written or, if either so requests, oral representations and any such representations have been considered.

(11) Where a hearing is held in the course of an inquiry, the appellant shall have the right to appear by a serving member of a police force or by counsel or a solicitor; and the respondent shall have the right to appear by an officer of the police force or by the clerk or other officer of the police authority or by counsel or a solicitor.

(12) Before making an order under the principal section the Secretary of State shall consider any report made to him under this paragraph, as well as the notice of appeal and any other documents

submitted to him by the appellant and the respondent in accordance with rules under this Schedule.

(13) The Secretary of State may, before making an order under the principal section, remit the case for further investigation by the person or persons who held the inquiry or, if he thinks fit, for further consideration by the person or persons whose decision is the subject of the appeal.

Notice and effect of orders

4.—(1) A copy of any order made by the Secretary of State, together with a written statement of his reasons for making it, shall as soon as made be sent to the appellant and the respondent together with, if an inquiry was held, a copy of the report of the person or persons who held the inquiry; and the order shall be final and binding upon all parties.

(2) Where an appeal is allowed or the punishment is varied by the Secretary of State, the order shall take effect by way of substitution for the decision appealed from, and as from the date of that decision; and where the effect of the order is to reinstate the appellant in the force or in his rank, he shall, for the purpose of reckoning service for pension, and, to such extent (if any) as may be determined by the order, for the purpose of pay, be deemed to have served in the force or in that rank, as the case may be, continuously from the date of the decision to the date of his reinstatement and, if he were suspended for a period immediately preceding the date of the decision, the order shall deal with the suspension.

(3) Any costs payable under the principal section shall be subject to taxation in such manner as the Secretary of State may direct.

Rules

5.—(1) The Secretary of State may make rules as to the procedure on appeals and at inquiries under this Schedule and in particular, but without prejudice to the generality of this provision, may make rules—

(*a*) prescribing the form and content of the notice of appeal and the documents to be submitted by the appellant and the time within which such documents are to be submitted; and

(*b*) prescribing the documents to be submitted and the time within which they are to be submitted by the respondent; and

(*c*) providing for the person or persons holding an inquiry to receive evidence or representations in writing instead of holding a hearing.

(2) Any rules made under this paragraph shall be laid before Parliament after being made."

General

Restrictions on subsequent proceedings

104.—(1) Where a member of a police force has been convicted or acquitted of a criminal offence he shall not be liable to be charged with any offence against discipline which is in substance the same as the offence of which he has been convicted or acquitted.

(2) Subsection (1) above shall not be construed as applying to a charge in respect of an offence against discipline which consists in having been found guilty of a criminal offence.

(3) Subject to subsection (4) below, no statement made by any person for the purpose of the informal resolution of a complaint shall be admissible in any subsequent criminal, civil or disciplinary proceedings.

(4) A statement is not rendered inadmissible by subsection (3) above if it consists of or includes an admission relating to a matter which does not fall to be resolved informally.

Guidelines concerning discipline, complaints etc.

105.—(1) The Secretary of State may issue guidance to chief officers of police and to other police officers concerning the discharge of their functions—

(*a*) under this Part of this Act, and

(*b*) otherwise in connection with discipline.

and police officers shall have regard to any such guidance in the discharge of their functions.

(2) Guidance may not be issued under subsection (1) above in relation to the handling of a particular case.

(3) A failure on the part of a police officer to have regard to any guidance issued under subsection (1) above when determining—

(*a*) whether an officer has committed an offence against discipline; or

(*b*) the punishment to be awarded for such an offence,

shall be admissible in evidence on any appeal from the determination.

(4) In discharging their functions under section 93 above the Authority shall have regard to any guidance given to them by the Secretary of State with respect to such matters affecting the preferring and withdrawing of disciplinary charges as are for the time being the subject of guidance under subsection (1) above, and shall have regard in particular, but without prejudice to the generality of this subsection, to any such guidance as to the principles to be applied in cases that involve any question of criminal proceedings and are not governed by section 104 above.

(5) The report of the Authority under section 97(3) above shall contain a statement of any guidance given to the Authority under subsection (4) above during the year to which the report relates.

PART X

POLICE—GENERAL

Arrangements for obtaining the views of the community on policing

106.—(1) Arrangements shall be made in each police area for obtaining the views of people in that area about matters concerning the policing of the area and for obtaining their co-operation with the police in preventing crime in the area.

(2) Except as provided by subsections (3) to (7) below, arrangements for each police area shall be made by the police authority after consulting the chief constable as to the arrangements that would be appropriate.

(3) The Secretary of State shall issue guidance to the Commissioner of Police of the Metropolis concerning arrangements for the Metropolitan Police District; and the Commissioner shall make such arrangements after taking account of that guidance.

(4) The Commissioner shall make separate arrangements—

(*a*) for each London borough;

(*b*) for each district which falls wholly within the Metropolitan Police District; and

(*c*) for each part of a district which falls partly within that District.

(5) The Commissioner shall consult the council of each London borough as to the arrangements that would be appropriate for the borough.

(6) The Commissioner shall consult the council of each such district as is mentioned in subsection (4)(*b*) above as to the arrangements that would be appropriate for the district.

(7) The Commissioner shall consult the council of each such district as is mentioned in subsection (4)(*c*) above as to the arrangements that would be appropriate for the part of the district for which it falls to him to make arrangements.

(8) The Common Council of the City of London shall issue guidance to the Commissioner of Police for the City of London concerning arrangements for the City; and the Commissioner shall make such arrangements after taking account of that guidance.

(9) A body or person whose duty it is to make arrangements under this section shall review the arrangements so made from time to time.

(10) If it appears to the Secretary of State that arrangements in a police area are not adequate for the purposes set out in subsection (1) above, he may require the body or person whose duty it is to make arrangements in that area to submit a report to him concerning the arrangements.

(11) After considering the report the Secretary of State may require the body or person who submitted it to review the arrangements and submit a further report to him concerning them.

(12) A body or person whose duty it is to make arrangements shall be under the same duties to consult when reviewing arrangements as when making them.

Police officers performing duties of higher rank

107.—(1) For the purpose of any provision of this Act or any other Act under which a power in respect of the investigation of offences or the treatment of persons in police custody is exercisable only by or with the authority of a police officer of at least the rank of superintendent, an officer of the rank of chief inspector shall be treated as holding the rank of superintendent if he has been authorised by an officer of at least the rank of chief superintendent to exercise the power or, as the case may be, to give his authority for its exercise.

(2) For the purpose of any provision of this Act or any other Act under which such a power is exercisable only by or with the authority of an officer of at least the rank of inspector, an officer of the rank of sergeant shall be treated as holding the rank of inspector if he has been authorised by an officer of at least the rank of chief superintendent to exercise the power or, as the case may be, to give his authority for its exercise.

Deputy chief constables

108.—(1) The office of deputy chief constable is hereby abolished.

(2) In section 6 of the Police Act 1964—

    (*a*) in subsection (1), after the word "a" there shall be inserted the words "person holding the rank of"; and

    (*b*) in subsection (4), for the words from the beginning to "of", in the second place where it occurs, there shall be substituted the words "Appointments or promotions to the rank of deputy chief constable or".

(3) The following section shall be inserted after that section—

"Deputy chief constables—supplementary

6A.—(1) Any police force maintained under section 1 of this Act may include more than one person holding the rank of deputy chief constable, but only if the additional person or persons holding that rank—

    (*a*) was a deputy chief constable before a period—

        (i) of central service; or

        (ii) of overseas service, as defined in section 3 of the Police (Overseas Service) Act 1945; or

        (iii) of service in pursuance of an appointment under section 10 of the Overseas Development and Co-operation Act 1980 as an officer to whom that section applied; or

    (*b*) became a deputy chief constable by virtue of section 58(2) of this Act.

(2) If there is more than one person who holds the rank of deputy chief constable in a police force maintained under section 1 of this Act, one of the persons who hold it shall be designated as the officer having the powers and duties conferred on a deputy chief constable by section 6(1) of this Act.

(3) A person shall be designated under subsection (2) of this section by the police authority after consultation with the chief constable and subject to the approval of the Secretary of State.".

(4) In section 5 of the Police (Scotland) Act 1967—

    (*a*) in subsection (1), after the word "a" there shall be inserted the words "person holding the rank of";

    (*b*) subsection (3) shall be omitted; and

    (*c*) in subsection (5), for the words from the beginning to "of", in the second place where it occurs, there shall be substituted the words "Appointments or promotions to the rank of deputy chief constable or".

(5) The following section shall be inserted after that section—

"Deputy chief constables—supplementary

    5A.—(1) Any police force may include more than one person holding the rank of deputy chief constable, but only if the additional person or persons holding that rank—

    (*a*) was a deputy chief constable before a period—

        (i) of central service; or

        (ii) of overseas service, as defined in section 3 of the Police (Overseas Service) Act 1945; or

        (iii) of service in pursuance of an appointment under section 10 of the Overseas Development and Co-operation Act 1980 as an officer to whom that section applied; or

    (*b*) became a deputy chief constable by virtue of section 23(2) of this Act.

(2) If there is more than one person in a police force who holds the rank of deputy chief constable, one of the persons who hold it shall be designated as the officer having the powers and duties conferred on a deputy chief constable by section 5(1) of this Act.

(3) A person shall be designated under subsection (2) of this section by the police authority after consultation with the chief constable and subject to the approval of the Secretary of State.".

(6) In section 58(2) of the Police Act 1964 and section 23(2) of the Police (Scotland) Act 1967 (under both of which a chief constable affected by an amalgamation holds the rank of assistant chief constable) for the word "assistant" there shall be substituted the word "deputy".

Amendments relating to Police Federations

109. In section 44 of the Police Act 1964—
   (*a*) in subsection (1), for the word "and", in the last place where
   it occurs, there shall be substituted the words "affecting individuals, except as provided by subsection (1A) below, and
   questions of";
   (*b*) the following subsections shall be inserted after that
   subsection—
       "(1A) A Police Federation may represent a member of a
       police force at any disciplinary proceedings or on an appeal
       from any such proceedings.
       (1B) Except on an appeal to the Secretary of State or as
       provided by section 102 of the Police and Criminal Evidence
       Act 1984, a member of a police force may only be repre-
       sented under subsection (1A) above by another member of
       a police force."; and
   (*c*) in subsection (3), after the word "Federations", in the first
   place where it occurs, there shall be inserted the words "or
   authorise the Federations to make rules concerning such matters relating to their constitution and proceedings as may be
   specified in the regulations."

Functions of special constables in Scotland

110. Subsection (6) of section 17 of the Police (Scotland) Act 1967
(restriction on functions of special constables) is hereby repealed.

Regulations for Police Forces and Police Cadets—Scotland

111.—(1) In section 26 of the Police (Scotland) Act 1967 (regulations
as to government and administration of police forces)—
   (*a*) after subsection (1) there shall be inserted the following
   subsection—
       "(1A) Regulations under this section may authorise the
       Secretary of State, the police authority or the chief constable
       to make provision for any purpose specified in the regula-
       tions."; and
   (*b*) at the end there shall be inserted the following subsection—
       "(10) Any statutory instrument made under this section
       shall be subject to annulment in pursuance of a resolution
       of either House of Parliament.".
   (2) In section 27 of the said Act of 1967 (regulations for police cadets)
in subsection (3) for the word "(9)" there shall be substituted the words
"(1A), (9) and (10)".

Metropolitan police officers

112.—(1) An officer belonging to the metropolitan police force who is
assigned to the protection of any person or property in Scotland shall in
the discharge of that duty have the powers and privileges of a constable
of a police force maintained under the Police (Scotland) Act 1967.
   (2) An officer belonging to the metropolitan police force who is assigned
to the protection of any person or property in Northern Ireland shall in
the discharge of that duty have the powers and privileges of a constable
of the Royal Ulster Constabulary.

PART XI

MISCELLANEOUS AND SUPPLEMENTARY

Application of Act to Armed Forces

113.—(1) The Secretary of State may by order direct that any provision of this Act which relates to the investigation of offences conducted by police officers or to persons detained by the police shall apply, subject to such modifications as he may specify, to investigations of offences conducted under the Army Act 1955, the Air Force Act 1955 or the Naval Discipline Act 1957 or to persons under arrest under any of those Acts.

(2) Section 67(9) above shall not have effect in relation to investigations of an offence under the Army Act 1955, the Air Force Act 1955 or the Naval Discipline Act 1957.

(3) The Secretary of State shall issue a code of practice or a number of such codes, for persons other than police officers who are concerned with enquiries into offences under the Army Act 1955, the Air Force Act 1955 or the Naval Discipline Act 1957.

(4) Without prejudice to the generality of subsection (3) above, a code issued under that subsection may contain provisions, in connection with enquiries into such offences, as to the following matters—

(a) the tape-recording of interviews;

(b) searches of persons and premises; and

(c) the seizure of things found on searches.

(5) If the Secretary of State lays before both Houses of Parliament a draft of a code of practice under this section, he may by order bring the code into operation.

(6) An order bringing a code of practice into operation may contain such transitional provisions or savings as appear to the Secretary of State to be necessary or expedient in connection with the code of practice thereby brought into operation.

(7) The Secretary of State may from time to time revise the whole or any part of a code of practice issued under this section and issue that revised code, and the foregoing provisions of this section shall apply (with appropriate modifications) to such a revised code as they apply to the first issue of a code.

(8) A failure on the part of any person to comply with any provision of a code of practice issued under this section shall not of itself render him liable to any criminal or civil proceedings except those to which this subsection applies.

(9) Subsection (8) applies—

(a) to proceedings under any provision of the Army Act 1955 or the Air Force Act 1955 other than section 70; and

(b) to proceedings under any provision of the Naval Discipline Act 1957 other than section 42.

(10) In all criminal and civil proceedings any such code shall be admissible in evidence, and if any provision of such a code appears to the court or tribunal conducting the proceedings to be relevant to any question arising in the proceedings it shall be taken into account in determining that question.

(11) In subsection (10) above "criminal proceedings" includes—

(a) proceedings in the United Kingdom or elsewhere before a court-martial constituted under the Army Act 1955, the Air Force Act 1955 or the Naval Discipline Act 1957 or a disciplinary court constituted under section 50 of the said Act of 1957;

(b) proceedings before the Courts-Martial Appeal Court; and

(c) proceedings before a Standing Civilian Court.

(12) Parts VII and VIII of this Act have effect for the purposes of proceedings—

> (*a*) before a court-martial constituted under the Army Act 1955 or the Air Force Act 1955
> (*b*) before the Courts-Martial Appeal Court; and
> (*c*) before a Standing Civilian Court,

subject to any modifications which the Secretary of State may by order specify.

(13) An order under this section shall be made by statutory instrument and shall be subject to annulment in pursuance of a resolution of either House of Parliament.

Application of Act to Customs and Excise

114.—(1) "Arrested", "arresting", "arrest" and "to arrest" shall respectively be substituted for "detained", "detaining", "detention" and "to detain" wherever in the customs and excise Acts, as defined in section 1(1) of the Customs and Excise Management Act 1979, those words are used in relation to persons.

(2) The Treasury may by order direct—

> (*a*) that any provision of this Act which relates to the investigation of offences by police officers or to persons detained by the police shall apply, subject to such modifications as the order may specify, to investigations by officers of Customs and Excise of offences which relate to assigned matters, as defined in section 1 of the Customs and Excise Management Act 1979, or to persons detained by such officers; and
> (*b*) that, in relation to investigations of offences conducted by officers of Customs and Excise,
>> (i) this Act shall have effect as if the following section were inserted after section 14—
>> "Exception for customs and excise
>>
>> 14A. Material in the possession of a person who acquired or created it in the course of any trade, business, profession or other occupation or for the purpose of any paid or unpaid office and which relates to an assigned matter, as defined in section 1 of the Customs and Excise Management Act 1979, is neither excluded material nor special procedure material for the purposes of any enactment such as is mentioned in section 9(2) above."; and
>> (ii) section 55 above shall have effect as if it related only to things such as are mentioned in subsection (1)(*a*) of that section.

(3) Nothing in any order under subsection (2) above shall be taken to limit any powers exercisable under section 164 of the Customs and Excise Management Act 1979.

(4) In this section "officers of Customs and Excise" means officers commissioned by the Commissioners of Customs and Excise under section 6(3) of the Customs and Excise Management Act 1979.

(5) An order under this section shall be made by statutory instrument and shall be subject to annulment in pursuance of a resolution of either House of Parliament.

Expenses

115. Any expenses of a Minister of the Crown incurred in consequence of the provisions of this Act, including any increase attributable to those provisions in sums payable under any other Act, shall be defrayed out of money provided by Parliament.

Meaning of "serious arrestable offence"

116.—(1) This section has effect for determining whether an offence is a serious arrestable offence for the purposes of this Act.

(2) The following arrestable offences are always serious—
>   (*a*) an offence (whether at common law or under any enactment) specified in Part I of Schedule 5 to this Act; and
>   (*b*) an offence under an enactment specified in Part II of that Schedule.

(3) Subject to subsections (4) and (5) below, any other arrestable offence is serious only if its commission.
>   (*a*) has led to any of the consequences specified in subsection (6) below; or
>   (*b*) is intended to lead to any of those consequences.

(4) An arrestable offence which consists of making a threat is serious if carrying out the threat would be likely to lead to any of the consequences specified in subsection (6) below.

(5) An offence under section 1, 9 or 10 of the Prevention of Terrorism (Temporary Provisions) Act 1984 is always a serious arrestable offence for the purposes of section 56 or 58 above, and an attempt or conspiracy to commit any such offence is also always a serious arrestable offence for those purposes.

(6) The consequences mentioned in subsections (3) and (4) above are—
>   (*a*) serious harm to the security of the State or to public order;
>   (*b*) serious interference with the administration of justice or with the investigation of offences or of a particular offence;
>   (*c*) the death of any person;
>   (*d*) serious injury to any person;
>   (*e*) substantial financial gain to any person; and
>   (*f*) serious financial loss to any person.

(7) Loss is serious for the purposes of this section if, having regard to all the circumstances, it is serious for the person who suffers it.

(8) In this section "injury" includes any disease and any impairment of a person's physical or mental condition.

Power of constable to use reasonable force

117. Where any provision of this Act—
>   (*a*) confers a power on a constable; and
>   (*b*) does not provide that the power may only be exercised with the consent of some person, other than a police officer,

the officer may use reasonable force, if necessary, in the exercise of the power.

General interpretation

118.—(1) In this Act—
>   "arrestable offence" has the meaning assigned to it by section 24(1) above;
>   "designated police station" has the meaning assigned to it by section 35
>   "document" has the same meaning as in Part I of the Civil Evidence Act 1968;
>   "intimate search " means a search which consists of the physical examination of a person's body orifices"

"item subject to legal privilege" has the meaning assigned to it by section 10 above;

"parent or guardian" means—

(*a*) in the case of a child or young person in the care of a local authority, that authority; and

(*b*) in the case of a child or young person in the care of a voluntary organisation in which parental rights and duties with respect to him are vested by virtue of a resolution under section 64(1) of the Child Care Act 1980, that organisation;

"premises" has the meaning assigned to it by section 23 above;

"recordable offence" means any offence to which regulations under section 27 above apply;

"vessel" includes any ship, boat, raft or other apparatus constructed or adapted for floating on water.

(2) A person is in police detention for the purposes of this Act if

(*a*) he has been taken to a police station after being arrested for an offence; or

(*b*) he is arrested at a police station after attending voluntarily at the station or accompanying a constable to it; and—

(*a*) is detained there; or

(*b*) is detained elsewhere in the charge of a constable,

except that a person who is at a court after being charged is not in police detention for those purposes.

Amendments and repeals

119.—(1) The enactments mentioned in Schedule 6 to this Act shall have effect with the amendments there specified.

(2) The enactments mentioned in Schedule 7 to this Act (which include enactments already obsolete or unnecessary) are repealed to the extent specified in the third column of that Schedule.

(3) The repeals in Parts II and IV of Schedule 7 to this Act have effect only in relation to criminal proceedings.

Extent

120.—(1) Subject to the following provisions of this section, this Act extends to England and Wales only.

(2) The following extend to Scotland only—

section 108(4) and (5);

section 110;

section 111;

section 112(1); and

section 119(2), so far as it relates to the provisions of the Pedlars Act 1871 repealed by Part VI of Schedule 7.

(3) The following extend to Northern Ireland only—

section 6(4); and

section 112(2).

(4) The following extend to England and Wales and Scotland—

section 6(1) and (2);

section 7;

section 83(3), so far as it relates to paragraph 8 of Schedule 4;

section 108(1) and (6);

section 109; and

section 119(2), so far as it relates to section 19 of the Pedlars Act 1871.

(5) The following extend to England and Wales, Scotland and Northern Ireland—

section 6(3);

section 83(3), so far as it relates to paragraph 7(1) of Schedule 4; and
section 114(1).

(6) So far as they relate to proceedings before courts-martial and Standing Civilian Courts, the relevant provisions extend to any place at which such proceedings may be held:

(7) So far as they relate to proceedings before the Courts-Martial Appeal Court, the relevant provisions extend to any place at which such proceedings may be held.

(8) In this section "the relevant provisions" means—

(*a*) subsection (11) of section 67 above;

(*b*) subsection (12) of that section so far as it relates to subsection (11);

(*c*) Parts VII and VIII of this Act except paragraph 10 of Schedule 3;

(*d*) subsections (2), (8) to (11) and (12) of section 113 above; and

(*e*) subsection (6) of that section so far as it relates to an order under subsection (5).

(9) Except as provided by the foregoing provisions of this section, section 113 above extends to any place to which the Army Act 1955, the Air Force Act 1955 or the Naval Discipline Act 1957 extends.

(10) Section 118(1), so far as it relates to any provision amended by Part II of Schedule 6, extends to any place to which that provision extends.

(11) Section 119(2), so far as it relates—

(*a*) to any provision contained in—
the Army Act 1955;
the Air Force Act 1955;
the Armed Forces Act 1981, or
the Value Added Tax Act 1983,

(*b*) to any provision mentioned in Part VI of Schedule 7, other than section 18 of the Pedlars Act 1871,

extends to any place to which that provision extends.

(12) So far as any of the following—
section 115;
in section 118; the definition of "document";
this section;
section 121, and
section 122,

has effect in relation to any other provision of this Act, it extends to any place to which that provision extends.

Commencement

121.—(1) This Act, except section 120 above, this section and section 122 below, shall come into operation on such day as the Secretary of State may by order made by statutory instrument appoint, and different days may be so appointed for different provisions and for different purposes.

(2) Different days may be appointed under this section for the coming into force of section 60 above in different areas.

(3) When an order under this section provides by virtue of subsection (2) above that section 60 above shall come into force in an area specified in the order, the duty imposed on the Secretary of State by that section shall be construed as a duty to make an order under it in relation to interviews in that area.

(4) An order under this section may make such transitional provision as appears to the Secretary of State to be necessary or expedient in connection with the provisions thereby brought into operation.

Short title

122. This Act may be cited as the Police and Criminal Evidence Act 1984.

SCHEDULES

SCHEDULE 1   Section 9

SPECIAL PROCEDURE

Making of orders by circuit judge

1. If on an application made by a constable a circuit judge is satisfied that one or other of the sets of access conditions is fulfilled, he may make an order under paragraph 4 below.

2. The first set of access conditions is fulfilled if—
   (*a*) there are reasonable grounds for believing—
     (i) that a serious arrestable offence has been committed;
     (ii) that there is material which consists of special procedure material or includes special procedure material and does not also include excluded material on premises specified in the application;
     (iii) that the material is likely to be of substantial value (whether by itself or together with other material) to the investigation in connection with which the application is made; and
     (iv) that the material is likely to be relevant evidence;
   (*b*) other methods of obtaining the material—
     (i) have been tried without success; or
     (ii) have not been tried because it appeared that they were bound to fail; and
   (*c*) it is in the public interest, having regard—
     (i) to the benefit likely to accrue to the investigation if the material is obtained; and
     (ii) to the circumstances under which the person in possession of the material holds it,
     that the material should be produced or that access to it should be given.

3. The second set of access conditions is fulfilled if—
   (*a*) there are reasonable grounds for believing that there is material which consists of or includes excluded material or special procedure material on premises specified in the application;
   (*b*) but for section 9(2) above a search of the premises for that material could have been authorised by the issue of a warrant to a constable under an enactment other than this Schedule; and
   (*c*) the issue of such a warrant would have been appropriate.

4. An order under this paragraph is an order that the person who appears to the circuit judge to be in possession of the material to which the application relates shall—
   (*a*) produce it to a constable for him to take it away; or
   (*b*) give a constable access to it,
not later than the end of the period of seven days from the date of the order or the end of such longer period as the order may specify.

5. Where the material consists of information contained in a computer,
   (*a*) an order under paragraph 4 above shall have effect as an order to produce the material in a form in which it can be taken away and in which it is visible and legible, and
   (*b*) an order under paragraph 4(*b*) above shall have effect as an order to give a constable access to the material in a form in which it is visible and legible.

6. For the purposes of sections 21 and 22 above material produced in pursuance of an order under paragraph 4(*a*) above shall be treated as if it were material seized by a constable.

239

Notices of applications for orders

7. An application for an order under paragraph 4 above shall be made inter partes.

8. Notice of an application for such an order may be served on a person either by delivering it to him or by leaving it at his proper address or by sending it by post to him in a registered letter or by the recorded delivery service.

9. Such a notice may be served—

    (*a*) on a body corporate, by serving it on the body's secretary or clerk or other similar officer; and

    (*b*) on a partnership, by serving it on one of the partners.

10. For the purposes of this Schedule, and of section 7 of the Interpretation Act 1978 in its application to this Schedule, the proper address of a person, in the case of secretary or clerk or other similar officer of a body corporate, shall be that of the registered or principal office of that body, in the case of a partner of a firm shall be that of the principal office of the firm, and in any other case shall be the last known address of the person to be served.

11. Where notice of an application for an order under paragraph 4 above has been served on a person, he shall not conceal, destroy, alter or dispose of the material to which the application relates except—

    (*a*) with the leave of a judge; or

    (*b*) with the written permission of a constable,

until—

        (i) the application is dismissed or abandoned; or

        (ii) he has complied with an order under paragraph 4 above made on the application.

Issue of warrants by circuit judge

12. If on an application made by a constable a circuit judge—

    (*a*) is satisfied—

        (i) that either set of access conditions is fulfilled; and

        (ii) that any of the further conditions set out in paragraph 14 below is also fulfilled; or

    (*b*) is satisfied—

        (i) that the second set of access conditions is fulfilled; and

        (ii) that an order under paragraph 4 above relating to the material has not been complied with,

he may issue a warrant authorising a constable to enter and search the premises.

13. A constable may seize and retain anything for which a search has been authorised under paragraph 12 above.

14. The further conditions mentioned in paragraph 12(*a*)(ii) above are—

    (*a*) that it is not practicable to communicate with any person entitled to grant entry to the premises to which the application relates;

    (*b*) that it is practicable to communicate with a person entitled to grant entry to the premises but it is not practicable to communicate with any person entitled to grant access to the material;

    (*c*) that the material contains information which—

        (i) is subject to a restriction or obligation such as is mentioned in section 11(2)(*b*) above; and

        (ii) is likely to be disclosed in breach of it if a warrant is not issued;

    (*d*) that service of notice of an application for an order under paragraph 4 above may seriously prejudice the investigation.

15.—(1) If a person fails to comply with an order under paragraph 4 above, a circuit judge may deal with him as if he had committed a contempt of the Crown Court.

(2) Any enactment relating to contempt of the Crown Court shall have effect in relation to such a failure as if it were such a contempt.

Costs

16. The costs of any application under this Schedule and of anything done or to be done in pursuance of an order made under it shall be in the discretion of the judge.

Section 26	**SCHEDULE 2**

PRESERVED POWERS OF ARREST

1892 c.43.	Section 17(2) of the Military Lands Act 1892.
1911 c.27.	Section 12(1) of the Protection of Animals Act 1911.
1920 c.55.	Section 2 of the Emergency Powers Act 1920.
1936 c.6.	Section 7(3) of the Public Order Act 1936.
1952 c.52.	Section 49 of the Prison Act 1952.
1952 c.67.	Section 13 of the Visiting Forces Act 1952.
1955 c.18.	Sections 186 and 190B of the Army Act 1955.
1955 c.19.	Sections 186 and 190B of the Air Force Act 1955.
1957 c.53.	Sections 104 and 105 of the Naval Discipline Act 1957.
1959 c.37.	Section 1(3) of the Street Offences Act 1959.
1969 c.54.	Sections 28(2) and 32 of the Children and Young Persons Act 1969.
1971 c.77.	Section 24(2) of the Immigration Act 1971 and paragraphs 17, 24 and 33 of Schedule 2 and paragraph 7 of Schedule 3 to that Act.
1972 c.20.	Sections 5(5), 7 and 100 of the Road Traffic Act 1972.
1976 c.63.	Section 7 of the Bail Act 1976.
1977 c.45.	Sections 6(6), 7(11), 8(4), 9(7) and 10(5) of the Criminal Law Act 1977.
1980 c.5.	Section 16 of the Child Care Act 1980.
1980 c.9.	Schedule 5 to the Reserve Forces Act 1980.
1981 c.22.	Sections 60(5) and 61(1) of the Animal Health Act 1981.
1983 c.20.	Sections 18, 35(10), 36(8), 38(7), 136(1) and 138 of the Mental Health Act 1983.
1984 c.8.	Section 12 and 13 of the Prevention of Terrorism (Temporary Provisions) Act 1984.
1984 c.47.	Section 5(5) of the Repatriation of Prisoners Act 1984.

Section 68	**SCHEDULE 3**

PROVISIONS SUPPLEMENTARY TO SECTIONS 68 AND 69

PART I

PROVISIONS SUPPLEMENTARY TO SECTION 68

1. Section 68(1) above applies whether the information contained in the document was supplied directly or indirectly but, if it was supplied indirectly, only if each person through whom it was supplied was acting under a duty; and applies also where the person compiling the record is himself the person by whom the information is supplied.

2. Where—
    (a) a document setting out the evidence which a person could be expected to give as a witness has been prepared for the purpose of any pending or contemplated proceedings; and
    (b) it falls within subsection (1) of section 68 above,
a statement contained in it shall not be given in evidence by virtue of that section without the leave of the court, and the court shall not give leave unless it is of the opinion that the statement ought to be admitted in the interests of justice, having regard—
    (i) to the circumstances in which leave is sought and in particular to the contents of the statement; and
    (ii) to any likelihood that the accused will be prejudiced by its admission in the absence of the person who supplied the information on which it is based.

3. Where in any proceedings a statement based on information supplied by any person is given in evidence by virtue of section 68 above—
    (a) any evidence which, if that person had been called as a witness, would have been admissible as relevant to his credibility as a witness shall be admissible for that purpose in those proceedings;
    (b) evidence may, with the leave of the court, be given of any matter which, if that person had been called as a witness, could have been put to him in cross-examination as relevant to his credibility as a witness but of which evidence could not have been adduced by the cross-examining party; and

    (*c*) evidence tending to prove that that person has, whether before or after supplying the information, made a statement (whether oral or otherwise) which is inconsistent with that information shall be admissible for the purpose of showing that he has contradicted himself.

4. A statement which is admissible by virtue of section 68 above shall not be capable of corroborating evidence given by the person who supplied the information on which the statement is based.

5. In deciding for the purposes of section 68(2)(*a*)(i) above whether a person is unfit to attend as a witness the court may act on a certificate purporting to be signed by a registered medical practitioner.

6. Any reference in section 68 above or this Part of this Schedule to a person acting under a duty includes a reference to a person acting in the course of any trade, business, profession or other occupation in which he is engaged or employed or for the purposes of any paid or unpaid office held by him.

7. In estimating the weight, if any, to be attached to a statement admissible in evidence by virtue of section 68 above regard shall be had to all the circumstances from which any inference can reasonably be drawn as to the accuracy or otherwise of the statement and, in particular—

    (*a*) to the question whether or not the person who supplied the information from which the record containing the statement was compiled did so contemporaneously with the occurrence or existence of the facts dealt with in that information; and

    (*b*) to the question whether or not that person, or any other person concerned with compiling or keeping the record containing the statement, had any incentive to conceal or misrepresent the facts.

Part II

Provisions Supplementary to Section 69

8. In any proceedings where it is desired to give a statement in evidence in accordance with section 69 above, a certificate—

    (*a*) identifying the document containing the statement and describing the manner in which it was produced;

    (*b*) giving such particulars of any device involved in the production of that document as may be appropriate for the purpose of showing that the document was produced by a computer;

    (*c*) dealing with any of the matters mentioned in subsection (1) of section 69 above; and

    (*d*) purporting to be signed by a person occupying a responsible position in relation to the operation of the computer,

shall be evidence of anything stated in it; and for the purposes of this paragraph it shall be sufficient for a matter to be stated to the best of the knowledge and belief of the person stating it.

9. Notwithstanding paragraph 8 above, a court may require oral evidence to be given of anything of which evidence could be given by a certificate under that paragraph.

10. Any person who in a certificate tendered under paragraph 8 above in a magistrates' court, the Crown Court or the Court of Appeal makes a statement which he knows to be false or does not believe to be true shall be guilty of an offence and liable—

    (*a*) on conviction on indictment to imprisonment for a term not exceeding two years or to a fine or to both;

    (*b*) on summary conviction to imprisonment for a term not exceeding six months or to a fine not exceeding the statutory maximum (as defined in section 74 of the Criminal Justice Act 1982) or to both.

11. In estimating the weight, if any, to be attached to a statement regard shall be had to all the circumstances from which any inference can reasonably be drawn as to the accuracy or otherwise of the statement and, in particular—

    (*a*) to the question whether or not the information which the information contained in the statement reproduces or is derived from was supplied to the relevant computer, or recorded for the purpose of being supplied to it, contemporaneously with the occurrence or existence of the facts dealt with in that information; and

    (*b*) to the question whether or not any person concerned with the supply of information to that computer, or with the operation of that computer or any equipment by means of which the document containing the statement was produced by it, had any incentive to conceal or misrepresent the facts.

12. For the purposes of paragraph 11 above information shall be taken to be supplied to a computer whether it is supplied directly or (with or without human intervention) by means of any appropriate equipment.

PART III

PROVISIONS SUPPLEMENTARY TO SECTIONS 68 AND 69

13. Where in any proceedings a statement contained in a document is admissible in evidence by virtue of section 68 above or in accordance with section 69 above it may be proved—

    (*a*) by the production of that document; or

    (*b*) (whether or not that document is still in existence) by the production of a copy of that document, or of the material part of it,

authenticated in such manner as the court may approve.

14. For the purpose of deciding whether or not a statement is so admissible the court may draw any reasonable inference—

    (*a*) from the circumstances in which the statement was made or otherwise came into being; or

    (*b*) from any other circumstances, including the form and contents of the document in which the statement is contained.

15. Provision may be made by rules of court for supplementing the provisions of section 68 or 69 above or this Schedule.

Section 82   **SCHEDULE 4**

THE POLICE COMPLAINTS AUTHORITY

PART I–GENERAL

Constitution of Authority

1.—(1) The Police Complaints Authority shall consist of a chairman and not less than 8 other members.

(2) The chairman shall be appointed by Her Majesty.

(3) The other members shall be appointed by the Secretary of State.

(4) The members of the Authority shall not include any person who is or has been a constable in any part of the United Kingdom.

(5) Persons may be appointed as whole-time or part-time members of the Authority.

(6) The Secretary of State shall appoint 2 of the members of the Authority to be deputy chairmen of the Authority.

Incorporation and status of Authority

2.—(1) The Authority shall be a body corporate.

(2) It is hereby declared that the Authority are not to be regarded as the servant or agent of the Crown or as enjoying any status, privilege or immunity of the Crown; and the Authority's property shall not be regarded as property of or property held on behalf of the Crown.

Members

3.—(1) Subject to the following provisions of this Schedule, a person shall hold an office to which he is appointed under paragraph 1(2), (3) or (6) above in accordance with the terms of his appointment.

(2) A person shall not be appointed to such an office for more than 3 years at a time.

(3) A person may at any time resign such an office.

(4) The Secretary of State may at any time remove a person from such an office if satisfied that—

    (*a*) he has without reasonable excuse failed to carry out his duties for a continuous period of 3 months beginning not earlier than 6 months before that time; or

    (*b*) he has been convicted of a criminal offence; or

    (*c*) he has become bankrupt or made an arrangement with his creditors; or

    (*d*) he is incapacitated by physical or mental illness; or

    (*e*) he is otherwise unable or unfit to perform his duties.

4. The Secretary of State may pay, or make such payments towards the provision of, such remuneration, pensions, allowances or gratuities to or in respect of persons appointed to office under paragraph 1(2), (3) or (6) above or any of them as, with the consent of the Treasury, he may determine.

5. Where a person ceases to hold such an office otherwise than on the expiry of his term of office, and it appears to the Secretary of State that there are special circumstances which make it right for that person to receive compensation, the Secretary of State may, with the consent of the Treasury, direct the Authority to make to the person a payment of such amount as, with the consent of the Treasury, the Secretary of State may determine.

Staff

6. The Authority may, after consultation with the Secretary of State, appoint such officers and servants as the Authority think fit, subject to the approval of the Treasury as to numbers and as to remuneration and other terms and conditions of service.

7.—(1) Employment by the Authority shall be included among the kinds of employment to which a superannuation scheme under section 1 of the Superannuation Act 1972 can apply, and accordingly in Schedule 1 to that Act, at the end of the list of "Other Bodies" there shall be inserted—

"Police Complaints Authority"

(2) Where a person who is employed by the Authority and is by reference to that employment a participant in a scheme under section 1 of the said Act of 1972 is appointed to an office under paragraph 1(2), (3) or (6) above, the Treasury may determine that his service in that office shall be treated for the purposes of the scheme as service as an employee of the Authority; and his rights under the scheme shall not be affected by paragraph 4 above.

8. The Employers' Liability (Compulsory Insurance) Act 1969 shall not require insurance to be effected by the Authority.

Power of Authority to set up regional offices

9.—(1) If it appears to the Authority that it is necessary to do so in order to discharge their duties efficiently, the Authority may, with the consent of the Secretary of State and the Treasury, set up a regional office in any place in England and Wales.

(2) The Authority may delegate any of their functions to a regional office.

Proceedings

10.—(1) Subject to the provisions of this Act, the arrangements for the proceedings of the Authority (including the quorum for meetings) shall be such as the Authority may determine.

(2) The arrangements may, with the approval of the Secretary of State, provide for the discharge, under the general direction of the Authority, of any of the Authority's functions by a committee or by one or more of the members, officers or servants of the Authority.

11. The validity of any proceedings of the Authority shall not be affected—

    (*a*) by any defect in the appointment
        (i) of the chairman;
       (ii) of the deputy chairman; or
      (iii) of any other member or
    (*b*) by any vacancy
        (i) in the office of chairman;
       (ii) among the other members; or
      (iii) in the office of deputy chairman.

Finance

12. The Secretary of State shall pay to the Authority expenses incurred or to be incurred by the Authority under paragraphs 5 and 6 above and, with the consent of the Treasury, shall pay to the Authority such sums as the Secretary of State thinks fit for enabling the Authority to meet other expenses.

13.—(1) It shall be the duty of the Authority—

    (*a*) to keep proper accounts and proper records in relation to the accounts;
    (*b*) to prepare in respect of each financial year of the Authority a statement of accounts in such form as the Secretary of State may direct with the approval of the Treasury; and
    (*c*) to send copies of the statement to the Secretary of State and the Comptroller

and Auditor General before the end of the month of August next following the financial year to which the statement relates.

(2) The Comptroller and Auditor General shall examine, certify and report on each statement received by him in pursuance of this paragraph and shall lay copies of each statement and of his report before Parliament.

(3) The financial year of the Authority shall be the 12 months ending on 31st March.

PART II

TRANSITIONAL

Information received by Police Complaints Board

14.—(1) No information received by the Police Complaints Board in connection with any complaint shall be disclosed by any person who has been a member, officer or servant of the Board except—

    (*a*) to the Secretary of State or to a member, officer or servant of the Authority or, so far as may be necessary for the proper discharge of the functions of the Authority, to other persons; or

    (*b*) for the purposes of any criminal, civil or disciplinary proceedings.

(2) Any person who discloses information in contravention of this paragraph shall be guilty of an offence and liable on summary conviction to a fine of an amount not exceeding level 5 on the standard scale, as defined in section 75 of the Criminal Justice Act 1982.

Property, rights and liabilities

15.—(1) On the day on which section 83 above comes into operation all property, rights and liabilities which immediately before that day were property, rights and liabilities of the Police Complaints Board shall vest in the Authority by virtue of this paragraph and without further assurance.

(2) Section 12 of the Finance Act 1895 (which requires Acts to be stamped as conveyances on sale in certain cases) shall not apply to any transfer of property effected by this paragraph.

Proceedings

16. Proceedings in any court to which the Police Complaints Board is a party and which are pending immediately before the date on which section 83 above comes into operation may be continued on and after that day by the Authority.

Payments to former members of Police Complaints Board

17. Where a person—

    (*a*) ceases to be a member of the Police Complaints Board by reason of its abolition; and

    (*b*) does not become a member of the Authority,

the Secretary of State may, with the consent of the Treasury, make to the person a payment of such amount as, with the consent of the Treasury, the Secretary of State may determine.

General

18. Paragraphs 14 to 17 above are without prejudice to the generality of section 121(4) above.

Section 116   **SCHEDULE 5**

SERIOUS ARRESTABLE OFFENCES

PART I

OFFENCES MENTIONED IN SECTION 116(2)(*a*)

1. Treason.
2. Murder.
3. Manslaughter.
4. Rape.
5. Kidnapping.

6. Incest with a girl under the age of 13.
7. Buggery with—
    (*a*)   a boy under the age of 16; or
    (*b*)   a person who has not consented.
8. Indecent assault which constitutes an act of indecency.

PART II

OFFENCES MENTIONED IN SECTION 116(2)(b)

Explosive Substances Act 1883 (c.3)

1. Section 2 (causing explosion likely to endanger life or property).

Sexual Offences Act 1956 (c.69)

2. Section 5 (intercourse with a girl under the age of 13)

Firearms Act 1968 (c.27)

3. Section 16 (possession of firearm with intent to injure).
4. Section 17(1) (use of firearms and imitation firearms to resist arrest).
5. Section 18 (carrying firearms with criminal intent).

Road Traffic Act 1972 (c.20)

6. Section 1 (causing death by reckless driving).

Taking of Hostages Act 1982 (c.28)

7. Section 1 (hostage-taking).

Aviation Security Act 1982 (c.36)

8. Section 1 (hi-jacking).

Section 118   **SCHEDULE 6**

CONSEQUENTIAL AMENDMENTS

PART I

ENGLAND AND WALES

Game Act 1831 (32)

1. The following section shall be inserted after section 31 of the Game Act 1831—
"Powers of constables in relation to trespassers
    31A. The powers conferred by section 31 above to require a person found on land as mentioned in that section to quit the land and to tell his Christian name, surname, and place of abode shall also be exercisable by a police constable.".

Metropolitan Police Act 1839 (c.47)

2. In section 39 of the Metropolitan Police Act 1839 (fairs within the metropolitan police district) after the word "amusement" there shall be inserted the words "shall be guilty of an offence".

Railway Regulation Act 1840 (c.97)

3. In section 16 of the Railway Regulation Act 1840 (persons obstructing officers of railway company or trespassing upon railway) for the words from "and" in the third place where it occurs to "justice," in the third place where it occurs there shall be substituted the words ", upon conviction by a magistrates' court, at the discretion of the court,".

London Hackney Carriages Act 1843 (c.86)

4. In section 27 of the London Hackney Carriages Act 1843 (no person to act as driver of carriage without consent of proprietor) for the words after "constable" there shall be substituted the words "if necessary, to take charge of the carriage and every horse in charge of any person unlawfully acting as a driver and to deposit the same in some place of safe custody until the same can be applied for by the proprietor.".

Town Gardens Protection Act 1863 (c.13)

5. In section 5 of the Town Gardens Protection Act 1863 (penalty for injuring garden) for the words from the beginning to "district" there shall be substituted the words "Any person who throws any rubbish into any such garden, or trespasses therein, or gets over the railings or fence, or steals or damages the flowers or plants, or commits any nuisance therein, shall be guilty of an offence and".

Parks Regulation Act 1872 (c.15)

6. The following section shall be substituted for section 5 of the Parks Regulation Act 1872 (apprehension of offender whose name or residence is not known)—
  "5. Any person who—
  (a) within the view of a park constable acts in contravention of any of the said regulations in the park where the park constable has jurisdiction; and
  (b) when required by any park constable or by any police constable to give his name and address gives a false name or false address,
  shall be liable on summary conviction to a penalty of an amount not exceeding level 1 on the standard scale, as defined in section 75 of the Criminal Justice Act 1982.".

Dogs (Protection of Livestock) Act 1953 (c.28)

7. In the Dogs (Protection of Livestock) Act 1953 the following section shall be inserted after section 2—
  "Power of justice of the peace to authorise entry and search
  2A. If on an application made by a constable a justice of the peace is satisfied that there are reasonable grounds for believing—
  (a) that an offence under this Act has been committed; and
  (b) that the dog in respect of which the offence has been committed is on premises specified in the application,
  he may issue a warrant authorising a constable to enter and search the premises in order to identify the dog."

Army Act 1955 (c.18)
Air Force Act 1955 (c.19)

8. The following subsection shall be substituted for section 195(3) of the Army Act 1955 and section 195(3) of the Air Force Act 1955—
  "(3) A constable may seize any property which he has reasonable grounds for suspecting of having been the subject of an offence against this section."

"Sexual Offences Act 1956 (c.69)

9. At the end of section 41 of the Sexual Offences Act 1956 (power to arrest in cases of soliciting by men) there shall be added the words "but a constable may only do so in accordance with section 24 of the Police and Criminal Evidence Act 1984."

Game Laws (Amendment) Act 1960 (c.30)

10. In subsection (1) of section 2 of the Game Laws (Amendment) Act 1960 (power of police to enter on land) for the words "purpose of exercising any power conferred on him by the foregoing section" there shall be substituted the words "purpose—
  (a) of exercising in relation to him the powers under section 31 of the Game Act 1831 which section 31A of that Act confers on police constables; or
  (b) of arresting him in accordance with section 25 of the Police and Criminal Evidence Act 1984.".

11. In subsection (1) of section 4 of that Act (enforcement powers) for the words from "under", in the first place where it occurs, to "thirty-one" there shall be substituted the words ", in accordance with section 25 of the Police and Criminal Evidence Act 1984, for an

offence under section one or section nine of the Night Poaching Act 1828, or under section thirty".

Betting, Gaming and Lotteries Act 1963 (c.2)

12. The following subsection shall be substituted for subsection (2) of section 8 of the Betting, Gaming and Lotteries Act 1963 (prohibition of betting in streets and public places)—
"(2) Where a person is found committing an offence under this section, any constable may seize and detain any article liable to be forfeited under this section.".

Deer Act 1963 (c.36)

13. In subsection (2) of section 5 of the Deer Act 1963 (enforcement powers) after the word "subsection" there shall be inserted the words "or arresting a person in accordance with section 25 of the Police and Criminal Evidence Act 1984, for an offence under this Act".

Police Act 1964 (c.48)

14. In section 7(1) of the Police Act 1964 (other members of police forces) after the words "chief constable" there shall be inserted the words ", deputy chief constable".
15. In section 29(2) of that Act (removal of chief constables) for the words "the deputy or an assistant chief constable" there shall be substituted the words "a deputy or assistant chief constable".
16. In section 43(5) of that Act (central service) after the word "constabulary" there shall be inserted the words "or with the Police Complaints Authority."

Criminal Law Act 1967 (c.58)

17. The following subsection shall be inserted after section 4(1) of the Criminal Law Act 1967—
"(1A) In this section and section 5 below 'arrestable offence' has the meaning assigned to it by section 24 of the Police and Criminal Evidence Act 1984.".

Theatres Act 1968 (c.54)

18. In section 15(1) of the Theatres Act 1968 (powers of entry and inspection) for the words "fourteen days" there shall be substituted the words "one month".

Children and Young Persons Act 1969 (c.54)

19. In the Children and Young Persons Act 1969—
  (a) in section 28(4), for the words "a police officer not below the rank of inspector or by the police officer in charge of" there shall be substituted the words "the custody officer at"; and
  (b) the following section shall be substituted for section 29—

  "Recognisance on release of arrested child or young person
  29. A child or young person arrested in pursuance of a warrant shall not be released unless he or his parent or guardian (with or without sureties) enters into a recognisance for such amount as the custody officer at the police station where he is detained considers will secure his attendance at the hearing of the charge; and the recognisance entered into in pursuance of this section may, if the custody officer thinks fit, be conditioned for the attendance of the parent or guardian at the hearing in addition to the child or young person."

Immigration Act 1971 (c.77)

20. In section 25(3) of the Immigration Act 1971 for the words "A constable or" there shall be substituted the word "An".

Criminal Justice Act 1972 (c.71)

21. In subsection (1) of section 34 of the Criminal Justice Act 1972 (powers of constable to take drunken offender to treatment centre) for the words from the beginning to "section the" there shall be substituted the words "On arresting an offender for an offence under—
  (a) section 12 of the Licensing Act 1872; or
  (b) section 91(1) of the Criminal Justice Act 1967,

Child Care Act 1980 *(c.5)*

22. In subsection (1)(*b*) of section 73 of the Child Care Act 1980 (provisions as to places of safety etc.) for the words "section 29(3) of the Children and Young Persons Act 1969" there shall be substituted the words "section 38(6) of the Police and Criminal Evidence Act 1984".

Deer Act 1980 *(c.49)*

23. In subsection (2) of section 4 of the Deer Act 1980 (enforcement powers) after the word "above" there shall be inserted the words "or arresting a person, in accordance with section 25 of the Police and Criminal Evidence Act 1984, for an offence under this Act".

Animal Health Act 1981 *(c.22)*

24. In subsection (5) of section 60 of the Animal Health Act 1981 (enforcement powers) for the words "a constable or other officer" there shall be substituted the words "an officer other than a constable".

Wildlife and Countryside Act 1981 *(c.69)*

25. In subsection (2) of section 19 of the Wildlife and Countryside Act 1981 (enforcement powers) after the words "subsection (1)" there shall be inserted the words "or arresting a person in accordance with section 25 of the Police and Criminal Evidence Act 1984 for such an offence".

Mental Health Act 1983 *(c.20)*

26. In section 135(4) of the Mental Health Act 1983 for the words "the constable to whom it is addressed", in both places where they occur, there shall be substituted the words "a constable".

Prevention of Terrorism (Temporary Provisions) Act 1984 *(c.8)*

27. In paragraph 4 of Schedule 3 to the Prevention of Terrorism (Temporary Provisions) Act 1984 (search warrants)—
   (*a*) in sub-paragraph (4)—
        (i) for the word "If" there shall be substituted the words "Subject to sub-paragraph (4A) below, if"; and
        (ii) at the end there shall be added the words "or which could have been so given but for section 9(2) of the Police and Criminal Evidence Act 1984"; and
   (*b*) the following sub-paragraph shall be inserted after sub-paragraph (4)—
        "(4A) An order given under sub-paragraph (4) above may not authorise a search for items subject to legal privilege within the meaning of section 10 of the Police and Criminal Evidence Act 1984."

PART II

OTHER AMENDMENTS

Army Act 1955 *(c.18)*

28.—(1) The Army Act 1955 shall be amended as follows.
(2) In section 99—
   (*a*) in subsection (1), after the word "below" there shall be inserted the words "and to service modifications"; and
   (*b*) the following subsections shall be inserted after that subsection—
        "(1A) In this section 'service modifications' means such modifications as the Secretary of State may by regulations made by statutory instrument prescribe, being modifications which appear to him to be necessary or proper for the purposes of proceedings before a court-martial; and it is hereby declared that in this section—
        'rules' includes rules contained in or made by virtue of an enactment; and
        'enactment' includes an enactment contained in an Act passed after this Act.
        (1B) Regulations under subsection (1A) above may not modify section 99A below.
        (1C) Regulations under subsection (1A) above shall be subject to annulment in pursuance of a resolution of either House of Parliament.".

(3) In section 99A(1) for the word "Section" there shall be substituted the words "Without prejudice to section 99 above, section".

(4) The following section shall be inserted after section 200—

"False statements in computer record certificates

200A.—(1) Any person who in a certificate tendered under paragraph 8 of Schedule 3 to the Police and Criminal Evidence Act 1984 (computer records) in evidence before a court-martial makes a statement which he knows to be false or does not believe to be true shall be guilty of an offence and liable—

    (*a*) on conviction on indictment to imprisonment for a term not exceeding two years or to a fine or to both;

    (*b*) on summary conviction to imprisonment for a term not exceeding six months or to a fine not exceeding the statutory maximum or to both.

(2) In this section "statutory maximum" has the meaning given by section 74 of the Criminal Justice Act 1982."

Air Force Act 1955 (c.19)

29.—(1) The Air Force Act 1955 shall be amended as follows.

(2) In section 99—

    (*a*) in subsection (1), after the word "below" there shall be inserted the words "and to service modifications"; and

    (*b*) the following subsections shall be inserted after that subsection—

"(1A) In this section 'service modifications' means such modifications as the Secretary of State may by regulations made by statutory instrument prescribe, being modifications which appear to him to be necessary or proper for the purposes of proceedings before a court-martial; and it is hereby declared that in this section—

'rules' includes rules contained in or made by virtue of an enactment; and

'enactment' includes an enactment contained in an Act passed after this Act.

(1B) Regulations under subsection (1A) above may not modify section 99A below.

(1C) Regulations under subsection (1A) above shall be subject to annulment in pursuance of a resolution of either House of Parliament.".

(3) In section 99A(1) for the word "Section" there shall be substituted the words "Without prejudice to section 99 above, section".

(4) The following section shall be inserted after section 200—

"False statements in computer record certificates

200A.—(1) Any person who in a certificate tendered under paragraph 8 of Schedule 3 to the Police and Criminal Evidence Act 1984 (computer records) in evidence before a court-martial makes a statement which he knows to be false or does not believe to be true shall be guilty of an offence and liable—

    (*a*) on conviction on indictment to imprisonment for a term not exceeding two years or to a fine or to both;

    (*b*) on summary conviction to imprisonment for a term not exceeding six months or to a fine not exceeding the statutory maximum or to both.

(2) In this section "statutory maximum" has the meaning given by section 74 of the Criminal Justice Act 1982.".

Police (Scotland) Act 1967 (c.77)

30. In section 6(2) of the Police (Scotland) Act 1967 (constables below rank of assistant chief constable) for the words "an assistant chief constable or a constable holding the office of deputy chief constable" there shall be substituted the words "a deputy chief constable or an assistant chief constable".

31. In section 7(1) of that Act (ranks) after the words "chief constable," there shall be inserted the words "deputy chief constable,".

32. In section 26(7) of that Act (disciplinary authority) immediately before the words "deputy chief constable" there shall be inserted the word "any".

33. In section 31(2) of that Act (compulsory retirement of chief constable etc.) for the words "the deputy or an assistant chief constable" there shall be substituted the words "a deputy or assistant chief constable".

Courts-Martial (Appeals) Act 1968 (c.20)

34. The following section shall be inserted after section 37 of the Courts-Martial (Appeals) Act 1968—
"False statements in computer record certificates.
37A.—(1) Any person who in a certificate tendered under paragraph 8 of Schedule 3 to the Police and Criminal Evidence Act 1984 (computer records) in evidence before the Appeal Court makes a statement which he knows to be false or does not believe to be true shall be guilty of an offence and liable—
(*a*) on conviction on indictment to imprisonment for a term not exceeding two years or to a fine or to both;
(*b*) on summary conviction to imprisonment for a term not exceeding six months or to a fine not exceeding the statutory maximum or to both.
(2) Proceedings for an offence under this section committed outside the United Kingdom may be taken, and the offence may for all incidental purposes be treated as having been committed, in any place in the United Kingdom,
(3) In this section "statutory maximum" has the meaning given by section 74 of the Criminal Justice Act 1982."

House of Commons Disqualification Act 1975 (c.24)

Northern Ireland Assembly Disqualification Act 1975 (c.25)

35. In Part II of Schedule 1 to the House of Commons Disqualification Act 1975 and Part II of Schedule 1 to the Northern Ireland Assembly Disqualification Act 1975 (bodies of which all members are disqualified under those Acts) there shall be inserted at the appropriate place in alphabetical order—
"The Police Complaints Authority".

Armed Forces Act 1976 (c.52)

36. The following paragraph shall be inserted after paragraph 17 of Schedule 3 to the Armed Forces Act 1976 (Standing Civilian Courts)—
"17A. Section 200A of that Act (false statements in computer record certificates) shall have effect as if the reference to a court-martial in subsection (1) included a reference to a Standing Civilian Court.".

Customs and Excise Management Act 1979 (c.2)

37. The following subsection shall be subsituted for section 138(4) of the Customs and Excise Management Act 1979—
"(4) Where any person has been arrested by a person who is not an officer—
(*a*) by virtue of this section; or
(*b*) by virtue of section 24 of the Police and Criminal Evidence Act 1984 in its application to the Customs and Excise Acts,
the person arresting him shall give notice of the arrest to an officer at the nearest convenient office of customs and excise.".

38. In section 161 of that Act—
(*a*) in subsection (3), for the words from "that officer" to the end of the subsection there shall be substituted the words "any officer and any person accompanying an officer to enter and search the building or place named in the warrant within one month from that day"; and
(*b*) in subsection (4), for the words "person named in a warrant under subsection (3) above" there shall be substituted the words "other person so authorised".

Betting and Gaming Duties Act 1981 (c.63)

39. In the following provisions of the Betting and Gaming Duties Act 1981, namely—
(*a*) section 15(2);
(*b*) paragraph 16(1) of Schedule 1;
(*c*) paragraph 17(1) of Schedule 3; and
(*d*) paragraph 17(1) of Schedule 4,
for the words "fourteen days" there shall be substituted the words "one month".

Car Tax Act 1983 (c.53)

40. In paragraph 7(3) of Schedule 1 to the Car Tax Act 1983 for the words "fourteen days" there shall be substituted the words "one month".

Value Added Tax Act 1983 (c.55)

41. In Schedule 7 to the Value Added Tax Act 1983—
   (*a*) the following sub-paragraph shall be substituted for paragraph 7(5)—
       "(5) A statement contained in a document produced by a computer shall not by virtue of sub-paragraph (3) of this paragraph be admissible in evidence—
           (*a*) in civil proceedings in England and Wales, except in accordance with sections 5 and 6 of the Civil Evidence Act 1968;
           (*b*) in criminal proceedings in England and Wales except in accordance with sections 68 to 70 of the Police and Criminal Evidence Act 1983;
           (*c*) in civil proceedings in Scotland, except in accordance with sections 13 and 14 of the Law Reform (Miscellaneous Provisions) (Scotland) Act 1968;
           (*d*) in criminal proceedings in Scotland, except in accordance with the said sections 13 and 14, which shall, for the purposes of this paragraph, apply with the necessary modifications to such proceedings;
           (*e*) in civil proceedings in Northern Ireland, except in accordance with sections 2 and 3 of the Civil Evidence Act (Northern Ireland) 1971; and
           (*f*) in criminal proceedings in Northern Ireland, except in accordance with the said sections 2 and 3, which shall, for the purposes of this paragraph, apply with the necessary modifications to such proceedings.";
   (*b*) in paragraph 7(6), for the words from "under the corresponding" to the end of the sub-paragraph there shall be substituted the words "section 13(4) of the Law Reform (Miscellaneous Provisions) (Scotland) Act 1968 or section 2(4) of the Civil Evidence Act (Northern Ireland) 1971"; and
   (*c*) in paragraph 10(3), for the words "14 days" there shall be substituted the words "one month".

SCHEDULE 7   Section 18.

Repeals

Part I

Enactments Repealed in Consequence of Parts I to V

Chapter	Short title	Extent of repeal
5 Geo. 4. c.83.	Vagrancy Act 1824	Section 8 Section 13
1 & 2 Will. 4. c.32.	Game Act 1831.	In section 31, the words "or for any police constable".
2 & 3 Vict. c.47.	Metropolitan Police Act 1839.	Section 34. In section 38, the words from "it" to "and" in the sixth place where it occurs. In section 39, the words "to take into custody". In section 47, the words "take into custody" and the words ", and every person so found". In section 54, the words from "And" to the end of the section. In section 62, the words from "may" in the first place where it occurs to "and" in the second place where it occurs. Sections 63–67.

Chapter	Short title	Extent of repeal
3 & 4 Vict. c.50.	Canals (Offences) Act 1840.	The whole Act,
5 & 6 Vict. c.55.	Railway Regulation Act 1842.	In section 17, the words "or for any special constable duly appointed,".
8 & 9 Vict. c.20.	Railways Clauses Consolidation Act 1845.	In section 104, the words "and all constables, gaolers, and police officers,".
10 & 11 Vict. c.89.	Town Police Clauses Act 1847.	In section 15, the words "may be taken into custody, without a warrant, by any constable, or" and the words from "Provided" to the end of the section. In section 28, the words from "and" in the first place where it occurs to "offence" in the second place where it occurs.
14 & 15 Vict. c.19.	Prevention of offences Act 1851	Section 11
23 & 24 Vict. c.32.	Ecclesiastical Courts Jurisdiction Act 1860.	In section 3, the words "constable or".
24 & 25 Vict. c.100.	Offences against the Person Act 1861.	In section 65, the words "in the daytime".
34 & 35 Vict. c.96.	Pedlars Act 1871.	Sections 18 and 19.
35 & 36 Vict. c.93.	Pawnbrokers Act 1872.	In section 36, the words ", within the hours of business,".
38 & 39 Vict. c.17.	Explosives Act 1875.	In section 78, the words "a constable, or".
52 & 53 Vict. c.18.	Indecent Advertisements Act 1889.	Section 6.
52 & 53 Vict. c.57.	Regulation of Railways Act 1889.	In section 5(2), the words "or any constable".
8 Edw. 7. c.66.	Public Meeting Act 1908.	In section 1, in subsection (3) the words from "and" in the sixth place where it occurs to the end of the subsection.
1 & 2 Geo. 5. c.28.	Official Secrets Act 1911.	In section 9(1), the words "named therein".
15 & 16 Geo. 5. c.71.	Public Health Act 1925.	Section 74(2) and (3).
23 & 24 Geo. 5. c.12.	Children and Young Persons Act 1933.	Section 10(2). Section 13(1) and (2). In section 40, in subsection (1) the words "named therein" and in subsection (4) the words "addressed to and".
11 & 12 Geo. 6, c.58.	Criminal Justice Act 1948.	Section 68.
1 & 2 Eliz. 2. c.14.	Prevention of Crime Act 1953.	Section 1(3).
3 & 4 Eliz. 2. c.28.	Children and Young Persons (Harmful Publications) Act 1955.	In section 3(1), the words "named therein".
4 & 5 Eliz. 2. c.69.	Sexual Offences Act 1956.	Section 40. In section 43(1), the word "named".
5 & 6 Eliz. 2. c.53.	Naval Discipline Act 1957.	In section 106(1), the words from "may" in the first place where it occurs to "and".
7 & 8 Eliz. 2. c.66.	Obscene Publications Act 1959.	In section 3(1), the words ", within fourteen days from the date of the warrant,".
8 & 9 Eliz. 2, c.36.	Game Laws (Amendment) Act 1960.	Section 1.
1963 c.2.	Betting, Gaming and Lotteries Act 1963.	In section 51(1), the words "at any time within fourteen days from the time of the issue of the warrant" and the words "arrest and".

Schedule 7—*continued*

Chapter	Short title	Extent of repeal
1963 c.36.	Deer Act 1963.	Section 5(1)(c).
1964 c.26.	Licensing Act 1964.	Section 187(5).
1967 c.58.	Criminal Law Act 1967.	Section 2.
1968 c.27.	Firearms Act 1968.	In section 46(1), the words "named therein". Section 50.
1968 c.52.	Caravan Sites Act 1968.	Section 11(5).
1968 c.60.	Theft Act 1968.	Section 12(3). Section 26(2).
1968 c.65.	Gaming Act 1968.	Section 5(2). In section 43, in subsection (4), the words "at any time within fourteen days from the time of the issue of the warrant", and in subsection (5)(b), the words "arrest and".
1970 c.30.	Conservation of Seals Act 1970.	Section 4(1)(a).
1971 c.38.	Misuse of Drugs Act 1971.	Section 24.
1971 c.77.	Immigration Act 1971.	In Schedule 2, in paragraph 17(2), the words "acting for the police area in which the premises are situated," and the words "at any time or times within one month from the date of the warrant".
1972 c.20.	Road Traffic Act 1972.	Section 19(3). Section 164(2).
1972 c.27.	Road Traffic (Foreign Vehicles) Act 1972.	Section 3(2).
1972 c.71	Criminal Justice Act	Section 34(3)
1973 c.57.	Badgers Act 1973.	Section 10(1)(b).
1974 c.6.	Biological Weapons Act 1974.	In section 4(1), the words "named therein".
1976 c.32.	Lotteries and Amusements Act 1976.	In section 19, the words "at any time within 14 days from the time of the issue of the warrant".
1976 c.58.	International Carriage of Perishable Foodstuffs Act 1976.	Section 11(6).
1977 c.45.	Criminal Law Act 1977.	Section 11. Section 62.
1979 c.2.	Customs and Excise Management Act 1979.	In section 138, in subsections (1) and (2), the words "or constable".
1980 c.43.	Magistrates' Courts Act 1980.	Section 49.
1980 c.49.	Deer Act 1980.	Section 4(1)(c).
1980 c.66.	Highways Act 1980.	Section 137(2).
1980 c.x.	County of Merseyside Act 1980.	Section 33
1980 c.xi.	West Midlands County Council Act 1980.	Section 42.
1981 c.14.	Public Passenger Vehicles Act 1981.	Section 25(2).
1981 c.22.	Animal Health Act 1981.	In section 60, subsection (3), in subsection (4) the words "or apprehending", subsection (6) and in subsection (5) the words "constable or" in the second place when they occur.
1981 c.42.	Indecent Displays (Control) Act 1981.	Section 2(1). In section 2(3), the words "within fourteen days from the date of issue of the warrant".

Schedule 7—*continued*

Chapter	Short title	Extent of repeal
1981 c.47.	Criminal Attempts Act 1981.	Section 9(4).
1981 c.69.	Wildlife and Countryside Act 1981.	Section 19(1)(*c*).
1982 c.48.	Criminal Justice Act 1982.	Section 34
1983 c.2.	Representation of the People Act 1983.	In section 97(3), the words from "and" in the fifth place where it occurs to "him" in the third place where it occurs. In Schedule 1, paragraph 36.
1983 c.20.	Mental Health Act 1983.	In section 135, in subsections (1) and (2), the words "named in the warrant".

Part II

Enactments Repealed in Relation to Criminal Proceedings in Consequence of Part VII

Chapter	Short title	Extent of repeal
1971 c.liv.	Cornwall County Council Act 1971.	Section 98(4).
1972 c.xlvii.	Hampshire County Council Act 1972.	Section 86(2).

Part III

Enactments Repealed Generally in Consequence of Part VII

Chapter	Short title	Extent of repeal
3 & 4 Eliz. 2. c.18.	Army Act 1955.	In section 198(1), the words "of this section and of sections 198A and 198B of this Act". Sections 198A and 198B.
3 & 4 Eliz. 2. c.19.	Air Force Act 1955.	In section 198(1), the words "of this section and of sections 198A and 198B of this Act". Sections 198A and 198B
1965 c.20.	Criminal Evidence Act 1965.	The whole Act.
1969 c.48.	Post Office Act 1969.	In section 93(4), the words "the Criminal Evidence Act 1965 and". In Schedule 4, paragraph 77.
1981 c.55.	Armed Forces Act 1981.	Section 9.
1981 c.xviii.	County of Kent Act 1981.	Section 82.
1983 c.55.	Value Added Tax Act 1983.	In Schedule 7, paragraph 7(7) and (8).

PART IV

ENACTMENTS REPEALED IN RELATION TO CRIMINAL PROCEEDINGS IN CONSEQUENCE OF PART VIII

Chapter	Short title	Extent of repeal
14 & 15 Vict. c.99.	Evidence Act 1851.	Section 13.
28 & 29 Vict. c.18.	Criminal Procedure Act 1865.	In section 6 the words from "and a certificate" onwards.
34 & 35 Vict. c.112.	Prevention of Crimes Act 1871.	Section 18 except the words "A previous conviction in any one part of the United Kingdom may be proved against a prisoner in any other part of the United Kingdom."

PART V

ENACTMENTS REPEALED GENERALLY IN CONSEQUENCE OF PART VIII

Chapter	Short title	Extent of repeal
16 & 17 Vict. c.83.	Evidence (Amendment) Act 1853.	Section 3.
46 & 47 Vict. c.3.	Explosive Substances Act 1883.	Section 4(2).
58 & 59 Vict. c.24.	Law of Distress Amendment Act 1895.	Section 5.
61 & 62 Vict. c.36.	Criminal Evidence Act 1898.	In section 1, the words "and the wife or husband, as the case may be, of the person so charged", the words (in paragraph (*b*)) "or of the wife or husband, as the case may be, of the person so charged" and paragraphs (*c*) and (*d*). Section 4. In section 6(1), the words from "notwithstanding" to the end. The Schedule.
4 & 5 Geo. 5. c.58.	Criminal Justice Administration Act 1914.	Section 28(3).
19 & 20 Geo. 5. c.34.	Infant Life (Preservation) Act 1929.	Section 2(5).
23 & 24 Geo. 5. c.12.	Children and Young Persons Act 1933	Section 15. Section 26(5).
4 & 5 Eliz. 2. c.69.	Sexual Offences Act 1956.	Section 12(2) and (3). Section 15(4) and (5). Section 16(2) and (3). Section 39. In Schedule 3 the entry relating to section 15 of the Children and Young Persons Act 1933.
8 & 9 Eliz. 2. c.33.	Indecency with Children Act 1960.	In section 1, subsection (2) and in subsection (3) the words "except in section 15 (which relates to the competence as a witness of the wife or husband of the accused)".
1965 c.72.	Matrimonial Causes Act 1965.	Section 43(1).
1968 c.60.	Theft Act 1968.	Section 30(3).
1970 c.55.	Family Income Supplements Act 1970.	Section 12(5).

Schedule 7—*continued*

Chapter	Short title	Extent of repeal
1973 c.38.	Social Security Act 1973.	In Schedule 23, paragraph 4.
1975 c.14.	Social Security Act 1975.	Section 147(6).
1975 c.16.	Industrial Injuries and Diseases (Old Cases) Act 1975.	Section 10(4).
1975 c.61.	Child Benefit Act 1975.	Section 11(8).
1976 c.71.	Supplementary Benefits Act 1976.	Section 26(5).
1977 c.45.	Criminal Law Act 1977.	In section 54(3) the words "subsection (2) (competence of spouse of accused to give evidence)".
1978 c.37.	Protection of Children Act 1978.	Section 2(1).
1979 c.18.	Social Security Act 1979.	Section 16.
1980 c.43.	Magistrates' Courts Act 1980.	In Schedule 7, paragraph 4.
1982 c.24.	Social Security and Housing Benefits Act 1982.	Section 21(6).

PART VI

MISCELLANEOUS REPEALS

Chapter	Short title	Extent of repeal
2 & 3 Vict. c.47.	Metropolitan Police Act 1839.	Section 7.
34 & 35 Vict. c. 96.	Pedlars Act 1871.	In section 18, the words from "or" where secondly occurring to "Act," and the words from "and forthwith" to the end of the section.
1964 c.48.	Police Act 1964.	Section 49. Section 50.
1967 c.77.	Police (Scotland) Act 1967.	Section 5(3) and section 17(6).
1972 c.11.	Superannuation Act 1972.	In Schedule 1, the reference to the Police Complaints Board.
1975 c.24.	House of Commons Disqualification Act 1975.	In Part II of Schedule 1, the entry relating to the Police Complaints Board.
1975 c.25.	Northern Ireland Assembly Disqualification Act 1975.	In Part II of Schedule 1, the entry relating to the Police Complaints Board.
1976 c.46.	Police Act 1976.	Section 1(1) to (4). Sections 2 to 13. Section 14(2). In the Schedule, paragraphs 1 to 3, in paragraph 4, the words "remuneration" and "allowances" and paragraphs 5 to 13.

CODES OF PRACTICE

CODES OF PRACTICE

Codes of Practice

CODES OF PRACTICE

CODE OF PRACTICE FOR THE DETENTION, TREATMENT AND QUESTIONING OF PERSONS BY THE POLICE

1 General

1.1 All persons in custody must be dealt with expeditiously, and released as soon as the need for detention has ceased to apply.

1.2 This code of practice must be readily available at all police stations for consultation by police officers, detained persons and members of the public.

1.3 The Notes for Guidance included in this and the other codes are not provisions of this code, but are guidance to police officers and others about its application and interpretation. Provisions in the Annexes to the codes are provisions of those codes.

1.4 If an officer has any suspicion, or is told in good faith that a person of any age may be mentally ill or mentally handicapped, or mentally incapable of understanding the significance of questions put to him or his replies, then that person shall be treated as a mentally ill or mentally handicapped person for the purposes of this code.

1.5 If anyone appears to be under the age of 17 then he shall be treated as a juvenile for the purposes of this code in the absence of clear evidence to show that he is older.

1.6 If a person appears to be blind or seriously visually handicapped, deaf, unable to communicate orally with the officer dealing with him at the time, he should be treated as such for the purposes of this Code in the absence of clear evidence to the contrary.

1.7 In this code "the appropriate adult" means:
    (a) in the case of a juvenile, (i) his parent or guardian (or, if he is in care, the care authority or organisation or (ii) a social worker or (iii) failing either of the above another responsible adult who is not a police officer or employed by the police; and
    (b) in the case of a person who is mentally ill or mentally handicapped,
        (i) a relative, guardian or other person responsible for his care or custody; (ii) someone who is not a police officer or employed by the police who has experience of dealing with mentally ill or mentally handicapped persons; or (iii) failing either of the above, some other responsible adult who is not a police officer or employed by the police. [See Note 1C]

1.8 Whenever this code requires a person to be given certain information he does not have to be given it if he is incapable at the time of understanding what is said to him or is violent or likely to become violent or is in urgent need of medical attention, but he must be given it as soon as practicable.

1.9 Any reference to a custody officer in this or the other codes includes an officer who is performing the functions of a custody officer.

1.10 This Code applies to persons who are in custody at police stations whether or not they have been arrested for an offence except section 16 which applies solely to persons in police detention.

Notes for guidance

1A Although certain sections of this code (e.g. section 9—Treatment of detained persons) apply specifically to persons in custody at police stations, those there voluntarily to assist with an investigation should be treated with no less consideration (e.g. offered refreshments at appropriate times) and enjoy an absolute right to obtain legal advice or communicate with anyone outside the police station.

1B This Code does not affect the principle that all citizens have a duty to help police officers to prevent crime and discover offenders. This is a civic rather than a legal duty; but when a police officer is trying to discover whether, or by whom, an offence has been committed he is entitled to question any person from whom he thinks useful information can be obtained, subject to the restrictions imposed by this Code. A person's declaration that he is unwilling to reply does not alter this entitlement.

1C In the case of persons who are mentally ill or mentally handicapped, it may in certain circumstances be more satisfactory for all concerned if the appropriate adult is someone who has experience or training in their care rather than a relative lacking such qualifications. But if the person himself prefers a relative to a better qualified stranger his wishes should if practicable be respected.

2 Custody records

2.1 A separate custody record must be opened as soon as practicable for each person who is brought to a police station under arrest or arrested at the police station having attended there voluntarily. All information which has to be recorded under this code must be recorded as soon as practicable, in the custody record unless otherwise specified.

2.2 In the case of any action requiring the authority of an officer of a specified rank, his name and rank must be noted in the custody record.

2.3 The custody officer is responsible for the accuracy and completeness of the custody record and for ensuring that the record or a copy of the record accompanies a detained person if he is transferred to another police station. The record shall show the time of and reason for transfer and the time a person is released from detention.

2.4 When a person leaves police detention he or his legal representative shall be supplied on request with a copy of the custody record as soon as practicable. This entitlement lasts for 12 months after his release.

2.5 All entries in custody and written interview records (except those identifying the person to whom the record relates) must be timed and signed by the maker.

2.6 Any refusal by a person to sign either a custody or an interview record when asked to do so in accordance with the provisions of this code must itself be recorded.

Note for Guidance

2A The person who has been detained, the appropriate adult or a legal representative who gives reasonable notice of a request to inspect the original custody record should be allowed to do so.

3 Initial action

(a) *Detained persons: normal procedure*

3.1 When a person is brought to a police station under arrest or arrested at the police station having attended there voluntarily the custody officer must inform him of the following rights and that they need not be exercised immediately:

(i) the right to have someone informed of his detention in accordance with section 5 below;

(ii) the right to consult a solicitor in accordance with section 6 below; and

(iii) the right to consult this and the other codes of practice. [See Note 3D]

3.2 The custody officer must also give the person a written notice setting out the above three rights, the right to a copy of the custody record in accordance with paragraph 2.4 above and the caution in the terms prescribed in section 10 below. The custody officer shall ask him to sign the custody record to acknowledge receipt of this notice.

3.3 If the custody officer authorises a person's detention he must inform him of the grounds as soon as practicable and in any case before he has been questioned about any offence.

3.4 The person shall be asked to sign on the custody record to signify whether or not he wants legal advice at this point.

(b) *Detained persons: special groups*

3.5 If the person does not understand English or appears to be deaf and the custody officer cannot communicate with him then the custody officer must as soon as practicable call an interpreter, and ask him to provide the information required above.

3.6 If the person is a juvenile is mentally handicapped or is suffering from mental illness then the custody officer must as soon as practicable inform the appropriate adult of the grounds for his detention and his whereabouts, and ask the adult to come to the police station to see the person. If the appropriate adult is already at the police station when information is given to the person as required in paragraphs 3.1–3.3 above, then the information must be given to the detained person in his presence. If the appropriate adult is not at the police station when the information is given the information must be given to the detained person again in the presence of the appropriate adult once that person arrives.

3.7 If the person is blind or seriously visually handicapped or is unable to read, the custody officer should ensure that his solicitor, relative, the appropriate adult or some other person likely to take an interest in him is available to help in checking any documentation. Where this code requires written consent or signification, then this person who is assisting may be asked to sign instead.

3.8 In the case of a juvenile who is known to be subject to a supervision order, reasonable steps must be taken to inform the person supervising him.

(c) *Persons attending a police station voluntarily*

3.9 Any person attending a police station voluntarily for the purpose of assisting with an investigation may leave at will unless placed under arrest. If it is decided that he would not be allowed to do so then he must be informed at once that he is under arrest and brought before the custody officer. If he is not placed under arrest but is cautioned in accordance with section 10 below, the officer who gives the caution must, at the same time, inform him that he is not under arrest, that he is not obliged to remain at the police station and that he may obtain legal advice if he wishes.

(d) *Documentation*

3.10 The grounds for a person's detention shall be recorded, in his presence if practicable.

3.11 Action taken under paragraphs 3.6 or 3.8 shall be recorded.

Notes for guidance

3A If the juvenile is in the care of a local authority or voluntary organisation but is living with his parents or other adults responsible for his welfare then, although there is no legal obligation on the police to inform them, they as well as the authority or organisation should normally be contacted unless suspected of involvement in the offence concerned. Even if a juvenile in care is not living with his parents, consideration should be given to informing them as well.

3B Section 7 of this code contains special additional provision for Commonwealth citizens and foreign nationals.

3C Most Local Authority Social Services Departments, can supply a list of interpreters who have the necessary skills and experience to interpret for the deaf at police interviews.

3D The right to consult the codes of practice under paragraph 3.1 above does not entitle the person concerned to delay unreasonably necessary investigative or administrative action while he does so.

4 Detained persons' property

(a) *Action*

4.1 The custody officer is responsible for:
  (a) ascertaining:
    (i) what property a detained person has with him when he comes to the police station (whether on arrest, re-detention or answering to bail, commitment to prison custody on the order of sentence of a court, on lodgement at the police station with a view to his production in court from such custody, or on arrival at a police station or transfer from detention at another station or from hospital);
    (ii) what property he might have acquired for an unlawful purpose while in custody.
  (b) the safekeeping of any property which is taken from him and which remains at the police station.
To these ends the custody officer may search him or authorise his being searched to the extent that he considers necessary (provided that a search of intimate parts of the body or involving the removal of more than outer clothing may only be made in accordance with Annex A to this Code). A search may only be carried out by an officer of the same sex as the person searched.

4.2 A detained person may retain clothing and personal effects at his own risk unless the custody officer considers that he may use them to cause harm to himself or others, interfere with evidence, damage property or effect an escape or they are needed as evidence. In this event the custody officer can withhold such articles as he considers necessary. If he does so he must tell the person why.

4.3 Personal effects are those items which a person may need to use or refer to while in detention but do not include cash.

(b) *Documentation*

4.4 The custody officer is responsible for recording all property brought to a police station that a detained person had with him or had taken from him on arrest. The detained person shall be allowed to check and sign the record of property as correct.

4.5 If a detained person is not allowed to keep any article taken from him either on arrest or on detention, the reason must be recorded.

Notes for guidance

4A Paragraph 4.1 is not to be taken as requiring each detained person to be searched. Where, for example, a person is to be detained for only a short period and is not to be placed in a cell, the custody officer may at his discretion decide not to search the person. In such a case the custody record will be endorsed "not searched" and the person will be invited to sign the entry. Where the person detained refuses to sign, the custody officer will be obliged to ascertain what property he has on him in accordance with paragraph 4.1.

4B Paragraph 4.4 does not require the custody officer to record on the custody record, property in the possession of the person on arrest, if by virtue of its nature, quantity or size, it is not practicable to remove it to the police station.

4C Paragraph 4.1 above is not to be taken as requiring that items of clothing worn by the person be recorded unless withheld by the custody officer in accordance with paragraph 4.2.

5 The right not to be held incommunicado

(a) *Action*

5.1 Any person to whom paragraphs 2.1 and 3.9 apply may on request have one person known to him or who is likely to take an interest in his welfare informed at public expense as soon as practicable of his whereabouts. If the person cannot be contacted the detained person may choose up to two alternatives. If they too cannot be contacted the custody officer has discretion to allow further attempts until the information has been conveyed. [See Notes 5C and 5D]

5.2 The exercise of the above right in respect of each of the persons nominated may be delayed only in accordance with Annex B (p. 279 below) to this code.

5.3 The above right may be exercised on each occasion that a person is taken to another police station.

5.4 Detained persons may receive visits at the custody officer's discretion. [See Note 5B]

5.5 Where an inquiry as to the whereabouts of a detained person is made by friend, relative, or person with an interest in his welfare, this information shall be given, if he agrees and if Annex B does not apply. [See Note 5D]

5.6 The person shall be supplied on request with writing materials. Any letter or other message shall be sent as soon as practicable unless Annex B (p. 279 below) applies.

5.7 He may also speak on the telephone to one person unless Annex B applies. [See Note 5E]

5.8 Before any letter or message is sent, or telephone call made the person shall be informed that what he says in any letter, call or message (other than in the case of a communication to a solicitor) may be given in evidence. A telephone call may be terminated if it is being abused. The costs can be at public expense at the discretion of the custody officer.

(b) *Documentation*

5.9 A record must be kept of (a) any request made under this section and the action taken on it; (b) any letters or messages sent, calls made or visits received; and (c) any refusal on the part of a person to have information about himself or his whereabouts given to an outside inquirer.

Notes for guidance

5A An interpreter may make a telephone call or write a letter on a person's behalf.

5B In the exercise of his discretion the custody officer should allow visits where possible in the light of the availability of sufficient manpower to supervise a visit and any possible hindrance to the investigation.

5C If the person does not know of anyone to contact for advice or support or cannot contact a friend or relative the custody officer should bear in mind any local voluntary bodies other organisations who might be able to offer help in such cases. But if it is specifically legal advice that is wanted, then paragraph 6.1 below will apply.

5D In some circumstances it may not be appropriate to use the telephone to disclose information under paragraphs 5.1 and 5.5 above.

5E The telephone call at paragraph 5.7 is in addition to any communication at paragraphs 5.1 and 6.1.

6 The right to legal advice

(a) *Action*

6.1 Any person to whom paragraphs 2.1 and 3.9 apply may at any time consult and communicate privately, whether in person, in writing or on the telephone:

(a) with a solicitor of his own choice;

(b) with the duty solicitor (where a Duty Solicitor Scheme is in operation);

(c) with a solicitor selected by him from a list of solicitors who have indicated that they are available for the purpose of providing legal advice.

Persons to whom paragraphs 2.1 and 3.9 apply shall be informed in writing of these options and of the fact that option (b) will always be free of charge; and that the other options will also be free of charge unless the suspect agrees otherwise with his solicitor.

6.2 The exercise of the above right may be delayed only in accordance with Annex B (p. 279 below) to this code.

6.3 A person who asks for legal advice may not be interviewed or continue to be interviewed until he has received it unless:

(a) Annex B applies; or

(b) an officer of the rank of superintendent or above has reasonable grounds to believe that (i) delay will involve an immediate risk of harm to persons or serious loss of or damage to property; or that (ii) awaiting the arrival of a solicitor would cause unreasonable delay to the processes of investigation; or (iii) the person has given his agreement in writing or on tape that the interview may be commenced at once. [See Notes 6A and 6B]

6.4 Where 6.3(b)(i) applies, once sufficient information to avert the risk has been obtained, questioning must cease until the person has received legal advice or 6.3(a), (b)(ii) or (iii) apply.

6.5 Where a person has been permitted to consult a solicitor and the solicitor is available at the time the interview begins or is in progress, he must be allowed to have his solicitor present while he is interviewed.

6.6 The solicitor may only be required to leave the interview if his conduct is such that the investigating officer is unable properly to put questions to the suspect. [See Note 6C]

6.7 If the investigating officer considers that a solicitor is acting in such a way, he will stop the interview and consult an officer not below the rank of superintendent, if he is readily available, and otherwise an officer not below the rank of inspector who is not connected with the investigation. After speaking to the solicitor the officer will decide whether or not the interview should continue in the presence of that solicitor. If he decides that it should not, the suspect will be given the opportunity to consult another solicitor before the interview continues and that solicitor will be given an opportunity to be present at the interview.

6.8 The removal of a solicitor from an interview is a serious step and if it occurs, the officer of superintendent rank or above who took the decision will consider whether the incident should be reported to The Law Society. If the decision to remove the solicitor has been taken by an officer below the rank of superintendent, the facts must be reported to an officer of superintendent rank or above who will similarly consider whether a report to The Law Society would be appropriate.

6.9 In this code "solicitor" means a solicitor qualified to practice in accordance with the Solicitors Act 1974. If a solicitor wishes to send a clerk or legal executive to provide advice on his behalf, then the clerk or legal executive shall be admitted to the police station for this purpose unless an officer of the rank of inspector or above considers that such a visit will hinder the investigation of crime and directs otherwise. If no such direction is given then the provisions of paragraphs 6.3–6.6 apply. [See Note 6D]

6.10 If the inspector refuses access to a clerk or legal executive or a decision is taken that such a person should not be permitted to remain at an interview, he must forthwith notify a solicitor on whose behalf the clerk or legal executive was to have acted or was acting, and give him an opportunity of making alternative arrangements.

(b) *Documentation*

6.11 Any request for legal advice and the action taken on it shall be recorded.

6.12 If a person has asked for legal advice and an interview is commenced in the absence of a solicitor or his representative (or the solicitor or his representative has been required to leave an interview), a record shall be made in the interview record.

Notes for guidance

6A In considering whether paragraph 6.3(b)(i) and (ii) applies, the officer should where practicable ask the solicitor for an estimate of the time that he is likely to take in coming to the station, and relate this information to the time for which detention is permitted, the time of day (*i.e.* whether the period of rest required by paragraph 12.2 is imminent) and the requirements of other investigations in progress. If it appears that it will be necessary to begin an interview before the solicitor's arrival he should be given an indication of how long police would be able to wait before paragraph 6.3(b) (i) and (ii) applies so that he has an opportunity to make arrangements for legal advice to be provided by someone else.

6B Procedures under section 8 of the Road Traffic Act 1972 do not constitute interviewing for the purposes of this code.

6C In considering whether paragraph 6.5 applies, a solicitor is not guilty of misconduct if he seeks to challenge an improper question to his client or the manner in which it is put or he wishes to give his client further legal advice, and should not be required to leave an interview unless his interference with its conduct clearly goes beyond this.

6D A clerk or legal executive should normally be afforded the same facilities as a solicitor. However if a clerk or legal executive acts improperly or has done so in the past, he should be reminded that he has no more rights or privileges than any other member of the public and may be so treated.

6E In a case when an officer takes the decision to exclude a solicitor, he must be in a position to satisfy the court that the decision was properly made. In order to do this he may need to witness what is happening himself.

7 Citizens of independent Commonwealth countries or foreign nationals

(a) *Action*

7.1 A citizen of an independent Commonwealth country or a national of a foreign country (including the Republic of Ireland) may communicate at any time with his High Commissioner, Embassy or Consulate.

7.2 If a citizen of an independent Commonwealth country has been detained for more than 24 hours he must be asked if he wishes the police to inform his High Commission in London of his whereabouts and the grounds for his detention. If so the custody officer is responsible for ensuring that the High Commission is informed by telephone.

7.3 If a national of a foreign country with which a Consular Convention is in force is detained, the appropriate consulate shall be informed as soon as practicable, subject to paragraph 7.6 below.

7.4 Any other foreign national who is detained must be informed as soon as practicable of his right to communicate with his consul if he so wishes. He must also be informed that the police will notify his consul of his arrest if he wishes.

7.5 Consular officers may visit one of their nationals who is in police detention to talk to him and, if required, to arrange for legal advice. Such visits shall take place out of the hearing of a police officer.

7.6 Notwithstanding the provisions of consular conventions, where the person is a political refugee (whether for reasons of race, nationality, political opinion or religion) or is seeking political asylum, a consular officer shall not be informed of the arrest of one of his nationals or given access to or information about him except at the person's express request.

(b) *Documentation*

7.7 A record shall be made when a person is informed of his rights under this section and of any communications with a High Commission, Embassy or Consulate.

Notes for guidance

   7A The exercise of the rights in this section may not be interfered with even though Annex B (p. 279 below) applies.

   7B A list of countries with which a Consular Convention is in force is set out in the Home Office Consolidated Circular to the Police on Crime and Kindred Matters.

8 Conditions of detention

(a) *Action*

8.1 So far as is practicable, not more than one person shall be detained in each cell.

8.2 Cells in use must be adequately heated, cleaned and ventilated. They must be adequately lit, subject to such dimming as is compatible with safety and security to allow persons detained overnight to sleep. No additional restraints should be used within a locked cell.

8.3 Blankets, mattresses, pillows and other bedding supplied should be of a reasonable standard and in a clean and sanitary condition. [See Note 8B]

8.4 Access to toilet and washing facilities must be provided.

8.5 If it is necessary to remove a person's clothes for the purposes of investigation, for hygiene or health reasons or for cleaning, replacement clothing of a reasonable standard of comfort and cleanliness shall be provided. A person may not be interviewed unless adequate clothing has been offered to him.

8.6 At least two light meals and one main meal shall be offered in any period of 24 hours. Wherever necessary, advice shall be sought from the police surgeon on medical or dietary matters. As far as practicable, meals provided shall offer a varied diet and meet any special dietary needs or religious beliefs that the person may have; he may also have meals supplied by his family or friends at his or their own expense. [See Note 8B]

8.7 Brief outdoor exercise shall be offered daily if practicable.

8.8 A juvenile shall not be placed in police cells unless no other secure accommodation is available and the custody officer considers that it is not practicable to supervise him if he is not placed in a cell. He may not be placed in a cell with a detained adult.

8.9 Reasonable force may be used if necessary for the following purposes:

    (i) to secure compliance with reasonable instructions, including instructions given in pursuance of the provisions of a code of practice; or

   (ii) to prevent escape, injury, damage to property or the destruction of evidence.

(b) *Documentation*

8.10 Persons detained should be visited every hour, and those who are drunk every half an hour. [See Note 8A]

8.11 A record must be kept of replacement clothing and meals offered.

8.12 If a juvenile is placed in a cell, the grounds must be recorded.

8A Whenever possible juveniles and other persons at risk should be visited more regularly.

8B The provisions in paragraphs 8.3 and 8.6 respectively regarding bedding and a varied diet are of particular importance in the case of a person detained under the Prevention of Terrorism (Temporary Provisions) Act 1984. This is because such a person is likely to remain in police custody for some time.

9 Treatment of detained persons

(a) *General*

9.1 If a complaint is made by or on behalf of a detained person about his treatment since his arrest, or it comes to the notice of any officer that he may have been treated improperly, a report must be made as soon as practicable to an officer of the rank of inspector or above who is not connected with the investigation. If the matter concerns a possible assault or the possibility of unnecessary or unreasonable use of force then the police surgeon must also be called as soon as practicable.

(b) *Medical treatment*

9.2 The custody officer must immediately call the police surgeon (or, in urgent cases, send the person to hospital or call the nearest available medical practitioner) if a person brought to a police station or already detained there:
  (a) appears to be suffering from physical or mental illness; or
  (b) is injured; or
  (c) does not show signs of sensibility and awareness or fails to respond normally to questions or conversation (other than through drunkenness alone); or
  (d) otherwise appears to need medical attention.
This applies even if the person makes no request for medical attention and whether or not he has recently had medical treatment elsewhere (unless brought to the station direct from hospital). [See Note 9A]

9.3 If it appears to the custody officer, or he is told, that a person brought to the police station under arrest may be suffering from an infectious disease of any significance he must take steps to isolate the person and his property until he has obtained medical directions as to where the person should be taken, whether fumigation should take place and what precautions should be taken by officers who have been or will be in contact with him.

9.4 If a detained person requests a medical examination the police surgeon must be called as soon as practicable. He may in addition be examined by a medical practitioner of his own choice at his own expense.

9.5 If a person is required to take or apply any medication in compliance with medical directions, the custody officer is responsible for its safe keeping and for ensuring that he is given the opportunity to take or apply it at the appropriate times. No police officer may administer controlled drugs subject to the Misuse of Drugs Act 1981 for this purpose: a person may administer such drugs to himself only under the personal supervision of the police surgeon.

9.6 If a detained person has in his possession or claims to need medication relating to a heart condition, diabetes, epilepsy or a condition of comparable potential seriousness then, even though paragraph 9.2 may not apply, the advice of the police surgeon must be obtained.

9.7 A record must be made of any arrangements made for an examination by a police surgeon under paragraph 9.2 above and of any complaint reported under that paragraph together with any relevant remarks by the custody officer.

(c) *Documentation*

9.8 A record must be kept of any request for a medical examination under paragraph 9.4, of the arrangements for any examination made, and of any medical directions to the police.

9.9 Subject to the requirements of section 4 above the custody record shall include not only a record of all medication that a detained person has in his possession on arrival at the police station but also a note of any such medication he claims he needs but does not have with him.

Notes for guidance

9A The need to call a police surgeon need not apply to minor ailments.

9B It is important to remember that a person who appears to be drunk or behaving abnormally may be suffering from illness or the effect of drugs or may have sustained injury (particularly head injury) which is not apparent, and that someone needing or addicted to certain drugs may experience harmful effects within a short time of being deprived of their supply. Police should therefore always call the police surgeon when in any doubt, and act with all due speed.

9C If a medical practitioner does not record his clinical findings in the custody record, the record must show where they are recorded.

9D All officers dealing with detained persons are of course under a duty to observe not only the above provisions but also those set out in the Police Discipline Code.

10 Cautions

(a) *Where a caution must be given*

10.1 A person whom there are grounds to suspect of an offence other than an offence for which a fixed penalty may be offered must be cautioned before any questions about it (or further questions if it is his answers to previous questions that provide grounds for suspicion) are put to him for the purpose of obtaining evidence which may be given to a court in a prosecution. He therefore need not be cautioned if questions are put for other purposes, for example, to establish his identity, his ownership of any vehicle or the need to search him in the exercise of powers of stop and search.

10.2 When a person who is not under arrest is initially cautioned before or during an interview at a police station or other premises, he must at the same time be told that he is not under arrest, is not obliged to remain with the officer and may obtain legal advice if he wishes.

10.3 A person must be cautioned upon arrest for an offence unless (a) it is impracticable to do so by reason of his condition or behaviour at the time; or (b) he has already been cautioned immediately prior to arrest in accordance with paragraph 10.1 above.

(b) *Action—general*

10.4 The caution shall be in the following terms: "You do not have to say anything unless you wish to do so, but what you say may be given in evidence." Minor deviations do not constitute a breach of this requirement provided that the sense of the caution is preserved. [See Notes 10C and 10D]

10.5 When there is a break in questioning under caution the interviewing officer must ensure that the person being questioned is aware that he remains under caution. If there is any doubt the caution should be given again in full when the interview resumes. [See Note 10A]

(c) *Documentation*

10.6 A record shall be made when a caution is given under this section, either in the officer's pocket book or in the interview record as appropriate.

Notes for guidance

10A In considering whether or not to caution again after a break; the officer may have to satisfy a court that the person understood that he was still under caution when the interview resumed.

10B It is not necessary to give or repeat a caution when informing a person who is not under arrest that he may be prosecuted for an offence.

10C If it appears that a person does not understand what the caution means the officer who has given it should go on to explain it in his own words.

10D In case anyone who is given a caution is unclear about its significance the officer concerned should explain that the caution is given in pursuance of the general principle of English law that a person need not answer any questions or provide any information which might tend to incriminate him, and that no adverse inferences from this silence may be drawn at any trial that takes place. The person should not, however, be left with the false impression that non-cooperation will have no effect on his immediate treatment as, for example, his refusal to provide his name and address when charged with an offence may render him liable to detention.

11 Interviews—general

11.1 No police officer may try to obtain answers to questions or to elicit a statement by the use of oppression, or shall indicate, except in answer to a direct question, what action will be taken on the part of the police if the person being interviewed answers questions, makes a statement or refuses to do either. If the person directly asks the officer what action will be taken in the event of his answering questions, making a statement or refusing to do either, then the officer may inform the person what action he proposes to take in that event provided that that action is itself proper and warranted.

11.2 As soon as a police officer who is making inquiries of any person about an offence believes that a prosecution should be brought against him and that there is sufficient evidence for it to succeed, he shall without delay cease to question him.

11.3 (a) An accurate record must be made of each interview with a person suspected of an offence, whether or not the interview takes place at a police station. (b) If the interview takes place in the police station or other premises: (i) the record must state the place of the interview, the time it begins and ends, the time the record is made (if different), any breaks in the interview and the names of all those present, and must be made on the forms provided for this purpose or in the officer's pocket book or in accordance with the code of practice for the tape recording of police interviews with suspects; (ii) the record must be made during the course of the interview unless in the investigating officer's view this would not be practicable or would interfere with the conduct of the interview and must constitute either a verbatim record of what has been said or, failing this, an account of the interview which, though not verbatim, adequately and accurately summarizes it.

11.4 If an interview record is not made during the course of the interview it must be made as soon as is practicable after its completion.

11.5 Written interview records must be timed and signed by the maker.

11.6 If an interview record is not completed in the course of the interview the reason must be recorded in the officer's pocket book.

11.7 Any refusal by a person to sign an interview record when asked to do so in accordance with the provisions of this code must itself be recorded.

12 Interviews in police stations

(a) *Action*

12.1 If a police officer wishes to interview, or conduct enquiries which require the presence of, a detained person the custody officer is responsible for deciding whether to deliver him into his custody.

12.2 In any period of 24 hours a detained person must be allowed a continuous period of at least 8 hours for rest, free from questioning, travel or any interruption arising out of the investigation concerned. This period should normally be at night. The period of rest may not be interrupted or delayed unless there are reasonable grounds for believing that it would:

  (i) involve a risk of harm to persons or serious loss of or damage to property; or

 (ii) delay unnecessarily the person's release from custody;

(iii) otherwise prejudice the outcome of the investigation.

12.3 A detained person may not be supplied with intoxicating liquor except on medical directions. No person who is unfit through drink or drugs to the extent that he is unable to appreciate the significance of questions put to him and his answers may be questioned about an alleged offence in that condition except in accordance with Annex C (p. 280 below). [See Note 12C]

12.4 As far as practicable interviews shall take place in interview rooms, which must be adequately heated, lit and ventilated.

12.5 Persons being questioned or making statements shall not be required to stand.

12.6 Before the commencement of an interview each interviewing officer shall identify himself and any other officers present by name and rank to the person being interviewed.

12.7 Breaks from interviewing shall be made at recognised meal times. Short breaks for refreshments shall also be provided at intervals of approximately two hours subject to the interviewing officer's discretion to delay a break if there are reasonable grounds for believing that it would:

  (i) involve a risk of harm to persons or serious loss of or damage to property; or

 (ii) delay unnecessarily the person's release from custody; or

(iii) otherwise prejudice the outcome of the investigation.

12.8 If in the course of the interview a complaint is made by the person being questioned or on his behalf concerning the provisions of this code then the interviewing officer shall:—

  (i) record it in the interview record; and

 (ii) inform the custody officer, who is then responsible for dealing with it in accordance with section 9 of this code.

(b) *Documentation*

12.9 A record must be made of the times at which a detained person is not in the custody of the custody officer, and why; and of the reason for any refusal to deliver him out of that custody.

12.10 A record must be made of any intoxicating liquor supplied to a detained person, in accordance with paragraph 12.3 above.

12.11 Any decision to delay a break in an interview must be recorded, with grounds, in the interview record.

12.12 Where the person interviewed is in the police station at the time that a written record of the interview is made, he shall be given the opportunity to read it and to sign it as correct or to indicate the respects in which he considers it inaccurate, but no person shall be kept in custody for this sole purpose. If the interview is tape recorded the arrangements set out in the Procedural Guidance or any tape recording code of practice apply. [See Note 12B]

12.13 All written statements made at police stations after caution shall be written on the forms provided for the purpose.

12.14 All written statements made after caution shall be taken in accordance with Annex D (p. 281 below) to this code.

12.15 Where the appropriate adult or another third party is present at an interview and is still in the police station at the time that a written record of the interview is made he shall be asked to read it (or any written statement taken down by a police officer) and sign it as correct or to indicate the respects in which he considers it inaccurate. If the person refuses to read or sign the record as accurate or to indicate the respects in which he considers it inaccurate the senior officer present shall record on the record itself, in the presence of the person concerned, what has happened. If the interview is tape recorded the arrangements set out in the Procedural Guidance or any tape recording code of practice apply.

Notes for guidance

12A The purpose of any interview is to obtain from the person concerned his explanation of the facts, and not necessarily to obtain an admission.

12B If the interview has been contemporaneously recorded and the record signed by the person interviewed in accordance with paragraph 12.12 above, or has been tape recorded, it is normally unnecessary to ask for a written statement. Statements under caution should normally be taken in these circumstances only at the person's express wish. An officer may, however, ask him whether or not he wants to make such a statement.

12C The police surgeon can give advice about whether or not a person is fit to be interviewed under paragraph 12.3 above.

13 Persons at risk: juveniles, the mentally ill and the mentally handicapped

13.1 A juvenile or a person who is mentally ill or mentally handicapped, whether suspected of crime or not, must not be interviewed or asked to provide or sign a written statement in the absence of the appropriate adult unless Annex C (p. 280 below) applies. If he is cautioned under section 10 above in the absence of the appropriate adult the caution must be repeated in the adult's presence (unless the interview has by then already finished).

13.2 If, having been informed of the right to legal advice under paragraph 3.6 above, the appropriate adult considers that legal advice should be taken, then the provisions of section 6 of this code apply.

13.3 Juveniles may only be interviewed at their place of education in exceptional circumstances and then only when the principal or his nominee agrees and is present.

Notes for guidance

13A Where the parents or guardians of a person at risk are themselves suspected of involvement in the offence concerned, or are the victims of it, it may be desirable for the appropriate adult to be some other person.

13B It is important to bear in mind that, although juveniles or person who are mentally ill or mentally handicapped are often capable of providing reliable evidence, they may without knowing or wishing to do so, be particularly prone in certain circumstances to provide information which is unreliable, misleading or self-incriminating. Special care should therefore always be exercised in questioning such a person, and the safeguards set out in the code applied, if there is any doubt about a person's age, mental state or capacity. Because of the risk of unreliable evidence it is also important to obtain corroboration of any facts admitted wherever possible.

13C The appropriate adult should be informed that he is not expected to act simply as an observer. The purposes of his presence are, first, to advise the person being questioned and to observe whether or not the interview is being conducted fairly; and, second to facilitate communication with the person being interviewed.

13D Officers are reminded that a juvenile should not be arrested at his place of education unless this is unavoidable. In this case the principal or his nominee must be informed.

14 Interpreters

(a) *Foreign languages*

14.1 If a person has difficulty in understanding English and either the interviewing officer cannot himself speak the person's own language or the person wishes an interpreter to be present, he must not be interviewed in the absence of a person capable of acting as interpreter unless Annex C applies.

14.2 The interviewing officer shall ensure that the interpreter makes a note of the interview at the time in the language of the person being interviewed for use in the event of his being called to give evidence, and certifies its accuracy. The person shall be given an opportunity to read it or have it read to him and sign it as correct or to indicate the respects in which he considers it inaccurate. If the interview is tape recorded the arrangements set out in the Procedural Guidance or any tape recording code of practice apply.

14.3 In the case of a person making a statement in a language other than English
  (a) the interpreter shall take down the statement in the language in which it is made;
  (b) the person making the statement shall be invited to sign the statement; and
  (c) an official English translation shall be made in due course.

(b) *The deaf*

14.4 If a person is deaf or there is doubt about his hearing ability he must not be interviewed in the absence of an interpreter unless he agrees in writing to be interviewed without one or Annex C applies. (Information on obtaining the services of a suitably qualified interpreter for the deaf is given in Note for Guidance 3C.)

14.5 The interviewing officer shall ensure that the interpreter makes a note of the interview at the time for use in the event of his being called to give evidence and certifies its accuracy. The person shall be given an opportunity to read it and sign it as correct or to indicate the respects in which he considers it inaccurate.

(c) *Additional rules for detained persons*

14.6 All reasonable attempts should be made to make clear to the detained person that interpreters will be provided at public expense.

14.7 Where paragraph 6.1 applies and the person concerned cannot communicate with the solicitor, whether because of language or having difficulties, an interpreter must be called. The interpreter may not be a police officer when interpretation is needed for the purposes of obtaining legal advice. In all other cases a police officer may only interpret if he first obtains the detained person's (or the appropriate adult's) agreement in writing or if the interview is tape recorded in accordance with the relevant code of practice or Procedural Guidance.

14.8 When a person who has difficulty in understanding English is charged with an offence, and the custody officer cannot himself speak the persons language, arrangements must be made for an interpreter to explain as soon as practicable the offence concerned and any other information given by the custody officer.

14.9 Action taken to call an interpreter under this section and any agreement to be interviewed in the absence of an interpreter must be recorded.

Note for guidance

14A If the interpreter is needed as a prosecution witness at the person's trial, a second interpreter must act as the court interpreter.

15 Questioning: special restrictions

15.1 If a person has been arrested by one police force on behalf of another and the lawful period of detention in accordance with section 41 of the Police and

Criminal Evidence Act 1984 in respect of that offence has not yet commenced, no questions may be put to him about the offence concerned while he is in transit between the forces except in order to clarify any voluntary statement made by him.

15.2 If a person is in police detention at a hospital he may not be questioned without the agreement of the responsible doctor. [See Note 15A]

Note for guidance

15A If questioning takes place at a hospital under paragraph 15.2 (or on the way to or from a hospital), the period concerned counts towards the total period of detention permitted.

16 Reviews and extensions of detention

(a) *Action*

16.1 The review officer is responsible under section 40 of the Police and Criminal Evidence Act 1984 for determining whether or not a person's detention continues to be necessary. In reaching a decision he shall provide an opportunity to make representations to the detained person himself (unless unfit to do so because of his condition or behaviour) and his solicitor or the appropriate adult if available at the time. Other persons having an interest in the person's welfare may make representations at the review officer's discretion.

16.2 The same persons may make representations to the officer determining whether further detention should be authorised under section 42 of the Act.

(b) *Documentation*

16.3 The grounds for and extent of any delay in conducting a review shall be recorded.

16.4 Any written representations shall be retained.

16.5 A record shall be made as soon as practicable of the outcome of each review and application for a warrant of further detention or its extension.

Notes for guidance

16A An application for a warrant of further detention or its extension should be made between 10 a.m. and 9 p.m., and if possible during normal court hours. It will not be practicable to arrange for a court to sit specially outside these hours. If it appears possible that a special sitting may be needed (either at a weekend, Bank/Public Holidays or on a weekday outside normal court hours but between 10 a.m. and 9 p.m.) then the clerk to the justices should be given notice and informed of this possibility, while the court is sitting if possible.

16B If the only practicable way, in the circumstances, of conducting a review is over the telephone then this is permissible, provided that the requirements of section 40 of the Police and Criminal Evidence Act 1984 are observed.

17 Charging of detained persons

(a) *Action*

17.1 When an officer considers that there is sufficient evidence to prosecute a detained person he should without delay bring him before the custody officer who shall then be responsible for considering whether or not he should be charged. Any resulting action should be taken in the presence of the appropriate adult if the person is a juvenile or a person who is mentally handicapped or suffering from mental illness.

17.2 When a person is charged with or informed that he may be prosecuted for an offence he shall be cautioned in the terms of paragraph 10.4 above.

17.3 A charged person shall be given at the time he is charged a written notice showing particulars of the offence with which he is charged and including the name of the officer in the case, his police station and the station's reference number for the case. So far as possible the particulars of the charge shall be stated in simple terms, but they shall also show the precise offence in law with which he is charged. The notice shall begin with the following words:

> "You are charged with the offence(s) shown below. You do not have to say anything unless you wish to do so, but what you say may be given in evidence."

If the person is an arrested juvenile or is mentally ill or mentally handicapped the notice shall be given to the appropriate adult.

17.4 If at any time after a person has been charged with or informed he may be prosecuted for an offence a police officer wishes to bring to the notice of that person any written statement made by another person or the content of an interview with another person, he shall hand to that person a true copy of any such written statement or bring to his attention the content of the interview record, but shall say or do nothing to invite any reply or comment save to caution him in the terms of paragraph 10.4 above. If the person cannot read then the officer may read it to him. If the person is a juvenile or mentally ill or mentally handicapped the copy shall also be given or the interview record shown to the appropriate adult.

17.5 Questions relating to an offence may not be put to a person after he has been charged with that offence, or informed that he may be prosecuted for it, unless they are necessary for the purpose of preventing or minimising harm or loss to some other person or to the public or for clearing up an ambiguity in a previous answer or statement, or where it is in the interests of justice that the person should have put to him and have an opportunity to comment on information concerning the offence which has come to light since he was charged or informed that he might be prosecuted. Before any such questions are put he shall be cautioned in the terms of paragraph 10.4 above.

17.6 Where a juvenile is charged with an offence and the custody officer authorises his continuing detention he must try to make arrangements for the juvenile to be taken into the care of a local authority to be detained pending appearence in court unless he certifies that it is impracticable to do so in accordance with s.38(6) of the Police and Criminal Evidence Act 1984. [See Note 17A]

(b) *Documentation*

17.7 A record shall be made of anything a detained person says when charged.

17.8 Any questions put after charge and answers given relating to the offence shall be contemporaneously recorded in full on the forms provided and the record signed by that person or, if he refuses, by the interviewing officer and any third parties present. If the questions are tape recorded the arrangements set out in the Procedural Guidance or any tape recording code of practice apply.

17.9 If it is not practicable to make arrangements for the transfer of a juvenile into local authority care in accordance with paragraph 17.6 above the custody officer must record the reasons and make out a certificate to be produced before the court together with the juvenile.

Note for guidance

17A Neither a juvenile's unruliness nor the nature of the offence with which he is charged provides grounds for the custody officer to retain him in police custody rather than seek to arrange for his transfer to the care of the local authority.

ANNEX A [4.1]

Intimate and strip searches

(a) *Action*

1. Body orifices may be searched only if an officer of the rank of superintendent or above has reasonable grounds for believing (a) that an article which could cause physical injury to a detained person or others at the police station has been concealed or (b) that the person has concealed a Class A drug which he intended to supply to another or to export and (c) that in either case an intimate search is the only practicable means of removing it. The reasons why an intimate search is considered necessary shall be explained to the person before the search takes place.

2. An intimate search may only be carried out by a registered medical practitioner, State Registered Nurse, or State Enrolled Nurse unless an officer of at least the rank of superintendent considers that this is not practicable and the search is to take place under paragraph 1 (a) above.

3. An intimate search under paragraph 1 (a) above may take place only at a hospital, surgery, other medical premises or police station. A search under paragraph 1 (b) may take place only at a hospital, surgery or other medical premises.

4. An intimate search at a police station of a juvenile or a person who is mentally ill or mentally handicapped may take place only in the presence of the appropriate adult of the same sex. In the case of a juvenile the search may take place in the absence of the appropriate adult only if the juvenile signifies in the presence of the appropriate adult that he prefers the search to be done in his absence and the appropriate adult agrees.

5. A strip search (that is a search involving the removal of more than outer clothing) may take place only if this is thought by the custody officer to be necessary to remove an article which the detained person would not be allowed to keep.

6. An intimate search under paragraph 1(a) above which is not carried out by a medical practitioner or a strip search must be carried out by a police officer of the same sex as the person to be searched. No person of the opposite sex who is not a medical practitioner or nurse shall be present, nor shall anyone whose presence is unnecessary.

(b) *Documentation*

7. In the case of an intimate search the custody officer shall as soon as practicable record which parts of the person's body were searched, who carried out the search, who was present, the reasons for the search and its result.

8. In the case of a strip search he shall record the reasons for the search and its result.

9. If an intimate search is carried out by a police officer, the reason why it is impracticable for a suitably qualified person to conduct it must be recorded.

ANNEX B

Delay in notifying arrest or allowing access to legal advice

(A) Persons detained under the Police and Criminal Evidence Act 1984

(a) *Action*

1. The rights set out in sections 5 and 6 of the code may be delayed if the person has been detained in connection with a serious arrestable offence, has not

279

yet been charged with an offence and an officer of the rank of superintendent or above has reasonable grounds for believing that the exercise of the rights:

   (i) will lead to interference with or harm to evidence connected with a serious arrestable offence or interference with or physical harm to other persons: or

  (ii) will lead to the alerting of other persons suspected of having committed such an offence but not yet arrested for it; or

 (iii) will hinder the recovery of property obtained in consequence of the commission of such an offence.

2. Access to a solicitor may not be delayed on the grounds that he might advise the person not to answer any questions or that the solicitor was initially asked to attend the police station by someone else, provided that the person himself then wishes to see the solicitor.

3. These rights may be delayed only for as long as necessary and in no case beyond 36 hours after the lawful period of detention under section 41 of the Police and Criminal Evidence Act 1984 has commenced irrespective of whether the person remains at a police station or is transferred to a hospital. If the above grounds cease to apply within this time, the person must as soon as practicable be asked if he wishes to exercise either right and action taken in accordance with the relevant section of the code.

4. A detained person must be permitted to consult a solicitor for a reasonable time before any court hearing.

(b) *Documentation*

5. The grounds for action under this Annex shall be recorded and the person informed of them as soon as practicable.

(B) Persons detained under the Prevention of Terrorism (Temporary Provisions) Act 1984

(a) *Action*

6. The rights set out in sections 5 and 6 of this code may be suspended if paragraph 1 above applies or if an officer of the rank of superintendent or above has reasonable grounds for believing that the exercise of either right:—

  (a) will lead to interference with the gathering of information about the commission, preparation or instigation of acts of terrorism; or

  (b) by alerting any person, will make it more difficult to prevent an act of terrorism or to secure the apprehension, prosecution or conviction of any person in connection with the commission, preparation or instigation of an act of terrorism.

7. Paragraph 3 above applies except that the delay permitted is 48 and not 36 hours. The custody officer must remind any such person who has been detained for 48 hours of his right to consult a solicitor and ask him whether he wishes to exercise it.

(b) *Documentation*

8. Paragraph 5 above applies.

9. Any reply given by a person under paragraph 7 above must be recorded and the person asked to endorse the record.

Notes for guidance

  B1 Even if Annex B applies in the case of a juvenile or a person who is mentally ill or mentally handicapped, action to inform the appropriate adult must nevertheless be taken in accordance with paragraph 3.6 of the code.

B2 In the case of foreign nationals and Commonwealth citizens, see paragraph 7A.

ANNEX C

Urgent interviews

1. If and only if an officer of the rank of superintendent or above considers that delay will involve an immediate risk of harm to persons or serious loss of or serious damage to property:

   (a) a person heavily under the influence of drink or drugs may be interviewed in that state; or

   (b) an arrested juvenile or a person who is mentally ill or mentally handicapped may be interviewed in the absence of the appropriate adult; or

   (c) a person who has difficulty in understanding English or who has a hearing disability may be interviewed in the absence of an interpreter.

2. Questioning in these circumstances may not continue once sufficient information to avert the immediate risk has been obtained.

3. A record shall be made of the grounds for any decision to interview a person under paragraph 1 above.

Note for guidance

C1 The special groups referred to in Annex C are all particularly vulnerable. The provisions of the Annex, which override safeguards designed to protect them and to minimise the risk of interviews producing unreliable evidence, should be applied only in exceptional cases of need.

ANNEX D

Written statements under caution [12.14]

(a) *Written by a person under caution*

1. A person shall always be given the opportunity to write down himself what he wants to say.

2. Where the person wishes to write it himself, he shall be asked to write out and sign, before writing what he wants to say, the following:

> "I make this statement of my own free will. I understand that I need not say anything unless I wish to do so and that whatever I say may be given in evidence."

3. Any person writing his own statement shall be allowed to do so without any prompting except that a police officer may indicate to him which matters are material or question any ambiguity in the statement.

(b) *Written by a police officer*

4. If a person says that he would like someone to write it for him, a police officer shall, write the statement, but, before starting, he must ask him to sign, or make his mark, to the following:

> "I, ... , wish to make a statement. I want someone to write down what I say. I understand that I need not say anything unless I wish to do so and that what I say may be given in evidence."

5. Where a police officer writes the statement, he must take down the exact words spoken by the person making the statement; he must not edit or paraphrase it. Any questions that are necessary (e.g. to make it more intelligible) and the answers given must be recorded contemporaneously on the statement form.

6. When the writing of a statement by a police officer is finished the person making it shall be asked to read it and to make any corrections, alterations or additions he wishes. When he has finished reading it he shall be asked to write and sign or make his mark on the following certificate at the end of the statement:

> "I have read the above statement, and I have been able to correct, alter or add anything I wish. This statement is true. I have made it of my own free will."

7. If the person making the statement cannot read, or refuses to read it, or to write the above mentioned certificate at the end of it or to sign it, the senior police officer present shall read it over to him and ask him whether he would like to correct, alter or add anything and to put his signature or make his mark at the end. The police officer shall then certify on the statement itself what has occurred.

ANNEX E

Summary of provisions relating to the mentally ill and mentally handicapped

1. If an officer has any suspicion or is told in good faith that a person of any age, whether or not in custody, may be mentally ill or mentally handicapped, or cannot understand the significance of questions put to him or his replies, then he shall be treated as a mentally ill or mentally handicapped person.

2. In the case of a person who is mentally ill or mentally handicapped, 'the appropriate adult' means
   (a) a relative, guardian or some other person responsible for his care or custody; or
   (b) someone who is not a police officer or employed by the police who has experience of dealing with mentally ill or mentally handicapped persons; or
   (c) failing either of the above, some other responsible adult who is not a police officer or employed by the police.

3. If the custody officer authorises the detention of a person who is mentally handicapped or is suffering from mental illness or mental handicap he must as soon as practicable inform the appropriate adult of the grounds for the person's detention and his whereabouts, and ask the adult to come to the police station to see the person. If the appropriate adult is already at the police station when information is given as required in paragraphs 3.1 to 3.3 the information must be given to the detained person in his presence. If the appropriate adult is not at the police station when the information is given then the information must be given to the detained person again in the presence of the appropriate adult once that person arrives. [3.6]

4. If a person brought to a police appears to be suffering from mental illness, or is incoherent other than through drunkenness alone, or if a detained person subsequently appears to be mentally ill, the custody officer must immediately call the police surgeon or, in urgent cases send the person to hospital or call the nearest available medical practitioner. [9.2]

5. A mentally ill or mentally handicapped person must not be interviewed or asked to provide or sign a written statement in the absence of the appropriate adult unless an officer of the rank of superintendent or above considers that delay will involve an immediate risk of harm to persons or serious loss of or serious damage to property. Questioning in these circumstances may not continue in the absence of the appropriate adult once sufficient information to avert the risk has been obtained. A record shall be made of the grounds for any decision to begin an interview in these circumstances. [13.1 and Annex C]

6. If the appropriate adult, having been informed of the right to legal advice, considers that legal advice should be taken, the provisions of section 6 of the code

apply as if the mentally ill or mentally handicapped person had requested access to legal advice. [13.2]

7. If the detention of a mentally ill or mentally handicapped person is reviewed by a review officer or a superintendent, the appropriate adult must, if available at the time, be given an opportunity to make representations to the officer about the need for continuing detention. [16.1 and 16.2]

8. If the custody officer charges a mentally ill or mentally handicapped person with an offence or takes such other action as is appropriate when there is sufficient evidence for a prosecution this must be done in the presence of the appropriate adult. A copy of the written notice embodying any charge must be given to the appropriate adult. [17.1 to 17.3]

9. An intimate search of a person who is mentally ill or mentally handicapped may take place only in the presence of the appropriate adult of the same sex. [Annex A, paragraph 4]

Notes for guidance

E1 It is important to bear in mind that although persons who are mentally ill or mentally handicapped are often capable of providing reliable evidence, they may, without knowing or wishing to do so, be particularly prone in certain circumstances to provide information which is unreliable, misleading or self-incriminating. Special care should therefore always be exercised in questioning such a person, and the appropriate adult involved if there is any doubt a person's mental state or capacity. Because of the risk of unreliable evidence it is important to obtain corroboration of any facts admitted wherever possible. [Note 13B]

E2 Because of the risks referred to in Note E1, which the presence of the appropriate adult is intended to minimise, officers of superintendent rank should exercise their discretion to authorise the commencement of an interview in the adult's absence only in exceptional cases, where there is a strict need to avert an immediate risk of serious harm. [1b and Note C1 of Annex C]

E3 The appropriate adult should be informed that he is not expected to act simply as an observer. The purposes of his presence are, first, to advise the person being interviewed and to observe whether or not the interview is being conducted properly and fairly; and, second, to facilitate communication with the person being interviewed. [Note 13C]

E4 It may in certain circumstances be more satisfactory for all concerned if the appropriate adult is someone who has experience or training in the care of mentally ill or mentally handicapped persons rather than a relative lacking such qualifications. But if the person himself prefers a relative to a better qualified stranger his wishes should if practicable be respected. [Note 1C]

CODE OF PRACTICE FOR THE IDENTIFICATION OF PERSONS BY POLICE OFFICERS

1 General

[Paragraphs 1.1 to 1.5 are identical to paragraphs 1.2 to 1.5 and 1.7 in the Questioning Code (p. 263 above). They are not repeated here.]

1.6 Any reference to a custody officer in this Code includes an officer who is performing the functions of a custody officer. Any reference to a solicitor in this code includes a clerk or legal executive except in Annex A, paragraph 7.

1.7 Where a record is made under this code of any action requiring the authority of an officer of specified rank, his name and rank must be included in the record.

1.8 All records must be timed.

1.9 In the case of a detained person records are to be made in his custody record unless otherwise specified.

1.10 In the case of any procedure requiring a suspect's consent, the consent of a person who is mentally ill or mentally handicapped is only valid if given in the presence of the appropriate adult; and in the case of a juvenile the consent of his parent or guardian is required as well as his own (unless he is under 14, in which case the consent of his parent or guardian is sufficient in its own right). [See Note 1A]

1.11 In the case of any procedure requiring information to be given to a suspect, it must be given in the presence of the appropriate adult if the suspect is mentally ill, mentally handicapped or a juvenile. If the suspect is deaf or there is doubt about his hearing ability or ability to understand English and the officer cannot himself speak the person's language, the information must be given through an interpreter.

1.12 Any procedure involving the participation of a person who is mentally ill, mentally handicapped or a juvenile (whether as a suspect or witness) must take place in the presence of the appropriate adult; but the adult must not be allowed to prompt any identification of a suspect by a witness.

1.13 Nothing in this code affects any procedure to identify a person under:
   (i) sections 5–12 of the Road Traffic Act 1972, as amended;
   (ii) paragraph 18 of Schedule 2 to the Immigration Act 1971; or
   (iii) paragraph 5 of Schedule 3 to the Prevention of Terrorism (Temporary Provisions) Act 1984.

1.14 In this code references to photographs include optical disc computer print- outs.

Note for guidance

   1A For the purposes of paragraph 1.10 above consent may be given, in the case of a juvenile in the care of a local authority or voluntary organisation, by that authority or organisation.

2 Identification by witnesses

(a) *Suspect at the police station—the decision as to the method of identification*

2.1 In a case which involves disputed identification evidence a parade must be held if the suspect asks for one and it is practicable to hold one. A parade may also be held, if the officer in charge of the investigation considers that it would be useful.

2.2 Arrangements for the parade and its conduct shall be the responsibility of an officer in uniform not below the rank of inspector who is not involved with the investigation ("the identification officer"). No officer involved with the investigation of the case against the suspect may take any part in the arrangements for or the conduct of the parade.

2.3 A parade need not be held if the identification officer considers that, whether by reason of the unusual appearance of the suspect or for some other reason, it would not be practicable to assemble sufficient people who resembled him to make a fair parade.

2.4 If a suspect refuses or, having agreed, fails to attend an identification parade or the holding of a parade is impracticable, arrangements must if practicable be made to allow the witness an opportunity of seeing him in a group of people. Such a group identification may also be arranged if the officer in charge of the investigation considers, whether because of fear on the part of the witness or for some other reason, that it is in the circumstances more satisfactory than a parade.

2.5 If neither a parade nor a group identification procedure is arranged, the suspect may be confronted by the witness. Such a confrontation does not require the suspect's consent, but may not take place unless neither group procedure is practicable, whether because the suspect has withheld his consent to them or for some other reason.

2.6 A witness must not be shown photographs or photofit or identikit pictures for identification purposes if there is a suspect already available to be asked to stand on a parade or participate in a group identification.

(b) *Notice to suspect*

2.7 Before (a) a parade takes place or (b) group identification is arranged, the identification officer shall explain to the suspect:—

  (i) the purpose of the parade or group identification
 (ii) the procedures for holding it (including his right to have a solicitor or friend present);
(iii) where appropriate the special arrangements for juveniles;
 (iv) where appropriate the special arrangements for mentally ill and mentally handicapped persons;
  (v) the fact that he does not have to take part in either procedure and, if it is proposed to hold a group identification, his entitlement to a parade if this can practicably be arranged; and
 (vi) the fact that, if he does not consent to take part in a parade or other group identification, he may be confronted by a witness and his refusal may be given in evidence in any subsequent trial, where a witness might be given an opportunity of identifying him in court.

2.8 This information must also be contained in a written notice which must be handed to the suspect. The identification officer shall give the suspect a reasonable opportunity to read the notice, after which he shall be asked to sign a second copy of the notice to indicate whether or not he is willing to attend the parade or participate in the group identification. The signed copy shall be retained by the identification officer.

(c) *The conduct of a parade or other group identification*

2.9 Any parade or other group identification must be carried out in accordance with Annex A (p. 288 below).

(d) *Confrontation by a witness*

2.10 Any confrontation must be carried out in accordance with Annex B (p. 290 below).

(e) *Street identification*

2.11 A police officer may take a witness to a particular neighbourhood or place to observe the persons there to see whether he can identify the person whom he said he saw on the relevant occasion. Care should be taken however not to direct the witness's attention to any individual. Where the subject is at a police station, the provisions of paragraphs 2.1 to 2.10 must apply.

(f) *The showing of photographs etc*

2.12 If photographs or photofit, identikit or similar pictures are shown to a witness for identification purposes this must be done in accordance with Annex C (p. 291 below).

(g) *Documentation*

2.13 The identification officer will make a record or the parade or group identification on the form provided.

2.14 If the identification officer considers that it is not practicable to hold a parade he shall tell the suspect why and record the reason.

2.15 A record shall be made of a person's refusal to take part in a parade or other group identification.

3 Identification by fingerprints

(a) *Action*

3.1 A person's fingerprints may be taken only with his written consent or if paragraph 3.2 applies. If he is at a police station consent must be in writing. In either case the person must be informed of the reason before they are taken and that they will be destroyed if paragraph 3.4 applies and that he may witness their destruction if he asks to do so within one month upon being cleared or informed that he will not be prosecuted.

3.2 Fingerprints may be taken from any person over the age of ten years without consent if:—

(i) before he has been charged or reported for an offence he is in police detention and an officer of the rank of superintendent or above has reasonable grounds to believe that fingerprints will tend to confirm or disprove his involvement in the commission of a particular offence; or

(ii) he has been charged with or reported for a recordable offence and has not had his fingerprints taken in the course of the investigation; or

(iii) he has been convicted of a recordable offence and his fingerprints have not been taken as a result of (i) or (ii). [See Note 3A]

3.3 Reasonable force may be used if necessary.

3.4 The fingerprints of a person and all copies of them taken in that case must be destroyed:

(a) if he is prosecuted for the offence concerned and cleared; or

(b) if he is not prosecuted (unless he admits the offence and is cautioned for it).

An opportunity of witnessing the destruction must be given to him if he wishes and if in accordance with paragraph 3.1 he applies within one month of being cleared or informed that he will not be prosecuted.

3.5 References to fingerprints include palm prints.

(b) *Documentation*

3.6 A record must be made as soon as possible of the reason for taking a person's fingerprints without consent and of their destruction. If force is used a record shall be made of the circumstances and those present.

3A   References to recordable offences in this code relate to those offences for which convictions are recorded in national police records.

4 Identification by photographs

(a) *Action*

4.1 The photograph of a person who has been arrested may be taken at a police station only with his written consent or if paragraph 4.2 applies. In either case he must be informed of the reason for taking it and that the photograph will be destroyed if paragraph 4.5 applies and that he may ask to witness its destruction.

4.2 The photograph of a person who has been arrested may be taken without consent:

   (i)   if he is arrested at the same time as other persons or at a time when it is likely that other persons will be arrested, and a photograph is necessary to establish who was arrested, at what time and at what place; or

   (ii) if he has been charged with or reported for a recordable offence and has not yet been released or brought before a court; or

   (iii) if he is convicted of such an offence and his photograph is not already on record as a result of (i) or (ii). There is no power of arrest to take a photograph in pursuance of this provision which applies only where the person is in custody as a result of the exercise of another power (*e.g.* arrest for fingerprinting under s.27 of the Police and Criminal Evidence Act 1984). [See Note 3A]

4.3 Force may not be used to take a photograph.

4.4 Where a person's photograph has been taken in accordance with this section, the photograph, negatives and all copies of it taken in that particular case must be destroyed as soon as practicable:

   (a)   if he is prosecuted for the offence concerned and cleared; or

   (b)   if he is not prosecuted (unless he admits the offence and is cautioned for it).

An opportunity of witnessing the destruction must be given to him if he so requests provided they have not already been destroyed.

(b) *Documentation*

4.5 A record must be made as soon as possible of the reason for taking a person's photograph under this section without consent and of the destruction of any photographs.

5 Identification by body samples, swabs and impressions

(a) *Action*

5.1 A detained suspect's dental impressions and samples of his blood, pubic hair, semen, urine and saliva or any other tissue fluid or genital or rectal swabs may be taken from him only with his written consent and if an officer of the rank of superintendent or above considers that the offence concerned is a serious arrestable offence and that there are reasonable grounds for suspecting that such an impression, sample or swab will tend to confirm or disprove the suspect's involvement in it. Before the impression, sample or swab is taken the person must be informed of the grounds on which the required authority has been given including the nature of the suspected offence.

5.2 Before a person is asked to provide an intimate sample or swab he must be warned that a refusal may be treated, in any proceedings against him, as corroborating relevant prosecution evidence. [See Note 5A]

5.3 Except for samples of urine or saliva, the above samples and swabs may be taken only by a registered medical or dental practitioner as appropriate.

5.4 A non-intimate sample, as defined in paragraph 5.11 or a body impression other than fingerprints, may be taken from a detained suspect only with his written consent or if paragraph 5.5 below applies. Even if he consents, an officer of the rank of inspector or above must have reasonable grounds to believe that such a sample or impression will tend to confirm or disprove the suspect's involvement in a particular offence.

5.5 A non-intimate sample or a body impression may be taken without consent if the offence in connection with which the suspect is detained is a serious arrestable offence and an officer of the rank of superintendent or above has reasonable grounds for believing that the sample or impression will tend to confirm or disprove his involvement in it.

5.6 The suspect must be informed before the sample or impression is taken, of the grounds on which the relevant authority has been given, including the nature of the suspected offence, and that the sample or impression will be destroyed if paragraph 5.8 applies.

5.7 When paragraph 5.5 applies reasonable force may be used if necessary to take non-intimate samples and body impressions.

5.8 Where a sample or impression has been taken in accordance with this section, it and all copies of it taken in that particular case must be destroyed:

    (a) if he is prosecuted for the offence concerned and cleared; or

    (b) if he is not prosecuted (unless he admits the offence and is cautioned for it).

(b) *Documentation*

5.9 A record must be made as soon as practicable of the reason for taking a sample or impression and of its destruction. If force is used a record shall be made of the circumstances and those present. Consent to the taking of a sample or impression must be recorded in writing.

5.10 A record must be made of the giving of a warning required by paragraph 5.2 above.

(c) *General*

5.11 'Non-intimate sample' means:

    (i) hair (other than pubic hair);

    (ii) nail clippings or scrapings;

    (iii) swabs taken from parts of the body other than body orifices; or

    (iv) a footprint or a similar impression of any part of a person's body other than a part of his hand.

5.12 Where clothing needs to be removed in circumstances likely to cause embarrassment to the person, no person of the opposite sex who is not a medical practitioner or nurse shall be present, nor shall anyone whose presence is unnecessary.

Note for Guidance

    5A In warning a person who refuses to provide an intimate sample or swab in accordance with paragraph 5.2, the following form of words may be helpful:

        "You do not have to provide this sample/allow this swab to be taken, but I must warn you that if you do not do so, a court may treat such a refusal as supporting any relevant evidence against you".

ANNEX A

Identification parades and group identifications

(a) *General*

1. A suspect must be given a reasonable opportunity to have a solicitor or friend present, and the identification officer shall ask him to indicate on a second copy of the Notice to Suspect whether or not he so wishes.

2. A parade may take place either in a normal room or in one equipped with a screen permitting witnesses to see members of the parade without being seen. The procedure for the composition and conduct of the parade are the same in both cases, subject to paragraph 7 below, except that a parade involving a screen may take place only when the suspect's solicitor, friend or appropriate adult is present or the parade recorded on video.

(b) *Parades involving prison inmates*

3. If an inmate is required for identification, and there are no security problems about his leaving the establishment, he may be asked to participate in a parade. (Group identification, however may not be arranged other than in the establishment or inside a police station.)

4. A parade may be held in a Prison Department establishment, but shall be conducted as far as practicable under normal parade rules. Members of the public shall make up the parade unless there are serious security or control objections to their admission to the establishment. In such cases, or if a group identification is arranged within the establishment, other inmates may participate.

(c) *Conduct of a parade*

5. Immediately before the parade, the identification officer must remind the suspect of the procedures governing its conduct and caution him in the terms of paragraph 10.4 of the code of practice for the detention, treatment and questioning of persons by the police.

6. All unauthorised persons must be strictly excluded from the place where the identification parade is held.

7. Once the parade has been formed, everything afterwards in respect of it shall take place in the presence and hearing of the suspect and of any interpreter, solicitor, friend or appropriate adult who is present (unless the parade involves a screen, in which case everything said to or by any witness at the place where a parade is held must be said in the hearing and presence of the suspect's solicitor, friend or appropriate adult or be recorded on video).

8. The parade shall consist of at least eight persons (in addition to the suspect) who so far as possible resemble the suspect in age, height, general appearance and position in life. One suspect only shall be included in a parade unless there are two suspects of roughly similar appearance in which case they may be paraded together with at least twelve other persons. In no circumstances shall more than two suspects be included in one parade and where there are separate parades they shall be made up of different persons.

9. Where all members of a similar group are possible suspects, separate parades shall be held for each member of the group unless there are two suspects of similar appearance when they may appear on the same parade with at least twelve other members of the group who are not suspects. Where police officers in uniform form an identification parade, any numerals or other identifying badge shall be concealed.

10. When the suspect is brought in to the place where the parade is to be held, he shall be asked by the identification officer whether he has any objection to the arrangements for the parade or to any of the other participants in it. The suspect may obtain advice from his solicitor or friend, if present, before the parade

proceeds. Where practicable, steps shall be taken to remove the grounds for objection. Where it is not practicable to do so, the officer shall explain to the suspect why his objections cannot be met.

11. The suspect may select his own position in the line. Where there is more than one witness, the identification officer must tell the suspect, after each witness has left the room, that he can if he wishes change position in the line. Each position in the line must be clearly numbered, whether by means of a numeral laid on the floor in front of each parade member or by other means.

12. The identification officer is responsible for ensuring that, before they attend the parade, witnesses do not:—

   (i)   communicate with each other about the case or overhear a witness who has already seen the parade;

   (ii) see any member of the parade;

   (iii) on that occasion, see or are reminded of any photograph or description of the suspect or given any other indication of his identity; or

   (iv) see the suspect in any circumstances, either before or after the parade.

13. The officer conducting a witness to a parade must not discuss with him the composition of the parade, and in particular he must not disclose whether a previous witness has made any identification.

14. Witnesses shall be brought in one at a time. Immediately before the witness inspects the parade, the identification officer shall tell him that the person he saw may or may not be on the parade and if he cannot make a positive identification he should say so. The officer shall then ask him to walk along the parade at least twice, taking as much care and time as he wishes. When he has done so the officer shall ask him whether the person he saw in person on an earlier relevant occasion is on the parade.

15. The witness should make an identification by indicating the number of the person concerned.

16. If the witness makes an identification after the parade has ended the suspect and, if present, his solicitor, interpreter, or friend shall be informed. Where this occurs consideration should be given to allowing the witness a second opportunity to identify the suspect.

17. If a witness wishes to hear any parade member speak, adopt any specified posture or see him move the identification officer shall first ask whether he can identify any persons on the parade on the basis of appearance only. When the request is to hear members of the parade speak, the witness shall be reminded that the participants in the parade have been chosen on the basis of physical appearance only. Members of the parade may then be asked to comply with the witness's request to hear them speak, to see them move or to adopt any specified posture.

18. When the last witness has left, the suspect shall be asked by the identification officer whether he wishes to make any comments on the conduct of the parade.

(d) *Conduct of a group identification*

19. The arrangements for a group identification are the sole responsibility of the identification officer and must as far as practicable satisfy the requirements of (c) above.

(e) *Documentation*

20. If a parade is held without a solicitor or a friend of the suspect being present a colour photograph of the parade shall be taken unless any of the parade members objects. A copy of the photograph shall be supplied on request to the suspect or his solicitor within a reasonable time.

21. Where a photograph is taken in accordance with paragraph 20, at the conclusion of the proceedings the negative will be destroyed.

22. If the identification officer asks any person to leave a parade because he is interfering with its conduct the circumstances shall be recorded.

23. A record must be made of all those present at a parade or group identification whose names are known to the police.

24. If prison inmates make up a parade the circumstances must be recorded.

25. A record of the conduct of any parade or group identification must be made on the forms provided.

ANNEX B

Confrontation by a witness [2.10]

1. The identification officer is responsible for the conduct of any confrontation of a suspect by a witness.

2. The suspect shall be confronted independently by each witness, who shall be asked "Is this the person?" Confrontation must take place in the presence of the suspect's solicitor, interpreter or friend, where he has one, unless this would cause unreasonable delay.

ANNEX C

The showing of photographs [2.12]

(a) *Action*

1. An officer of the rank of sergeant or above shall be responsible for supervising and directing the showing of photographs. The actual showing may be done by a constable.

2. Only one witness shall be shown photographs at any one time. He shall be given as much privacy as practicable and shall not be allowed to communicate with or overhear any other witness in the case.

3. The witness shall be shown not less than twelve photographs at a time. These photographs shall either be in an album or loose photographs mounted in a frame and shall, as far as possible, all be of a similar type. If the photographs include that of a person suspected of the offence concerned by the police, the other photographs in the group shall have as close resemblance to the suspect as possible.

4. When the witness is shown the photographs, he shall be told that the photograph of the person whom he has said that he has seen previously may or may not be amongst them. He shall not be prompted or guided in any way but shall be left to make any selection without help.

5. If a witness makes a positive identification from photographs, then, unless the person identified is otherwise eliminated from enquiries, other witnesses shall not be shown photographs. But both they and the witness who has made the identification shall be asked to attend an identification parade or group identification if practicable unless there is no dispute about the identification of the suspect.

6. Where the use of a photofit, identikit or similar picture has led to there being a suspect available who can be asked to appear on a parade, or participate in a group identification the picture shall not be shown to other potential witnesses.

7. Where a witness attending an identification parade has previously been shown photographs or photofit, identikit or similar pictures then the suspect and his solicitor must be informed of this fact before any committal proceedings or summary trial.

8. Any photographs used shall be retained for production in court if necessary, whether or not an identification is made.

(b) *Documentation*

9. Whether or not an identification is made, a record shall be kept of the showing of photographs and of any comment made by the witness.

CODE OF PRACTICE FOR THE SEARCHING OF PREMISES BY POLICE OFFICERS AND THE SEIZURE OF PROPERTY FOUND BY POLICE OFFICERS ON PERSONS OR PREMISES

1 General

1.1 and 1.2 are similar to 1.2 and 1.3 in the Questioning Code (p. 263 above) and are not repeated here.

1.3 This code applies to the following searches of premises:

(a) searches of premises undertaken for the purpose of an investigation into an alleged offence with the occupier's consent other than routine scenes of crime searches and searches following the activation of burglar or fire alarms or bomb threat calls;

(b) searches of premises under the powers conferred by sections 17, 18 and 32 of the Police and Criminal Evidence Act 1984;

(c) searches of premises undertaken in pursuance of a search warrant issued in accordance with section 15 of or Schedule 1 to that Act.

"Premises" is a wide term which may include vessels and, in certain circumstances, vehicles.

2 Search warrants and production orders

(a) *Action to be taken before an application is made*

2.1 Where information is received which appears to justify an application the officer concerned must take reasonable steps to check that the information is accurate, recent and has not been provided maliciously or irresponsibly. An application may not be made on the basis of information from an anonymous source where corroboration has not been sought.

2.2 The officer shall ascertain as specifically as is possible in the circumstances the nature of the articles concerned and their location.

2.3 The officer shall also make enquiries to establish what, if anything, is known about the likely occupier of the premises and the nature of the premises themselves; and whether they have been previously searched and if so how recently; and to obtain any other information relevant to the application.

2.4 No application for a search warrant may be made without the authority of an officer of at least the rank of inspector (or, in a case of urgency where no officer of this rank is readily available, the senior officer on duty). No application for a production order under Schedule 1 to the Police and Criminal Evidence Act 1984 may be made without the authority of an officer of at least the rank of superintendent.

2.5 Except in a case of urgency, if there is reason to believe that a search might have an adverse effect on relations between the police and the community then the local police community liaison officer shall be consulted before it takes place.

(b) *The making of application*

2.6 An application for a search warrant must be supported by an information in writing, stating:
  (i) the enactment under which the application is made;
  (ii) as specifically as is reasonably practicable the premises to be searched and the object of the search; and
  (iii) the grounds on which the application is made (including, where the

292

purpose of the proposed search is to find evidence of an alleged offence, an indication of how the evidence relates to the investigation).

2.7 An application for a search warrant under paragraph 12(a) of Schedule 1 to the Police and Criminal Evidence Act 1984 shall also, where appropriate, indicate why it is believed that service of notice of an application for a production order may seriously prejudice the investigation.

2.8 If an application is refused, no further application may be made for a warrant to search those premises unless supported by additional grounds.

(c) *Note for guidance*

2A The identity of an informant need not be disclosed when making an application but the officer concerned should be prepared to deal with any questions the magistrate or judge may have about the accuracy of previous information provided by that source or other related matters.

3 Entry without warrant

(a) *Making an arrest*

3.1 The conditions under which an officer may enter and search premises without warrant for the purpose of making an arrest are as set out in section 17 of the Police and Criminal Evidence Act 1984.

(b) *Search, after arrest, of premises in which arrest takes place*

3.2 The powers of an officer to search premises in which he has arrested a person are as set out in section 32 of the Police and Criminal Evidence Act 1984.

(c) *Search, after arrest, of premises of arrested person*

3.3 The powers of an officer to search the premises of a person who has been arrested for an arrestable offence are as set out in section 18 of the Police and Criminal Evidence Act 1984. The record of the search required by section 18(7) of the Act shall be made in the custody record where there is one.

4 Search with consent

4.1 Subject to paragraph 4.3 below, if it is proposed to search premises with the consent of a person entitled to grant entry to the premises the consent must be given in writing. [See Note 4B]

4.2 Before seeking consent the officer in charge shall state the purpose of the proposed search and inform the person concerned that he is not obliged to consent and that anything seized may be produced in evidence. If, at the time, the person is not suspected of an offence the officer shall tell him so when stating the purpose of the search.

4.3 It is unnecessary to seek consent under paragraphs 4.1 and 4.2 above where in the circumstances this would cause disproportionate inconvenience to the person concerned. [See Note 4C]

Notes for guidance

4A In the case of a lodging house or similar accommodation a search should not be made on the basis solely of the landlord's consent unless the tenant is unavailable and the matter is urgent.

4B Where it is intended to search premises under authority of a warrant or a power of entry and search without warrant, and cooperation of the occupier of the premises is obtained in accordance with paragraph 5.4 below, there is no additional requirement to obtain written consent as at paragraph 4.1 above.

4C Paragraph 4.3 is intended, in particular, to apply to circumstances where to seek consent would cause disproportionate inconvenience to the person concerned. For example, police have arrested someone in the night after a pursuit and it is necessary to make a brief check of gardens along the route of the pursuit to see whether stolen or incriminating articles have been discarded.

5 Searching of premises: general considerations

(a) *Time of searches*

5.1 Searches made under warrant must be made within one month from the date of issue of the warrant.

5.2 Searches must be made at a reasonable hour unless this might frustrate the purpose of the search. [See Note 5A]

5.3 A warrant authorises an entry on one occasion only.

(b) *Entry other than with consent*

5.4 The officer in charge shall first attempt to communicate with the occupier or any other person entitled to grant access to the premises by explaining the authority under which he seeks entry to the premises and ask the occupier to allow him to do so, unless:

   (i) the premises to be searched are known to be unoccupied;
  (ii) the occupier or any other person entitled to grant access is known to be absent; or
 (iii) there are reasonable grounds to believe that to alert the occupier or any other person entitled to grant access by attempting to communicate with him would frustrate the object of the search or endanger the officers concerned or other persons.

5.5 Where the premises are occupied the officer shall, before a search after entry begins, identify himself and, if not in uniform, produce his warrant card; and state the purpose of the search and the grounds for undertaking it.

5.6 Reasonable force may be used if necessary to enter premises if the officer in charge is satisfied that the premises are those specified in any warrant or other written authority and where:

   (i) the occupier or any other person entitled to grant access has refused a request to allow entry to his premises;
  (ii) it is impossible to communicate with the occupier or any other person entitled to grant access; or
 (iii) any of the provisions of paragraph 5.4 (i) to (iii) apply.

5.7 Where the search is to be made under warrant the occupier shall, if present, be given a copy of it. If he is not present the copy shall be left in a prominent place on the premises. The warrant itself shall be endorsed to show that this has been done.

(c) *Search*

5.8 Premises may be searched only to the extent necessary to achieve the object of the search, having regard to the size and nature of whatever is sought. A search under warrant may not continue under the authority of that warrant once all the things specified in it have been found, or the officer in charge of the search is satisfied that they are not on the premises.

5.9 Searches must be conducted with due consideration for the property and privacy of the occupier of the premises searched, and with no more disturbance than necessary. Reasonable force may be used only where this is necessary because the co-operation of the occupier cannot be obtained or is insufficient for the purpose.

5.10 If the occupier wishes to ask a friend, neighbour or other person to witness the search then he must be allowed to do so, unless the officer in charge has reasonable grounds to believe that this would seriously hinder the investigation. A search need not be delayed for this purpose unreasonably.

(d) *Leaving premises*

5.11 If premises have been entered by force the officer in charge shall, before leaving them, satisfy himself that they are secure either by arranging for the occupier or his agent to be present or by any other appropriate means.

(e) *Search under Schedule 1 to the Police and Criminal Evidence Act 1984*

5.12 An officer of the rank of inspector or above shall take charge of and be present at any search made under a warrant issued under Schedule 1 to the Police and Criminal Evidence Act 1984. He is responsible for ensuring that the search is conducted with discretion and in such a manner as to cause the least possible disruption to any business or other activities carried on in the premises.

5.13 After satisfying himself that material may not be taken from the premises without his knowledge, the officer in charge of the search shall ask for the documents or other records concerned to be produced. He may also, if he considers it to be necessary, ask to see the index to files held on the premises, if there is one; and the officers conducting the search may inspect any files which, according to the index, appear to contain any of the material sought. A more extensive search of the premises may be made only if the person responsible for them refuses to produce the material sought, or to allow access to the index; if it appears that the index is inaccurate or incomplete; or if for any other reason the officer in charge has reasonable grounds to believe that such a search is necessary in order to find the material sought. [See Note 5B]

Notes for guidance

5A   In determining at what time to make a search the officer in charge should have regard, among other considerations, to the times of day at which the occupier of the premises is likely to be present, and should not search at a time when he, or any other person on the premises, is likely to be asleep unless not doing so is likely to frustrate the purpose of the search.

5B   In asking for documents to be produced in accordance with paragraphs 5.13 above, officers should direct the request to a person in authority and with responsibility for the documents.

5C   If the wrong premises are searched by mistake, everything possible should be done at the earliest opportunity to allay any sense of grievance. In appropriate cases assistance should be given to obtain compensation.

6 Seizure of property

(a) *Seizure*

6.1 Subject to paragraph 6.2 below, an officer who is searching any premises under any statutory power (whether under a warrant or not) or with the consent of the occupier may seize anything covered by the warrant. He may also seize anything which he has reasonable grounds for believing is evidence of an offence, or has been obtained in consequence of the commission of an offence, where seizure is necessary to prevent its concealment, alteration, loss, damage or destruction.

6.2 No item may be seized which is subject to legal professional privilege (as defined in section 11 of the Police and Criminal Evidence Act 1984).

6.3 An officer who decides that it is not appropriate to seize property because of an explanation given by the person holding it, but who has reasonable grounds for believing that it has been obtained in consequence of the commission of an offence by some person, shall inform the holder of his suspicions and shall explain that if he disposes of the property he may be liable to civil or criminal proceedings.

6.4 An officer may photograph or copy, or have photographed or copied, any document or other article which he has power to seize in accordance with paragraph 6.1 above.

6.5 Where an officer considers that a computer may contain information that could be used in evidence, he may require the information to be produced in a form that can be taken away and in which it is visible and legible.

(b) *Retention*

6.6 Subject to paragraph 6.7 below anything which has been seized in accordance with the above provisions may be retained only for as long as is necessary in the circumstances. It may be retained, among other purposes:
  (i) for use as evidence at a trial for an offence;
  (ii) for forensic examination or for other investigation in connection with an offence; or
  (iii) where there are reasonable grounds for believing that it has been stolen or obtained by the commission of an offence in order to establish its lawful owner.

6.7 Property shall not be retained in accordance with paragraphs 6.6 (i) and (ii) (*i.e.* for use as evidence or for the purposes of investigation) if a photograph or copy would suffice for those purposes.

(c) *Rights of owner etc*

6.8 If property is retained the person who had custody or control of it immediately prior to its seizure must, on request, be provided with a list or description of the property within a reasonable time.

6.9 He or his representative must be allowed supervised access to the property to examine it or have it photographed or copied, or must be provided with a photograph or copy, in either case within a reasonable time of any request and at his own expense, unless the officer in charge of an investigation has reasonable grounds for believing that this would prejudice the investigation of an offence or any criminal proceedings. In this case a record of the grounds must be made.

Note for guidance

  6A Any person claiming property seized by the police may apply to a magistrates' court under the Police (Property) Act 1897 for its possession, and should, where appropriate, be advised of this procedure.

7 Action to be taken after searches

7.1 Where premises have been searched in circumstances to which this code applies, other than in the circumstances covered by paragraph 4.3 above, the officer in charge of the search shall, on arrival at a police station, make or have made a record of the search. The record shall include:
  (i) the address of the premises searched;
  (ii) the date, time and duration of the search;
  (iii) the authority under which the search was made. Where the search was made in the exercise of a statutory power to search premises without warrant the record shall include the power under which the search was made; and where the search was made under warrant, or with written consent, a copy of the warrant or consent shall be appended to the record or kept in a place identified in the record;
  (iv) the names of the officers who conducted the search;
  (v) the names of any persons on the premises if they are known;

  (vi) either a list of any articles seized or a note of where such a list is kept and, if not covered by a warrant, the reason for their seizure;

  (vii) whether force was used and, if so, the reason why it was used;

  (viii) details of any damage caused during the search, and the circumstances in which it was caused.

7.2 Where premises have been searched under warrant, the warrant shall be endorsed to show:

  (i) whether any articles specified in the warrant were found;

  (ii) whether any other articles were seized;

  (iii) the date and time at which it was executed;

  (iv) the names of the officers who executed it; and

  (v) whether a copy was handed to the occupier or left on the premises and if so where on them.

7.3 Any warrant which has been executed or which has not been executed within one month of its issue shall be returned, if it was issued by a justice of the peace, to the clerk to the justices for the petty sessions area concerned or, if issued by a judge, to the appropriate officer of the court from which he issued it.

8 Search registers

8.1 A search register shall be maintained at each sub-divisional police station. All records which are required to be made by this code shall be made, copied or referred to in the register.

9 Scope

9.1 This code applies to the following searches of premises (other than of vehicles only):

  (a) searches of premises undertaken for the purposes of an investigation into an alleged offence with the occupier's consent other than routine scenes of crime searches and searches following the activation of burglar or fire alarms or bomb threat calls;

  (b) searches of premises under powers conferred by sections 17, 18 and 32 of the Police and Criminal Evidence Act 1984;

  (c) searches of premises undertaken in pursuance of a search warrant issued in accordance with section 15 of or Schedule 1 to that Act.

CODE OF PRACTICE FOR THE EXERCISE OF POWERS OF STOP AND SEARCH BY POLICE OFFICERS

1 General

1.1 This code of practice must be readily available at all police stations for consultation by police officers, detained persons and members of the public.

1.2 The Notes for Guidance included are not provisions of this code, but are guidance to police officers and others about its application and interpretation. Provisions in the Annexes to the code are provisions of this code.

1.3 This code governs the exercise by police officers of statutory powers to search a person without first arresting him or to search a vehicle without first arresting him or to search a vehicle without making an arrest. The main stop and search powers in existence at the time when this code was made are set out in Annex A but that list should not be regarded as definitive.

1.4 This Code does not apply to the following powers of stop and search:
(i) Aviation Security Act 1982, ss.27, 27(2);
(ii) Police and Criminal Evidence Act 1984, s.6 (which relates specifically to powers of statutory undertakers on the premises of the statutory undertakers).

1.5 The exercise of the powers to which this Code applies requires reasonable grounds to suspect that articles of a particular kind are being carried. Annex B to this Code provides guidance about this.

1.6 Nothing in this code affects the ability of an officer to speak to or question a person in the course of his duties without detaining him or exercising any element of compulsion.

Note for guidance

1A It is important to ensure that powers of stop and search are used responsibly and sparingly and only where reasonable grounds for suspicion genuinely exist. Over use of the powers is as likely to be harmful to police effort in the long-term as misuse; both can lead to mistrust of the police among sections of the community. It is also particularly important to ensure that any person searched must be treated courteously and considerately if police action is not to be resented.

2 Action before a search is carried out

2.1 Where an officer has the reasonable grounds for suspicion necessary to exercise a power of stop and search he may detain the person concerned for the purposes of and with a view to searching him. There is no power to stop or detain a person against his will in order to find grounds for a search.

2.2 Before carrying out a search the officer may question the person about his behaviour or his presence in circumstances which gave rise to the suspicion, since he may have a satisfactory explanation which will make a search unnecessary. If, as a result of any questioning preparatory to a search or other circumstances which come to the attention of the officer, there cease to be reasonable grounds for suspecting that an article of a kind for which there is a power of stop and search is being carried, no search may take place.

2.3 The reasonable grounds for suspicion which are necessary for the exercise of the initial power to detain may be confirmed or eliminated as a result of the questioning of a person detained for the purposes of a search (or such questioning may reveal reasonable grounds to suspect the possession of a different kind of unlawful article from that originally suspected); but the reasonable grounds for suspicion, without which any subsequent search or detention for the purposes of a search is unlawful, cannot be retrospectively provided by such questioning during his detention or by his refusal to answer any question put to him.

2.4 Before any search of a detained person or attended vehicle takes place the officer must give the person to be searched or in charge of the vehicle the following information:

    (i) his name and the name of the police station to which he is attached;

    (ii) the object of the search; and

    (iii) his grounds for undertaking it.

2.5 If the officer is not in uniform he must show his warrant card.

2.6 Unless it appears to the officer that it will not be practicable to make a record of the search he must also inform the person who has been searched (or the owner or person in charge of a vehicle that has been searched, as the case may be) is entitled to a copy of the record of the search if he asks for it within a year. If the person wishes to have a copy and is not given one on the spot, he should be advised to apply to the officer's police station.

2.7 If the person to be searched, or in charge of a vehicle to be searched, does not understand what is being said, the officer must take reasonable steps to bring the information in paragraphs 2.4 and 2.6 to his attention. If the person has someone with him then the officer must establish whether that person can interpret.

Note for guidance

2A In some circumstances preparatory questioning may be unnecessary, but in general a brief conversation or exchange will be desirable as a means of avoiding unsuccessful searches. Where a person is lawfully detained for the purpose of a search, but no search in the event takes place, the detention will not thereby have been rendered unlawful.

3. Conduct of the search

3.1 Every reasonable effort must be made to reduce to the minimum the embarrassment that a person being searched may experience.

3.2 Although force may only be used as a last resort, reasonable force may be used if necessary to conduct a search or to detain a person or vehicle for the purposes of a search. A compulsory search may be made only if it has been established that the person is unwilling to cooperate (*e.g.* by opening a bag).

3.3 The length of time for which a person or vehicle may be detained will depend on the circumstances, but must in all circumstances be reasonable and not extend beyond the time taken for the search. The thoroughness and extent of a search must depend on what is suspected of being carried, and by whom. If the suspicion relates to a particular article, for example an offensive weapon, which is seen to be slipped into a person's pocket then, in the absence of other grounds for suspicion or an opportunity for the article to be moved elsewhere, the search must be confined to that pocket. In the case of a small article which can readily be concealed, such as a drug and which might be concealed anywhere on the person, a more extensive search may be necessary.

3.4 The search must be conducted at the place where the person or vehicle was first detained or nearby.

3.5 Searches in public must be restricted to superficial examination of outer clothing. There is no power to require a person to remove any clothing in public other than an outer coat, jacket or gloves. Where on reasonable grounds it is considered necessary to conduct a more thorough search, *e.g.* by asking someone to take off a tee-shirt or headgear, this should be done out of public view (*e.g.* in a police van or a nearby police station if there is one). Any search involving the removal of more than an outer coat, jacket, gloves, headgear or footwear may only be made by an officer of the same sex as the person searched and may not be made in the presence of anyone of the opposite sex. [See Note 3A]

Notes for guidance

3A A search in the street itself should be regarded as being in public for the purposes of paragraph 3.5 above, even though it may be empty at the time a search begins. Although there is no power to require a person to do so there is nothing to prevent an officer from asking a person voluntarily to remove more than outer clothing in public.

3B As a search of a person in public should be a superficial examination of outer clothing, such searches should normally be capable of completion within one minute or so.

4 Action after a search is carried out

(a) *General*

4.1 An officer who has carried out a search must make a written record. In some cases this may not be possible such as in situations involving public disorder occurring in seaside areas during Bank Holiday weekends or the search of football supporters entering or leaving a ground. [See Note 4A]

4.2 The record must be completed as soon as practicable: on the spot unless circumstances (*e.g.* other immediate duties or very inclement weather) make this impracticable.

4.3 The record must be made on the form provided for this purpose (the national search record).

4.4 In order to complete the search record the officer should normally seek the name, address, and date of birth of the person searched. But there is no obligation under the search procedures on a person to provide these details and no power to detain him if he is unwilling so to do.

4.5 The following information can always and must be included in the record of a search even if the person does not wish to identify himself or give his date of birth:

   (i) the name of the person searched, or (if he withholds it) a description of him, together in all cases with an indication of;

  (ii) when the person searched is White, Afro-Caribbean or Asian, a notification to that effect;

 (iii) where a vehicle is searched, a description of it;

 (iv) the object of the search;

  (v) the grounds for making it;

 (vi) the date and time when it was made;

(vii) the place where it was made;

(viii) its results;

 (ix) a note of any injury or damage to property resulting from it;

  (x) the identity of the officer making it. [See Note 4B]

4.6 A record is required for each person and each vehicle searched. If, for example, a person is in a vehicle and both are searched, two records must be completed.

4.7 The record of the grounds for making a search must, briefly but informatively, explain the reason for suspecting the person concerned, whether by reference to his behaviour or other circumstances.

(b) *Unattended vehicles*

4.8 After searching an unattended vehicle, or anything in or on it, an officer must leave a notice in it (or on it if things in or on it have been searched without opening it) recording the fact that it has been searched.

4.9 The notice should include the name of the police station to which the officer concerned is attached and state where a copy of the record of the search may be obtained and where any application for compensation should be directed.

4.10 The vehicle must if practicable be left secure.

Notes for guidance

4A Nothing in this code affects the routine searching of a person entering sports grounds or other premises with their consent, or as a condition of entry.

4B When a search is conducted by more than one officer the identity of all officers engaged in the search must be recorded on the search record.

ANNEX A

Power / *Unlawful articles* / General

Power	Object of Search	Extent of Search	Where exercisable
1 Public Stores Act 1875, s.6	HM Stores stolen or unlawfully obtained	Persons, vehicles and vessels	Anywhere where the constabulary powers are exercisable*
2 Firearms Act 1968, s.47	Firearms	Persons and vehicles	A public place**
3 Misuse of Drugs Act 1971 s.23	Controlled drugs	Persons and vehicles	Anywhere
4 Customs and Excise Management Act 1979, ss.163–164	Goods: (a) on which duty has not been paid; (b) being unlawfully removed, imported or exported; (c) otherwise liable to forfeiture to HM Customs and Excise	Persons, vehicles and vessels [(a),(b)]; Vehicles and vessels only [(c)]	Anywhere where the constabulary powers are exercisable*
5 Police and Criminal Evidence Act 1984, s.1	Stolen goods; articles for use in certain Theft Act offences; offensive weapons	Persons and vehicles	Where there is public access***
Police and Criminal Evidence Act 1984, s.6(3) (by a UKEA constable in respect of property owned or controlled by British Nuclear Fuels Ltd.)	HM Stores (in the form of goods and chattels belonging to British Nuclear Fuels Ltd.)	As at 1. above	As at 1. above

Evidence of Game and Wildlife Offences			
6 Poaching Prevention Act 1862, s.2	Game or poaching equipment	Persons and vehicles	A public place
7 Deer Acts 1963, s.5 and 1980, s.4	Evidence of offences under the Act	Persons and vehicles	Anywhere except dwellings
8 Conservation of Seals Act 1970, s.4	Seals or hunting equipment	Vehicles only	Anywhere
9 Badgers Act 1973, s.10	Evidence of offences under the Act	Persons and vehicles	Anywhere
10 Wildlife and Countryside Act 1981, s.19	Evidence of wildlife offences	Persons and vehicles	Anywhere except dwellings
Other			
11 Prevention of Terrorism (Temporary Provisions) Act 1984, Sched. 3	Evidence of offences under the Act	Persons and vehicles	Anywhere

* Including, in the case of a vessel, territorial waters.
** Anywhere in the case of reasonable suspicion of offences of carrying firearms with criminal intent or trespassing with firearms.
*** Any place where the public is at the time entitled to go or places other than dwellings where people have ready access at the time (unless land attached to a dwelling where the person or vehicle is permitted to be).

ANNEX B [1.5]

Reasonable grounds for suspicion

1. Reasonable suspicion does not require certainty that an unlawful article is being carried; nor does the officer concerned have to be satisfied of this beyond reasonable doubt. Reasonable suspicion, in contrast to mere suspicion, must be founded on fact. There must be some concrete basis for the officer's suspicion, related to the individual person concerned, which can be considered and evaluated by an objective third person. Mere suspicion, in contrast, is a hunch or instinct which cannot be explained or justified to an objective third person. An officer who has such a hunch or instinct may well be justified in continuing to keep the person under observation or speak to him, but additional grounds which bring up mere suspicion to the level of reasonable suspicion are needed before he may exercise the powers dealt with in this code.

2. Reasonable suspicion may arise from the nature of the property observed or being carried or suspected of being carried coupled with other factors including the time, the place and the suspicious behaviour of the person concerned or those with him. The decision to search must be based on all the facts which, to a careful officer, bear on the likelihood that an article of a certain kind will be found, and not only on what can be seen at the time. So an officer with prior knowledge of the behaviour of someone he sees in a certain situation, or acting on information received (such as a description of a suspected offender) may have reasonable grounds for searching him although another officer would not.

3. Reasonable suspicion cannot be supported on the basis simply of a higher than average chance that the person has committed or is committing an offence, for example because he belongs to a group within which offenders of a certain kind are relatively common, or because of a combination of factors such as these. For example, a person's colour of itself can never be a reasonable ground for suspicion. The mere fact alone that a person is carrying a particular kind of property or is dressed in a certain way or has a certain hairstyle is likewise not of itself sufficient. Nor is the fact that a person is known to have a previous conviction for unlawful possession of an article.

4. The degree or level of suspicion required to establish the reasonable grounds justifying the exercise of powers of stop and search is no less than the degree or level of suspicion required to effect an arrest without warrant for any of the suspected offences to which these powers relate. The powers of stop and search provide an opportunity to establish the commission or otherwise of certain kinds of offences without arrest and may therefore render arrest unnecessary.

5. Paragraph 4 above is subject to the principle that where a police officer has reasonable grounds to suspect that a person is in *innocent* possession of a stolen or prohibited article, the power of stop and search exists notwithstanding that there would be no power of arrest. However every effort should be made to secure the voluntary production of the article before the power is resorted to.

APPENDIX

APPENDIX

THE RELATIONSHIP BETWEEN CRIMINAL AND DISCIPLINARY PROCEEDINGS: REVISED GUIDANCE TO CHIEF OFFICERS*

5.9. A police officer is subject to the criminal law and to a discipline code. As a result, alleged misconduct may render him liable to both criminal and disciplinary proceedings. It is necessary that where both these systems may apply, they are operated in ways which are neither unfair to the officer nor offensive to the public interest. In deciding whether to prefer a disciplinary charge the effect of any criminal proceedings which have already taken place has to be distinguished from the effect of any decision by the Director of Public Prosecutions that criminal proceedings should not be brought.

Where criminal proceedings have already taken place
5.10. Here it has to be examined whether section 11 of the Police Act 1976 operates. The section provides that an officer brought before the courts on a criminal charge should not, whether acquitted or convicted, thereafter be charged with a disciplinary offence which is in substance the same (save that criminal conduct itself constitutes a disciplinary offence). This is because, since the required standard of proof in disciplinary proceedings is the same as that in criminal proceedings, to bring a disciplinary charge following a criminal charge would be in effect to try the officer twice for the same offence. This is the only statutory bar to discipline proceedings and the sole situation in which it is appropriate to say that "double jeopardy" obtains.

5.11. In considering whether section 11 operates, close attention should be paid to the similarity in the elements of the criminal charge and the possible disciplinary charge. In some cases they may not be as similar as appears at first sight: the mental element of the criminal offence may be lacking in the disciplinary offence, or the conduct involved may differ. Where this is so, there is no bar to disciplinary proceedings, because the two offences are not in substance the same. As examples, in criminal proceedings against a police officer for corruption it is necessary to establish that the officer agreed to show favour to the person from whom he agreed to accept a gift or consideration, but this element is absent from the disciplinary offence of accepting a gratuity; a criminal charge of perjury involves proof that an allegedly false statement was material to the proceedings in which it was made, but a disciplinary charge of falsehood does not; and a Theft Act charge will require proof of an intention permanently to deprive a person of his property or permanently to evade payment of a debt, whereas these elements are absent from disciplinary offences relating to the care of property or failure to discharge debts. By contrast, the criminal charge of assault and the disciplinary charge of unnecessary violence is the most common example of such charges being in substance the same.

5.12. There will also be cases where an acquittal on a criminal charge may be very relevant to the question whether to prefer a disciplinary charge, notwithstanding that the charges are not in substance the same so that section 11 of the 1976 Act does not operate. This will be so, in particular, when a matter essential to the proof of the disciplinary charge was in issue in the criminal proceedings and was apparently resolved in the officer's favour. In the first example quoted in paragraph

* *Police Complaints and Discipline Procedures*, Home Office, Cmnd. 9072, (1983).

5.11, if the essential issue in a trial for corruption was whether the officer received a gift, rather than whether he showed favour in return for a gift, it may not be appropriate to prefer a disciplinary charge of accepting a gratuity following an acquittal in the criminal proceedings.

Where the Director has decided that criminal proceedings should not be brought

5.13. Here section 11 of the 1976 Act does not operate and all cases fall to be considered individually on their merits. However, account should be taken of such a decision by the Director if the criminal offence which he has considered is in substance the same as the disciplinary offence under consideration (*i.e.* the sort of examination outlined in paragraph 5.11 will be relevant here also) *and* his decision is on the grounds that the available evidence is insufficient: if the Director has decided that the evidence is insufficient for criminal prosecution it is for consideration whether it is sufficient for disciplinary proceedings. Ultimately, however, having considered each case on its merits, the disciplinary authority is free to bring proceedings if it thinks in all the circumstances that it is fair and appropriate to do so.

5.14. In a separate category are cases where the alleged misconduct is fairly trivial when regarded as a criminal offence, but far more serious in the context of a disciplined service. Cases of common assault, minor thefts of police property and the use of bad language to a member of the public might fall within this category. In such cases, the Director may decide that the offence is not such as to merit prosecution (he may use the expression that it would not be in the public interest to bring a criminal charge). If this is so, his decision is not relevant to the question whether disciplinary proceedings should be brought, since he has not expressed the view that the evidence is insufficient to justify criminal proceedings. It follows, therefore, that the disciplinary authority is free to take what action it thinks appropriate in such instances without further regard to the Director's decision.

Attitude of complainant

5.15. It can normally be assumed that a person who has made a complaint against a police officer will be prepared to substantiate that complaint in criminal or disciplinary proceedings. Machinery is available to secure the attendance of reluctant witnesses at both criminal and disciplinary hearings. Complainants should not be asked to express a preference for criminal or disciplinary proceedings, or for attending one type of hearing rather than the other. Any unsolicited expression of the complainant's feelings should nevertheless be recorded.

INDEX

INDEX

Note—Roman type is used to indicate pages in the Commentary, **bold** type to indicate sections of the Police and Criminal Evidence Act and *italic* type to indicate paragraphs in the Codes of Practice and pages in this book on which they appear. The abbreviation *N for G* stands for Notes for Guidance.